ML Binding

This textbook has an ML-BINDING designed for exceptional durability and long lasting use. The ML-BINDING is distinguished by:

Extensive Testing for Durability

The ML-Binding has endured highly sophisticated testing that approximates the wear and tear of heavy classroom use.

Reinforced Stress Points

A specially designed reinforced endsheet assembly strengthens the joint area and relieves stress on the first and last signatures. This also enables the book to stay open easily.

Maximum Cover Adhesion

Latex-impregnated kraft liners are the strongest available providing superb adhesion to the backbone and cover of the book.

Flexible Spine for Ease of Use

Tubular liners add strength and also enhance flexibility at normal stress points on the spine of the book.

The ML-BINDING exceeds the Manufacturing Standards and Specifications set forth by the National Association of State Textbook Administrators.

McDougal, Littell

ENGLISH

Dear Student,

You are entering a challenging and exciting period of your life. Your view of the world is becoming more mature and more complex. The textbooks you use should reflect this growth. They should encourage you to think new thoughts and explore new ideas. Most of all, your textbooks should help you discover and develop your own special talents and skills.

McDougal, Littell English was created to help you achieve these goals. The photos, fine art, and literature selections were chosen to fire your imagination and expand your knowledge of the world. The text was designed to appeal to your interests and abilities while at the same time challenging you to improve your writing and speaking skills.

We hope you will enjoy working with the images and ideas in this book. More important, we hope that using the book will give you confidence in your abilities and an eagerness to try out new ideas. In the process, you will even discover that language can be lively, exciting, and even fun.

The Editors

*"The more we see, the more
we must be able to imagine. . ."*

Gotthold Ephraim Lessing

McDougal, Littell
English

Red Level

ML

McDougal, Littell & Company

Evanston, Illinois
New York   Dallas   Sacramento   Raleigh

Allan A. Glatthorn
Brenda C. Rosen

Consultants

Naomi Arabian, District Curriculum Coordinator of Middle School Reading, Fresno Unified School District, Fresno, California

David R. Collins, English/Creative Writing Instructor, Moline Senior High School, Moline, Illinois

Sr. Mary Dawson, IHM, Director of Curriculum and Instruction, Diocese of Rockville Centre, Education Department, Rockville Centre, New York

Dr. Joy C. Fowles, Coordinator for Secondary Education, Clear Creek Independent School District, League City, Texas

Richard Fluck, Superintendent, Cary School District 26, Cary, Illinois

Dr. Donald Gray, Professor of English, Indiana University, Bloomington, Indiana

Elizabeth W. McDonald, Secondary Language Arts Consultant, Pontiac, Michigan

Judy Powers Money, English Teacher, Fort Recovery High School, Fort Recovery, Ohio

Janet Morrow, Teacher Specialist, Staff Development, Mesa Public Schools, Maricopa, Arizona

Debra Olsen, Teacher, Garside Junior High School, Las Vegas, Nevada

Jerome Smiley, English Coordinator, Elmont Memorial Junior and Senior High Schools, Elmont, New York

Sr. Mary Theiss, SSSF, Coordinator of Curriculum, Archdiocese of Milwaukee, Milwaukee, Wisconsin

Mary Ellen Tindall, Project Consultant, Wayne-Westland Community Schools, Westland, Michigan

Gay D. Wells, Supervisor of Language Arts, Neshaminy School District, Langhorne, Pennsylvania

Cover Photograph: Mark Tomalty/Masterfile
Cover Quote: from *Laocoön* by Gotthold Ephraim Lessing (1729–1781)
Acknowledgments: See page 697

ISBN 0-8123-5747-7

Composition

Beginning with You

Choosing a Process for Writing

Writing for Different Purposes

Resources and Skills

Grammar, Usage, and Mechanics

Chapter 22 Using Nouns   422

Chapter 23 Using Pronouns   444

Writer's Handbook 652

Index 683

Acknowledgments 697

Featured Writers

Paul Annixter

David Attenborough

Natalie Babbitt

John Christopher

June Counsel

Kyle Counts

Emily Dickinson

Penelope Farmer

Hanako Fukuda

Don Herbert

George Laycock

Sisel Keyn Lodding

Julian Nava

Robert O'Brien

Carl Sagan

Mary Shelley

Gene Siskel

Zilpha Snyder

Elizabeth Speare

B. J. Walker

Jonathan Weiner

E. B. White

Richard Zoglin

Longer Literature Selections

Composition

Writing, like painting, is a process of exploration and discovery. Both writers and painters travel through feelings, thoughts, and visions—searching and experimenting. In the end, they share their discoveries. The painter shares through colors, shapes, and images; the writer shares through words.

1
Using the Senses in Writing

Imagine eating an apple that had no taste, no smell, and no crunch. It wouldn't be any more appetizing than the paper this picture is printed on. Your five senses allow you to experience your world more fully—to see it, feel it, hear it. When you share your world with others, it is important to describe how things look, taste, smell, feel, and sound.

In this chapter you will learn to use your senses to observe your world more closely. Then you will find how you can share in writing what you have learned while observing.

1
Sight

Artists, detectives, and scientists make a career out of their attention to detail. They see the same things everyone else sees—but they notice more than most people because they look more carefully. When detectives observe a car, for example, they are likely to notice its color, make, model, year, license number, and general condition. The detectives would probably see whether the car had any decals, stickers, dents, or rust. They might also notice the color of the car, contents, and condition of the car's interior. Perhaps they would note whether the car made an unusual sound as it passed by. Likewise, a good artist will interpret and reproduce the details of a scene—the small objects, colors, shapes, and textures that help compose the overall picture.

Good writers also learn to pay special attention to things around them. They make notes in order to remember the size, shape, color, and condition of things. They also notice how things sound, feel, taste, and smell. Then, when they describe things in their writing, they use the details they remember, so their descriptions are clear and interesting.

To practice looking more carefully at things around you, study the picture of the scene above. Take time to examine everything carefully. Pretend that you are in the scene. Study the overall

picture and the small details. Then answer the questions that
follow. Use the sight words on pages 15–17 to make your
answers vivid and precise.

1. What kind of day is it? What is the weather like? What
   season do you think it is? Why?
2. What is happening here? Describe the scene from near to the
   horizon. Describe what the people in the photograph are
   doing.
3. What colors are shown in this picture? What color appears
   most often? What colors are absent?
4. Which things in the photograph attract your attention? What
   size and shape are they? Which things are less noticeable?
   What size and shape are they?

Now look at the picture on this page.
Use your sense of sight as you
answer the questions that follow.

1. What object is being magnified?
2. How does the object look when
   it is not magnified? Describe
   the color, size, and shape.
   Describe details you can see
   without a magnifying glass.
3. How does the object look when
   magnified? Describe additional
   colors and shapes that you can
   see. Can you see details that
   you didn't notice before?
   Describe them.

Writing Activity Using Sight Words

Begin to keep a writing journal. It will be a place for you to
experiment with and to develop writing ideas. Choose four of the
following things and describe them in your journal. Use sight
words and describe details as well as general appearances.

a garden	your favorite outfit	a hockey stick
a woods	a shopping center	a quiet street
your pet	an amusement park	a snowstorm

2
Hearing

We hear so many sounds each day that we learn to ignore many of them. Yet all kinds of sounds, from background music to loud noises, affect us and influence the way we feel. By learning to listen carefully, you can become more attuned to and aware of your surroundings. This awareness will help you to enliven your descriptions of things.

Study the photograph of the traffic and street scene. Imagine that you are there. Then use your memory and imagination to help you answer the following questions. Use the hearing words on page 18 to make your answers more colorful and interesting.

1. What sounds do the motors of the cars, the buses, and the trucks make?
2. What sounds from brakes, mufflers and horns do you hear?
3. What sounds do the tires make as they slap the tarred street and roll across loose manhole covers?
4. Describe other sounds you might hear—such as the flag rippling in the wind.

Writing Activity Using Hearing Words

Choose three of the familiar sounds listed. Try to hear them in your mind, and describe them in your writer's journal.

fire	rain on a roof	flying airplane
doorbell	dog barking	running water
skating	footsteps	windshield wipers
owl	sawing wood	ringing phone

3
Touch

You react more immediately to your sense of touch than to any other sense. You pull away instantly when you touch something too hot or sharp. You know at once when you are cold or wet or dizzy or in pain.

The sense of touch is so much a part of you that you may find it difficult to describe physical sensations. One way to describe a feeling effectively is to compare it to something else.

The water felt like an icy sea of snow.

The photograph on this page shows an activity that is experienced through the sense of touch. Imagine yourself in this scene. Then answer the questions below. Use the touch words on page 19 to help you think of interesting comparisons.

1. What does the water feel like as it splashes against your face?
2. Is the water getting in your eyes? your nose? your mouth? How does this feel?
3. Describe the sensations in your arm and leg muscles as you churn through the water.
4. What does the swimming cap feel like?
5. Imagine climbing out of the pool. How does the air feel on your wet skin?

Writing Activity **Using Touch Words**

Choose three of the following things, and describe them in your writing journal. In describing how each thing feels, use new and interesting comparisons that appeal to the sense of touch.

a pillow	clay	a balloon
a peach	an egg	walking barefoot
a plastic bag	a callus	riding on a bus

4
Taste and Smell

You probably have trouble tasting your food when your nose is stuffy, and you may get a taste for food just because it smells good. Maybe some things smell good to you because of the tastes they represent. Other things smell so odd, that you may be reluctant to taste them. The senses of taste and smell are very closely linked. By referring to them, you can give your reader very strong impressions of the things you want to describe.

Study the picture on this page. Use the taste and smell words on page 19 to help you answer the following questions.

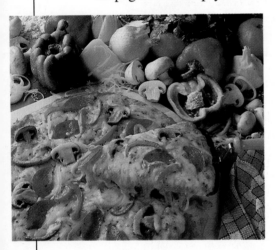

1. The pizza is hot and fresh. How does it smell? What ingredients have the strongest smell?
2. How does the sauce on the pizza smell? How does it taste? How does it change the taste of other ingredients?
3. How do the tomatoes smell and taste when they are raw? How do they smell when they are cooked? How do they taste in combination with other ingredients?
4. How does the cheese smell? How does it taste? Do the taste and smell of the cheese become stronger when hot and melted?

Writing Activity **Smell and Taste Words**

Choose four of the foods listed or four of your own choice and describe how each of the foods you chose tastes and smells. Record your descriptions in your writer's journal.

popcorn	cake	cooked cabbage	a pickle
whole milk	vegetable soup	tacos	bread
spinach	apples	tomato sauce	fish

Starting from Literature

from *Born Free*

Joy Adamson

The following selection is from Joy Adamson's journal-like account of a young lioness, Elsa, who was raised by the writer and her husband. As you read it, notice Adamson's use of sensory words and images.

Sense of
sight
introduced

*I*n the soft darkness above, the stars sparkled brilliantly—and in the Northern Frontier they always seem to me to be twice as big as anywhere else. Now I hear a deep vibrating sound like that of distant aircraft; this meant that elephants were making their way to the river. Luckily, the wind was in our favor; and the rumbling soon ceased.

Sense of
hearing
introduced

Suddenly, the unmistakable grunts of lion became audible. At first they were very far away, then gradually, they grew louder and louder. What could Elsa be thinking about all this? In fact, she seemed utterly unconcerned at the approach of her own kind. She tore at her meat, gnawing slices off with her molars, then she rolled on her back, all four paws in the air, and dozed off, while I sat listening to the chuckling of hyena, the yelping of jackal, and the magnificent chorus of the lions.

Sense of
touch
introduced

It is very hot at that season, so Elsa spent part of the day in the water; then, when the sun made this uncomfortable for her, she would rest in the reeds, at intervals rolling lazily into the river, where she landed with a great splash. As we knew that crocodiles were plentiful in the Uaso Nyiro this caused us some concern, but none ever approached her.

Elsa was always full of mischief; sharing her fun with us, she would splash us whenever she found us off guard, or she would jump quickly out of the water, pounce on us, wet as she was, and we would find ourselves rolling in the sand with our cameras, field glasses, and rifles pressed down by her heavy dripping body. She used her paws in a variety of ways. She would use them in gentle caresses, but she could also deliver a playful well-aimed smack at full speed, and she knew a little ju-jitsu trick which unfailingly laid us flat on our backs. No matter how prepared we were for the act, she would give just a small twist to our ankles with her paw and down we went. . . .

Elsa was not afraid of the sound of a shot, and she grew to know that "bang" meant a dead bird. She loved retrieving, especially guinea fowl, whose quills she crunched, though she very rarely ate the flesh and never the feathers. The first bird was always hers; she would carry it proudly in her mouth till she found this uncomfortable, then she placed it at my feet and looked at me, as though to say: "Please carry it for me," then, so long as I dangled it in front of her nose, she trotted good-naturedly after it.

The Dream. Henri Rousseau. Detail.

Often, it was touching to see her torn between her hunting instinct and her wish to please us. Anything moving seemed to her, as it would to most dogs, just asking to be chased; but, as yet, her instinct to kill had not fully developed. Of course, we had been careful never to show her her goat meat alive. She had plenty of opportunity of seeing wild animals, but as we were usually with her when this happened, she gave chase merely in play and always came back to us after a short time, rubbed her head against our knees, and told us with a low miaow about the game. . . .

It was an exciting moment when the cub met her first elephant, an anxious one too, for poor Elsa had no mother to warn her against these animals who regard lions as the only enemies of their young and therefore sometimes kill them. One day Nuru, who had taken her out for her morning walk, came back panting to say that Elsa was "playing with an elephant." We took our rifles and he guided us to the scene. There we saw a great old elephant, his head buried in a bush, enjoying his breakfast. Suddenly Elsa, who had crept up from behind, took a playful swipe at one of his hind legs. A scream of shocked surprise and injured dignity followed this piece of impertinence. Then the elephant backed from the bush and charged. Elsa hopped nimbly out of his way and, quite unimpressed, began to stalk him. It was a very funny though an alarming sight, and we could only hope that we should not need to use our guns. Luckily, after a time, both became bored with the game; the old elephant went back to his meal and Elsa lay down, close by, and went to sleep. . . .

By now we had established a routine for Elsa. The mornings were cool; it was then that we often watched the impala antelope leaping gracefully on the rifle range and listened to the chorus of the awakening birds. As soon as it got light Nuru released Elsa and both walked a short distance into the bush. The cub, full of unspent energy, chased everything she could find. . . .

About teatime the two of them returned and we took over. First, Elsa had some milk, then we wandered into the hills or walked in the plain; she climbed trees, appeared to sharpen her claws, followed exciting scents or stalked Grant's

Sense of smell introduced

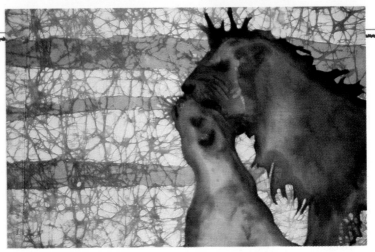

Lions. A batik by Danielle J. Turzanski, student artist.

gazelle and gerenuk, which sometimes played hide-and-seek with her. Much to our surprise, she was fascinated by tortoises, which she rolled over and over; she loved playing, and never did she miss an opportunity of starting a game with us—we were her "pride" and she shared everything with us.

As darkness fell we returned home and took her to her enclosure, where her evening meal awaited her. It consisted of large quantities of raw meat, mostly sheep and goat; she got her roughage by breaking up the rib bones and the cartilages. . . .

Later, I sat with Elsa, played with her, sketching her, or reading. These evenings were our most intimate time, and I believe that her love for us was mostly fostered in these hours when, fed and happy, she could doze off with my thumb still in her mouth. It was only on moonlight nights that she became restless; then she padded along the wire, listening intently, her nostrils quivering to catch the faintest scent which might bring a message from the mysterious night outside.

Trying Out Sensory Writing   Look around you and choose an object to describe. Study the object with your senses. How does it look, sound, taste, smell, feel? How is this object different than any others of its kind? Write a brief but precise description of your object. Choose your words carefully so that they truly describe what you observe.

A List of Sight Words

Colors

reds
pink
salmon
rose
coral
raspberry
strawberry
cherry
crimson
cardinal
vermilion
ruby
garnet
wine
maroon
burgundy

blues
sky
sapphire
azure
porcelain
turquoise
aqua
aquamarine
peacock
cobalt
royal
navy

yellows
peach
apricot
butter
buttercup
lemon
canary
gold
topaz
ochre
sulphur
mustard
butterscotch
orange
tangerine
persimmon

purples
lavender
lilac
orchid
mauve
plum
mulberry
magenta
violet

grays
ashen
dove
steel
silver
platinum

greens
celery
mint
apple
lime
kelly
emerald
olive
pistachio
chartreuse

whites
snow
milky
marble
cream
ivory
oyster
pearl

blacks
jet
ebony
licorice
charcoal

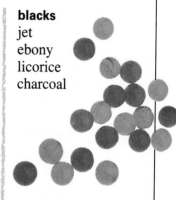

browns
sandy
almond
amber
tawny
hazel
cinnamon
nutmeg
chocolate
coffee
copper
rust
ginger
bronze
walnut
mahogany
beige
buff

Movements

fast
hurry
run
scamper
skip
scramble
dart
spring
spin
sprint
stride
streak
propel
trot
gallop
drive
dash
bolt
careen
rush
race
zoom
zip
ram
speed
chase
hurl
swat
flick
whisk
rip
shove
swerve

smash
drop
plummet
bounce
dive
swoop
plunge
swing
fly
sail

slow
creep
crawl
plod
slouch
lumber
tiptoe
bend
amble
saunter
loiter
stray
slink
stalk
edge
sneak

stagger
lope
canter
waddle
drag
sway
soar
lift
drift
droop
heave

Shapes

flat
round
domed
curved
wavy
globular
scalloped
ruffled
frilled
crimped
crinkled
flared
oval
conical
cylindrical
tubular
hollow
rotund
chubby
portly
fat
swollen

lumpy
clustered
padded
tufted
top-heavy
pendulous
jutting
irregular
proportioned
angular
triangular
rectangular
hexagonal
octagonal
square
pyramidical
tapering
branching
twiggy
split
broken
spindly
skinny
thin
wiry
shapely
winged
shapeless

Appearance

dotted	dull	jammed	jeweled
freckled	dark	packed	sturdy
spotted	dismal	bruised	hardy
blotched	rotted	tied	healthy
wrinkled	old	stretched	fragile
patterned	used	tall	sickly
mottled	worn	erect	tiny
flowery	untidy	lean	timid
striped	shabby	slender	nervous
bright	messy	supple	wild
clear	cheap	lively	dramatic
shiny	ugly	muscular	irresistible
glowing	ramshackle	robust	perky
glossy	tired	strong	imposing
shimmering	exhausted	frail	stately
fluid	arid	pale	large
sparkling	awkward	small	immense
iridescent	crooked	miniature	gigantic
glassy	loose	shy	decorative
flashy	curved	frightened	opulent
glazed	straight	bold	lavish
sheer	orderly	tantalizing	exotic
transparent	formal	energetic	fiery
translucent	crisp	arrogant	fresh
opaque	pretty	regal	scrubbed
muddy	lithe	elegant	handsome
grimy	flat	huge	calm
young	stout	massive	radiant
drab	wide	showy	blazing
dingy	rigid	dazzling	clean
	narrow		tidy
	overloaded		pleasant
	congested		serene
	cluttered		
	crowded		

A List of Hearing Words

Loud Sounds

crash	discord
thud	jangle
bump	rasp
boom	clash
thunder	clamor
bang	tumult
smash	riot
explode	racket
roar	brawl
scream	bedlam
screech	pandemonium
shout	hubbub
yell	blatant
whistle	deafening
whine	raucous
squawk	earsplitting
bark	piercing
bawl	rowdy
bluster	disorderly
rage	
blare	**Soft Sounds**
rumble	
grate	sigh
slam	murmur
clap	whisper
stomp	whir
stamp	rustle
noise	twitter
	patter
	hum
	mutter
	snap
	hiss

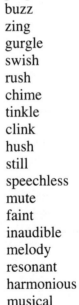

crackle
bleat
peep
buzz
zing
gurgle
swish
rush
chime
tinkle
clink
hush
still
speechless
mute
faint
inaudible
melody
resonant
harmonious
musical

Speech Sounds

stutter
stammer
giggle
guffaw
laugh
sing
yell
scream
screech
snort
bellow
growl
chatter
murmur
whisper
whimper
talk
speak
drawl

A List of Touch Words

cool	oily	feathery
cold	waxy	fuzzy
icy	fleshy	hairy
lukewarm	rubbery	prickly
tepid	tough	gritty
warm	crisp	sandy
hot	elastic	rough
steamy	leathery	sharp
sticky	silky	thick
damp	satiny	pulpy
wet	velvety	dry
slippery	smooth	dull
spongy	soft	thin
mushy	woolly	fragile
	furry	tender

A List of Taste and Smell Words

buttery	medicinal	savory
salty	fishy	sharp
bitter	spicy	gamy
bittersweet	peppery	fishy
sweet	gingery	briny
hearty	hot	acrid
mellow	burnt	burnt
sugary	overripe	gaseous
crisp	spoiled	reeking
ripe	rotten	putrid
bland	acidic	rancid
tasteless	fragrant	sickly
sour	aromatic	stagnant
vinegary	perfumed	moldy
fruity	heady	musty
tangy	fresh	mildewy
unripe	earthy	damp
raw	piney	dank
alkaline	pungent	stench
	tempting	

Creative Writing

A Have you ever wondered what it would be like if you could not see? Even familiar things and places might seem different to you. Ask someone to blindfold you. Explore a small section of a familiar room in your home or school. Let your other four senses lead you around instead of your eyes. Does the area feel or smell or sound the way you expected? How does your foot or shoe sound hitting the floor? What aromas do you smell? How does the back of your chair feel? Write a paragraph describing any new sensations that you discovered using only four senses.

B Our eyes are one of the most powerful tools we have for taking in the world around us. Our minds record colors, shapes, and textures through our eyes. Often, however, we look at things but do not "see" them. Have you ever passed a place day after day and then suddenly realized how striking it was? Think of something you see every day and take a new look at it. "See" it through different eyes. Describe it using only your sense of sight.

C Inside your mind, create a scene where the sounds interest you. Imagine that you are there. Tune in the sounds—much as you would tune in to your favorite radio station. What do you hear? In writing, describe the scene only by the sounds that you hear. Try to make the sounds and the scene come alive.

Application and Review

A **Identifying the Senses** Identify the sense (sight, hearing, smell, touch, or taste) that is associated with each of the following words.

1. crackle
2. whisper
3. tart
4. bounce
5. musty
6. gurgle
7. spongy
8. shimmering
9. salty
10. rough
11. sugary
12. yellow

B **Improving Writing with Sensory Details** Read and improve the following paragraph by adding details that appeal to the senses. For example, the house might be creaky and dark.

In the basement of the house down the street, a girl was working in a laboratory. The lab was filled with bottles of liquid and other equipment. The girl tasted a few of the liquids, then chose two of the potions. She mixed them together to form a new liquid, then drank it. All of a sudden, an explosion shook the house and smoke filled the room. A creature appeared in place of the young scientist. It moved around the room, as if it were looking for something. It knocked over tables and bottles, turning the room into a mess. The creature finally found the bottle it had been searching for, and disappeared through the door into the night.

C **Using Sensory Words** Write three words or phrases that describe each of these locations, using three different senses for each place.

1. a campfire
2. a baseball game
3. a kitchen
4. a cafeteria

2
Clear Thinking and Writing

The seashore is more than just the place where land and sea meet. Hidden in the sand and beneath the waves are many wonders for you to discover.

Similarly, you have within you many ideas waiting to be discovered. To explore them, you need to understand your thinking processes and learn how to tap your own creativity. In this chapter you will study the techniques and strategies you can use to find, explore, and develop ideas for writing.

1
Finding Ideas

Most people think that artists, writers, or inventors rely on inspiration to find ideas. Creative people, however, know better. They know that if you wait for inspiration to strike, you may find yourself waiting a very long time. Good writers share this knowledge. They work hard to find ideas for writing.

You can search for ideas by examining your inner world or by exploring the people, places, and things around you. When you look *inside* yourself by searching through your memories, your knowledge, and your experiences, you use a thinking skill called **reflecting**. When you look *outside* yourself to find ideas, you use a thinking skilled called **gleaning**.

Consider the following situation.

> The Polk School Computer Club wanted to purchase a new printer. However, their treasury was nearly empty and the price had just gone up. At a meeting, club members were asked to write down ideas for raising money. These ideas would be discussed at the next meeting.

> Marta approached this problem by reflecting. She sat down with a sheet of paper and a pencil. Then she wrote down every idea on the subject of fundraising that popped into her head.

> Julio approached this problem by gleaning. He asked friends what they would do to raise money. He went to the library and got a pamphlet called *Fundraising*. He also came up with an idea one evening while watching a commercial for blue jeans. The club might print and sell T-shirts.

Reflecting

When you reflect, begin by choosing a focus, or starting point for your thoughts. Once you have a focus, let your mind wander from that starting point. Then see where your thoughts take you. Three strategies for reflecting follow.

Brainstorming This technique involves listing whatever words or phrases come to mind when you think about your topic. You keep adding to your list until you run out of ideas. The goal is to get all your ideas out quickly. Then you go back and underline a word or phrase that might be a good idea for writing. Because brainstorming is an efficient way of generating ideas, small groups use it as well as individuals.

Freewriting This technique resembles brainstorming, but it requires that you write nonstop. To use this technique follow these steps.

1. Write your focus, or starting point, on paper.
2. Then write whatever comes to mind as you think about your focus. Write nonstop—without lifting your pen or pencil from the paper.
3. Write as much as you can in three to five minutes. Let your thoughts go. Don't worry about using complete sentences or proper spelling and punctuation.

Here's how Marta used freewriting to come up with ways for the computer club to raise money.

> Fundraising . . . variety shows . . . we could have kids perform and charge admission—Could we use the auditorium? Selling cookies for the Girl Scouts . . . once my youth group held a car wash, wonder if our advisor could give me any ideas? She knows a lot about business—How do businesses raise money anyway? Selling things mostly—what could we sell? Pastries? posters? how about raffle tickets?

Clustering This technique involves thinking of additional ideas that relate to a central idea or focus. Like freewriting, all you need is your focus, a sheet of paper, and a pen or pencil. Then follow the next three steps.

1. Write your focus, or starting point, in the center of your paper. Circle it.
2. Think about your focus. Write outside the circle any related ideas that pop into your head. Circle these and draw lines connecting the related ideas to the main circle.

3. Think about the related ideas. Write down other new ideas that occur to you. Circle these and draw connecting lines between the new and the related ideas.

Following is how one student used clustering to come up with ideas for a composition about television.

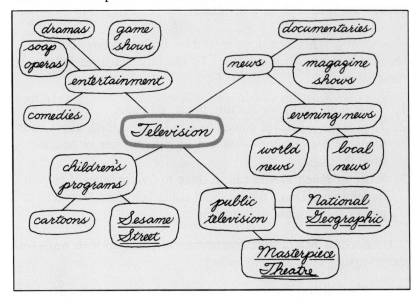

Gleaning

The word *gleaning* means "gathering, or taking in." One way to use this skill is to begin as you would when reflecting. First come up with a focus, or starting point. Then, as you go through your daily life, keep your focus in mind. Talk to people about your focus. Read about it. Look for related ideas in all that happens around you.

Sometimes gleaning works without your having a focus at all. You are simply going through your day, not thinking of anything in particular, when suddenly something happens that gives you an interesting idea. In fact, some of the best ideas come to people in this way. Many songs, for example, have been inspired by a word or a sound that struck the musician as being special somehow.

Always be open to potential ideas in whatever happens around you. When an interesting idea suggests itself, jot the idea down in a notebook or journal.

Use reflecting and gleaning

- to find ideas for writing and speech assignments
- to find solutions to practical problems
- to discover possibilities for new inventions and creations

Writing Activities *Reflecting and Gleaning*

A Choose one subject from the following list. Use freewriting to record your thoughts about the subject. You may wish to keep these and the following activities in your writer's journal.

robots	carnivals	homework
basketball	cats	video games
sneakers	school lockers	insects

B Choose one of the following subjects. Use clustering to record your thoughts about the subject.

dragons	holidays	water
Mexico	fire	costumes
football	movies	horses

C You have been told to write a paper on some topic related to the future. Using "the future" as your focus, spend a day gleaning ideas for the topic of your paper. Use the following sources of ideas to come up with four possible topics.

1. friends, relatives, or teachers
2. observation of things at home or at school
3. books, magazines, or newspapers
4. radio, television, or movies

D Using the ideas that you developed in the preceding activities, decide on a topic you would like to write about. Research your topic. Then write a short composition about it.

2
Exploring Ideas

Once you have an idea to explore or a problem to solve, you can think it through in many different ways. However, all of these ways depend on two basic thinking skills: **listing features** and **making connections**.

Listing Features

Whenever you have to do some careful thinking, begin by listing all the things involved—the people, places, objects, events, and ideas. Then list the features of these things. Use the observation skills you learned in Chapter 1. Following are some features to look for.

size	height	smell
shape	depth	feel
color	width	duration
parts	taste	function
weight	sound	condition
age	quantity	importance or value

Here's a situation in which Eric used the skill of listing features.

Eric witnessed a hit-and-run accident involving a neighborhood dog. A police officer arrived on the scene, talked to Eric, and asked for a detailed description of the driver and the car.

Eric told the officer that the car was a blue '84 Sundancer with a rusted rear fender, and the letters *HL* were on the license plate. Eric also noticed that the car was missing a hubcap on the front end of the driver's side.

Eric also told the officer that he didn't see the driver's face, but he did notice that the driver was a red-haired man. Although he couldn't be sure, Eric guessed that the man was young because he had a red plaid bandana tied around his head, and he had on a white sweat shirt.

In his report to the police officer, how many features did Eric remember about the car and the driver?

Making Connections

Whenever you think about more than one person, place, object, event, or idea, consider the connections, or relationships, between them. Doing so will help you organize information, draw conclusions, and develop new ideas. Following are some of the most important connections, or relationships.

Relationships in Time	Ask yourself, "When did each event or action happen?"
Relationships in Space	Ask yourself, "Where is each thing in relation to the others?"
Relationships of Degree	Ask yourself, "Is one greater or lesser than another in some way? Is one harder or softer? Is one more or less important?"
Relationships of Cause and Effect	Ask yourself, "Does one cause the other? Is one an effect of the other?"

Here's a situation in which Paula used the skill of making connections.

> For her science class, Paula prepared a slide show on the planets in the solar system. Her science teacher provided her with slides of the planets. Then Paula gathered information on each planet from encyclopedias, books, and magazines. Next she had to figure out the best order for presenting her slides.
> To do this, she thought about the relationships among the planets. She realized that she could discuss them in terms of size, temperature, or position in space. Paula finally decided to present the planets according to their distance from the sun. She would start with the planet nearest the sun, Mercury, and end with the planet furthest from the sun, Pluto.

Think of some other ways in which Paula could have organized her slide presentation.

Grammar in Action

People, places, objects, events, and ideas are named by nouns and pronouns. Using precise nouns and pronouns helps you to focus your thinking. See pages 424 and 446. In the following sentence, the nouns are italicized.

The *anaconda* is a *snake* found in *South America*.

Features are often named by adjectives and other describing words. Using such words helps to make your thinking more vivid and concrete. See pages 508–523. In the following sentences, the adjectives are italicized.

The anaconda is the *longest* and *heaviest* snake in the *entire* world. It can weigh *950* pounds and reach $37\frac{1}{2}$ feet.

Writing Activity In the following sentences, which of the italicized words describe things? Which describe features?

Cobras are *cold-blooded, poisonous snakes*.
Even some of the *small reptiles* are very *dangerous*.
A *rattlesnake* has *two hollow fangs* in its *upper jaw*.
Scientists think that the *black mamba* of Africa is the *fastest snake* in the world.

Applying Thinking Skills

- When gathering information for a paragraph, composition, speech, or report, follow these steps. First list the people, places, objects, events, and ideas you want to write about. Then list details that describe the features of each one.
- When you acquire new information from reading, listening, or new experiences, look for relationships among the details. Identifying these connections will help you draw conclusions, develop new ideas, and go beyond the information you have. You will be able to choose the best order for organizing the material.

Writing Activities *Exploring Ideas*

A Before you go shopping, you should have a clear idea about what you are looking for. Suppose you want to buy one of the items listed below. List the features that you would want the item to have. Then write a paragraph describing it.

a wristwatch   an article of clothing
a notebook   a radio/cassette player
a bicycle   a piece of sports equipment

B Make a list of the things that you want to accomplish next week. Organize this list in time order (the first thing you want to do, the second, and so on). Then make a second list organized according to degree of importance (most important, next most important, and so on).

C Choose some place that is special to you. List the things in that place, in order, according to their relationships in space (left to right, right to left, top to bottom, bottom to top, near to far, or far to near).

D Place the items in each of the following groups in a logical order. Be ready to explain why you organized the items in the way you did.

1. San Francisco, New York City, Chicago, Kansas City
2. visit to the doctor, treatment, sickness, recovery
3. New Year's Day, Columbus Day, Thanksgiving, Labor Day
4. water, ice, steam
5. write a rough draft, find a topic, revise the draft, gather information
6. door, coffee table, sofa, window, piano
7. poodle, Great Dane, Chihuahua, German shepherd
8. washing clothes, sorting clothes, adding detergent, folding clothes, drying clothes, turning on the washing machine, placing the clothes inside the machine

E Think of a time when you were very successful in school or in some outside activity. List the things that caused you to be successful. Then write a paragraph explaining how to be successful at this activity.

3
Using Strategies

Adventurers and scientists must do some exploring before they make discoveries. In the same way, you must explore your ideas to learn more about them. There are many possible strategies, or plans, for exploring and developing ideas. Two such strategies are **analyzing** and **inquiring**.

Analyzing

To analyze something, you divide it into parts. Then you study each part carefully. Therefore, when you want to analyze something, follow the basic steps below.

1. Divide the thing or idea into its parts.
2. List the features of these parts.
3. Examine the connections, or relationships, among the parts.
4. Examine the connections, or relationships, between each part and the whole.

Here's how Karen used this strategy to solve a problem.

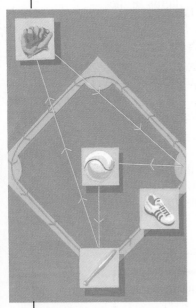

Karen is the manager of the girls' softball team at Roosevelt Junior High. When her team lost its first three games of the season, Karen decided to try to figure out why. To do this, she first divided the game of softball into its parts: pitching, batting, fielding, and base running. Then she considered the features of her team.

The team's batting, fielding, and base running were all excellent. However, the team's pitching was not so good. This poor pitching was obviously connected to the team's losing. Therefore, the coach recruited one new pitcher and started special training sessions for the other pitchers. The team won its next six games.

Inquiring

To inquire, you simply ask questions. Usually these questions begin with the words *who, what, where, when, why,* and *how.* These are the same kind of questions that reporters answer when they write newspaper articles.

What happened?	a fire, house destroyed, no one hurt
Where did it happen?	in Chicago, on the West Side, at the home of Mr. George Zagaras
Who was injured?	no one seriously, a firefighter treated for smoke inhalation but released
When did it happen?	at 2:00 P.M. on Tuesday
Why wasn't anyone injured?	Mr. Zagaras heard smoke alarm and fled the house
How did the fire start?	firefighters uncertain, possibly faulty wiring

Here's how Andrew used this strategy to accomplish a task at school.

Andrew is a member of the drama club at Lake Township Middle School. The sponsor of the club asked Andrew to write an announcement to be read over the public address system. The announcement would tell students about upcoming auditions for a musical. Andrew prepared the following list of questions.

Who can audition?
What will they be auditioning for?
When and *where* will auditions be held?
Why should students audition?
How can students interested in auditioning learn
more about it?

Then Andrew answered each question and used the answers to write his announcement.

Other Strategies for Exploring Ideas

Following are some additional strategies, or plans, for exploring and developing ideas.

Comparing and Contrasting Use this strategy to discover how things are alike or different. Follow the steps below.

1. List the things you want to compare and contrast.
    going to the movies   watching television
2. List the features of the things.
    going to the movies: big screen, refreshments, new films, costs money, entertaining escape away from home
    watching television: small screen, refreshments (in the refrigerator), old films, doesn't cost any money, entertaining escape at home
3. Look for similarities between the things (compare them).
    Both activities involve watching films on a screen.
    Both can involve refreshments.
    Both provide an entertaining escape.
4. Look for differences between the things (contrast them).
    The screen in a movie theater is larger.
    Going to the movies costs money, but watching television doesn't.
    Movie theaters show mostly new films, but television shows mostly old ones.

For more information on comparing and contrasting, see pages 221–227 in Chapter 11.

Classifying When you organize ideas into groups, you are classifying them. Follow these steps.

1. List the things that you want to classify.
    pets: gerbils, canaries, dogs, cats, snakes, turtles, rabbits, hamsters, horses
2. Think of features that some of the things have that the others don't have.
    Some require cages; others don't.
    Some can be easily trained; others cannot be trained.
3. Divide your list into groups, or classes.
    Caged Pets   Uncaged Pets

Writing Activities *Analyzing and Inquiring*

A Analysis is especially useful when thinking about a process—anything that happens in stages over a period of time. Think about one of the following processes. First divide the process into its parts. That is, list each step in the process. Then describe or list the features of each step in the process. Organize the steps according to their relationship in time (first, second, third, and so on). Write a paragraph that describes the process.

a. cooking something such as an omelette or a pizza
b. making something such as a kite or a paper airplane
c. studying for a test in English, math, or science
d. using something, like a computer or a VCR
e. cleaning your room

B Choose some special event that you would like to write a newspaper article about. For example, you could write about a school track meet, a local concert, or a school play. Before attending the event, prepare a list of questions beginning with *who, what, where, when, why,* and *how.* During or after the event, write the answers to your questions. Then write a short newspaper article reporting the event.

Come to the Meet!
WASHINGTON JR HI VS TAFT JR HI
MONDAY, JUNE 3, 3:00

4
Thinking Creatively

Creative thinking involves coming up with ideas that are new, original, and unexpected. By using creative thinking, you can create a song, a story, a work of art, or an invention. You can find a new and original solution to a problem. You can find new ways to approach everyday tasks. The following example shows how one student used creative thinking to solve a problem involving a conflict of time.

Devin was always busy. On two nights a week, she had to babysit for her three-year-old nephew. On one night a week, she had a piano lesson. Every night she had to practice for a couple hours, because she hoped to be able to get into a good music school

Writing Inside Out

Cheryl Johnson-Odim is a poet and a professor of Afro-American Studies at the University of Wisconsin at Madison. Following are some of her thoughts on writing and how writing ideas come to her.

"Poetry is something I do for myself. It's not writing dictated by deadlines or anything except my own needs and time. It's very personal. Also, poetry is writing in which I feel really free to express how I feel and not just what I think. You can be creative in your use of language. You can use words that would not ordinarily be used in a certain way. There is a lot of freedom in writing poetry."

some day. However, in recent weeks her grades had been slipping because she didn't have enough time to study. She realized that she had to come up with a creative solution to this problem.

The next morning Devin rode to school on the bus—as she did every morning and every afternoon. She turned off the music on her pocket cassette player that she listened to on headphones. She knew she had to think of something to get her grades back up. As she fingered the earphones of her cassette player, she suddenly found the solution to her problem.

She decided to take half an hour each day, right after school, to record her notes from class on a tape. Then, on her way to and from school, she would listen to the tapes of her notes. As a result, she would know her notes very well, and her test scores were bound to improve.

"There are so many different things about poetry that you can feel. It can be the way you use words. It can be the phrases you use, or it can be the rhythm of the poem."

"I'll wake up in the middle of the night with a poem in my mind, and I have to get up and write at least a few lines so that the next day I can get up and do it. My poetry—I feel like it just comes into my head, and I can be stimulated by some experience in my life or if something happens in somebody else's life. I have written poems as a result of watching the news. I never think I'm going to write a poem and then sit down and begin to craft it. It just sort of turns around in my head until it comes, and when it comes, I just write it out."

"Poetry is not work. It's pleasure writing. There are certain lines that really turn me on because I like language. I like words. It's funny, you know, a lot of people who like words don't like poetry. They think they don't. I mean, look at kids who like rap songs. I mean, that's poetry."

Creative Approaches to Thinking

Devin solved her problem by using something—a portable tape player—in a new way. Using things in new ways is one of the many creative approaches to thinking. To begin thinking creatively, try the following suggestions.

First, be open to new ideas. Turn off that part of your mind that evaluates and criticizes. Play with ideas without worrying about whether they seem foolish or silly. Remember that the first people who built flying machines were considered strange and eccentric by more "sensible" people.

Second, learn to observe things closely. Creative people look at the world with fresh eyes. By doing so, they see new connections between things, as Devin saw a possible connection between listening to tapes and studying for her classes.

Third, use your imagination. Creative people continually ask themselves the question "What if?" In other words, they ask questions such as the following.

1. What if I combined these two objects that are normally separate? (One fast food chain combined a spoon and a fork to make a *spork*.)
2. What if I used this object in a new or unusual way? (A hair dryer could be used to dry paint.)
3. What if this person, place, object, event, or idea had never existed or happened? (Imagine the world without the telephone.)
4. What if I changed just one part of this thing or situation? (Sun roofs changed the way people thought about cars.)
5. What if I changed what this object is made of? What if I changed its shape in some way? (One couple invented a baby bottle with a hole in the middle so that a baby could hold it easily.)
6. What if the relationships between certain people, places, objects, or events were different? (Imagine yourself suddenly becoming the teacher and your teacher becoming a student.)
7. What if I changed the location of something? (Imagine your town or city being relocated suddenly to a South Pacific island.)
8. What if people changed their roles or actions in some way? (Imagine something happening so that everyone could only walk backwards.)

9. What if I put these opposing ideas together? (Imagine a concert with a famous rock singer and a symphony orchestra.)

Applying Thinking Skills

Use creative thinking

- to come up with ideas for writing, speeches, projects, inventions, or works of art
- to solve problems and make decisions
- to come up with new ways of viewing yourself and the world around you

---

Writing Activities *Thinking Creatively*

A Each of the following passages gives an example of creative thinking. Explain which "What if" question or questions were asked in each situation.

1. Automobile tires used to be made of rubber. However, rubber was very expensive. As a result, someone had the idea of making them out of petroleum products instead.
2. Dennis had to write a short story for his English class. He wrote about a world that was just like ours except that the dinosaurs had not died out.

B Choose one of the "What if" questions on pages 38–39. Use that question to think of a new product that a business might make and sell. Write a paragraph describing the product.

C Following are some problems that need creative solutions. Brainstorm alone or with friends. Ask "What if" questions about them. Then list ideas that you have for solving or beginning to solve these problems.

1. hunger in the world
2. air and water pollution
3. overcrowding in cities
4. future energy shortages

Creative Writing

A Freewriting can be a fun, productive way to get your creative juices flowing before actually writing out the lines of a poem. You might discover some unexpected connections or comparisons to use in your poem. Select a topic for a poem, either on your own or from the list below. Take one minute for freewriting on that subject, writing down everything that comes into your mind. Try not to stop writing for even a second, and don't worry about spelling or grammar. Use the ideas you come up with as a starting point for an original poem. Write the poem, adding other ideas as you go along.

happiness
snow
the color red
tigers
your mother
babies
anger
water
a sport
a friend
dancing
love
paper
silence

Flight. Hans Hoffman.

B New inventions are often the result of freewriting or brainstorming. For example, you might see a common object around your home or classroom and think of new uses for it. Or, you might be thinking about everyday activities, such as driving, walking, or talking, and think of ways to make those activities easier or more fun. For one minute, think about an activity or an object and write down everything that comes to mind. Try to discover something new about it by asking yourself, "What if. . . ?" Write a description of your new invention.

English and Health

Often, the people we love have bad habits such as smoking, drinking, or overeating which we cannot get them to stop. Nagging doesn't help, nor does lecturing. So what can we do about a friend or parent whose health worries us?

Sometimes it takes a group of people working together to solve problems like these. For example, Alateen is an organization that brings together teenagers who face alcoholism problems in their families. The group meets regularly and helps teens brainstorm about this problem. By brainstorming, they can pool their ideas and help each other out.

To brainstorm, you start with a question or problem, analyze it, and think of all the possible solutions. The goal is to agree on the best possible approach. Remember that listening can be as important as speaking in this situation. You need to be able to hear and use the ideas of the entire group.

Activity

Choose one of the following health problems. Divide into groups. Then brainstorm with one group to find the best possible solution. Share and compare the various group solutions.

A Your friend lives on cookies and orange soda, hasn't eaten a vegetable in weeks, and never exercises. How do you convince him or her to eat better and exercise regularly without hurting any feelings?

B Some kids are starting to smoke cigarettes in the school restroom. The smoke hurts your eyes, and you know it's not good for them either. You and your friends don't feel comfortable walking into the restroom anymore. What can you and your friends do?

> # ALATEEN
>
> ## 3:30
> ## Room 212
>
> ## Meeting Today
> If there is a problem in your family, help yourself by helping others.
> Come brainstorm with us!

Application and Review

A Using Brainstorming Look over the following brainstorming ideas. What object or subject is the starting point for each list?

1. Keeps me informed, comes every day, sports section, newsprint gets on my hands, comics, movie listings.
2. Tells about products, commercials, billboards, uses testimony from famous people, jingles, persuasion, slogans sometimes funny.
3. Strawberry, triple dips, trucks with bells and whistles, drips in summertime, might fall off cone, can't choose.

B Recognizing Features and Making Connections Read and think about the following lists. Identify the feature that connects the items in each list.

1. Chicago, New York City, Dallas, Los Angeles, Miami
2. Chair, horse, pants, table, boy, girl, spider
3. Judge, lawyer, gavel, witnesses, defendant, evidence
4. Stop sign, octopus, $2.00 in quarters, octagon
5. Star, headlight, sun, diamonds
6. Blood, stoplight, heart, strawberry
7. France, Russia, Japan, England, Italy, Mexico
8. Quarterback, wide receiver, safety, running back, guard

C Using Inquiry Read the following school announcement. Identify five questions that might have been asked by the speaker before writing this report.

> The boys' basketball team won their fifth straight game on Friday afternoon against the Central Wildcats by a score of 52–31. Steve Miller was the leading scorer with fifteen points. Coach Wagner reports that the team has strong shooters and a good defense. Their next game is after school today in the North gym at 4:00. It's against the Cardinals, so make sure you're there to cheer on our team!

Starting Points

Ideas for Writing

Starting Points provides pictures and quotes to assist you in your search for interesting writing topics. Use these pages, and the questions below, to unlock your writer's imagination.

Pictures

1. What do I see in this picture? How could I describe it?
2. Can I do further research on this subject?
3. What feelings, memories, or ideas does the picture bring to mind?
4. What might have happened *before* the scene in the picture or just *after* it?
5. Describe the people in this picture. Would they make good characters in a story?
6. Does the picture remind me of another issue or experience worth exploring?

Quotations

1. What is the main point of the quotation? Do I agree with it?
2. How does this quotation apply to my own life?
3. Does the quotation remind me of anyone?
4. Can I think of an example that supports this quotation?

Feel free to go beyond *Starting Points.* Apply these questions to any of the photos, art, and ideas that appear throughout the text.

Invention

This artist's concept shows a cutaway view of two U.S. modules of a permanently occupied space station planned for the future.

There are three ways to get to the top of a tree: 1) climb it; 2) sit on an acorn; or, 3) make friends with a big bird.

Robert Maidment

Augustus Herring's early flying machine.

A SAFE FALLS ON THE HEAD OF PROFESSOR BUTTS AND KNOCKS OUT AN IDEA FOR HIS LATEST SIMPLE FLY SWATTER.
CARBOLIC ACID(A) DRIPS ON STRING(B) CAUSING IT TO BREAK AND RELEASE ELASTIC OF BEAN SHOOTER (C) WHICH PROJECTS BALL(D) INTO BUNCH OF GARLIC(E) CAUSING IT TO FALL INTO SYRUP CAN(F) AND SPLASH SYRUP VIOLENTLY AGAINST SIDE WALL. FLY(G) BUZZES WITH GLEE AND GOES FOR SYRUP, HIS FAVORITE DISH. BUTLER-DOG(H) MISTAKES HUM OF FLY'S WINGS FOR DOOR BUZZER AND RUNS TO MEET VISITOR, PULLING ROPE(I) WHICH TURNS STOP-GO SIGNAL(J) AND CAUSES BASEBALL BAT(K) TO SOCK FLY WHO FALLS TO FLOOR UNCONSCIOUS.
AS FLY DROPS TO FLOOR PET TROUT(L) JUMPS FOR HIM, MISSES, AND LANDS IN NET(M). WEIGHT OF FISH FORCES SHOE(N) DOWN ON FALLEN FLY AND PUTS HIM OUT OF THE RUNNING FOR ALL TIME.
IF THE FISH CATCHES THE FLY, THE SHOE CAN BE USED FOR CRACKING NUTS.

Invention by Rube Goldberg.

The universe is full of wonderful things
patiently waiting for our wits to grow sharper.

Eden Philpotts

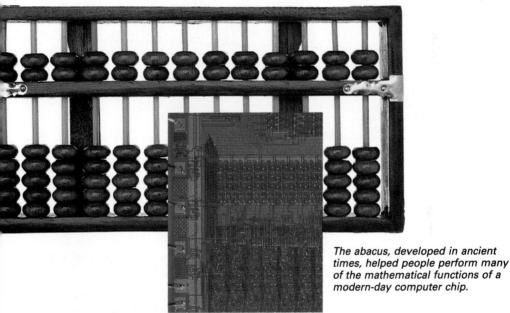

The abacus, developed in ancient times, helped people perform many of the mathematical functions of a modern-day computer chip.

It is better to know some of the questions than all of the answers.

James Thurber

More Ideas to Explore

Great Inventors
Useless Inventions
An Invention that
  Changed the World
Life Without an
  Important Invention
Mad Scientists

45

Starting Points

Achievement

One is not born a genius, one becomes a genius.

Simone De Beauvoir

What you can achieve
is only limited by what
you can dream.

Richard Rutan

The best part of greatness, and perhaps the biggest part, is humility.

Red Smith

Jesse White Tumbling Team, Chicago, Illinois.

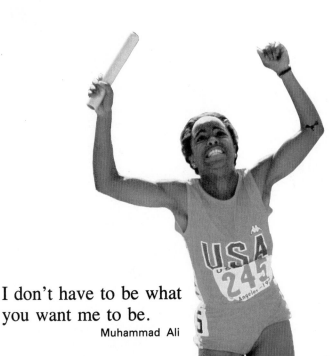

I don't have to be what you want me to be.

Muhammad Ali

Evelyn Ashford, winner of the 1984 Olympic gold medal for the 100-meter run.

More Ideas to Explore

Teams and Teamwork
Heroes
Competition and Cooperation
Practice
Obstacles and Challenges

Travel

Rod Taylor in H. G. Wells' The Time Machine.

Advice to Travelers

A burro once, sent by express,
His shipping ticket on his bridle,
Ate up his name and his address
And in some warehouse, standing idle,
He waited till he like to died.
The moral hardly needs the showing:
Don't keep things locked up deep inside—
Say who you are and where you're going.

Walker Gibson

"Would you tell me, please, which way I ought to go from here?" "That depends a good deal on where you want to get to," said the Cat.

ALICE IN WONDERLAND

Lewis Carroll

This painting by Alfred Russell shows Sacajawea guiding Lewis and Clark from Mandan Indian territory through the Rocky Mountains.

When you go by on a train, everything looks beautiful.

Edward Hopper

More Ideas to Explore

Wonders of the World
Pioneers and Explorers
Time Travel
Tourism
Great Getaways
Under the Sea and Into the Air

Starting Points

America

Some canyons are natural features of the land, and others have been made by human hands.

Freedom breeds freedom. Nothing else does.

Anne Roe

Spacious Skies

A great city is that which has the greatest men and women.

Walt Whitman

America is woven of many strands. . . . Our fate is to become one, and yet many.

Ralph Ellison

More Ideas to Explore

Exploring America
The American Dream
Regions of America
Problems and Solutions
The Pilgrim Spirit

Friends

What a gamble friendship is!
E.B. White

The only way to have a friend is to be one.
Ralph Waldo Emerson

I'm with you, pal

Forget injuries. Never forget kindnesses.

Confucius

The comic friendship between Stan Laurel and Oliver Hardy delighted movie audiences of the 1920's and 1930's.

Winter, Spring, Summer or Fall
All you have to do is call
And I'll be there,
You've got a friend.

Carole King

More Ideas to Explore

Best Friends
Popularity
Secrets
Peer Pressure
Sharing

Starting Points

Animals

You were once wild here. Don't let them tame you!
Isadora Duncan

When elephants fight it is
the grass that suffers.
Kikuyu Proverb

The terrifying and lovable King Kong thrilled movie audiences from 1933 into the present.

Animals are such agreeable friends—they ask no questions, they pass no criticisms.

George Eliot

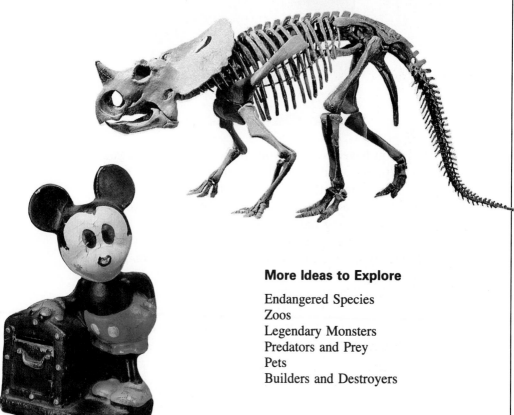

More Ideas to Explore

Endangered Species
Zoos
Legendary Monsters
Predators and Prey
Pets
Builders and Destroyers

3
Prewriting

You have gathered your provisions, checked your equipment, and planned your route. Now you are ready to step off on your mountain adventure.

Writing experiences are adventures too. Like hiking, writing requires advanced planning to help you decide exactly what you want to do. As you write, you take time to explore different paths and new opportunities.

This chapter introduces the steps of the writing process. It explains the first step, prewriting, which helps you choose a topic, gather information, and organize ideas for your writing adventures.

1
The Writing Process

There are as many ways to write as there are writers and things to write about. However, most writers find that they complete the following basic stages while writing.

Prewriting This is the planning stage. You choose a subject, determine your purpose, identify your audience, and decide what form to use for your writing. During prewriting you also explore possibilities, gather information, and organize your ideas.

Drafting In this stage you set down your ideas on paper, without worrying about errors. You may refine your work as it progresses by crossing out, rewriting, or moving sentences. As you write you may look back at your notes to check details.

Revising, or Editing When you revise or edit your paper, your first step is to judge its strengths and weaknesses. This can be done by self-editing, by working with a peer editor, or by reading your writing aloud to an audience. Then you make changes that are needed to clarify your meaning or improve your organization. Finishing touches are added in a separate substage called proofreading. When you proofread, you correct errors in spelling, grammar, usage, and mechanics.

Publishing and Presenting This stage occurs whenever you share your writing with others. There are many ways of publishing and presenting, from class magazines to oral readings.

A Flexible Process

The stages of the writing process are flexible. Often they overlap, go in circles, and run into each other. While drafting, you may realize that you need more details about your subject, so you circle back to prewriting. You may also move ahead to revise as you draft. The diagram on the next page illustrates the flexible nature of the writing process.

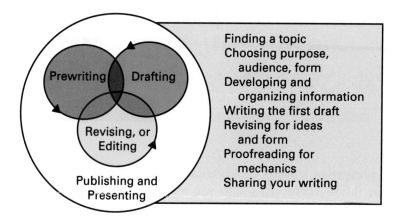

Finding a topic
Choosing purpose, audience, form
Developing and organizing information
Writing the first draft
Revising for ideas and form
Proofreading for mechanics
Sharing your writing

A Problem-Solving Tool

You may better understand the writing process if you think of it as a way of solving problems in writing. The flexible stages of the process may be viewed as problem-solving steps.

In prewriting, you **identify the task or problem** by deciding what your writing needs to accomplish. Then you **examine alternatives** by exploring different topics or forms for writing. To complete your prewriting, you **choose an approach**.

In the drafting stage, you **try out the approach**. You may experiment with different approaches. You might also share an early draft of your story with a classmate.

In the revising, or editing, stage you **evaluate results**. You judge the effectiveness of your paper, perhaps asking others to judge it also. If needed, you revise your paper.

Writing Activity *The Writing Process*

Answer the following questions to help you understand the writing process you use now.

1. How do you choose a subject to write about?
2. What kind of planning or prewriting do you usually do?
3. Do you draft with a pencil, pen, typewriter, or word processor? Do you revise as you draft?
4. Do you ever read your work aloud while revising? What other revising techniques do you use?
5. How carefully do you proofread your writing?
6. Who is your favorite audience when you share your writing? Has a piece of your writing ever been published?

2
Prewriting: Planning Your Writing

The prewriting stage is an important one that includes several different tasks. These tasks help you plan your writing in detail. During prewriting, you should think about four main questions. In answering them, you will use many of the thinking skills you learned in Chapter 2.

What Will I Write About? You will do your best writing when you write about things you know or that you are interested in learning about. There are several useful techniques for discovering ideas for writing that are inside your own mind and in your surroundings. One is keeping a notebook or journal of your thoughts, ideas, observations, and feelings. Reading your journal entries can help you find subjects for writing. You might also try freewriting or clustering (see pages 25–26). Your journal is a good place to practice these thinking skills.

Another useful technique is gleaning ideas from people, places, and things in your daily life, as described on page 26. While reading, talking to friends, or even watching television, you should be open to potential subjects for writing. Finally, you might use creative thinking, as explained on pages 36–39, to come up with completely new subjects or ideas. This approach is especially helpful when you are writing stories or poems or when you are trying to think of a new angle on an old subject.

Here is how Mark used the gleaning technique when trying to think of a subject for an article to publish in his class magazine.

> While watching a television special in which a young magician performed a modern version of one of Houdini's classic magic tricks, Mark had an idea. He thought, "I'm interested in magic. Maybe I can write about Houdini."

Once you have an idea, you have to set limits by narrowing your focus to a topic that you can cover thoroughly. One way to begin is by analyzing your subject (see page 32). Dividing your subject into parts may help you choose which part to develop in your writing. Another way is by inquiring (described on page 33). After listing questions about your subject, you might decide to concentrate on answering only one question in your writing, such as why something happened.

Mark used inquiring to set limits. He started by writing the following list of questions about Houdini.

> Who was Houdini?
> Why is Houdini so famous?
> Where did Houdini learn to perform magic tricks?
> What tricks did Houdini do?
> Where did Houdini perform his tricks?
> How did Houdini perform his tricks?

Mark found a book on Houdini in the library. While looking through the book, Mark realized that he was most interested in two of his questions—what tricks Houdini did, and how he did them. "Maybe I should write about one famous trick and explain how Houdini did it," he thought. He noticed an interesting photograph of Houdini hanging upside down in a straightjacket above a busy street. The photograph convinced Mark to focus on how Houdini got out of the straightjacket.

What Is My Main Purpose in Writing? There are four main purposes for writing: **to express yourself**, **to entertain**, **to inform**, and **to persuade**. Sometimes the topic itself determines the purpose. Suppose, for example, that Mark had decided to write an article comparing Houdini with the magician he had seen on television. Then his purpose might have been to persuade the reader that Houdini was a better magician.

At other times you decide on the purpose of your writing by reflecting on your thoughts and feelings about your subject. To help you determine your purpose, answer these questions:

> Why does this subject appeal to me?
> Why do I want others to know about it?
> What effect do I want my writing to have on my audience?

On the next page, see how Mark answered these questions.

I am interested in magic, so I think my classmates will be interested in it, too. Houdini was a world-famous magician. I want my classmates to know who Houdini was and what kinds of tricks he did. I will explain how Houdini escaped from a straightjacket, because this trick was one of his most spectacular feats. My main purpose is to inform my classmates about Houdini and to convince them that he was a great magician.

Who Are the Readers in My Audience? Sometimes you can choose your audience. For example, when you write a letter to a friend or relative, you choose that person to be your audience. At other times, your audience is chosen for you. If your teacher asks you to write an article for the class magazine, your audience has been chosen for you. There are many possible audiences with whom you can share your writing. These include the people who read your town newspaper or those who read a special-interest magazine or newsletter. They include the teachers and students

Writing Inside Out

Do you remember watching *Sesame Street* with Big Bird, Ernie, María, and Mr. Snuffleupagus? Today, many of the characters are the same as you remember. Others, however, have changed. One big change on *Sesame Street* has been Gordon and Susan's adoption of a little boy named Miles.

When Miles was added to the show, a team of researchers had to prepare for his arrival. Margarita Perez was an important member of this team. Ms. Perez is an expert on child development. She lives in New York and works for the Children's Television Workshop. Ms. Perez is one of the people who decides what will be taught each day on

who read your school newspaper or literary magazine and members of a club or a class.

Once you know your audience, you analyze who your readers are so that you can suit your writing to them. You decide what part of your subject might interest them, what information they might need, and what level of language would be most appropriate. For example, since some of the students in his class might not have heard of Houdini, Mark decided to include in his article background information on who Houdini was and why he was so famous.

What Form Will I Use? The **form** is the type of writing in which your message is expressed. The most common forms are stories, plays, poems, magazine and newspaper articles, school reports, editorials, and letters. You determine which form to use by thinking about the other prewriting decisions you have made concerning topic, purpose, and audience. Sometimes your topic determines the form. For instance, Mark might have decided to write an imaginative account of a meeting between Houdini and

Sesame Street. She is also responsible for giving ideas to the men and women who write *Sesame Street* scripts. For example, in 1985, when Miles was adopted, she wrote all about him, explaining his adoption, his likes, dislikes, growth, and development. It was almost like making up a character for a novel—except Miles was a real baby.

We asked Ms. Perez how she collects ideas when she has to write about a topic such as Miles's adoption. She explained: "First, I find out as much about a topic as I can, whether it's in books, calling people up to talk to them, or going through the library. Finding out as much about it, to understand what all the questions are, is really important.

"Second, I ask what do I want to emphasize. So now I know, for example, everything there is about adoption—who the experts are. Then, I ask what is the most important message?

"Third, how do I write it so the writers can use it? It can't be a cold, dry report. How can I make it come alive and be real? It's like fiction writing in a way."

the magician who is now performing his tricks. The form best suited for that topic is a story or play. At other times the purpose determines the form. Since Mark's purpose was to inform, an article was the best choice. The audience can also indicate what form you should use. If Mark had decided to write to the magician, asking him about his interest in Houdini, his form would have been a letter.

Using the Prewriting Process Sometimes one or more of the four prewriting questions will be answered for you. For instance, Mark's teacher asked him to write an article (form) for his class magazine (audience). He used the prewriting questions to determine his topic and purpose.

If you do not have the limits set for you, reflect on the four questions in any order. For instance, you might decide first that you want to write something for young children (audience). Then you determine that you want to write a story (form) about a young girl who wants to be a magician (topic). Your story will illustrate that with hard work and dedication, a person can accomplish any goal (purpose).

Writing Activities *Planning*

A Below are several statements. Tell whether each is about topic, purpose, audience, form, or a combination of these.

1. I think I'll write a play.
2. I feel like writing something entertaining for children.
3. I'd like to write something about mountain climbing.
4. I have to write a report for science class.
5. I'd like other people to see that movie.

B **Writing in Process** Use a thinking technique such as freewriting, clustering, or gleaning to come up with an idea for a short composition. As a possible source of ideas, look through *Starting Points: Ideas for Writing* (pages 43–55). Then, by analyzing or inquiring, narrow your subject to a topic that you can cover thoroughly. Answer the other prewriting questions to determine your purpose, audience, and form. Make a special writing folder, and save your notes in it. You will refer back to these notes in future exercises. You will also use this folder in other chapters to store notes, drafts, and revisions.

3
Gathering Information

Once you have planned your writing, you must gather information. For writing to inform, explain, or persuade, you gather information by reflecting, analyzing, inquiring, and gleaning. For more imaginative writing, such as stories, plays, and poems, you will have to create characters, settings, or images. You can do this by using your imagination or by finding similar people and things in real life. Jot down all the details that you can. Use the inquiring technique to ask questions about the who, what, where, when, why, and how of your idea. You will learn more about narratives in Chapter 10.

Using Reflecting to Gather Information

One good way to begin gathering information is by **reflecting** on what you already know about your topic. For instance, you might try **freewriting** to help you discover what details you know and what details you will have to find by some other method. Here is some freewriting that Mark did about Houdini.

> Let's see what I know about Houdini already. He was a famous magician. He performed miraculous escapes. I think he escaped from chains, handcuffs, straightjackets, and a box thrown into a river. I saw a picture of him in a straightjacket hanging upside down from a crane over a busy street. The cars on the street were old-fashioned, so this must have been a long time ago. I'd better check the date. A huge crowd was staring up at him. He must have been popular.

Using Analyzing and Inquiring to Gather Information

Another important technique for gathering information about your topic is **analyzing**. When you analyze, you divide your topic into its parts. On the next page read how Mark analyzed the topic for his article.

Who Houdini was and when he lived are parts of the background information. His escapes from chains, handcuffs, a straightjacket, and a box are all variations of his most famous trick, "The Escape." Details of how he did the trick can be grouped together as an explanation.

After you have analyzed your topic, use **inquiring** to make a list of questions your reader will want to have answered about each part. Here are the notes Mark made to show the parts of his topic and the questions he will try to answer about each part.

Topic: How the famous magician Houdini escaped from a straightjacket.

Parts and Questions:
Part 1: Background information on Houdini
    1. When did Houdini live and when was he popular?
    2. What were Houdini's most famous tricks?
Part 2: A description of Houdini performing his straightjacket escape
    3. Where did Houdini perform this trick?
    4. How did the audience react to the trick?
Part 3: How Houdini escaped from the straightjacket
    5. What special equipment did Houdini use?
    6. What techniques did Houdini use?

Using Gleaning to Gather Information

Probably the most useful technique for gathering information for an article or report is **gleaning.** Notice that in his freewriting, Mark had already started gleaning information about Houdini from the picture he had seen. Then Mark went back to the book he had found on Houdini to find the answers to the questions he had listed. He read parts of the book and studied the photographs.

As he read and studied, he thought about and evaluated each step. He asked himself, "Is this information directly related to my topic? How can I use it? Under which part can I use it?" He wrote the information that he might need in his writing notebook. On the next page is a list of notes Mark made for the second part of his article.

1. First escape from straightjacket—performed inside curtained cabinet
2. Once Houdini escaped from a jail cell in just a few minutes—ten pairs of handcuffs locked on his arms
3. Later Houdini performed straightjacket escape as publicity stunt—outdoors, spectacular
4. Straightjacket escape performed inside cabinet—audience did not believe Houdini escaped without help
5. Houdini revealed secret of his straightjacket escape in magazine article
6. Houdini escaped from a straightjacket in about three minutes—hanging upside down
7. Straightjacket escape performed in full view, audience went wild

Houdini escape act, Washington, D.C., 1921.

You can also use gleaning to gather information from sources other than books. For instance, Mark decided to interview his uncle, an amateur magician, about Houdini. To get ready for his interview, Mark prepared a list of questions to ask. He wrote down his uncle's answers. He also showed his uncle the other notes he had made and asked for advice on his article. Mark was already sharing his writing.

Writing Activities *Asking Questions*

A Choose one of the topics listed below. Write five questions you would want answered in a short composition about the topic. Review the section on inquiring on page 66 to help you think of questions. Then tell how you might find the answers.

1. Computers in the classroom
2. Farming in the future
3. Making and keeping a friend
4. Life on other planets

B Writing in Process Take out your notes from Activity B on page 64. Here are some ways to develop your writing idea. Use freewriting to find out how much you already know about your topic. Use analyzing to divide your topic into parts. Use inquiring to list questions you need to answer about each part of the topic. Use gleaning to gather information about your topic. Keep your notes in your writing folder.

4
Organizing Your Ideas

Once you have gathered information about your topic, you need to organize the information so that it makes sense to your readers. When you organize material, you complete two main tasks. First you arrange your information in a logical order. Second, you decide what information should be deleted and what information you still need.

Ideas can be organized in many ways. To choose a method of organization, look for relationships among your ideas.

Relationships in Time Sometimes your ideas are events that occur at different times. If so, you can use **chronological order**. Look on page 67 at Mark's notes. Notice that some are about Houdini performing his straightjacket escape inside a curtained cabinet (notes 1 and 4). Others tell about Houdini performing the escape later in his career in full view of his audience (notes 3, 6, and 7). Since the curtained escapes occurred before the public escapes, it is logical for Mark to arrange these ideas in chronological order.

Relationships by Position Sometimes the details you have gathered are related to one another by position. If so, you can use **spatial order**. Consider how Mark might have written about Houdini's outdoor escape. First, he might have described Houdini dangling upside down, then the crane from which he was hanging, and next the building which supported the crane. Last would be the crowd filling the street below.

Relationships of Amount or Degree At other times your details differ from one another in degree. You can arrange them in **order of familiarity** or in **order of importance** by starting with the least familiar or least important idea and ending with the most familiar or most important idea. For example, when he wrote about the tricks Houdini did, Mark could have begun with Houdini's least famous or least impressive trick and led up to his most famous or most impressive trick.

Adding and Deleting Information After organizing your ideas, make sure that each detail fits your topic and purpose. Look again on page 67 at the list of notes Mark made for his article. Notice that note 2 is about Houdini's escape from a jail cell. Since the purpose of Mark's report is to explain Houdini's straightjacket escape, this detail should be deleted.

You will also need to make sure that you have enough details to fulfill your statement of purpose. Look at the material from your readers' point of view and ask yourself whether all their questions have been answered. In looking at his notes, Mark decided that his readers would want to know why Houdini performed this stunt, so he added the following note to his list.

8. Houdini used straightjacket escape to get free publicity for 1915 tour to Kansas City, Oakland, and Los Angeles

Writing Activities *Organizing Notes*

A Paula made these notes for a report that she was writing on hiking in the Grand Canyon. Read the notes carefully. Tell what method of organization is most logical for the notes. Then, using that organization, arrange the notes in order.

- Bright Angel Trail finally reaches the Colorado River and the narrow Kaibab Suspension Bridge.
- A good place to rest along the trail is Indian Garden, a cottonwood oasis 3,100 feet below the rim.
- Bright Angel Trail starts into the canyon from Grand Canyon Village on the South Rim.
- Across the bridge is Bright Angel Campground where weary hikers can spend the night.

B Writing in Process Take out the notes you gathered for Activity B on page 67. Decide which method of organization is best suited for each part of your composition. Arrange your notes in the order you have chosen. Add additional information you think your reader will need and delete any details that do not fit your topic or purpose. Save your final notes in your folder.

Crossroads

English and Math

   Planning is an important part of any task—whether you want
to write a story, put together a puzzle, or solve a math problem.
In fact, planning is particularly important in math because you
must think about the processes you need to use. Should you add?
subtract? multiply? divide? And which should you do first? In
fact, the problems you face every day are often like math
problems, and planning can also help you solve them.
   Whatever the problem, you will find that the process of
solving it often includes the steps below:

1. Study all of the information carefully, looking for numbers
   and facts.
2. Think of a similar problem that you've solved.
3. Think about how the numbers and facts are related and use a
   sketch, diagram, or mental map to outline the problem.
4. Make a guess, or do the mathematical computations.
5. Check your answers.

Activities

   Solve the following problems using the steps above.

A If A equals 1,352, and B equals 2,060, and C equals 523,
   what is the value of A + B − 2C?

B Peter, Karen, Jeff, and Susan are the first names of my
   mother, father, sister, and brother. I am older than Karen,
   and Jeff is younger than I am. How is each person related to
   me?

C At the grocery store, three different brands of yogurt are on
   sale. The first costs $.58 and weighs 8 ounces. The second
   costs $.81 and weighs 9 ounces, and the third costs $.49 and
   weighs 6 ounces. Which is the best buy?

Application and Review

A Identifying the Stages of the Writing Process Read the following list of writing activities. Tell whether each activity is most likely to be prewriting, drafting, revising, or presenting.

1. Reading a story to a friend
2. Freewriting or clustering
3. Correcting errors in spelling or grammar
4. Taking notes from various sources
5. Publishing your article in a school paper
6. Putting your ideas together on paper
7. Proofreading

B Planning Your Writing Read the draft below. Identify its subject (*what*), purpose (*why*), audience (*who*), and form (*how*).

> Dear Allyson,
>   Hi there! Karen told me that you weren't coming to my birthday party, and I'm upset! Everyone's going to be there (even Michael), and it's going to be a lot of fun. There will be great music and dancing. Please change your mind, and come!
>   Terri

C Organizing Ideas Read the following notes taken for a written report. Tell what method of organization (chronological order, spatial order, order of familiarity, or order of importance) is best for these items. Rearrange the notes in a logical order.

1. A little while later, the scene changed and we were floating over green pastures and trickling streams.
2. We arrived at the launch pad right at dawn to prepare the hot air balloon for flight.
3. All too soon, after only an hour in the air, it was time to leave our bird's eye view of life, and return to the ground.
4. The balloon slowly drifted over a thick forest of tall pines.
5. By 6:30, the heated gas had inflated the balloon, and we were ready to lift off.

4
Drafting

Imagine you are asked to design the world's tallest skyscraper. How will you do it? You might have a general idea in mind when you sit down at your drafting table, but your table will probably become littered with discarded plans before you settle on a final design.

Drafting, whether you design a building or a composition, is the process of getting your ideas down on paper. You add, delete, and change ideas as you draft, using a method that works best for you. In this chapter you will learn about the approaches you can try.

1
Getting Ready to Write

Think for a moment about two good cooks making stew. One follows the recipe exactly, carefully measuring every ingredient. This cook stops often to wipe up spills and put things away. The other cook seldom consults the recipe, tossing in a dash of this and a handful of that, depending on what is fresh and in stock. This cook cleans up at the end when the stew is ready for the oven. The two cooks work differently, but both end with a good product.

Writers work in a similar way. As you will learn in this chapter, there are many ways of drafting a piece of writing. The method you choose will be determined by your purpose and by the style of writing that is most comfortable for you. Like the first cook, you might prefer a precise and careful method. On the other hand, like the second cook, your style might be more informal. The writing that results, like the stews prepared by the two cooks, can be equally successful.

Take Stock As you prepare to begin drafting, you should first use reflecting to take stock of the prewriting choices you have made. Ask yourself questions to make sure your writing is planned as you want. Here are some questions to consider:

> Have I narrowed my topic?
> Is my information arranged logically?
> Do I have enough information?
> Do I know my purpose?
> Have I analyzed my audience?
> Have I chosen the right form?

As Mark prepares to draft his article on Houdini, he thinks about these questions. He decides that his topic is sufficiently narrow, and that he is satisfied with how he has analyzed his audience and determined his purpose and form. He reads over his notes (see page 67), adding more information about Houdini's background. He realizes, however, that he has not yet decided how to organize his explanation of Houdini's escape from a straightjacket. Looking over his notes, he decides he will explain Houdini's technique as a series of steps arranged in chronological, or time, order.

Find a Time and Place The next step in preparing to draft is choosing a good time and place. Writing takes concentration. You will probably do your best work when you have a block of time without interruptions. You should think about finding a good place to write. The desk in your room, the library, or even a quiet place outside can be a good choice.

Choose and Gather Materials Once you have set aside a good time and place, the next step is choosing writing materials and gathering them together. Some writers prefer to draft in pencil, erasing to keep their rough drafts as neat as possible. Others like the free flow of writing with a pen. They make changes by crossing out or by drawing arrows. Today, many writers are switching from pencil and paper to the typewriter or word processor. Typewriters produce readable drafts that can be revised later in pencil or pen. Word processors allow writers to revise their work as they draft, by making it easy to eliminate mistakes and to move words and sentences around on the screen before the final copy is printed.

You might find that you like having a dictionary nearby, or that a thesaurus helps you to choose just the right word. For some writing projects, you might also need a reference book like an atlas or an encyclopedia to check details. Mark decides that he wants his book on Houdini close at hand, so that he can look at the photographs while he describes them. You will also want to have your prewriting notes or note cards handy.

Writing Activity *Reviewing Your Plan*

Writing in Process Take out your writing folder and look over the notes you made for your composition in Chapter 3. Answer the questions listed under *Take Stock* on page 74 to check whether you are satisfied with your planning. Add additional information to your notes if needed and go over your plan of organization. Save your notes in the folder. Decide what materials you need to begin drafting, and gather them together.

2
Methods of Drafting

When you draft, your goal is to get your ideas down in sentences and paragraphs. You can experiment freely, cross out ideas, add details, and reorganize sentences and paragraphs. You can postpone thinking about errors in spelling, grammar, usage, and mechanics until the revising stage, if you wish. If your draft gets stalled, you can even start all over again.

There is no single way of drafting. The method you choose should fit your personal style and the requirements of the writing you are doing. Here is a description of the most common methods of drafting. Experiment with those methods to find the one that is best for you.

The Loosely Structured Draft When you write a loosely structured draft, you work from rough prewriting notes. As you write, you experiment with ideas and organization. This method works best when you are not exactly sure what you want to say or how you want to say it.

Here is a loosely structured draft Mark wrote of the paragraph that describes the picture of Houdini performing his straightjacket escape. Notice that Mark changes his plan of organization while drafting this paragraph. His thoughts are shown in the bubbles.

I should add a transition. → *Above their heads*

A crane sits on top of a tall building. Strong

ropes from the crane are attached to a pulley. A man

upside down

hangs from the pulley. His feet are tied together.

His arms are crossed over his chest and bound by a

straightjacket. A huge crowd fills the street. Mainly

I should describe the crowd first.

men in straw hats and shirtsleeves. They are all

looking up.

The Highly Structured Draft When you write a highly structured draft, you work from very complete prewriting notes. As you write, you follow your writing plan carefully, changing little of the content and organization. This approach often works best for reports or other detailed expository papers.

Here is an example of how Mark might have written a highly structured draft from his notes on page 67.

When Houdini first started performing his
on stage ← I should be more specific.
straightjacket escape, he did the trick inside a
curtained cabinet. The audience was not excited by
his feat, however, since they could not believe that
Houdini had escaped without help. Later in his
career, Houdini began performing this trick outdoors
I shouldn't say "outdoor" twice.
as a spectacular outdoor publicity stunt. In 1915, he
used the stunt to get people interested in the magic
in theaters
shows he would be performing in Kansas City,
Oakland, and Los Angeles. When Houdini escaped
I should end with the crowd's reaction.
in full view of his audience, the crowd went wild.
He escaped in three minutes.

Bridge Building When you use this drafting method, you begin with three or four main ideas or situations. During drafting, you work on building logical bridges between the ideas. For example, Mark could have started one section of his paper knowing only that he wanted to cover three main ideas: 1) Houdini was a magician and escape artist; 2) He played in theaters around the world; 3) He performed many of his escapes in public.

Instead of making more detailed notes at this point, Mark could have just started writing, developing his paragraph from the information in his head. However, at some point he would think, "Well, Houdini was a magician but he wasn't so famous. That might be a good lead-in to the idea of public escapes. I can end the first paragraph saying that despite his skill, Houdini was not well known. Then I can begin the next paragraph, 'To increase his popularity, Houdini began doing stunts in public.'"

The bridge-building method is a good one to use if you are writing from personal experience or knowledge, or if detailed planning is difficult for you. It is something like freewriting. You learn what you want to say as you are saying it.

The Quick Draft or the Slow Draft? Whichever drafting method you choose, you can complete your draft in one of two main ways—the quick draft or the slow draft. When you write a quick draft, you can use prewriting notes if you have them. However, your goal is to get all your ideas down on paper quickly. Once your draft is complete, you can go back over it several times to refine ideas, reorganize, add or delete information, and correct errors. Like freewriting, the quick draft is a good choice when writing will help you discover what you want to say. It is also helpful if frequent stopping interrupts your flow of thought.

When you use the slow draft method, you work slowly and carefully, drafting one sentence or paragraph at a time. You use prewriting notes if you have them. You generally revise as you go along. This is a good method if you feel uncomfortable about leaving an idea unfinished.

Writing Activities *Drafting*

A Andrea made the following prewriting notes for a paragraph she is writing about scuba diving. Choose a drafting method and write a paragraph using Andrea's notes.

- tropical reef, a beautiful place to dive
- diver hangs weightless in clear sunlit water
- brightly colored corals
- spiny lobster under coral covered rock
- bubbles rise from diver's regulator

B **Writing in Process** Look over your notes from Activity B on page 69. Use one drafting method to write a first draft about your topic. Keep the draft in your writing folder.

3
Reflecting After Drafting

When you have finished drafting, it is often a good idea to delay the start of the revising stage of the writing process for a day or two. This will give you a chance to reflect, or think, about what you have written. Use one of the following techniques when you are reflecting.

Read Your Draft Silently When you read your draft silently, try to imagine that you are the reader, not the writer. Ask yourself questions as you read, such as "What does that sentence mean?" or "Why do you think that?" Try to identify places where the reader might be confused, or might need additional information.

Read Your Draft Aloud When you read a draft aloud, you can often hear problems you might miss if you were reading silently. You might catch missing words or ideas, awkward phrases or sentences, and problems with organization.

Share Your Draft Sharing your draft with a relative or friend is another good way of gathering information before revising. Your reader should question you about anything in the draft that doesn't make sense or that isn't detailed enough. For school assignments, you might try trading drafts with another student working on the assignment.

As you use these reflecting techniques, look for answers to the following questions.

Checklist for Reflecting After Drafting
1. Do I need more information, or can some information be deleted?
2. Will everything be clear to the reader?
3. Are there any missing words or ideas?
4. Can I identify awkward words or sentences?
5. Are there any problems with the logical order?

Speaking and Listening

When reporters write a story for the newspapers, they almost always have to talk to at least one person before writing. The purpose of these interviews is to get complete information for the article. In your writing, you may need to locate people who know something about a particular topic. The best people for interviews are those who either saw or know something about what happened or who were part of the event. For example, they might be athletes who played in a big game, artists who are exhibiting their work, or passers-by who witnessed an event.

Next, you need to think up several questions to ask the person in an interview. For example, a good news reporter tries to ask the basic questions: *Who? What? When? Where? Why?* and *How?* As the person answers these questions, take notes on what they have to say.

Once the reporter completes an interview, he or she has to combine all of the information into one story. The reporter writes a draft of the story, making sure that all the details fit together logically and smoothly. Usually, an editor reads this draft and makes any final changes before the story goes to print.

Activity

Choose a recent event in your school, home, or town. Find a person who knows what happened and think of several questions to ask him or her. Remember to use *who, what, when, where, why,* and *how* in your questions. Then, interview the person and write a brief news article sharing your information.

Application and Review

A Preparing to Write Make a plan to begin drafting a composition about closed caption programming on television. Use the following three categories: *Taking Stock, Finding a Time and Place,* and *Choosing and Gathering Materials.* List at least two activities under each category.

B Identifying Methods of Drafting Read through the writing plans below. Tell which drafting style each describes: loosely structured, highly structured, or bridge building.

1. The school newspaper only has room for one sports article in this issue, but you discover that the volleyball team, the swim team, and the basketball squad are all having winning seasons. You then decide to focus your article on the victories of these three teams.
2. One night you are awakened by a dream about a shipwreck at sea. You scribble a few notes on a pad and, the next day, begin writing a short story about the dream. Unsure about the plot, you try several ideas.
3. While writing a research paper on photosynthesis, you collect notes, and then construct an outline to follow as you draft your report.

C Reflecting After Drafting Read the paragraph below. Identify any problems that will need to be corrected during the revision stage. Look for spelling and punctuation errors, awkward phrases or sentences, and missing words or phrases. Think about additions that would improve the interest level of the paragraph.

> I must walked fifty miles this summer—behind a lawn mower! Each time my neibors get their lawns cut and trimmed. I walked away with ten dollars and a sun tan. It was a grate way to keep my legs strong but tired I got sometimes. I would drag the lawn mower home on my bicycle and collapse in the couch with a lemonade. Than Id start al over agin the next daye. What a summer?

5

Revising and Presenting

As you stand before your easel, all the false starts
and the rough sketches are behind you. Now it's
time to put the finishing touches on your painting.
You know you will be sharing your masterpiece
with the world, so you want to make sure everything
is right.

Writing that you plan to share also needs polishing. In Chapters 3 and 4 you learned how to gather
ideas and write your preliminary drafts. Now you
will learn to revise your work so that it presents
your thoughts clearly and completely. Then you will
be ready to share your written masterpiece with the
world.

1
Revising, or Editing

You probably have been revising your work all through the prewriting and drafting stages. Once you have finished drafting, however, it is time for your final revision.

Revising, also called editing, gives you the freedom to change anything about your draft that doesn't work well or that you think could be improved. You can also correct errors in spelling, grammar, usage, and mechanics. But your main tasks during revision are making sure that your ideas are expressed clearly, that your information is organized logically, and that you have chosen the right words to express your meaning.

Choosing a Method Choose a method of revising that suits your personal style and the kind of writing you are doing. Here are some common methods.

Methods of Revising

1. **Peer Editing** Share your draft with another student, preferably someone in your intended audience. Use your reader's questions and comments to help guide you during the revision.

2. **Group Questioning** Read your draft aloud to a group of students. Use their questions to help in your revision.

3. **Self-editing** Set your draft aside for a day or two. Then read it through carefully, silently or aloud. Correct any problems you discover.

4. **Teacher Conferences** Share your draft with your teacher, newspaper sponsor, or another member of your intended audience. Ask your reader specific questions about how to correct problems you have identified. For example, you may want to know if your language is colorful enough.

5. **Performance** If your writing explains how to do something, read your draft aloud while another student follows the directions. Look for instructions that are unclear, incomplete, or confusing.

Mark used a combination of these techniques when he revised his article on Houdini. He asked the editor of his class magazine to read his draft, and he had a conference with his teacher. Notice his thoughts as he revised.

When he was being ~~put~~ *buckeled* into the Straightjacket,

> This sentence is unnecessary.

Houdini expanded his chest. ~~His great chest~~

~~expansion helped him do underwater escapes.~~ This

slack   *To escape first*

gave him some ~~room~~ inside. He pushed on one

> I should add words to show chronological order.

force   *Then he tucked*

elbow to ~~push~~ it up toward his head ~~and pushed his~~

This brouht his arms in front of his lower body. Next

> This makes my explanation clearer.

head under the lower arm He undid the buckels on

and

the cuffs with his teeth. He ~~used~~ his hands encased

still in canvass to open the buckels on the back.

In less than three minutes

∧ Houdini was free.

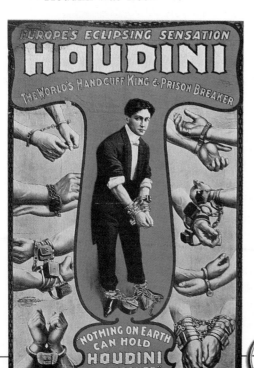

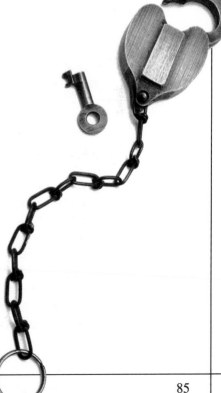

Revision Checklist The following questions may help you or a peer editor to evaluate your composition.

Revision and Peer-Editing Checklist
1. Is all essential information included? Are there any unnecessary or unrelated details?
2. Is each main idea clearly expressed and thoroughly developed?
3. Does the organization clearly show how ideas are related? Are transitions used to link ideas and paragraphs? Does anything seem out of place?
4. Are there any confusing sentences or paragraphs?
5. Are vivid and precise words used?
6. Do the tone, mood, and level of language suit the audience?

Writing Activities *Revising and Peer Editing*

A Revise the following paragraph that Jill wrote as part of a science report. Use the revision checklist as a guide. As you revise, find and delete one unrelated detail.

The turtle's shell is as protective as a suit of armor. It is a strong bony shell. The shell has two parts. The carapace is the domed top. There are openings where the head, legs, and tail poke out. The underneath part is called the plastron. Sea turtles can not hide in their shells. Sea turtles have flippers instead of legs. A freshwater turtle pulls back into its shell when it senses danger.

B **Writing in Process** Share the draft you wrote during Activity B on page 78 with a peer editor to get suggestions for revision. Then use the revision checklist to self-edit your draft. Save your draft in your writing folder.

2
Proofreading

Proofreading is the stage when you do your final polishing. It is the last step in your revision. At this point you pay close attention to finding and correcting problems with spelling, grammar, usage, and mechanics. You might find it helpful to proofread your work several times, each time looking for a different kind of error. Use a dictionary to correct spelling and hyphenation mistakes.

Proofreading Checklist As you proofread your draft, you should look for the answers to the following questions.

> ### Proofreading Checklist
> 1. Do all verbs agree with their subjects? (See pages 580–586.)
> 2. Do I have any run-on sentences? (See pages 413–414.)
> 3. Have I used the correct form of each pronoun? (See pages 446–458.)
> 4. Are all the adjectives and adverbs used correctly? (See pages 508–518 and 526–535.)
> 5. Are all the first words capitalized? Are all proper nouns and adjectives capitalized? (See pages 596–606.)
> 6. Does each sentence have the proper end mark? (See pages 614–615.)
> 7. Are commas, semi-colons, apostrophes, hyphens, and quotation marks used correctly? (See pages 620–641.)
> 8. Have I checked the spelling of all unfamiliar words in the dictionary? (See pages 336–340.)
> 9. Are all plurals and possessive forms spelled correctly? (See pages 435–437.)

Proofreading Symbols To change and correct your draft, use the symbols for proofreading from the chart on page 88 or from the chart on the inside back cover of this book.

Proofreading Symbols

∧	Add letters or words	⌒	Close up
⊙	Add a period	¶	Begin a new paragraph
≡	Capitalize a letter	⋏	Add a comma
/	Make a capital letter lowercase	∩	Trade the position of letters or words
	— or ⌿	Take out letters or words	

Mark proofread the revised paragraph from his article on Houdini. He used the proofreading checklist and symbols.

¶ When he was being buckeled into the Straightjacket, Houdini expanded his chest. This gave him some slack inside. To escape he first pushed on one elbow to force it up toward his head. Then he tucked his head under the lower arm this brouht his arms in front of his body. Next he undid the buckels on the cuffs with his teeth and used his hands encased still in canvass to open the buckels on the back. In less than three minutes Houdini was free.

Writing Activities *Proofreading*

A Proofread and rewrite the following paragraph.

On Salisbury plain in southern england is a wonderful circle arrangement of stones. The stones has been the subject of many stories, poem, and legends from as far back as the day of king Arthur. Many studys have tried to answer this question what do the stones mean. Modern astronomers have started solveing the mystery.

B **Writing in Process** Proofread the draft you revised in Activity B on page 86. Prepare a clean, final copy.

3
Publishing and Presenting

In this stage of the writing process you share your writing with others. Usually, you will publish your writing. But you may also choose another way of presenting your work. Here are a few suggestions.

Bulletin Boards   Your class, club, or library might use a bulletin board to post writing about a specific subject. The display could also contain drawings and photographs to illustrate the writing.

Booklets   Your class, club, or friends could put together a booklet. The booklet might contain writing about one subject, such as a common interest or hobby. Another kind of booklet might contain one type of writing, like poems or album reviews. You could illustrate the booklet with appropriate art work and duplicate the booklet in your school print shop.

Newspapers and Magazines   You could submit your writing to your school newspaper or magazine. Many local newspapers also accept student writing. You and your friends might even start a newspaper or magazine to publish writing about a specific topic.

Performances   You could adapt a story or poem to the form of a play and act it out for your class or club. You might like to read your writing aloud to an audience, perhaps with appropriate music in the background.

Letters   You could write a letter and mail it to a relative or friend, or submit it as a letter-to-the-editor of a magazine or newspaper. A group of students could also exchange letters with a club or class at a different school or in a different country.

You do not have to share everything you write, of course. Sometimes, you will write only for yourself and save your writings in a diary or journal. Other times, you will be writing mainly for your teachers. However, finding ways to share most things you write will make your writing more meaningful.

Mark will publish his article on Houdini in the class magazine. Here is the final copy of part of his article.

Student Model

When Houdini first started performing his straightjacket escape, he did the trick on stage inside a curtained cabinet. The audience was not excited by his feat, however, since they could not believe Houdini had escaped without help. Later in his career, Houdini began performing this trick as a spectacular outdoor publicity stunt.

On April 26, 1916, for example, a huge crowd of men in straw hats and shirtsleeves fills the streets of downtown Baltimore. They are looking up. Above their heads, a crane sits on top of a tall building. Strong ropes from the crane are attached to an iron hook. A man hangs upside down from the hook. His

Writing Inside Out

Doug Wood has written comedy sketches for stars such as Smokey Robinson, Chaka Khan, Pee Wee Herman, and Merv Griffin. Doug lives in Los Angeles, where he is an actor and writer who specializes in comedy. His credits include shows such as "Motown Review," "America," "The Fine Line," and "Star Search."

How did Doug get into acting and writing? Doug has known that he wanted to be an actor since he was six years old. He pursued his interest in acting throughout high school, college, and several drama schools. He began writing comedy material and eventually decided to head for Hollywood. When he left for Hollywood, he purchased a roundtrip ticket. He never used the return portion! Within a month, he was working on a television show. Doug's first love is acting, but these days he spends more time writing than acting.

feet are tied together. His arms are crossed over his chest and bound by a straightjacket.

At a signal, the man begins to struggle. His face gets redder as he thrashes in the air. In a minute and a half, he has forced his right arm over his head. In another twenty seconds, his left arm is free. Though his hands are still inside the canvas sleeves, he manages to unbuckle the jacket and ease it over his head. In under three minutes, the straightjacket drops to the street, as the crowd applauds wildly. Still upside down, Houdini takes a bow in mid-air.

Writing Activity *Presenting*

Writing in Process Choose one method of sharing and use it to share the writing you completed in Activity B on page 88.

What does a television writer do? In California Doug has worked as a comedy writer for several TV shows. He explains how a script comes together.

"In writing short skits for a variety show, the main goal is to write something funny that is also very current. Each day you come to work and spend the first few hours reading everything you can, from *Rolling Stone* magazine to the daily newspapers to *People* magazine. The week is spent first pitching ideas to the producers and head writers and then developing the ones that seem most interesting. When they decide which ones they like, a script for that week's show is compiled, and the rest of the week is spent rewriting, making revisions, attending rehearsals, and working with actors and producers until the taping of the show before a live audience."

How does a comedy writer know when a script is right? Doug says that the difference between comedy and drama is timing. In comedy, timing is absolutely essential for it to work. In that respect, Doug knows that a collaborator, or partner, is very valuable when writing comedy scripts: "It helps to have a collaborator because when your collaborator is doubled over with laughter, then you know it's funny."

4
Choosing a Process for Writing

You have learned that writing is a process made up of a series of stages—prewriting, drafting, revising, and presenting. These stages, however, are rarely completed in one neat, step-by-step sequence. The process may vary from writer to writer and with the type of writing being done.

The Writer How do you write? How do you go through the stages of writing? Do you write whatever comes to your mind, or do you plan very carefully? Do you revise as you write, or do you write without stopping and revise at the end?

The way you write depends in part on the kind of person you are. Some people, for example, are quite anxious to begin their actual writing. Instead of starting with prewriting, they begin with a first draft. On the other hand, some writers like to know exactly where they are going, and they follow a prewriting plan like a trusted road map. Others like to move back and forth from one stage to another.

The Type of Writing How you write also depends in part on what you are writing. You don't need to go through each stage of the writing process for every type of writing task. While a history report requires a great deal of research and planning, a social letter or a diary entry needs little planning.

Your purpose may also play an important role in how you write. An entertaining "I Was There" story about The Boston Tea Party might be done with little prewriting. Yet, an informative composition about the causes and effects of the Boston Tea Party would require much prewriting effort.

As you can see, there are many paths within the writing process. When you work through the chapters in this book, you will travel along several of those paths. You will experiment with the writing process and, with experience, find processes that best suit you, your purpose, and your material.

Speaking and Listening

Giving a speech is more than selecting a topic, writing the speech, and delivering it. A good speech has to take into account its audience. Some audiences are hoping to be entertained. Don't bore them with mountains of facts and figures. Other audiences want information. Give *them* the facts and figures. Some audiences already know a lot about your topic—don't insult them with repetition or misinformation. Other audiences are hungry for what only you know. Give it to them!

Whenever you give a speech, learn to analyze your audience before you begin writing. Ask yourself questions such as: What do I want to say? Who is going to be in the audience? Then, plan your speech accordingly. Remember that keeping the audience's attention is the only real goal of a good speech.

Activity

You have been asked to deliver a speech. Select a topic that tells how to do something, expresses a strong opinion, praises someone's accomplishment, or describes a special trip. Then choose two different audiences on your own or from those below. Prepare a speech for the first audience, and revise it so that it would be appropriate for the second group.

Audience: teachers, parents, friends, younger kids, students from another school, your classmates.

Creative Writing

A The fairy tales we know today, such as "Snow White" and "The Three Bears," were thought up hundreds of years ago in a very different place and time. While we still enjoy these tales, we might want to change some parts of them to fit modern times and places. Try to imagine what a present day Cinderella story would be like. Might the prince become a great star, the glass slipper a pink hightop sneaker, the royal ball an evening at a dance club? What do you think? How would changing the time affect the tale? Does one change lead to other changes throughout the story? Choose any fairy tale and rewrite it using the present as the setting. Note all of the changes you must make.

B In most science fiction stories and movies, the brave heroes and heroines always get our sympathy and our attention. What if that changed? What if science fiction stories were written through the eyes of the wicked villains? How would the story change? Rewrite any science fiction tale or write one of your own, making the villain the central character. Tell the story from the villain's point of view. You may discover some interesting things about human nature as you write.

Application and Review

A Recognizing Proofreading Symbols Rewrite the paragraph below by correcting the errors marked. Use the symbol chart in this chapter if necessary.

Located in Chicago, Illinois, the Sears tower is the World's tallest building. Its 110 storys plus antennas reach 1,707 feet into the air. The two buildings closest to this height are the World Trade Centre in New York City and the Amoco Building in Chicago. Millions and millions of people have visited the 103rd floor skydeck for the panoramic view of the city. High-speed elevators take them up in just over one minute and automatic window-washing machines go into action six to eight times a year to keep the clean view. During times of good visibility visitors can see four states.

B Using Proofreading Symbols Read the sentences below. Copy them and insert proofreading symbols wherever corrections are needed. (There are at least three errors per sentence.)

1. On my first day of skiing at copper Mountain I stayed on the the beginner and intermediate slopes.
2. The chair lift carried us up to the top of the run and we skiied down as fast as we could then we got right back in line.
3. The intermediate hills marked with blue squares and the Beginner ones with green circles so that skiiers would know wich kind of run they were on.

C Choosing a Process for Writing For each writing project below, tell whether it would most likely require more prewriting or more revising.

1. An essay question on an English test
2. A poem about your feelings
3. A letter to your parents
4. A report on ancient Greek mythology

6

Writing Paragraphs

A mixed-up jumble of puzzle pieces seems at first like a hopeless mess. As you sift through the pieces, however, you begin to sense patterns of shape and color. Eventually, all the pieces fall into place.

Writing a paragraph involves sifting through ideas and figuring out how they fit together. Just as a finished puzzle presents a complete picture, a finished paragraph presents a complete idea. In this chapter you will learn how to fit the puzzle pieces of a paragraph together to make paragraphs that are unified and coherent.

1
Understanding Paragraphs

News articles, short stories, reports, essays, and friendly letters have at least one thing in common. They all contain one or more paragraphs.

You can identify a paragraph easily because the first line is always indented. More importantly, a paragraph focuses on a single main idea. It also contains sentences that support that main idea. This information leads us to a definition: A **paragraph** is a group of related sentences that work together to explain or develop one main idea.

Read the following paragraphs and identify the one that is a well-developed paragraph. It should have a single main idea with related sentences.

> Chimpanzees seem to be natural showoffs. Captive young chimps not only learn easily all kinds of theatrical stunts, but they seem to delight in doing them and in the applause they earn. Even in their natural surroundings, in Africa, they are highly dramatic. When a group comes upon a good supply of fruit, young and old are likely to stamp and pound on the roots of large trees and raise a chorus of wild hoots and screams. Observers have described chimpanzee "carnivals" that went on for hours.

> The hot-air balloon races were exciting. We spread a blanket on the ground and waited. My sister had to baby-sit for the neighbors. Some people next to us ate egg rolls. Other people had sandwiches. A Boy Scout troop carried all the state flags of the balloonists. The mayor gave a welcoming speech.

If you decided that the first example is a well-developed paragraph, you are right. It was written by Dorothy E. Shuttlesworth, a professional writer. The first line is indented. It has a main idea—namely, that chimpanzees are natural showoffs. All the sentences relate to that main idea.

The second example is not a well-developed paragraph. The first sentence indicates that the paragraph will tell you about why the hot-air balloon races were exciting. However, none of the sentences that follow relate to or develop that idea.

Kinds of Paragraphs

You have just learned a general definition for a paragraph. However, there are many different kinds of paragraphs. A paragraph in a news story, for example, is not necessarily the same as a paragraph in a short story. Each may have a different purpose, a different development, or a somewhat different structure. Here is a chart describing four basic kinds of paragraphs you are likely to read and write. Often these types appear in combinations also. (You will learn more about each kind in other chapters.)

Kind	Purpose	Main Idea	Development
Narrative	To tell a story or describe an event	An incident or event important to the story	Details about setting, characters, actions, conflict
Descriptive	To create a picture with words	The person, place, or thing being described	Sensory details, specific details
Expository	To explain clearly	The subject being explained	Facts, examples, some descriptive details
Persuasive	To persuade	The writer's opinion	Reasons, facts, examples

Writing Activities Analyzing Paragraphs

A Read each paragraph and identify the main idea. Some of the paragraphs have a sentence that strays from the main idea. Identify each one and explain why it does not belong in the paragraph.

1.   Although early settlers had to work very hard, they were able to find some time for fun. Often when neighbors

The Quilting Party.

gathered together to help each other with some of the work, they made a party of it. They had quilting bees, house raisings, stump pullings, harvestings, and threshings. Some of these same activities can be seen today at folk festivals across the country. As they worked, the people talked, sang, and caught up on the news. When they finished the work, they all enjoyed a hearty meal.

2.   The cat was called Dragon, and the name was a good one. He was enormous, with a huge, broad head and a large mouth full of curving fangs, needle sharp. He had seven claws on each foot and a thick, furry tail which lashed angrily from side to side. In color he was orange and white, with glaring yellow eyes. When he was angry, he gave a high, strangled scream that froze all of us where we stood.

3.   People must band together to protect the world's tropical rain forests. Each year the rain forests are cut down for farms, ranches, and lumber. Scientists say that the acres of destroyed rain forest were home to possibly millions of plant and animal species. Each day, more acres and more species are being destroyed, never to be studied and recorded. They have been lost forever. A biologist from Costa Rica talked about a similar problem on television.

B Look at the chart on page 99 and then reread the paragraphs in Activity A. Decide if each one is a narrative, descriptive, expository, or persuasive paragraph, or a combination of these types. Be sure to consider each paragraph's purpose, main idea, and development.

2
Understanding the Topic Sentence

One of the best ways to make the main idea of a paragraph clear is to express it in a **topic sentence**. Usually, the topic sentence is the first sentence in the paragraph.

Notice how placing the topic sentence first in the following paragraph makes the main idea clear for the reader.

Professional Model

Everything about the Southwest seems big. The sky is vast and the deserts seem endless to someone walking or even driving through them. The mountains are rocky and almost impassable. From the top of Mt. Whitney in California (about 14,495 feet above sea level), a person can look down into Death Valley (about 282 feet below sea level). The Grand Canyon leaves the viewer breathless. The Painted Desert of Arizona must be seen to be believed. In Texas, the fertile grass-lands seem to go on forever along the horizon.

—Julian Nava

Sometimes the ideas in a paragraph can build up to the topic sentence. Then, the most effective place for the topic sentence is at the end. Notice how the sentences in the following paragraph lead up to the main idea in the last sentence.

Writing Model

When I was a child, there was a time for playing with marbles and flying kites. Then there was a time for playing hide-and-seek when we hoped that our parents would forget to call us inside for bed. The time for jumping in mounds of dried leaves and going on hayrides always ended too soon. It was quickly followed by the time for making snowmen and building snow forts. As children, we never measured the year by seasons; we measured it by our special times for play.

Writing Effective Topic Sentences

An effective topic sentence catches the reader's interest without being too obvious. Compare the following topic sentences:

> I am going to write about the problems of being the first-born child.

> Baby-sitting four rambunctious brothers while your parents shop for groceries is only one of the problems of being the first-born child.

The first topic sentence states the main idea, but it is dull and uninteresting. The second topic sentence catches the reader's interest by giving an example and stating the main idea. When you write a topic sentence, always think of an interesting way to state the main idea. Never begin with words such as "I am going to write about . . ." or "This paragraph is about . . . " or "The first thing I want to say is . . . ."

An effective topic sentence also is specific. That is, the main idea is narrow enough to be thoroughly developed in one paragraph. For instance, in the paragraph about the Southwest on page 101, the topic sentence would have been too broad if the writer only said "Everything about the Southwest is magnificent." It could never have been developed well, because the writer had not focused on a specific aspect of the Southwest's grandeur—its physical scale. Notice how the topic sentence states a specific main idea: *Everything about the Southwest seems big.* The reader knows that the paragraph will discuss the dimensions of the Southwest's geography. Then, all of the sentences in the paragraph relate to that main idea.

Topic Sentences Questionnaire
1. Does the sentence tell what the paragraph is about?
2. Is the main idea stated clearly?
3. Is the sentence interesting enough to catch the reader's attention?
4. Is the main idea narrow enough to be developed in one paragraph?
5. Does the sentence cover all the related ideas in the paragraph?

Writing Activities *Topic Sentences*

A Read each topic sentence below and ask yourself the first four questions in the Topic Sentences Questionnaire. If you answer *no* to any of the questions, rewrite the topic sentence.

1. A feeling of mystery filled me as I entered the cave.
2. A fascinating topic to write about is the different kinds of people you see walking down a busy street.
3. My paragraph is about the excitement of motorbike racing.
4. I see the world through the lens of my camera.
5. I would really like to write about the fact that this city needs a sports complex for kids.
6. The crackling fireplace and the brightly colored leaves strewn about our lawn remind me that autumn is my favorite season.
7. It is worthwhile to write about the need for computers in every classroom.
8. Would you like to hear about the toughest game of the season?
9. I would like to tell you about the death of a star.
10. How will our sun—a star—die?

Ancient cave painting

B Listed below are topics for paragraphs. For each one, write a topic sentence that expresses the main idea and meets the other requirements of page 102. Then choose one topic sentence and write at least three or four sentences related to the main idea.

1. One reason I like to jog (play baseball, collect stamps, or do some other sport or pastime)
2. Computers in the classroom
3. My favorite way to spend a rainy afternoon
4. Advantages of knowing how to sew
5. The best way to save money
6. Why I like (don't like) rock music
7. An important reason for studying science
8. A great vacation spot
9. A persuasive ad
10. What art means to me

3
Developing Paragraphs Fully

In addition to a well-written topic sentence, a paragraph must contain fully developed sentences that relate to the main idea. Once you have caught the reader's attention, you must keep the reader interested by providing more information and details in related sentences. As a general rule, you should try to include at least three sentences that support and develop your topic sentence.

Compare the following two paragraphs. Which is more interesting? Why?

Toys are a serious, competitive business. People buy toys for children all year long. Children learn about toys while watching television. Toy companies compete heavily for the money spent on toys each year. They must produce popular toys.

Toys are a serious, competitive business. At one time, people only bought toys for children's birthdays and holidays. Now, thanks to the large chains of toy stores and the year-round advertising on children's television programs, people are buying toys all year long. In 1980, people in the United States spent about seven billion dollars on toys. In 1985 they spent about twelve billion dollars! No wonder the toy companies compete to come up with the most popular toy each year.

Gathering Details

How can you make sure that you have enough information to write a fully developed paragraph? You can begin by asking six questions that apply to most topics: *Who? What? Where? When? Why?* and *How?* Use the answers to these questions to help develop your main idea. The following chart lists sample questions you can ask about your specific topic.

Five W's and How

Who?	Who said so? Who is involved? Who needs it?
What?	What happened? What should be done?
Where?	Where does it happen? Where should it be done?
When?	When did it happen? When was it done?
Why?	Why is it important? Why is it so?
How?	How was it done? How should it happen?

Kinds of Details

After you have answered the questions in the chart above, you should begin to select the kinds of details that best develop your paragraph. You may choose to use facts, examples, reasons, narrative details, or sensory details. You will probably find that you can use more than one kind of detail to develop your paragraph.

Facts   A fact is any specific piece of information. For instance, in the second paragraph about the toy business on page 104, the sentences citing the amount of money spent on toys in 1980 and 1985 are facts. They help support the idea that the toy business is serious and competitive.

Examples   An example is a specific case or incident that relates to the main idea. It usually is introduced by words such as *for instance, to illustrate,* or *for example*. Note the following topic sentence and example:

> Disease was a terrible hardship faced by the westward-bound pioneers. For example, during a cholera epidemic in 1853, Maria Belshaw recorded fifty-seven trailside graves over a two-week period.

Reasons   Reasons are logical statements that answer the question *Why?* If you were a restaurant critic persuading readers to try a new restaurant, you might give reasons such as the following:

> Cafe Olé serves excellent and tasty Mexican dishes at a reasonable cost. Furthermore, the atmosphere is pleasant and inviting. As you dine, strolling musicians play guitars and sing.

Narrative Details Narrative details provide information about the specific setting, characters, and actions that take place in a story. If you were writing about a woman in your neighborhood, you could include the following:

Professional Model   Miss Ernestine was a tall, lanky black woman. Her face was filled with laughter, but her eyes could darken and cloud over with anger when someone made her mad . . . It was on a Tuesday, almost two years ago, that she first moved to Andover Street. For months, no one said a word to her and she, too, kept her peace. Then one day, Sharif waved up at her as we passed her window. She smiled back. After that, we all waved everyday, and before long, she began to sit outside, waiting for us to come by. I guess that's how the stories started. We stopped and she talked. From her lips rolled story after story about life "down South." So captivated were we by these tales that we often sat on her steps for hours.   —B. J. Walker

Sensory Details Details that are based on the five senses are sensory details. If you were describing a favorite place, you could give many sensory details:

As I walk by the lake shore, the pungent smell of pine needles fills my lungs. At dawn a curtain of mist feels cool and soft on my arms.

Writing Activities **Developing Paragraphs**

Choose one of the following topic sentences and write at least three sentences that support and develop it.

1. Last Halloween night was both frightening and funny.
2. The state legislature should pass a law banning smoking in all public places.
3. Imagine how surprised I was when I actually enjoyed my first visit to a science museum.
4. When my parents set a rule, they always stick by it.
5. There are several simple ways to improve student morale at our school.

4
Achieving Paragraph Unity

A paragraph has **unity** when all the sentences tell about one main idea. If one sentence strays from that idea or contains an unrelated detail, the reader may become confused or disinterested. Some paragraphs lack unity because they are not about one idea. They ramble from one disconnected point to another.

> I think our community should attract more businesses so that more jobs would be available. My brother can't find a job in his field of sales. I would rather go into the travel business.

Some paragraphs lack unity because the writer mistakenly includes one or two sentences that do not belong. Which sentence in this paragraph destroys the unity? Why?

> Centuries ago, people were unsure about how the world was made. Some argued that the earth was flat. Others disagreed. The earth was round, they said. In our science class, we also had a debate about the shape of the earth. To solve the mystery, adventuresome men and women began to explore the land and the seas. Today we call these people geographers. In those days, they were called fools!

The *Genovese World Map,* 1467. Located at Biblioteca Nazionale, Florence.

Writing Activities *Achieving Paragraph Unity*

A Here are three groups of sentences. Each includes several sentences that work together to support one idea. Find the one sentence in each group that does not belong. Explain why it does not fit with the other sentences.

1. a. Last week, I helped some Cub Scouts build a tree house in an old oak tree.
    b. I used lumber left over from the garage Dad built.
    c. Friends of mine once built a wagon from a crate and old roller skates.
    d. Mr. Kane gave us a box of shingles for the roof.
    e. It only took two days to build the house.
2. a. The pitcher plant is a meat eater.
    b. Crawling insects are trapped in its hollow leaves.
    c. When the insects die, the plant absorbs them as food.
    d. Many interesting books have been written about how plants grow.
    e. The pitcher plant has an unusual diet.
3. a. When my sister practices the trumpet, I get a headache.
    b. Everyone in our family plays an instrument.
    c. I'm convinced that she has lost her sense of hearing.
    d. Each tortured note is louder than the one before it.
    e. Even the cat cringes when she plays.

B The following paragraph lacks unity. Identify the sentence or sentences that do not relate to the main idea. Then, revise the paragraph.

What would you find if you traveled to the center of the earth? First, you would pass through the earth's crust and mantle. The movie *Journey to the Center of the Earth* was about a similar passage. As you move through the mantle you would see places where water or other liquids lie in pools and where gases are trapped in pockets of rock. Then you reach the outer core and see the mantle resting on matter like a thick, liquid plastic. Plastic is not always hard. Finally, when you reach the inner core, the earth is solid again.

5
Achieving Paragraph Coherence

A paragraph has **coherence** when the sentences follow a logical order. You already know that each sentence must relate to the others in a paragraph, but each sentence must also flow logically from one idea to the next. The logical relationship between the sentences must be clear to the reader. Often, transitions can be used to connect sentences and to signal to the reader the order that is used.

Order in Paragraphs

One way to achieve coherence in a paragraph is to organize details in a way that suits your topic and purpose. Often, you will find that your ideas are related in one of the following kinds of order: chronological, spatial, or order of importance.

Chronological Order Chronological order is time order, the order in which events happen. A paragraph about an event or a process could easily be written in chronological order, moving from start to finish. Transition words such as *first, second, then, next,* and *finally* let the reader know how the sentences are related to the main idea.

Writing Model   Papier mâché sculpture can be made from just a few items. First, cut newspaper into one- or two-inch strips. Then, dip the paper into a mixture of water and white paste. (Use equal amounts of each.) Finally, mold the strips over a box, a hanger, or wadded newspaper. The shape you create will soon harden.

Spatial Order If you use spatial order, you describe the position of one part or object in relation to another. For example, if you describe a building, you could start at the bottom and move to the top. Or, you could move from front to back, from inside to outside, from left to right, and from near to far.

Entering City Hall is like traveling in a time machine. Outside, the century-old marble steps and columns greet you like an ancient caretaker. But once inside the majestic doors, you are met by clicking typewriters and beeping computers.

Order of Importance If you use order of importance to organize your paragraph, you can begin with the most important details and end with the least important details. You can also begin with the least important and end with the most important.

Professional Model

Yataro was more fortunate than the motherless, fatherless, little sparrow searching for food in the snow. He had a father. He had a warm house. And he had a friend—his grandmother. She was very old and not strong, but she loved Yataro and took care of him. Yataro's father was too busy to pay much attention to him, but his grandmother was always there when he needed her.

—Hanako Fukuda

The writer arranged the reasons why Yataro is fortunate in order from least important to most important. Yataro has a father and a warm house. But far more important to him is his grandmother.

Grammar in Action

When you think of coherence, it might help to think of glue. A coherent paragraph has all of its ideas and sentences "glued," or connected together. Conjunctions work like glue. For example, using words such as *and, but,* and *or* can help your sentences flow more logically.

> My morning started very badly. I overslept, *and* I was late for class. I actually caught a bus, *but* I did not make it to school on time. I missed my first class *and* the science test.

(For more information on conjunctions and combining sentences, see pages 134–151 and 554.)

Writing Activities *Paragraph Coherence*

A Use the topic sentence and details listed below to write a paragraph. Decide on an order that seems most suitable to the details. Use all the details, and add any transition words that help make the order clear.

The Olympics began many centuries ago in Greece.

1. The first modern Olympics were held in 1896.
2. No Olympics were held for more than 1500 years.
3. The earliest known Olympic games were held in 776 B.C.
4. The stadium of Olympia was located in western Greece.
5. After Rome conquered Greece the Olympics declined in quality.
6. The Olympics are held every four years.

B **Writing in Process** Brainstorm about topics for a paragraph. If you wish, use *Starting Points: Ideas for Writing* (pages 43–55). After selecting a topic, think of an audience and a purpose (for example, to persuade people in your community). Gather information by asking *who, what, when, where, why,* and *how* questions. Then write an effective topic sentence. Support and develop the topic sentence with related sentences. Revise and share a final copy with your audience.

Speaking and Listening

You've just learned that in a well-developed paragraph every sentence must support the topic sentence. In the same way, every action and conversation in a good play must support the main plot line. Ever since the art of drama began, tne plot, or plan of action, has consisted of a conflict or struggle that had to be resolved by the end of the play. When developing this plot, the playwright creates acts and scenes that fit together in a smooth and logical way. If there are any unrelated scenes, unimportant subplots, or unnecessary characters, the audience will be confused and bored. To hold the audience's attention, everything in the play must work together as a whole to tell the story.

Activity

As a class, discuss some of your favorite drama shows on television. Select one or two shows and have the class watch them. Evaluate each show using the following questions:

1. What is the main plot line (the conflict or struggle)?
2. Do all of the scenes support the main plot? Which do not?
3. Do the scenes fit together logically?
4. Do you recognize any unrelated scenes or unnecessary characters?

Scribble notes as you watch the show. Come to class the next day and discuss the show with your classmates.

Application and Review

A Recognizing Paragraph Types Read the topic sentences below. Identify which type of paragraph (narrative, descriptive, expository, persuasive) would most likely follow each one.

1. My youngest brother, with his pixie-like looks and lively antics, reminds me of a little elf.
2. Sara's experience makes her the perfect candidate for class president, and she deserves your vote.
3. The first passengers in a hot air balloon were farm animals, but this unique sport has been flying high ever since.
4. As the sky darkened, the old man proudly led the eager child into the tribal ring and signaled for the ceremonies to begin.

B Writing Effective Topic Sentences Rewrite the following dull topic sentences. Add details that will interest the reader.

1. I want to tell you about my first trip to the zoo.
2. This city would be a nice place to visit.

C Understanding Unity and Coherence Rewrite the following paragraph. Leave out the sentence that doesn't fit, and add transition words to improve the flow of the paragraph.

> Two outs in the bottom of the ninth inning, and I was up to win, or lose, the baseball championship. In my mind, I reviewed my brother's batting advice. I walked slowly up to home plate. I looked around to see where the outfielders were playing. I gave my bat a few good swings. The pitcher threw two perfect strikes in a row. Now I was really nervous. The ball was too high and "ball one" was called. I knew I couldn't strike out so I stared straight at the pitcher, ready for anything. She was wearing a yellow t-shirt that she had brought back from a trip to Florida. The pitch was great, but so was my batting! We all watched the ball sail through the air and over the back fence. The trophy was ours!

7

From Paragraph to Composition

Look at the single peacock feather in the picture above. A peacock's fan is made up of many of these beautiful feathers. Each feather has a special place in the overall design and contributes to the beauty of the whole.

A paragraph can also be part of a larger whole. In a composition, paragraphs work together to express a stronger, more complete idea than any one paragraph could on its own. In this chapter you will discover how to combine and organize paragraphs. You will use this skill to produce compositions as brilliant, dazzling, and unified as a peacock's fan.

1
Understanding the Parts of a Composition

You have learned that a paragraph is a group of sentences that work together to explain or support one idea. As you develop an idea, you may find that you need more than one paragraph to describe it. A **composition** is made up of several paragraphs. Like the sentences in a paragraph, the paragraphs in a composition work together to explain or support an idea. Also like a single paragraph, a composition may be narrative, descriptive, explanatory, or persuasive.

The paragraphs in a composition each serve a different purpose. The first paragraph in a composition is the **introductory paragraph**. It is similar to a topic sentence in a paragraph; both introduce the main idea. Next come the **body paragraphs**. They develop the main idea stated in the introductory paragraph. The last paragraph, or **conclusion**, ends the composition. Study this example of an explanatory composition.

Professional Model

Introductory Paragraph

Body Paragraphs

Reading the Water

If you want to catch more fish, learn how to read the water. Your favorite lake, pond, or stream is full of clues that point to fish. If you look for the clues before you start casting, your chances of catching fish are sure to improve.

Anglers who like to wade streams for bass or trout read the water carefully. Riffles where water bubbles over the rocks and flows into a quiet pool are good fishing places. Especially during the mornings and evenings, fish gather around riffles to feed. They lie pointed upstream, waiting for the current to carry food to them. Cast a bait or lure above the riffles, and let the current carry it into the pool with the natural foods. Do this carefully at the right time of day, with the right bait, and you'll learn that reading the water means more fish.

In the warmer, brighter times of day the fish, especially the bigger ones, may be hiding in deep holes. Fish like to rest in shady places. This may be beside a rock or beneath a half-sunken log. It may be along a rocky ledge dropping off into the stream or lake. . . .

Lakes, like fishing streams, can also be read by the fisherman who knows what to look for. Every lake has some fishing spots that are better than others. You can learn a lot just by looking at the surface of the lake. Are logs lying partly submerged on the edge of the lake? These are good hiding places for bass and other fish. Look around for other signs. The mouths of streams emptying into the lake, rocky ledges reaching into the water . . . and fields of stumps sticking from the water are all good places to fish.

Conclusion The more you study a lake or stream, the more fish you are going to catch. That is the best reason for learning to read the water.

—George Laycock

Now scan the composition again. Do you see how each paragraph fulfills a different purpose?

- The introductory paragraph tells you why you should learn to read water. Although the introduction comes first in a composition, it is not always written first. Some writers wait until they have written the entire composition before they write the introduction. Then they can be sure that their introduction includes all the major points covered in the composition.

- The body paragraphs describe what signs to look for. Each paragraph deals with a different type of water. In this composition, the writer uses a spatial order. He moves from place to place, from narrow streams to deep holes to lakes.

- The conclusion refers to the introductory paragraph. It restates the main idea, and signals that the writer has finished.

A Write a main idea of the composition entitled "Reading the Water." How does the writer treat that idea in the introduction, the body, and the conclusion?

B Writing in Process Turn to *Starting Points: Ideas for Writing* on page 43. Use any one of the pictures or ideas to brainstorm about things you have seen or done or places where you've been. Then read over your notes and choose one experience that could be developed into a composition. Think about the purpose of your composition. Once you have decided on the purpose, write the main idea of your composition. Save your notes in a writing folder. You will use them in a later activity.

Writing Inside Out

When a star football player like Willie Gault danced with ballerinas from the Chicago City Ballet, that was news. For public relations specialist Rena Zaid, it was the biggest news story she had seen in her two and a half years working with the Chicago City Ballet. Rena is a public relations specialist. She writes press releases, public service announcements, and brochures to increase the public's awareness of the ballet company. She is like an in-house reporter, getting out news and information about the Chicago City Ballet.

The ballet company does not pay for the newspaper space or radio and television time it gets. Instead, it must compete with thousands of other organizations who are all trying to get their messages across to the public. There are no guarantees that the ballet's announcements will be chosen, so Rena has to know

2
Planning a Composition

You can plan a composition by using many of the same techniques you use for planning paragraphs. First find a topic using one of the skills you learned in Chapter 2. Then develop the topic by using these three steps:

1. List details
2. Identify your main points
3. Organize your supporting information

what to say and how to write it. Here are some of her thoughts on writing:

"When I was younger, I loved to read. I think that's how I learned to write. I wasn't any smarter than anyone else. I just read so much that I knew how things were supposed to sound."

"My style is straightforward—I write what's happening and when, and I try to make it interesting at the same time."

"To write a press release, I just write *one, two, three, four, five,* and then right next to the number one, I write *date, time, place;* number two—*sponsored by;* number three—*other information;* number four—*closing;* and number five—*contact.* Then I just go and fill in all those things. It starts to take shape itself. In the last step, I write what I call the filler, which is just all the sentences that pull everything together into a press release and pretty much it writes itself at that point. A lot of times, I write key words on the side of the paper, words that are exciting to me and that I think would be catching, and I fit them in afterwards."

"I go over the release four to five times before I get it to where I do a final review of it."

The details you list will depend on the kind of writing you are doing. One student, Tony, wanted to write about his sister who joined the track team. He listed the main events of her experience.

> Stacy decided to become a runner
> Practiced every day
> We weren't sure she had a chance
> Stacy joined the track team
> She got sick and injured herself
>   the day of the race

When you read over your notes, try to decide how the ideas are related. Can certain details be grouped together? Do some ideas follow each other in a logical sequence? Such relationships will determine your order—chronological, spatial, or order of importance. For example, Tony realized that his notes could be put in three groups and then organized chronologically.

First Main Idea: Stacy's preparation for the track team
Second Main Idea: Her experiences on the team
Third Main Idea: The first race

Your final planning step is to expand your notes with details. These notes will be your guide as you write your composition.

First Main Idea   Stacy's preparation for the track team
                     Ran for miles every day, exercised
                     Watched races on TV
                     We weren't sure she had a chance

Second Main Idea   Her experiences on the team
                     Practiced all the time, was always tired,
                         sometimes got hurt
                     Family was worried about her

Third Main Idea   The first race
                     Family wasn't expecting much
                     Stacy tried hard—harder than anyone else

Writing Activity *Prewriting*

Writing in Process Look over your brainstorming from Activity B on page 118. Then list the details, identify the main ideas, add details, and organize your supporting details under the main ideas. Save your notes for the next activity.

3
Writing the Introduction

As you begin to draft any composition, keep one thing in mind: a composition can only be successful if someone reads it and understands it. Therefore, the beginning of a good composition should give the reader a clear idea of what the composition is about. It should also catch his or her interest. Of course, to know what will interest your reader, you will have to stop and think about who your audience will be.

This is a possible introductory paragraph to Tony's composition, which he titled "A Lesson from My Sister."

> My sister Stacy is a wonderful person. Once she did something that surprised the entire family. It had to do with running.

This paragraph tells what the composition is going to be about. However, it is not interesting enough to make the reader want to go any further. Following are some ways to make the introductory paragraph more interesting. Notice how each paragraph focuses on the same subject—Stacy as a runner. Yet each introduces that subject through a different technique.

Ask a Question
Have you ever done anything that everyone told you was impossible? My sister Stacy did. She wanted to be a runner, even though her family told her that she would never make it.

State an Interesting Fact
Runners have been pushing themselves to their limits since the first Olympic Games were held in ancient Greece. That was in 776 B.C. My sister Stacy belongs to this group of special athletes. She became a runner even when her family told her she would never make it.

Repeat an Interesting Quotation
A famous playwright once wrote, "To conquer without risk is to triumph without glory." My sister Stacy took this kind of risk when she decided to be a runner, even though the rest of the family told her she would never make it in track. We think she triumphed with glory!

Tell an   From the day she first saw the Olympic Games
Interesting on television, my sister Stacy had wanted to be a
Anecdote   runner. Her family would look at her stocky body
and short legs, and smile. Stacy was wonderful
and she might be any one of several things someday, but we knew she would never be a runner.
At least, that's what we thought back then.

These introductory paragraphs fulfill the two purposes of an
introduction. They tell the reader what the composition is going
to be about. They also tempt the reader to go beyond the opening
paragraph.

Writing Activities *Writing the Introduction*

A Rewrite each of the following introductions to tell the reader
what the composition will be about or to make the introduction
more interesting.

1.   I'd like to tell you about a memorable day in my life.
     When I awoke, I had no idea of the thrilling event that was to
     take place. It seemed that a usual morning passed, but around
     noon I began to feel that something different might happen.
2.   Dogs, cats, fish, and birds—I have all the usual pets.
     Recently, however, I acquired a pet that I like better than any
     of the others. My new pet is a chameleon.
3.   I have spent my entire life as the youngest member of my
     family. My older sister is now old enough to go to college,
     and my brother is old enough to drive a car. I have survived
     only by learning that being the youngest can have definite
     advantages.
4.   I am going to tell you about Eddie and his friend Horace.
     Eddie was five years old when we moved next door to him.
     One day, soon after we came, I was reading on our back
     porch when I heard him playing in his yard. I put down my
     book and went next door to see what he was doing.

B Writing in Process Look over your prewriting notes from
the Writing Activity on page 120. Think about your audience.
Who will read your composition? Then write a good introduction
for your composition. Make sure that it will appeal to your
audience.

4
Writing the Body

The body of a composition develops the main idea introduced in the first paragraph. The body is made up of several paragraphs. Each paragraph focuses on one main idea. Each paragraph also contains related details that expand the main idea of the paragraph and tell what that particular paragraph is about.

The body of your composition must also have coherence. In other words, each paragraph must follow smoothly and naturally from the one before it. To develop coherence, use transitions to connect the main idea in one paragraph with the main idea in the next paragraph. Below are examples of such transitions.

Transitions	
Transitions to Show Time	always, before, finally, first, immediately, last, later, meanwhile, now, sometimes, soon, then
Transitions to Show Place	above, around, beneath, down, here, there, inside, outside, near, over, under, within
Transitions to Show Order of Importance	at first, first, second, last, former, latter, primarily, secondarily
Transitions to Show Cause and Effect	as a result, because, therefore, so, for that reason

Here is the body of Tony's composition about his sister. Notice how each paragraph focuses on one main idea and how each paragraph is tied to the next one with a transition.

Student Model

Stacy ignored our doubts and began to get in shape for the school track meet. She exercised constantly, watched runners on sports programs, and read every book on running she could find. Every day she ran for miles around the neighbor-

hood. However, all of this work couldn't change her height or the length of her legs, and we told her not to be disappointed if she didn't make the team.

Then, much to our surprise, the coach of the track team let Stacy join the team, and from that day on, we saw very little of her. She practiced even on weekends, coming home exhausted. She caught a cold from running in bad weather and suffered through painful shinsplints. We all tried to persuade her to stop this nonsense before she really hurt herself. Again, Stacy ignored us.

Finally, the day came for her first meet. Since we all loved her, the entire family went to see her. We weren't expecting much, and we all got ready to lift her spirits after she lost. Then something strange happened. As the runners left the blocks, Stacy's short legs were moving twice as fast as anyone else's. Her face showed twice the effort. Her stocky body was giving everything it had!

In the first paragraph of the body of the composition, the main idea is expressed in the first sentence. It states Stacy's determination—regardless of her family's doubts.

The second paragraph also begins with the main idea. It hints at the fact that Stacy might surprise her family again, and it shows how hard she worked toward her goal. Since this composition is told in chronological order, time transitions were used. The transition *then* ties the first two body paragraphs together. It shows that the events in the second paragraph followed the events in the first paragraph.

The third paragraph also begins with a sentence that expresses the main idea of that paragraph. It states that the events in that paragraph will be about the track meet. The transition *finally* once again indicates that the events are being told in chronological order.

Grammar in Action

The word *transition* means "a passage" from one place or subject to another. A writer uses time and place transitions as a kind of verbal bridge. They help a reader make a connection from one idea to a second, related idea. Such time and place transitions are adverbs or prepositional phrases used as adverbs. (See pages 526 and 551.) Notice how ideas are connected by adverbs in the following fictional passage.

> Pauline Childs built GORTHA, a robot, to perform ordinary household tasks. Later, she added artificial intelligence to the robot. Within microseconds, GORTHA learned to play championship chess and write popular novels. The robot now refuses to clean, cook, or wash dishes. It has also become very demanding.

Writing Activity Continue the story of GORTHA and Pauline, or write about an invention that you think the world needs. Use time and place transitions to connect sentences as you describe and tell about the invention or GORTHA.

Writing Activities *Writing the Body*

A Identify the main idea in each paragraph of the body of the following composition entitled "Stepping into the Past." Then write the transitions that were used to link the paragraphs and to develop coherence.

The barn on the Patterson's deserted farm looked so old that it might fall down at any minute. Its doors swung open and shut in the strong afternoon breeze. The sides of the barn reminded me of my grandmother's patchwork quilts. Strips of red paint had curled up and had fallen to the ground, leaving some patches of grey. In other places there still were patches of red in different shades. The sun had faded its sides in uneven patterns.

Inside there were stalls for twelve horses that used to be the homes of some sturdy work horses and two horses that Mr. Patterson's children rode to school. The stalls were now covered with cobwebs, and the dried-out hay left on the floor smelled old and musty. Still hanging on one wall was an old harness for a work horse. It made me wonder if everyone had left in a hurry and had forgotten it. The leather strips of the harness were cracked from the heat, and its metal parts were rough and rusted.

Above the stalls was a loft. The wooden stairs that led to the loft was now missing several steps. Others were warped and unsafe. Farmer Patterson had once stored his hay there. I imagine that his children also had played hide-and-seek there on warm summer days when their chores were finished. Now it stood empty and silent except for the sound of a few mice running across the floor. The loft was dark except for a small beam of light that streamed from a cracked window on its southern side.

B **Writing in Process** Write the body of the composition you started in Activity B on page 122. Include at least three paragraphs. Be sure that each paragraph has a main idea and that you use transitions to connect the paragraphs. Remember to save your writing in your folder.

5
Writing the Conclusion

In addition to an introduction and a body, your composition also needs an ending. A conclusion may do one of three things. First, it may be a summary of what you have written. Second, it may be a short, interesting statement that indicates "The End" to the reader. Third, it may describe a result, as does the conclusion of the composition "A Lesson from My Sister."

Student Model

> No, Stacy didn't win the race—she came in third. But she had won the admiration of our entire family. Never again would we tell her what she was capable of doing. Stacy showed us if you refuse to believe in the word "impossible," anything can happen.

The conclusion is the last idea your reader will take from your composition. You will want to make it as clear, as important, and as interesting as your introduction.

Once you have written your conclusion, revise and proofread your entire composition. Turn back to the revision and proofreading checklists in Chapter 5 (pages 86–87). You can also use the short checklists below to help you.

Checklist: Revising Compositions
_ precise language
_ coherent order
_ use of transitions
_ unity of ideas
_ informative or interesting introduction
_ effective conclusion

Checklist: Proofreading Compositions
_ agreement of subjects and verbs
_ no run-on sentences or fragments
_ all parts of speech used correctly
_ capitalization and punctuation
_ spelling

You have now seen that a composition is divided into paragraphs. Each paragraph, including the introduction and conclusion, is built around a main idea that tells what that paragraph is about. Each sentence in a paragraph supplies supporting details about the main idea, just as each paragraph in the body relates to the main idea in the introduction. When all the ideas in the body paragraphs support your main idea, your composition will have unity.

Writing Activities *Writing the Conclusion*

A Read the following conclusions. Be prepared to tell which ones you think are well written and why.

1. I have now told you three good reasons why I think that children's TV shows need to be changed. The people who make the shows could easily improve them.

2. We walked out of the "Hall of the Presidents" with the eerie feeling that we really had heard Lincoln speak. It was as though we had traveled back in time and been able to feel what Americans of the 1800's had felt when they found themselves face-to-face with the great man. The experience lasted only a few minutes, but the memory of it will stay with us for years.

3. My brother and his trusty wheelchair had won the game for our side. Now no one who saw him that day is foolish enough to make sympathetic remarks about his situation. They've learned that he is not handicapped by his condition. He's just different and very special.

4. The incident I shared with Jamie was certainly strange. To this day, I don't know how she was able to figure out what I had written on that slip of paper. I'm still not sure if I believe in mental telepathy, though.

5. In 1736, the Persian ruler, Nadir Shad, captured Delhi and stripped the jewels from the "Peacock Throne." The throne itself was then broken up and carried away. The ruins of the palace and a marble memorial tablet where the throne once stood are all that now mark the scene of that faded beauty.

6. In conclusion, the computer has already had an impact on the way we live, work, and play. Yet, as an invention, it is a mere infant. Fifty years from now, it may become the most important invention in modern history.

7.   The huge balloon landed gently in the cornfield, and the
     brightly colored silk fluttered and sank. The balloonists
     clambered out of the basket and matter-of-factly began to
     unfasten the lines of the balloon. The magic was over, at least
     for today. Fortunately, the balloonists knew that soon, when
     the breezes stirred the clouds again, they would be floating
     through the sky once more, the bright circles of their balloons
     decorating the otherwise ordinary sky.

B **Writing in Process**   Write the conclusion of the
composition you started in Activity B on page 122. Then revise
and proofread your entire composition. For example, when
revising, look for vague language that you can replace with
precise words and phrases. You also might have to rearrange
some ideas or eliminate some sentences to create unity. Other
words or phrases may have to be added to develop coherence
between and within your paragraphs. When proofreading, check
for errors in grammar, usage, capitalization, punctuation, and
spelling. When you have finished, carefully write the final copy
of your composition. Then look for a way to publish your
composition or to share it with someone else.

English and Reading

One way to learn how to write a good composition is to read and study well-written examples of the same type. These examples are called models when you use them to help you to write your own material. Models are used in many different situations. Your science teacher might have shown you examples of lab reports written by last year's class, or your English book might include an example of a business letter so that you would know how to write your own. Both are models.

When you use a model, don't copy the exact words or ideas. Think of the model as an outline or skeleton structure for your own ideas and experiences. A model can be used to teach you how to write a new type of composition or poem, or to show you how to improve a form that you already know.

Activity

Many beginning writers use the work of authors they admire to help them get started. Pretend you want to be a professional writer. Select a poem or story you like, and use it as a model for a similar poem or story of your own. Write about your own ideas. Attach the model to your writing.

Untitled, Sandra M. Venus, Student Artist.

Application and Review

A Identifying the Parts of a Composition Read the sentences below and decide where you would most likely place each one in a composition: in the *introduction, body,* or *conclusion.*

1. My friend tried to teach me how to do a figure eight, but my tangled legs told me I had to stick to the basics.
2. Despite all the bumps and bruises, my first attempt at ice skating had been a success!
3. As I looked down at the sparkling new ice skates near my bed, a thrill went through me; today, I was finally going to learn how to skate.

B Organizing Details Arrange these ideas in logical order.

1. The seedlings grew taller and taller in the sunshine.
2. I cleared a patch of ground and loosened the dirt.
3. The clerk gave me advice about watering, weeding, and harvesting.
4. I bought a packet of seeds at the garden shop.
5. I watered the area until the young sprouts broke ground.
6. The seeds were planted in long straight rows.

C Using Transitions In each section below, the first sentence concludes one paragraph and the second sentence begins the next one. Write a transition word or group of words that best join the two paragraphs.

1. A woman at the post office told us not to worry about Grandfather's package being lost in the mail, so we continued to wait and wait.
   _____ , a week later, a small brown box came addressed to the Reilly children and we knew our surprise had arrived.
2. The castle was just like the brochure had described, beautiful inside and out.
   _____ , there was a clear blue moat and tall green pine trees encircling the entire retreat.

8
Improving Sentences in Your Writing

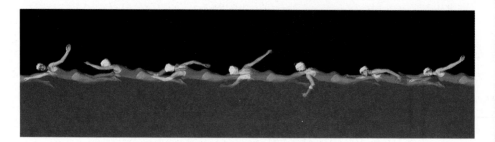

The graceful strokes of an experienced swimmer look effortless. However, many hours of practice were spent refining them.

Writers, too, must refine their work. At first, some sentences you write might be choppy or dull. Others might be stringy or padded. As you revise them, however, your sentences become smoother and the ideas they present become clearer.

This chapter explains how some sentences can be combined when they contain related ideas. It also explains how other sentences can be clarified by eliminating unnecessary words and phrases.

1
Combining Sentences and Sentence Parts

You have learned that a sentence is a group of words that expresses a single main idea. This definition, however, may be somewhat misleading. If you express each single idea in a sentence of its own, your writing can become choppy and dull. Your readers may not be sure of the relationships among those ideas. When you revise your writing, you should look for ways to combine ideas into clear, effective sentences.

Combining Sentences

Sometimes two sentences contain ideas that are equally important. They can be joined together to make one sentence.
If the ideas are similar, use a comma and the word *and*.

> Mammoth Cave is in Kentucky.
> Luray Caverns are in Virginia.

> Mammoth Cave is in Kentucky, **and** Luray Caverns are in Virginia.

If the ideas contrast, use a comma and the word *but*.

> Mammoth Cave is in a national park.
> Luray Caverns are privately owned.

> Mammoth Cave is in a national park, **but** Luray Caverns are privately owned.

If there is a choice between two ideas, use a comma and *or*.

> We could explore caves.
> On the other hand, we could go to the beach.

> We could explore caves, **or** we could go to the beach.

Combining Sentence Parts

Sometimes the ideas in two sentences are so closely related that some words are repeated. Your ideas may be more clearly expressed if you combine the sentences. Leave out the repeated words. The words you can use for combining sentence parts are *and*, *but*, and *or*.

For similar ideas, use *and* (repeated words or ideas are shown in italics).

> Andrew Campbell discovered Luray Caverns.
> William *Campbell also discovered Luray Caverns.*
>
> Andrew **and** William Campbell discovered Luray Caverns.

For contrasting ideas, use *but*.

> The Campbells were excited. *They* kept the cave a secret.
> The Campbells were excited **but** kept the cave a secret.

For a choice between ideas, use *or*.

> The cave might become a great tourist attraction.
> On the other hand, *the cave might* have little
>   commercial value.
>
> The cave might become a great tourist attraction **or** have
>   little commercial value.

Writing Activities *Combining Ideas*

A Rewrite each pair of sentences as one sentence. Use the word in parentheses. Eliminate the words in italics.

1. Stalactites are rock formations in caves. Stalagmites *also are rock formations in caves.* **(and)**
2. We may visit Luray Caverns this weekend. *We may visit* Mammoth Cave *instead.* **(or)**
3. The cold air in the first air-conditioned house did not come from an air conditioner. *The cold air came* from a shaft sunk into Luray Caverns. **(but)**

B Combine each pair of sentences. Decide on your own what combining word to use and what words, if any, to leave out.

1. Spelunking, or cave exploring, is exciting. It is also educational.
2. Spelunking seems easy. You should never go alone.
3. Be sure you know where you're going. You might not find your way out.

2
Adding Words to Sentences

Sometimes the ideas in two sentences are not equally important. You might have thought they were when you first wrote the sentences. When you revise, however, you see that only one word in the second sentence adds any meaning to the first.

You can add that one word to the first sentence. The result is a tighter and more effective way of expressing the idea.

> The Smithsonian has a special zoo. *It is an* insect *zoo.*
> The Smithsonian has a special **insect** zoo.

> A new specimen arrived at the zoo. *It arrived* recently.
> A new specimen arrived **recently** at the zoo.

> The zoo has many specimens. *Those specimens are* unusual.
> The zoo has many **unusual** specimens.

You can often add several words from different sentences to a single sentence. The words from the other sentences just add important details to the main idea. Notice that sometimes you need to use a comma or the word *and* when you add more than one word. See page 624 for rules on when to use a comma.

> The new specimen is a cockroach. *It is* huge. *It is* gray.
> The new specimen is a **huge, gray** cockroach.

> This cockroach has appeared in a race on television. *The cockroach is* fast. *The cockroach is* prize-winning.
> This **fast, prize-winning** cockroach has appeared in a race on television.

> The Smithsonian has displayed the cockroach. *The cockroach has been displayed* carefully and attractively.
> The Smithsonian has **carefully and attractively** displayed the cockroach.

Sometimes you need to change the form of an important word before adding it to another sentence. The usual change is to add an ending such as *-y, -ed, -ing,* or *-ly.*

Wasps gather around the faucet. *It has a* leak.
Wasps gather around the **leaky** faucet.

Some stingless flies have bodies that make
them look like stinging wasps. *Their bodies
have* stripes.
Some stingless flies have **striped** bodies that
make them look like stinging wasps.

The zoo attendant showed off a cricket
from China. *The cricket could* sing.
The zoo attendant showed off a **singing**
cricket from China.

The cricket rubbed its legs together to sing.
The song was loud.
The cricket rubbed its legs together to sing **loudly.**

Writing Activities *Adding Words*

A Combine each group of sentences. Eliminate the words in
italics and use any other clue that is given.

1. That insect had eight legs. *The insect was* strange.
2. That was a spider, not an insect. *The spider was* big. *It was*
   agile. (Use a comma.)
3. What is that bug? *It looks* odd. *It has* spots. (Add **-ed** to one
   of the words. Use a comma.)
4. It is some sort of beetle. *It can* fly. (Use **-ing**.)
5. That moth has antennae. *The antennae are covered with* fuzz.
   (Use **-y**.)
6. Farmers must act to save their crops from locusts. *Action
   must be* quick. (Use **-ly**.)

B Combine the following sentences by adding the important
words. Decide whether you need to change any words.

1. The botfly is an insect. It can fly.
2. Can you guess how fast this insect flies? The bug is speedy.
3. One speed of 800 miles an hour was proposed. That speed
   was an estimate.
4. At 800 miles an hour, an insect could kill a person. This
   would even be easy.

5. The speed estimate is wrong. That's obvious.
6. The botfly has been clocked at 24 miles an hour, however. The botfly is amazing.

C Rewrite the following passage. Combine sentences and sentence parts to make the passage more effective. Also look for single words that can be used in other sentences. The words in italics can be omitted. Groups of sentences that can be combined are enclosed in parentheses.

(Laura stopped. *She* leaned her bike against a tree.) (She had finally come to see the cave. Her brother *had come with her. The cave was* hidden.) Jake stopped his bike, but he did not get off. (His jaw had dropped open. His hand pointed to a spot high on the cliff.) (A wisp of smoke was drifting upward. *It was* thin *and* white.)

(Laura didn't remember any cave high up. Jake *also didn't remember such a cave.*) Someone or something must be up there. Jake began to shout hello, but Laura remained silent. (She approached the cave by the tree. *She did this* silently.) (A fire burned in the mouth of the cave. *The fire was* small.) (The smoke was not coming out of the cave. It was instead being drawn back into the dark interior.)

D Revise the following passage. Use what you know about combining sentences to make the passage more effective.

Jake heard the moaning. He heard it first. Like a quiet animal growl, the moaning drifted forward from the back of the cave. The cave was dark. Laura could not see beyond the fire. She stepped past it. She moved boldly. Jake tried to stop her. He was unsuccessful.

"I hear a voice," said Laura. "The voice is human." She went further into the cave. Jake joined her.

"Am I glad you're here!" said the voice. The voice was weak. "I broke my leg two days ago. I couldn't go for help."

Laura looked at the man in the firelight. The firelight was dim. "Were you exploring by yourself?" she asked.

"Yes, and I know that was stupid. I did find a natural chimney, however. This cliff is full of caves."

Laura went for help. Jake stayed with the injured man.

3
Adding Groups of Words

When you revise your work, you will often find that one sentence contains a group of words that merely gives details about part of another sentence. You can combine the two sentences in one of several ways.

Adding Groups of Words That Do Not Change

Some groups of words need no changes when combined into another sentence.

> *Commercials appear* on television and radio. Many people do not like these commercials.
> Many people do not like these commercials on television and radio.
>
> The ads interrupt a program. *They interrupt* in the middle of a good story or song.
> The ads interrupt a program in the middle of a good story or song.
>
> People see five or six commercials in a row. *This happens* during every station break.
> People see five or six commercials in a row during every station break.
> During every station break, people see five or six commercials in a row.

Adding Groups of Words with Commas

Sometimes a group of words merely renames a word or words in another sentence. When you add the group to the sentence, you must set it off with commas.

> Bulova paid only $9.00 for the first TV commercial. *Bulova is* a watch company.
> Bulova, **a watch company,** paid only $9.00 for the first TV commercial.

Adding Groups of Words with -ing and -ed

Sometimes you can add a group of words by adding *-ing* or *-ed* to a word. At other times, there is already a word that ends in *-ing* or *-ed*.

> Some commercials feature animals. *They* talk to each other.
> Some commercials feature animals **talking** to each other.

> Some commercials are interesting. *These are the ones* designed to entertain us.
> Some commercials **designed** to entertain us are interesting.

> New commercials get our attention. *The commercials* show respect for our intelligence.
> New commercials **showing** respect for our intelligence get our attention.

Writing Activities *Adding Word Groups*

A Combine each pair of sentences. Eliminate the words in italics. Use any other clues provided in parentheses.

1. Advertising executives have been concerned. *They are worried* about a special problem.
2. Many people now "zap" commercials with their remote control units. *The commercials are* unwanted.
3. Timex paid over $2 million for a commercial during a recent Super Bowl. *Timex is* another watch company. (Use commas.)
4. Some commercials barely name the product. *These commercials* fascinate *us*. (Use **-ing**.)

B Combine each pair of sentences. Use what you have learned to decide how to combine them.

1. We use remote controls to zap commercials. We zap them out of our lives.
2. Another device is used for zapping. The device is the VCR.
3. Advertisers are trying to make new commercials. The new commercials entertain enough to keep us watching.
4. Some commercials increase the sales of a product. Those are the ones most widely watched.

4
Combining with who, that, *or* which

Sometimes a writer introduces a person, place, or thing in one sentence and then gives additional information about that subject in a second sentence. Often you will find it possible to combine both sentences during a revision.

Adding Groups of Words Using who

A group of words that gives details about a person in another sentence can often be added to that sentence using the word *who*.

> Ellen Goodman wrote a funny article about food. *She* writes for a Boston newspaper.
> Ellen Goodman, **who** writes for a Boston newspaper, wrote a funny article about food.

> Any reader will enjoy the article. *The reader must* love food.
> Any reader **who** loves food will enjoy the article.

Notice that in the first example the added words are set off by commas. The added words merely give additional information about Ellen Goodman. The meaning of the sentence would be clear without them. In the second example, the added words help to identify a particular kind of reader. They do not merely give additional information. They are essential to the meaning of the sentence. Therefore, *who* is used without the commas.

Using that *and* which

A group of words that gives details about a thing or a place in a sentence is often introduced with the word *that* or *which*. Study the following examples.

> There is a cry that echoes through many American homes. The cry, which we hear all summer, is "There's nothing to eat in this house!"

In the first example, the words following *that* are essential to the meaning of the sentence. The word *that* is used to introduce the words, and no comma is used. In the second example, the words following *which* merely give additional information about the cry. The word *which* is used to introduce the words, and commas are used to set them off.

The words following *that* are important to the meaning of the sentence. You are not very likely to have put them in a sentence by themselves. You would probably add them in your first draft. The words following *which*, on the other hand, might have appeared in a second sentence in your first draft: *we hear the cry all summer*. *Which* can be used to combine sentences when the second sentence merely adds a detail.

Writing Activities *Using* who *or* which

A Combine each pair of sentences. Eliminate the italicized words, and follow the clues in parentheses.

1. According to Ellen Goodman, a few teen-agers are picky. *These teen-agers* have to fix their own snacks. (Use **who**.)
2. "Nothing to eat" means any item needing preparation. *This* includes most foods, of course. (Use commas and **which**.)
3. Canned tuna is not acceptable. *It* must be extracted and assembled into a sandwich. (Use commas and **which**.)
4. Goodman's article may not be fair to some teens. *It* is supposed to be humorous. (Use commas and **which**.)
5. My brother has no trouble finding food to eat. *He* is as hungry as any teen-ager. (Use commas and **who**.)
6. He makes elaborate snacks. Some of us find *these snacks* very tempting. (Use a comma and **which**.)

B Combine each pair of sentences. Decide whether to use *who* or *which*, and whether to use commas.

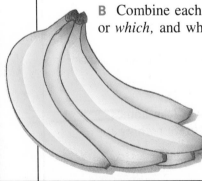

1. The banana is an extremely portable snack. It has its own protective packaging.
2. Nicki always carries a banana with her. She tends to get hungry just as school gets out.
3. The skin is not good to eat. Some people think the skin is poisonous.

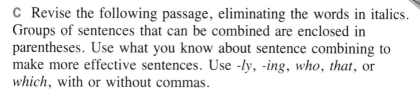

4. The banana contains some important minerals.
   It has only about a hundred calories.
5. Anyone will appreciate the banana.
   The person must care about nutrition.
6. Actually, those specks are "sugar spots."
   They show that the banana is ripe and sweet.

C Revise the following passage, eliminating the words in italics. Groups of sentences that can be combined are enclosed in parentheses. Use what you know about sentence combining to make more effective sentences. Use -*ly*, -*ing*, *who*, *that*, or *which*, with or without commas.

(The television chef smiled as the camera panned on her. *The smile was* broad.) She was standing completely at ease in the studio's immaculate kitchen. (Betty Moreno was the star of the show. *She* had owned and run several restaurants.)

("Today we will be making chicken and rice. *This* is very easy to do.") (First she filled a heavy pot. *She filled it* with water.) (Then she got out a pan. *It was the kind you* fry in.)

(Then Betty Moreno took a knife and started hacking away at the chicken. *The knife was* well-sharpened.) (As she hacked, she told jokes. *The jokes were* about chickens and cooking.) (She had a lot of trouble with the chicken. *The chicken was* a rubber prop from a comedy show.)

D Revise the following passage. Add groups of words to sentences to make the passage more effective.

Nervous perspiration began to show. The perspiration poured from Betty Moreno's forehead. She hacked at the chicken. Her hacking was furious. Somehow, the chicken wasn't cooperating. She thought it might be the knife. She got out her special stone. The stone was for sharpening. Soon the knife was razor-sharp. The rubber chicken finally got cut up.

Meanwhile, the water began to boil. The water was for the rice. Ms. Moreno had taken far too long with the chicken. This was a mistake. The water boiled away, and the pot started to blacken. Smoke alarms screeched. The experienced chef had burned the water! Ms. Moreno had not paid attention to the time. She had been concentrating on the chicken.

5
Avoiding Empty Sentences

Watch for **empty sentences** when you revise your work. There are two types of empty sentences. One type simply repeats an earlier idea. Another kind makes a claim that is not supported with a fact, a reason, or an example.

Sentences That Repeat an Idea

When you revise, eliminate repeated ideas by condensing or combining sentences. Examples of such revisions follow.

Faulty   The clan was in crisis. It was in serious trouble. (Crisis and trouble are similar ideas. Use just one.)

Revised   The clan was in crisis.

Faulty   Almost since childhood, Yola had been clan leader. She had inherited the position from her father. He had been the leader before her. (Since Yola had inherited the position, the third sentence is unnecessary.)

Revised   Almost since childhood, Yola had been clan leader. She had inherited the position from her father.

Faulty   Yola and the elders argued around the evening fire. The evening meal took place at the evening fire every day. They gathered together to eat their evening meal. As they ate, Yola and the elders debated. They could not agree on how to get more food.
(These sentences seem to wander through several ideas. The ideas should be combined.)

Revised   Gathered to eat around the evening fire, Yola and the elders argued about how to get more food.

Writing Activity **Avoiding Repetitions**

Revise the following sentences. Combine or leave out repeated ideas. There may be more than one way to revise each group.

1. The arguments became loud and angry. The quiet was broken. Yola held up her hand for silence.

2. Yola began to speak about similar times in the past. She told about other times the food supply had run out.
3. Of course we cannot survive without food. That much is certain. Without food, the clan will surely perish.
4. We must send our hunters farther away, to where the game is. They must travel to areas that are richer in animal life. Or, we can move the entire clan.
5. Everyone started muttering. They talked irritably among themselves. The clan had moved almost every year since Yola had taken over.

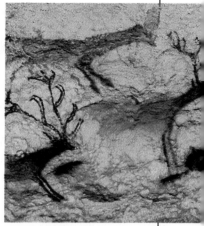

Cave painting from Lascaux, France.

Sentences with Unsupported Statements

Do not leave your reader asking, "Why?" Statements that are not supported by facts or examples produce empty writing.

What unsupported statements can you find in this paragraph?

> Stories can take place during every time period and with different types of settings. People of long ago and space explorers can both have interesting problems to solve. But stories about the past are boring. Space tales are better.

You may agree or disagree that stories about the past are boring or that space tales are better. However, the writer of the example never explains why anything is boring or better. As you revise your work, look for unsupported statements that need reasons, facts, or examples.

Writing Activity *Providing Reasons*

Revise the following items to provide reasons or facts.

1. Frozen pizza is the worst food in the world. Give me good old take-out any time.
2. Every student ought to have an after-school job. Merchants should get together and form a job bank.
3. TV has really gone downhill. There's nothing good to watch.
4. I like most pets. I hate cats, though. They are terrible.

6
Avoiding Stringy Sentences

A **stringy sentence** is a long series of statements strung together with *and*'s. With stringy sentences, your writing becomes confusing and loses its power. When you revise, sometimes you need to break up stringy sentences, combine some ideas, or use transitional words to show how the ideas are related. Then your reader can understand your ideas more clearly.

Stringy   Carron presented himself to the captain, and Carron smiled at her, and then she frowned back at him and his heart sank.

Revised   Carron smiled as he presented himself to the captain. When the captain frowned back at him, his heart sank.

Stringy   The captain's face was frightening, and her purple skin was dripping a kind of greenish oil, and when she frowned, her eyes sank into her skull and she looked like a giant prune.

Revised   The captain's face was frightening. Her purple skin dripped a kind of greenish oil. When she frowned, her eyes sank into her skull. Then she looked like a giant prune.

Writing Activities Stringy Sentences

A Revise sentences 1-10. Use the following guidelines as you revise and rewrite.

- Separate each sentence into two or more shorter sentences.
- Reduce the number of *and*'s.
- Try to show a logical connection between ideas. Use words like *when, then, but, with,* and *because.*
- Use sentence combining techniques when you can.

  1. Jen wanted to tell Pa about the lame mule, and she had waited all day, and then Pa got in from the fields, and he looked so tired and beat that she lost heart.

2. He cooked an egg every day for breakfast, and he would always hold it up and examine it and marvel at its perfect curves, and he would silently thank the chicken that had laid it.

3. Marc picked up his flute and played his new composition, and the audience became very silent, and you could almost hear the old electric clock grinding away in the back of the hall.

4. A computer won't automatically help you with your homework, and it won't balance your checkbook, and you really have to study to use one correctly.

5. A computer diskette can hold about ninety pages of typed material, and some can hold a lot more, and the large "hard disks" can hold 5,000 pages or more.

6. Maryann threw her pencil down, and she stormed out of the room, and then she stormed back in and she slammed down a stack of books and said, "Homework? I'll show you homework!"

7. Venus is our near neighbor, and Mars is our other near neighbor, and you can often see them in the morning or evening sky.

8. The suitcase tumbled open, and jar after jar of peanut butter and honey tumbled out, and they clattered noisily on the inspector's table, and she smiled.

9. Marvin's joints ached, and all the oil in the galaxy would not loosen them up, and most robots in such condition would be retired to the junk heap, and Marvin was worried.

10. Just beneath your skin are bundles of cells called receptors, and some can sense temperature, and some can sense pressure, and some can sense pain.

B Revise the following passage. Combine or condense any empty sentences. Eliminate unsupported statements or give facts or reasons for them. Separate stringy sentences and try to show a logical connection between ideas.

The best way to communicate with other folks is on a computer. It's a really good way to talk to people. You just hook up your computer to a telephone line, and soon you're talking to the

world, and it's all so friendly. You can talk through electronic bulletin boards or through subscription services. The subscription services have this feature called CB, and it stands for Citizens' Band, and it's like CB radio. The difference is that you have to type your "talk."

The CB can have a lot of strange talk on it. Lots of odd people like CB. But if you run into any, just wait an hour and try again, and a whole new bunch of people will be on, and then you can have fun.

Even better than the CB is something called a SIG, or special interest group. There are as many SIGs as there are interests. That's plenty of SIGs. You can sign on and ask about computers (of course), cooking, history, travel, and so on.

One writer has said that with a computer, you never have to be lonely, and I think he's right that you never have to be lonely. When I get on my CB, I can "talk" to anybody, and nobody cares about my age, and we all have a great time.

7
Avoiding Padded Sentences

A **padded sentence** contains words or phrases that do not contribute to its meaning. The padding is like the extra stuffing in a clown suit: it slows the sentence down and makes it seem lumpy and a little silly.

Some padding consists of extra words or phrases that repeat ideas. Other padding consists of large word groups that can be reduced to smaller phrases without damaging the thought or changing the meaning of the sentence.

Padding is not always incorrect. It just clutters up your writing and keeps your reader from fully understanding you. When you revise your work, look for padding that can be deleted.

Two of the most common padding expressions are *the fact that* and *what*. Following are examples of each type, as well as ways of reducing each.

"Fact" Expressions	Reduced
because of the fact that	because, since
on account of the fact that	because, since
in spite of the fact that	although
call your attention to the fact that	remind you

"What" Expressions	Reduced
what I want is	I want
what I mean is	(Just say it!)
what I want to say is	(Just say it!)

Sentences are smoother and less "lumpy" when you take the padding out.

Padded Our departure was delayed on account of the fact that the weather was too cold.

Revised Our departure was delayed because the weather was too cold.

Padded What the explorers did was search for a sea passage through the Northwest.

Revised The explorers searched for a sea passage through the Northwest.

Padded It so happens that the reason that computers are effective in helping to aid us in doing our work is that they are not impatient with our mistakes.

Revised Computers are effective helpers because they are not impatient with our mistakes.

Reducing Word Groups

Word groups beginning with *who is* and *which is* can often be simplified. Study the following examples.

Lengthy Jimmy Carter, who was our thirty-ninth President, served just one term.

Revised Jimmy Carter, our thirty-ninth President, served just one term.

Lengthy The computer, which is in the school office, is used for scheduling classes.

Revised The computer in the school office is used for scheduling classes.

Writing Activities *Padded Sentences*

A Revise each sentence. Get rid of "fact" and "what" expressions. Look for *who* or *which* word groups that can be simplified.

1. What many birds do is fly south for the winter.
2. Some birds do not fly south on account of the fact that they find enough food without making the long trip.
3. Audubon, who was a famous bird artist, set the standard for bird illustrations.
4. It was Roger Tory Peterson who worked out a system for identifying birds.
5. The system, which is called the Peterson System, is based on detailed illustrations.
6. What Peterson claims is that the system has been adopted all over the world.
7. The reason why the Peterson System works is that it has been worked out and revised over the years.
8. What I mean to say is that both Audubon and Peterson have made important contributions to bird study.

B Revise each of the following passages. You should see opportunities to use the following techniques:

- combine sentences and parts of sentences
- use *who* and *which* to combine sentences
- combine or condense "empty" sentences
- separate stringy sentences
- take the stuffing out of padded sentences

1. Do you think that paper is just made from wood? Wood used for paper is ground up and is treated with chemicals. There is more to it than that, however. Think of paper as a surface. The surface holds the printing. Paper can be coated. It can be coated with plastics. It can be coated with clay. Those coatings can provide ideal surfaces for printing.

2. Long ago, books were very precious, and they were made by writing them out by hand, and few people had them. Then what happened was that printing was invented. Each page would be carved on a block. The block was made of wood. Many copies of a page could be made.

3. A big revolution in printing happened about 1455. It was quite a major revolution. In that year Johannes Gutenberg invented movable type. He was a printer in Germany. Pages could be made up rapidly from Gutenberg's letters. The letters were separate. We would like to know more about how the invention came about. The printers of the time guarded their secrets jealously, however.

Illuminated text.
Gutenberg Bible, circa 1455.

4. Gutenberg's press eventually put books into everyone's hands. What I mean to say is that movable type made books affordable. I think that's very important. The latest revolution is "desktop publishing." Desktop publishing is already used in many large companies. With it, people can do their own typesetting and printing from a computer and a laser printer. A laser printer is a device that prints very sharp characters.

Creative Writing

A If you listen closely to conversations going on around you, you will see that people talk very differently. Some speak in exclamatory sentences and phrases: *Oh my gosh! You're kidding!* Some are always asking questions: *What am I going to do? What's up?* Others may speak boldly or timidly depending on their personality. In real life, we learn to identify people through these differences in their speech. In stories, authors often write out what people say to one another in a dialogue, so that readers can see the differences among characters. Consequently, writers spend a lot of time composing and then revising the dialogue in stories. The spoken words are placed within quotation marks and often separated from the rest of the action.

Choose a partner for this activity. Separately invent and describe a character, either a person or fantasy creature. Read each other's description and together write a dialogue in which the two characters meet and talk. The characters may be very different from one another; so think carefully about what they would say if they met. Try to write sentences that only your character would say. Afterwards, look over your sentences, changing any that do not fit your character's personality.

B Instead of writing out a dialogue in the form above, put the same dialogue into comic book form. Draw sketches of the characters and place them in several boxes in a row. Use bubbles to hold the words that the characters say to one another. If you choose this form, remember that dialogue is most important to the art of cartooning, so don't concentrate on the drawings.

Application and Review

A Combining Sentences Read the paragraphs below and combine sentences where needed to keep the writing clear and flowing.

The bloodhound is not the most intelligent dog in the world. It is an expert at following the trail of a specific person. Every individual has a distinct scent. This scent is like another sort of fingerprint. The dog can track down this scent. Bloodhounds are therefore valuable to police departments. Police use them to find lost children and criminals.

Bloodhounds, however, are unpopular because of their appearance. They are sad-looking. Even a bloodhound's eyelids are unattractive. They droop. The bloodhound does not even live up to its ferocious-sounding name. It is a gentle dog. The average adult bloodhound is twenty-six inches tall. They usually weigh ninety pounds.

B Improving Sentences Revise any sentences below that are empty, stringy, or padded.

1. The little girl was lost in the department store, so the police bloodhound sniffed the jacket that her mother was carrying, and the dog set out around the store to track down the girl's scent, and it quickly found her playing in the toy department and she didn't even realize that she was lost!
2. On account of the fact that many people think bloodhounds are ugly, what I want to say is that they're gentle and kind as well.
3. The bloodhound has the unique ability to track a person. It can follow a person's scent to find him or her. It's the only kind of dog that's worth owning in the world. It's one of the most remarkable of all animals!
4. James Thurber was a famous writer and he was a famous cartoonist and he drew many numbers of cartoons of bloodhounds.

9
Writing to Describe

A photograph is a good way to show friends what a farm looks like. "Showing" them through descriptive writing is another. Good descriptive writing lets your reader know exactly what people, places, and things are really like. It can make a reader imagine the smell of fresh cut hay in your description of a farm or hear the rumbling of a volcano when you write a report.

Description plays an important role in many kinds of writing. In this chapter you will improve your writing by creating specific images with words that appeal to the the senses.

1
Understanding Descriptive Writing

When you read good descriptive writing, the words seem to come to life. You're no longer just looking at marks on paper; you're seeing, hearing, smelling, tasting, and feeling all the things the words describe.

Description plays an important part in all kinds of writing, from stories and poems to articles and instructions. Good description can create strong moods and clear pictures of people, places, and things. Some writing includes entire paragraphs of description. More often, however, descriptive words and phrases are scattered throughout a piece of writing.

Read and Think Descriptive writing creates sensory images by using words and phrases that appeal to the senses of sight, sound, smell, taste, and touch. As you read the following selection, notice the words and phrases that appeal to your senses.

Professional Model

"It now seems clear," says Stebbins, "that the entire globe of the Sun is vibrating mechanically in and out, very much as a musical instrument vibrates when it makes a sound." The whole Sun is shaking and quivering, or *oscillating*. It is ringing like a bell!

From *Planet Earth* by Jonathan Weiner

The selection appeals to our senses of sight and sound. We "hear" music and bells; we "see" movement back and forth.

Description can also create a mood or feeling, such as fear or excitement. As you read the following selection, notice the mood that the description creates.

Literary Model

Her heart sank. This was Wethersfield! Just a narrow sandy stretch of shoreline, a few piles sunk in the river with rough planking for a platform. Out of the mist jutted a row of

cavernous wooden structures that must be
warehouses, and beyond that the dense, dripping
green of fields and woods. No town, not a house,
only a few men and boys and two yapping dogs
who had come to meet the boat.

—Elizabeth Speare

The selection creates a gloomy mood. Wethersfield is a misty
and depressing place, with rough planking, cavernous
warehouses, and yapping dogs. No wonder the character is so
disappointed when she first sees it.

Description can also bring characters to life. As you read the
following selection, try to get a picture of the woman and
imagine what she is like.

*Literary
Model*

Just then the door opened and a woman came
in; a tall, thin woman with her hair screwed up
on her head under a white cap like a nurse's cap,
her head very small like the knob on a knitting
needle. Her big white apron was starched to
shine; indeed, she shone all over as if newly
polished: shoes, hair, apron, even her nose.

—Penelope Farmer

The description creates a vivid picture of a tall, thin, and very
proper woman who likes neatness and order.

Think and Discuss Discuss the following questions with your
classmates.

1. What sort of mood does the first selection create? Which
   words help to create the mood?
2. Which senses does the second selection appeal to? Which
   words help you use those senses?
3. Do you think the woman in the third selection is mean or
   friendly? Why?

Follow Up Descriptive writing uses words and phrases that
appeal to our senses. Description plays an important part in many
kinds of writing. It can be used to create a mood or to depict
people, places, and things realistically. Keep these features of
descriptive writing in mind as you read the literature selection on
the next four pages.

Description in Literature

from *Kon-Tiki*

Thor Heyerdahl

I heard a wild war whoop from Knut, who was sitting aft behind the bamboo cabin. He bellowed "Shark!" till his voice cracked in a falsetto, and, as we had sharks swimming alongside the raft almost daily without creating such excitement, we all realized this must be something extra-special and flocked astern to Knut's assistance.

Knut had been squatting here, washing his pants in the swell, and when he looked up for a moment he was staring straight into the biggest and ugliest face any of us had ever seen in the whole of our lives. It was the head of a veritable sea monster, so huge and so hideous that, if the Old Man of the Sea himself had come up, he could not have made such an impression on us. The head was broad and flat like a frog's, with two small eyes right at the sides, and a toadlike jaw which was four or five feet wide and had long fringes drooping from the corners of the mouth. Behind the head was an enormous body ending in a long, thin tail with a pointed tail fin which stood straight up and showed that this sea monster was not any kind of whale. The body looked brownish under the water, but both head and body were thickly covered with small white spots.

The monster came quietly, lazily swimming after us from astern. It grinned like a bulldog, and lashed gently with its tail. The large, round dorsal fin projected clear of the water and sometimes the tail fin as well; and when the creature was in the trough of the swell, the water flowed about the broad back as though washing round a submerged reef. In front of the broad jaws swam a whole crowd of zebra-striped pilot fish in fan formation; and large remora fish and other parasites sat firmly attached to the huge body and traveled with it through the water, so that the whole thing looked like a curious zoological collection crowded round something that resembled a floating deep-water reef.

A twenty-five pound dolphin, attached to six of our largest fishhooks, was hanging behind the raft as bait for sharks; and a swarm of the pilot fish shot straight off, nosed the dolphin without touching it, and then hurried off to their lord and master, the sea king. Like a mechanical monster, it set its machinery going and came gliding at leisure toward the dolphin which lay, a beggarly trifle, before its jaws. We tried to pull the dolphin in, and the sea monster followed slowly, right up to the side of the raft. It did not open its mouth, but just let the dolphin bump against it, as if to throw open the whole door for such an insignificant scrap was not worthwhile. When the giant came close to the raft, it rubbed its back against the heavy steering oar, which was just lifted up out of the water; and now we had ample opportunity of studying the monster at the closest quarters—at such close quarters that I thought we had all gone mad, for we roared stupidly with laughter and shouted overexcitedly at the completely fantastic sight we saw. Walt Disney himself, with all his power of imagination, could not have created a more hair-raising sea monster than that which suddenly lay with its terrific jaws along the raft's side.

The monster was a whale shark, the largest shark and the largest fish known in the world today. It is exceedingly rare, but scattered specimens are observed here and there in the tropical oceans. The whale shark has an average length of fifty feet, and according to zoologists it weighs fifteen tons. It is said that large specimens can attain a length of sixty feet; one harpooned baby had a liver weighing six hundred pounds and a collection of three thousand teeth in each of its broad jaws.

Our monster was so large that, when it began to swim in circles round us and under the raft, its head was visible on one side while the whole of its tail stuck out on the other. And so incredibly grotesque, inert, and stupid did it appear when seen full-face, that we could not help shouting with laughter, although we realized that it had strength enough in its tail to smash both balsa logs and ropes to pieces if it attacked us. Again and again it described narrower and narrower circles just under the raft, while all we could do was to wait and see what might happen. While it appeared on the other side, it glided amiably under the steering oar

Specific details convey shark's size

Details support tense mood

and lifted it up in the air, while the oar blade slid along the creature's back. . . .

In reality, the whale shark went on encircling us for barely an hour, but to us the visit seemed to last a whole day. At last it became too exciting for Erik, who was standing at a corner of the raft with an eight-foot hand harpoon, and encouraged by ill-considering shouts, he raised the harpoon above his head. As the whale shark came gliding slowly toward him and its broad head moved right under the corner of the raft, Erik thrust the harpoon with all his giant strength down between his legs and deep into the whale shark's grisly head. It was a second or two before the giant understood properly what was happening. Then in a flash, the placid half-wit was transformed into a mountain of steel muscles.

We heard a swishing noise as the harpoon line rushed over the edge of the raft and saw a cascade of water as the giant stood on its head and plunged down into the depths.

Sensory language

The three men who were standing nearest were flung and burned by the line as it rushed through the air. The thick line, strong enough to hold a boat, was caught up on the side of the raft but snapped at once like a piece of twine; and a few seconds later a broken-off harpoon shaft came up to the surface two hundred yards away. A shoal of frightened pilot fish shot off through the water in a desperate attempt to keep up with their old lord and master. We waited a long time for the monster to come racing back like an infuriated submarine, but we never saw anything more of him.

Trying Out Descriptive Writing Thor Heyerdahl's detailed description of the "monster" adds excitement to the narrative. Now try your own descriptive skills. Think of an interesting person, place, or thing that you know well. Write a "word picture" of your subject in your journal. Concentrate on using precise details to make your description clear and lively.

2
Prewriting: Description

Before writing description, you should complete three steps. First, you should decide whether the situation calls for description. Then you should identify the feeling or mood that you want to create. Finally, you should collect the sensory details that you will use in your description.

Deciding to Use Description

Description can play an important role in almost any kind of writing. For example, pretend you are writing an editorial, protesting the construction of a shopping center near a meadow. Your editorial will be more convincing if you can describe just how beautiful and peaceful the meadow is now, without the shopping center, and how ugly and congested the meadow will be with the shopping center. Or pretend you want to write a science fiction story about a frightening creature. Nobody will be frightened by your creature unless you describe it well and bring it to life.

Both examples are situations where description can make your writing more powerful. However, not all situations call for description. In general, you should have a definite purpose for including description in your writing. For example, in persuasive writing, you should include description if it makes your argument more convincing. In expository writing, you should include description if it makes your subject clearer and easier to understand. In fiction writing, you should include descriptions of characters, objects, and settings that play a significant role in the story.

Identifying a Feeling or Mood

Once you have decided to describe something, you should identify the feeling or mood you want to create with your description. The feeling or **mood** will depend on what you want to say. Two writers describing the same thing may come up with completely different moods. For example, pretend that two writers describe the same street in a city. The first writer loves cities, so her description creates a mood of excitement and liveliness. The other writer hates cities, so his description creates a mood of confusion and fear. Both writers see the same street, but they see it through different eyes.

In general, select words and details that help create the mood you want. For example, if you're writing a mystery story, your descriptions should probably make readers feel puzzled, confused, and surprised. If you're writing an article about the extraordinary birds of the Amazon, your descriptions should probably create a mood of wonder and awe.

Collecting Sensory Details

The next step in writing description is to collect sensory details. With these details, you will be able to show your readers how something looks, sounds, smells, tastes, and feels. In Chapter 2, you learned thinking skills such as gleaning, noting features, analyzing, and inquiring that can help you gather and explore details for a topic.

Any person, place, or thing has dozens of details. If you were describing the details of a rock, for example, you could talk about its color, its size, its shape, its weight, its texture, and its smell. You could also describe what a rock sounds like when you drop it, how rough it is, where you found it, and what it looks like under a magnifying glass.

With so many details to choose from, where do you begin? The answer to that question will depend on the mood you want to create with your description. If you are writing a description of a prairie, you may want to create a mood of peace and solitude. You could create that mood with details such as the stillness of the air, the horizon stretching for miles in all directions, the wheat swaying slowly in the breeze, or the buffalo grazing in the sun.

Observation The first way to collect sensory details is to observe your subject carefully. If you are writing a description of a person, for example, you should study the person closely. What color is the person's hair? What does the person's voice sound like? What kinds of clothes does the person wear? How does the person move?

Memory Another way to collect sensory details is to use your memory. For instance, pretend that you want to describe a county fair that you attended last year. Try to remember everything you can about the fair. What sounds did you hear? What colors did you see? What did the exhibits smell like? What kinds of things did you eat?

Imagination The third way to collect sensory details is to use your imagination. If you are writing a fantasy about life on another planet, for example, you can make up any details you want. You can have red grass and green skies. The rain might fall constantly, the flowers might grow over ten feet tall, and the people might look like giant ostriches. Be creative and let your imagination run wild!

Listing Details

You can write down your details in a number of ways. One way is simply to list the details that you think are important. If you are describing an eclipse for a report, your list might look like this:

> chromosphere and corona only visible during
>   a total eclipse
> a red flash before the full eclipse
> a halo where the sun once was
> the sky gets dark

Another way to list details is to make up a chart with different categories. If you are describing a person, your chart might look like this:

General build	tall and thin
Height	six feet
Face	green eyes, large nose, short beard
Hair	black with gray streaks
Voice	deep and friendly
Movements	awkward, jerky
Skin	rough, hairy

You can also group your details by senses. Divide a page into five columns and label the columns: *sight, sound, smell, taste,* and *touch.* Then list the details in the correct columns. List only those details that support the mood you want to create.

Writing Activities *Prewriting*

A Collect details for two descriptions of the same place. The first description will describe the place's mood during the day; the second will describe the mood at night. Pick a place that you can observe carefully, such as your home, a local park, or a neighborhood street. Begin by observing the place during the day. Figure out what mood the place has, and then list the sensory details that support the mood. Next, observe the place at night and make a list of details that support the night mood. Finally, compare the two lists. How are the moods and details different? How are they the same?

B **Writing in Process** Find a person, place, or thing that you would like to describe. You might want to look through *Starting Points: Ideas for Writing* (pages 43–55) for a person, place, or thing that interests you, or you might use the brainstorming skills on pages 25–26. Perhaps you could describe someone you admire, a place you dislike, or a thing that fascinates you. Once you have decided on a topic, identify the mood you want to create and then make a list of sensory details that support the mood. Save your list in your writing folder. You will use it in a later activity.

3
Drafting: Organizing a Description

After you have finished the prewriting phase, you are ready to begin drafting your description. The first step in drafting is to organize your list of sensory details into a particular order. Look for relationships among the details, such as position, size, importance. Then find a method of organization that will lead your reader through your description in a logical way.

Spatial Order

When you use **spatial order**, you show where each detail is located in space. In particular, spatial order gives your reader a logical and well-organized picture of a scene. In describing a tree, for example, you might start with the roots, move up to the trunk, and end with the branches and leaves. Since your description of the trees moves from bottom to top, it is in bottom-top order. Other spatial orders include left-right, front-back, and inside-outside.

Read the following selection. Notice how the spatial order organizes your view of the scene.

Professional Model

But land beneath rain forests is often *not* fertile. The soil is old; eons of rains long ago leached away most of its chemicals and nutrients. The trees must now get most of their chemicals from the sky. Their leaves and bark tend to be thin and specially adapted to soak up nutrients from rainwater. Their roots are typically shallow, concentrated in the top few inches of the soil, where they soak up rain as soon as it falls. Some roots even grow up the trees, closer to the sky.

From *Planet Earth* by Jonathan Weiner

The description starts at the bottom of the scene and moves from the soil, to the leaves of the trees, back down to the roots, and finally up to the sky.

In spatial-order descriptions, certain words and phrases help you understand the order. The selection about the rain forest on the opposite page uses bottom-top, as well as top-bottom order. The words *beneath, up,* and *top* guide you up and down the scene. These words are called **transitions**. The chart shows common spatial orders and transitions.

Order	Transition Words
Top-bottom	at the top, near the bottom, under, above, below, on top
Inside-outside	on the outside, on the surface, just inside, within, inside
Left-right	on the left side, to the right, in between, next to
Front-back	at the front, in the back, behind, beyond

Order of Impression

When you use **order of impression**, you begin with the details an observer might notice first. Then you show the details that the observer might notice next, and so forth.

Some order-of-impression descriptions begin with a general impression and then give details that support the general impression. Other descriptions start with the details and build up to the general impression.

In the following selection, a girl named Melanie has just met another girl named April. Notice how Melanie's impressions of April are arranged.

Literary Model

At first glance April really was a surprise. Her hair was stacked up in a pile that seemed to be more pins than hair, and the whole thing teetered forward over her thin pale face. She was wearing a big, yellowish-white fur thing around her shoulders, and carrying a plastic purse almost as big as a suitcase. But most of all it was the eyelashes. They were black and bushy looking, and the ones on her left eye were higher up and sloped in a different direction. Melanie's mouth opened and closed a few times before anything came out. —Zilpha Snyder

The description begins by showing Melanie's general impression of April, which is one of surprise. Then the description gives details that support Melanie's impression: April's hair; her thin face; the fur; the plastic purse; the eyelashes.

Order of impression is often used to describe people, because we don't usually look at people in a particular spatial order. When Melanie meets April, for example, she doesn't start at April's shoes and work her way up to her hair. Instead, her eyes dart from one remarkable thing about April to another.

Writing Activities *Organizing a Description*

A Below are some sentences from paragraphs of description. Tell whether the paragraph probably used a spatial order or an order of impression. Explain your answers.

1. The bottom of the house was made of cinder block.
2. The first thing you notice about my dog is his long wagging tail.
3. To the left was a dense forest of trees capped with snow.
4. I finally became aware of her hands. They were smooth and soft, like a child's hands.
5. The right-hand wall was covered with shelves of books.
6. I heard the low rumbling even before I entered the darkened room.

B **Writing in Process** Examine the sensory details that you listed in Activity B on page 165. Use the details to draft two descriptions of the same subject. For the first description, use spatial order. For the second description, use order of impression. When you finish, compare the two descriptions. Which order seems better suited to the subject? Why?

4

Drafting and Revising: Descriptive Language

As you draft and revise a description, you will need to pay special attention to the descriptive language that you use. If your descriptive language is effective, your readers will be able to picture the things you describe. Good descriptive language creates sensory images and uses specific words.

Creating Sensory Images

A **sensory image** is a word or phrase that describes a sight, sound, smell, taste, or feeling. As you read the following selection, pay attention to the sensory images that the writer uses. Notice the words that create each sensory image.

Literary Model

> But one day a change came over the woods and the pond. Warm air, soft and kind, blew through the trees. . . . All the creatures that lived in the pond and in the woods were glad to feel the warmth. They heard and felt the breath of spring, and they stirred with new life and hope. There was a good, new smell in the air, a smell of earth waking after its long sleep.
>
> From *The Trumpet of the Swan* by E. B. White

The selection appeals to your senses of feeling and smell. You feel the warmth of the air and you smell the earth waking. Writers often focus on only one or two senses in describing a scene. The senses they choose depend on the mood they want to create. In this selection, the writer focuses on warmth and smell to create a joyful mood.

Using Specific Words

The more specific your words are, the more accurate and powerful your sensory images will be. For example, the sentence, "The snake moved along the ground," creates a weak sensory image. You don't know what kind of snake it is, or how it's moving, or what the ground looks like. Here's the same sentence with specific words: "The diamondback rattlesnake slithered noiselessly through the rocks along the path." That sentence creates a much stronger sensory image. Thanks to the specific words, you have a better picture of the scene.

Verbs You can use specific verbs to show actions clearly. Your characters don't have to just talk to each other, they can also scream, whisper, yell, mumble, lecture, command, and implore. In the following selection, notice how the specific verbs show the separate actions of the struggle.

Literary Model

> I made a grab at him. . . I almost got him off balance, but not quite. We swayed and struggled and then crashed together and rolled down into the ditch by the side of the road. There was some water in it, but we went on fighting, even after a voice challenged us from above.
>
> —John Christopher

Writing Inside Out

What do ex-English teachers do when they stop teaching English? Well, they might become professional writers like Cary Pepper, who lives and works in Brooklyn, New York. Mr. Pepper makes his living writing for other people. On a typical work day, he wakes up, relaxes over a cup of coffee, and then sits down at his typewriter for the next six to eight hours. Cary is lucky enough to be able to write about almost anything. He has written magazine articles, advertisements, brochures, catalogs, headlines for movie posters, and even the movie descriptions you read on videotapes.

Nouns You can use specific nouns to name the objects you describe. The more specific the nouns are, the more accurate the description will be. In the following selection, notice how the specific nouns help to create a powerful image.

Literary Model

> Over the years this clearing had grown over with a strange mixture of high, rank grass, tall weeds, berries, and wild flowers. In the summer it was a wild and beautiful place, bright with blooms and full of the smell of blackberry blossoms and purple clover. There were harsher plants as well—spiked jimson weeds and poisonous dark pokeberries, and bees droning everywhere.
>
> From *Mrs. Frisby and the Rats of Nimh* by **Robert O'Brien**

Adjectives and Adverbs You can use specific adjectives and adverbs to tell more about the things you describe. In the selection at the top of the next page, notice how the adjectives and adverbs tell more about the basic scene.

Although Mr. Pepper enjoys a great deal of success now, that was not always true. It took over three years for him to establish himself and earn a living as a writer. In fact, writing for magazines gave him his first real break into the world of professional writing. One day, he had the right idea at the right time for the right editor. He wrote his first article. That chance led to others and soon he was writing for publications like *TV Guide*, the *New York Times*, *American Film*, and *Advertising Age*.

There are days when Cary works all day. There are other days when he might take a walk, stare out a window, or see a movie. But a professional writer, Cary says, "is never not working." Everything is a possible inspiration—"You're always being nourished." For instance, Cary might see something as simple as a man wearing an emerald green tie and an orange sweater, and he might describe that later in a story or use it as an example in a magazine article. "To write," Cary says, "you must know things about the world out there."

And all at once the sun was uncomfortably hot, the dust oppressive, and the meager grass . . . somewhat ragged and forlorn. On the left stood the first house, a square and solid cottage with a touch-me-not appearance, surrounded by grass cut painfully to the quick and enclosed by a capable iron fence.

—Natalie Babbitt

Grammar in Action

You should avoid using too many adjectives and adverbs in your descriptions. Sentences with too many adjectives or adverbs sound ridiculous and overblown. Precise nouns and verbs are usually more effective (see pages 424 and 470). Consider the following pair of sentences. Which is stronger?

The strong, golden-haired dog ran quickly and effortlessly after the bouncing tennis ball.

The golden retriever sprinted after the tennis ball.

Writing Activities *Using Descriptive Language*

A The paragraph below contains few sensory images or specific words. Rewrite the paragraph so that it contains both sensory images and specific words.

I felt funny as I walked towards the house. It was an old house, and it didn't look very welcoming. I knocked on the door. The door wasn't in good shape either. A young boy opened the door. He looked really weird. He looked at me and said, "Can I help you?" His voice sounded funny.

B Writing in Process Revise one of the descriptions that you drafted for Activity B on page 168. Refer to your list of sensory details. Include sensory images and specific words in your revision. Save your work in your writing folder.

5
Revising a Description

Before you share your description with an audience, you will need to make a final revision. It is often helpful to put your draft aside for a while before trying to revise it. You may also find it useful to have someone serve as a peer editor.

You or your peer editor should use the revision checklist on page 174 to decide which parts of your draft need revision. Make the necessary changes, and then read your description again. After you finish, close your eyes and see if you can picture the things you have described. Then return to your revised draft and correct any awkward or unclear phrases or sentences.

Next, proofread your writing and correct any spelling or mechanical errors. Then prepare a final, clean copy.

Jane revised the following description. Her thoughts are shown in the blue bubbles.

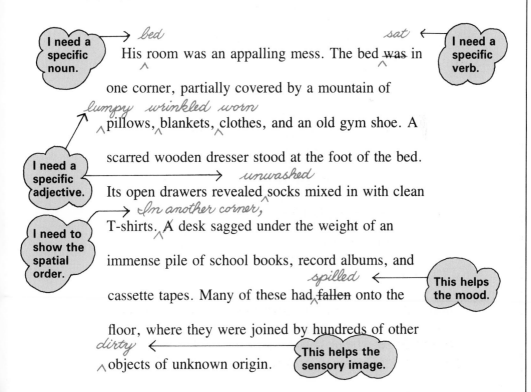

I need a specific noun. → *bed*

sat ← **I need a specific verb.**

His room was an appalling mess. The bed ~~was~~ in one corner, partially covered by a mountain of

lumpy wrinkled worn
ʌpillows, ʌblankets, ʌclothes, and an old gym shoe. A

I need a specific adjective.

scarred wooden dresser stood at the foot of the bed.
→ *unwashed*
Its open drawers revealed ʌsocks mixed in with clean

→ *In another corner,*
T-shirts. ʌA desk sagged under the weight of an

I need to show the spatial order.

immense pile of school books, record albums, and

spilled ← **This helps the mood.**

cassette tapes. Many of these had ~~fallen~~ onto the

floor, where they were joined by hundreds of other

dirty ←
ʌobjects of unknown origin. **This helps the sensory image.**

Revision and Peer-Editing Checklist

1. Does the description create a strong mood or feeling? Do the details support the mood? Are other details needed?
2. Is the description well organized? If the method of organization is spatial, is it easy for the reader to follow? Are transitions used effectively to show spatial relationships? If order of impression is used, does it show the impressions that an observer might have?
3. Does the description create sensory images? Are sensory words used that let readers see, hear, taste, smell, or feel the things that are described?
4. Are specific nouns, verbs, adjectives, and adverbs used? Are the words accurate and precise? Does the description avoid the overuse of adjectives and adverbs?

After you have made all of your revisions, you are ready to share your description with an audience. Can they picture the things you have described? Do they understand the mood you have created? If so, your description is a success.

Writing Activities *Revising a Description*

A Revise the following description to give it a more exciting mood. Add sensory images and specific words. Also rewrite the awkward sentences.

> A man entered the elevator. He had a mark on his face. He wore jeans and a sweatshirt. His hair was black. He smelled like a restaurant. His eyes looked from side to side. He was carrying a box. He turned to me and said, "Where is Apt G-5?" His voice was mean. His eyes were kind. I smiled and said, "Fifth floor—to your right." Just then the elevator door opened and I left.

B **Writing in Process** Make a final revision of the description you completed in Activity B on page 172. Try to answer all the questions in the checklist above. When you finish, share your description with an audience. Find out how well they can picture the things you describe. Also find out what kind of mood the description creates for them.

English and Social Studies

Have you ever walked into an unfamiliar room and felt instantly that you knew something about the person who lived there? It's quite possible because people leave hints and clues to their identity all around them. In fact, you might be able to come up with a fairly accurate description of the person living in that room just from the things you observed there.

Social scientists make it their business to observe the "things" that people use, along with the "things" that they leave behind. They use these observations to describe different kinds of so-cieties, both modern and ancient. It's a bit like being a detec-tive who fits together the pieces of a puzzle to solve a mystery. The challenge grows when the scientists study people who are no longer living. Imagination then becomes even more important to the task of re-creating these hidden lives, because the objects that they find may be unfamiliar to a modern person.

Ancient Greek and Italian vessels and urns.

Activity

Imagine that you are a social scientist, studying your classroom, a room in your home, or a room in someone else's home. Carefully observe everything in the room without touching anything. Write a description of the room's inhabitant(s) based only on the objects you see around you. What story does the room tell you?

Creative Writing

Imagination and exaggeration have teamed up to create many horrifying and outrageous creatures. Read on to discover (if you dare!) the horror felt by Dr. Von Frankenstein when he realized what a monster he had created:

> "His limbs were in proportion, and I had selected his features as beautiful. Beautiful! . . . His yellow skin scarcely covered the work of muscles and arteries beneath; his hair was of lustrous black, and flowing; his teeth of pearly whiteness; but these luxuriances only formed a more horrid contrast with his watery eyes, that seemed almost the same color as the dun-white sockets in which they were set, his shrivelled complexion and straight black lips."
>
> (*Frankenstein*, Mary Shelley, 1871)

Imagine that you have set out to create a modern-day Frankenstein, a monster more hideous than the Frankenstein created over a hundred years ago. Write a description of your creation in vivid, horrid detail for the world to read. Sketch a picture for those who are not too timid to take a look at the actual creature.

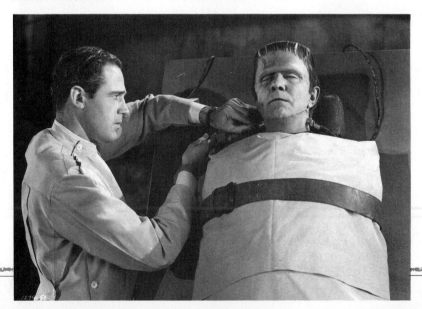

Application and Review

A Analyzing a Description Read the following paragraph.
Answer the questions below.

> Aunt Spiny was swelling! She was swelling and
> swelling and swelling! It's a trick that dragons do to
> frighten their enemies. She blew herself up until she
> was four times her normal size. Her crest stood up
> like spikes, and the frill around her neck that usually
> lay flat reared up like a huge steel ruff. Her scales
> turned black and crimson, and when she next spoke
> her voice hissed like rain falling on hot earth.
>
> —June Counsel

1. To which senses does the selection appeal? What specific
   words or images help you to use those senses?
2. What order does the author use to describe Aunt Spiny?

B Organizing a Description Read the following sentences from
a descriptive paragraph. Identify the topic sentence, then arrange
the facts in a logical order. Tell how you organized them.

- A strong tail helps the whale leap from the water.
- On top of the whale's head, the blowhole spurts water high
  into the air.
- The killer whale has a sleek, powerful body.
- Its dome-shaped black head barely breaks the water as it
  swims.
- Behind the blowhole, the whale has a single large dorsal fin.
- In sharp contrast to the black topside, the white underbelly of
  the killer whale gives it an impressive look.

C Using Specific Description Replace each word below with a
more specific word and write a sentence using each new word.

Nouns	Verbs
fish	talk
car	move
dessert	drink

10
Writing a Narrative

A mime in the park, an actor on stage, and a novelist at the typewriter are all doing the same thing—they're telling stories. Good storytellers like these can help their audiences experience people, places, and situations they might never encounter in their daily lives.

Narrative writing is writing that tells a story. The story might be true or imagined, serious or funny, long or short. In Chapter 9 you learned about writing to describe. Now you will learn to use your prewriting, drafting, revising, and sharing skills to create a narrative of your own.

1
Understanding the Narrative

Suppose you were away on vacation and wanted to write a letter to a friend back home. What would you write? You'd probably write a **narrative**, or story, about the interesting things that had happened to you.

Read and Think   Gina was on vacation and decided to write a letter to her friend Sean. As you read the body of her letter, look for the part of the letter that tells the story.

Student Model   How are things at home? I miss playing on the soccer team, but we're having a great time at my uncle's cottage. I'm even learning a few things—like how not to get into a canoe.

Early yesterday morning, my cousin Sonia and I walked down to the lake. We had planned to paddle to the cave before breakfast. Sonia asked me, "Have you been in a canoe before?"

I didn't want to sound dumb, especially since Sonia always acts like she can do anything, so I said, "Sure."

With my right foot, I stepped into the canoe. But my left foot stayed on the dock, and the canoe slowly drifted away from the dock. Sonia started laughing, and I didn't know what to do. Finally my feet decided for me. When the canoe drifted far enough from the dock, my feet slipped, and I fell into the water.

Sonia fished me out, and in the afternoon she taught me how to get into a canoe without getting into the lake first. Maybe I can teach *you*. When can you come?

Think and Discuss   Think about how you would answer the following questions about Gina's narrative. Discuss your answers with your classmates.

1. Is the story based on a real or imaginary event?

2. Who are the characters in the story Gina tells?
3. Where does the story take place? How do you know?
4. What happens to Gina in the story? Why does it happen?

Read and Think Here is another kind of narrative writing. This is the first part of a story by a published writer.

Literary Model

   I'm not sure I can tell you what you want to know about my brother; but everything about the pet fox is important, so I'll tell all that from the beginning.

   It goes back to a winter afternoon after I'd hunted the woods all day for a sign of our lost pet. I remember the way my mother looked up as I came into the kitchen. Without my speaking, she knew what had happened. For six hours I had walked, reading signs, looking for a delicate print in the damp soil or even a hair that might have told of a red fox passing that way—but I had found nothing.

   "Did you go up in the foothills?" Mom asked.

   I nodded. My face was stiff from heldback tears. My brother, Colin, who was going on twelve, got it all from one look at me and went into a heartbroken, almost silent, crying.

   Three weeks before, Bandit, the pet fox Colin and I had raised from a tiny kit, had disappeared, and not even a rumor had been heard of him since.

From "The Last Cover" by Paul Annixter

Think and Discuss Think about how this narrative is different from the story in Gina's letter. Then discuss these questions.

1. Who are the characters in this story?
2. What is the problem to be solved? How could it be solved?
3. Where and when does the story take place?

Follow Up You've seen that narratives can be created from events that really happened or from events a person imagines. Both kinds of narrative introduce a setting or story scene, a group of characters, and a series of events. Keep these features in mind as you read the following literature selection.

Narration in Literature

The Vigil

Jan Andrews

Characters and setting introduced

A long the dirt road that led through their small Newfoundland village, past the church and the schoolyard, and down onto the beach dashed Caitlin Roberts and her brother Kevin early one Saturday morning. . . .

A lock of Caitlin's long black hair fell across her face, and as she pushed it back, her gray eyes widened.

Beginning of plot

"Kev," she cried, pointing ahead. "Look!"

What she had seen sped them on, so that within seconds they were running as hard as they could towards where a huge, black shape was lying stranded.

"A whale," Kevin called. He kicked at a broad line of small, dead fish thrown up along the high water mark as he spoke. "Must have come after the capelin."

The great creature began to thrash and churn about at their approach. Stones and sand and spray were flung up from where the outgoing tide lapped around its tail, and its body writhed and twisted, carving deep into the sea bed. Its fins flapped as if, in some dreadful way, it were trying to walk. They paused, watching in horror.

Dialogue

"Won't get off, will it?" Caitlin said bleakly.

Kevin shook his head. "No," he answered. "Remember, last year, up by Twillingate? There was one there. It was on TV. Folks came from St. John's even, trying to push it off. Weren't no good."

He bent, picked up a stone, weighed it on his hand, and let it drop. The whale thrashed still more desperately. Air came sighing and steaming out of its blowhole, and a long, shuddering breath was sucked back in. . . .

They had almost reached the whale's side when they realized that, between the rocks at the cove's mouth, other whales were appearing. First one steam spout thrust itself upward and then another; then four dark enormous shapes rose from the water, arched through the mist, and plunged.

"They come to be with it," Kevin said. "Remember Mr. Jones telling us about that in science?"

"Shhh," Caitlin commanded. "Listen!"

Main event

From the blowhole of the whale on the beach a strange, high sound soared. It was answered by a succession of wavering notes, and again the shapes rose, this time closer to shore. Squeaks and cries and long, drawn whistles sounded on the cold, gray morning air.

"They're talking to each other," Caitlin said in awe.

Characters respond to event

As she looked at the creature on the beach and then out into the cove she realized her cheeks were wet with tears. Glancing round, she saw that Kevin was crying, too. He wiped his hand slowly across his eyes.

"They'll stay now till it's dead, won't they?" Caitlin asked through the lump in her throat.

"Yes, Mr. Jones told all about that, too. Yes, 'course they will."

As the communication between the whales went on, Kevin perched himself against a rock.

"Will you mind, Cat?" he said at last.

"Mind what?"

"When it's dead, and Dad and the men come to cut it. There's a wonderful lot of meat on a whale."

Caitlin hung her head to let her black hair shut out her vision for a while. "Sort of," she answered quietly. "But it'd only rot and stink otherwise, like the capelin."

"What if . . . ?"

The harshness in her brother's voice made her look up quickly. His round, usually cheerful face was pale and strained.

"What if what, now?" she asked.

"Well, if there'd been a gang of us, say. See, it'd have been different. We'd have yelled and laughed, and someone would've thrown a stone. Then we'd all have done it. Wouldn't have been like it is now. Not at all!"

The worry in Caitlin's gray eyes acknowledged the truth of his statement. He looked at his watch.

Problem introduced

"Some other kid's bound to come here before long," he said.

"Soon as one knows, they all will."

"We'll have to stay here then."

"We'll have to guard it."

"All day if need be."

Kevin hesitated. "Cat," he said. "We're not being daft, are we? I mean it's only an old whale and it's going to die anyway."

Doubt crept into Caitlin's mind. Already the drizzle was soaking through her jeans and running down her neck. She could feel the beginnings of cold and hunger, and fear of what the other kids in the village would say.

"I don't know," she muttered.

The whale on the beach let out another of its high strange cries, and once more the cry was answered. Brother and sister looked at each other. They knew then that they could not walk away.

Solution of problem

"We've got to, 'en't we?" Caitlin whispered.

Kevin nodded. "Yes. Yes, we have."

So it was that, with Caitlin and Kevin standing by on

land, and with its fellows waiting and calling to it from the sea, the whale on the beach came peacefully to the moment of its death. Gentle then was its passing; gentle and calm, like a cloud moving across the sun and breaking up and disappearing on a summer's day; certain as the tide that rose to wash cold and salt around it. For the first time, Caitlin put out a hand to touch the great body.

"The men'll come tomorrow, won't they?" she said softly. "They'll cut it. It'll be all a mess, and then nothing."

Kevin reached over and touched the dead animal, too. "I won't be sorry we stayed," he said. "Not ever."

Caitlin took a last look out into the cove. Somehow she could feel that already the other whales were swimming past the rocks and out into the open and away.

Conclusion   "No more will I," she said firmly. "No more will either of us."

Trying Out Narrative Writing Personal experiences are often a good source of narrative ideas. Write your own brief narrative based on an event that involved you, your friends, or your relatives. Then think about your narrative. What was easy to write? What was difficult? The rest of this chapter will help you to strengthen your narrative skills.

2
Prewriting: Finding Ideas for a Narrative

Before you begin writing, you need a story idea. This is a good time to use your thinking skills. You might glean story ideas from your own experience or from something you read. You might generate ideas by talking with friends or asking yourself *what-if* questions. See Chapter 2 (pages 24-39) for a discussion of such thinking skills.

Once the ideas start to come, get out a sheet of paper and a pencil. Using a method like freewriting or clustering, you can get your ideas down in a form you can work with.

Basically, you have three main starting points for finding ideas for your narrative: character, plot, and setting.

Start with a Character

Look for interesting characters among the people around you. You might be curious about people with a particular kind of job—say paramedics or street musicians. Your interest might be caught by a person's gesture, facial expression, or tone of voice. You might even try to imagine what a familiar person would be like in unfamiliar circumstances. For example, what were your parents like when they were your age? How would your best friend react to being lost in a strange city?

Once you find an interesting character, you need to do some thinking on paper about that character. In order to write a convincing story, you have to know the character thoroughly— his or her appearance, attitudes, feelings, hobbies, and goals. Make notes about how your character looks and acts, how he or she feels about things, and what this character does for fun. Even if you don't use all the details in your story, knowing them will make the story easier to write.

One good way to get ideas about a character is freewriting. Think about a character and write down whatever comes to mind. Don't worry about being neat or writing complete sentences. Just keep writing for a few minutes.

Start with a Plot

Most stories have a plot—a series of events that starts with a problem or a conflict and ends with a solution. You could start planning your story by coming up with a plot idea. You might begin with your own experience. Think of an important event or turning point in your life. You might glean plot ideas from magazines and newspapers. Start with an event that actually happened and change some of the details or characters. Imagine the situation that led to the event. You could also come up with a plot by using your imagination and asking a *what-if* question. For example, what if someone found a suitcase full of one-hundred-dollar bills lying beside the railroad tracks? What if someone suddenly gained the ability to hear the thoughts of other people?

To get a plot idea down on paper, think about the connections, or relationships, between events. Ask yourself what could lead to this situation. What might happen next? List the main events of your plot idea. Then put them in the order that they would happen.

Start with a Setting

Every narrative takes place in a particular place at a particular time. You might get ideas for a narrative by thinking about a setting—the where and when of a story. You might imagine unusual settings—a mountaintop in a blizzard or a deserted space station in the twenty-first century. Perhaps a place you know well—the school auditorium or a park by a lake—could be a good setting for a narrative.

If thinking about a special setting seems to be a good way for you to plan your narrative, get your ideas down on paper by using clustering. Think about the setting and write down the details that come to mind. Circle each detail and draw lines to show how the details are connected. Include details about the kinds of characters that might live and work in your setting. See Chapter 2 (pages 22–42) for more information on clustering and other brainstorming techniques.

Read the entry from Rod's journal that follows on the next page. It shows how Rod uses his own experience to come up with a story idea.

I love to be around Grandpa, even though he is kind of rough and crusty, and he's always offering advice. Especially about playing baseball. But why not? He was a great player and would have been in the major leagues if black players had been allowed back then. He's in such good shape, and looks like he still could play. I wonder how I might feel about him if I didn't know what he was when he was young?

Now answer these questions about the journal entry.

1. Did Rod use freewriting, listing, or clustering?
2. Did Rod focus on a character, plot, or setting?
3. What problem or conflict is emerging as a story idea?

Writing Activities *Finding Narrative Ideas*

A Choose two or three story starters from the following suggestions. Use freewriting, listing, or clustering to expand on each starter.

Character
1. An immigrant from Russia who moves to your town
2. A teen-ager who feels she needs to get a job to help out her family

Plot
1. Three strangers are stranded in a small airport.
2. A farm boy or girl spends a summer in New York City or in some other large city.

Setting
1. Half time in a locker room
2. A deserted beach on a foggy night

B **Writing in Process** Find at least two story ideas of your own. You can begin with a character, plot, or setting. If you wish, you may use one of the ideas from Activity A. You may also look through Starting Points (pages 43–55) or Ideas for Writing in the Writer's Handbook (pages 652–653) for story ideas. Use the suggestions in this lesson to help you think of ideas and get them down on paper. Save your story ideas in your writing folder for use in the next activity.

3
Prewriting: Developing a Narrative Idea

By starting with a character, plot, or setting, you came up with an idea for a story. By using a thinking technique such as freewriting, you began your planning. Now you can complete a plan for the story by developing the details. You may have decided whom the story will be about but not what will happen to that person. You may know where the story will take place but not what kinds of characters will meet there. Now it is time to plan these other aspects of your story.

Know Your Characters

Think about each of the characters in your story. Give each one a name. Decide how old each character is and what he or she looks like. Does the character have a family? What about friends? What problems does he or she face? Answer such questions in a brief sketch for each character in your story.

Focus the Setting

Every story takes place in a particular place at a particular time. As you plan the setting for your story, think about how it will affect your characters and plot. If you place your characters in an apartment, they'll act differently than if you put them in a steamy Amazon jungle, a snowed-in ski resort, or the audience of Ford's Theater on the night Lincoln was shot. You might develop your details according to the categories listed below:

Location (urban, suburban, or rural)
Geography (mountains, lakes, plains)
Weather (hot or cold, clear or stormy, calm or windy)
Conditions (an elegant home, a run-down tenement)
Time of day (early morning, suppertime, midnight)
Season (winter, spring, summer, fall)
Era (past, present, or future)
Atmosphere (eerie, lonely, carefree, hectic, dull)

Explore Plot Events

A plot is what happens in a story—the action or events. Usually, a plot advances from beginning to middle to end. The beginning introduces a problem. It becomes increasingly serious or complicated, but is solved at the end.

Constructing an effective plot takes thought. To fit events together, you might ask yourself when the events happened. You might ask yourself why the characters do what they do, and what will happen next. Ask such questions until you reach the end.

Organize with a Scenario

A good way to record your plan for a narrative is to complete a scenario. A **scenario** is a rough outline of your story. On the next two pages is Rod's scenario about his grandfather. Notice that Rod has made the main character a boy named Terry.

Writing Inside Out

Cheriff Morgan and Patrice Mozee are both police officers for a large metropolitan police force. When interviewed, both were working as instructors at the police academy. In teaching new recruits, both instructors stress how important writing reports is to everyday police work.

Officer Morgan: "Let me first say that police work itself is probably ninety percent writing reports. It is not like on television where all you see is the police officer chasing criminals. Once a criminal is caught, there are certain things that need to be done. In the course of arresting someone, I have to write an arrest report. The report will state the date and time of the arrest and where the arrest took place. In the narrative portion, I have to justify

Scenario for a Narrative

1. **Who are the characters?**
   - Terry, a boy about my age. He's tall for his age, athletic, and hopes someday to be a major-league baseball player. Terry loves practicing, and he works hard at pitching, catching, and batting. He has a good arm. But he isn't good at taking advice from people—he thinks he already knows everything he needs to know.
   - Terry's grandfather, an athletic, elderly man (about 67). He lives alone on his farm and has become stubborn and cranky around other people. When Grandpa was a young man, he was a professional baseball player (before black players were allowed in the major leagues). He is glad that Terry loves baseball, and wants to make friends with him. However, the grandfather's gruff manner gets in the way when he tries to help.

---

why I arrested that person. Besides the arrest report, I also have to complete a case report. There are certain elements about that crime, as related to me by the victim, that I have to include in that case report. Both the judge and the state's attorney will look at the reports that I've written."

Officer Mozee: "Case reports make or break criminals. If you haven't written properly in the case report, the criminal can be freed because of something you've either put in or left out of the report. In reality, by the time a person is arrested and has gone to jail, a police officer has already written anywhere from ten to twelve reports. So writing is basic to this job. It's everyday."

Officer Morgan: "Exactly. And it's necessary that the report be so accurate that six months later when you go to court on the case, you're able to read that report, refresh your memory about the crime, and be able to testify about what occurred."

Officer Mozee: "Once you write a report, it tells a lot about you as an individual police officer."

2. **What is the setting?**
   - Grandpa's farm early in the summer. The farm is small but homey. It is hundreds of miles from a big city and is a lonely, isolated, slow-moving, and quiet place.

3. **What are the events in the plot?**
   - Terry arrives for a three-week stay on Grandpa's farm.
   - Grandpa assigns Terry some farm chores, but Terry skips his chores to practice pitching. Grandpa tries to give Terry some pitching advice, but Terry runs off.
   - As he walks down the road, Terry meets a neighbor, who tells Terry about Grandpa's former baseball career.
   - Terry goes back to the farm and sees Grandpa differently.

Writing Activities *Developing a Narrative*

A Write a short scenario based on one of the ideas below.

1. A boy genius who is much younger and smaller than his classmates
2. A crowded beach with a summer storm approaching
3. A girl starts having dreams that come true
4. A small off-shore island

B **Writing in Process** Choose one of the story ideas you came up with for Activity B on page 188. Write a scenario for the idea. Follow the example that begins on page 191.

4
Drafting a Narrative

In writing the first draft of your narrative, use your scenario as a guide. Develop your draft in a loosely structured way, experimenting with ideas and organization as you write. Remember, stories often develop in unexpected ways. Characters take on lives of their own, and events don't always turn out the way you planned. Don't be afraid to make changes as you draft. Here are some suggestions to help you write a first draft.

Create a Strong Beginning

A good beginning serves two main purposes. It catches the reader's interest. It also gives the reader enough information to get into the story. One way to find out whether your beginning is effective is to show it to friends and ask them whether it makes them curious about your story.

You will be writing a short narrative, so you won't have space for an elaborate introduction. Just concentrate on getting the story started in an interesting way.

Read the beginning that Rod wrote for his story. Then discuss answers to the questions that follow it.

> The bus swirled a cloud of dust around Terry as it
> pulled away from him down the *country* road. He looked around.
> *Corn in every direction.*
> Why did his parents have to send him *away* to this, he
> wondered. Three weeks with *stiff, old* Grandpa. He would have
> been fine at home. At least he would have had something
> to do there.

I want to describe what he saw.

I want to make it clear that he's far from home.

I want to describe Grandpa.

1. Does this beginning catch your interest? How?
2. What information about characters, setting, and plot does Rod provide in this beginning?

Develop the Setting

Don't overwhelm your readers by trying to describe everything at once. Include only the important descriptive details, those that help establish a mood for your story or that help readers better understand the characters or the plot. Use any leftover details to help you figure out what your characters might do and say.

To make your description effective, appeal to your readers' senses. Use details that help them see, hear, feel, taste, and smell what's going on in the story. For instance, instead of telling your readers that a house looked spooky, *show* them. Describe the tangled lawn, the weather-beaten shutters, the musty smell, and the mournful creaking. Show your characters shivering from unexplained drafts.

Here is a part of Rod's first draft that shows the use of sensory details. You can see how his thoughts guided him as he worked. Read the draft, and then discuss answers to the questions that follow it.

Terry woke up to the ringing of a heavy skillet *cast-iron, wood-burning* against the top of the ⌃stove in the kitchen.

I want to be more specific.

He groaned and slowly pulled his pillow over his head, but he could still hear the ~~sounds~~ of ~~his~~ *clanging* pots and pans ⌃and *the whistle of the kettle.* ~~grandfather cooking.~~ He could smell dark strong coffee brewing and could hear the sizzle of

I want to use details that *show*, not tell.

something frying in the skillet. He wondered what *shadowy and still,* time it was. His room was ~~still dark~~ but he knew ⌃ that Grandpa would be calling him any minute.

I want to use the senses more.

1. How do these details help to develop the setting?
2. What do the details tell you about Terry and his grandfather?
3. Have the details that Rod added improved the development of the setting? How?

Show the Characters

Your story will become more interesting as you reveal more about your characters. The best way to reveal your characters' thoughts and feelings is to show the characters in action. Instead of telling your readers that someone is angry, describe the character's red face or clenched fist. Show the character slamming a door.

You can also show your characters through dialogue. Try to copy the way your characters would actually speak. Remember that people leave out words when they talk. They use slang. Remember, too, that different people speak in different ways. Someone might speak much more carefully and formally at work than at home. Here is a part of Rod's story in which he used action and dialogue to show his characters.

Just as Terry *pitched a fastball at* ~~released the ball toward~~ his

I want to show his pitching more vividly.

target, Grandpa came around the corner of the

barn. Terry *glared at Grandpa. Then he* grabbed the pail of chicken feed

I want to show Terry's anger.

and tried to act like he was on his way.

"Shouldn't leave chores undone," Grandpa said.

"I'm doing them."

"I can see you need the practice, though,"

Grandpa continued, almost as if he wasn't

listening. "Your windup is too choppy. Leg kick

is bad, too." *Grandpa did a leg kick like Terry's.*

I want to show Grandpa's actions.

Terry stared at Grandpa for a moment. Then

he turned toward the chicken coop. "I don't need

any advice from you," he muttered under his breath.

Grammar in Action

Quotation marks are an important part of much narrative writing. They make dialogue more understandable by showing readers which words have been spoken by which characters.

> "I never thought we'd make it home before Mom," Jackie said. "We've only got a few minutes to decorate."
>
> "Better hurry," warned Roger. "Where's the key?"
>
> "Wh-what key?" Jackie's face had a stricken look, and her hand moved to her mouth.
>
> Roger groaned, "Oh, no! Don't tell me you forgot to bring it!"

Notice that each character's words are enclosed in quotation marks and a new paragraph begins each time the speaker changes. Descriptive phrases like *Jackie's face had a stricken look* and words like *warned Roger* are placed outside the quotation marks. Only actual speech is enclosed in quotation marks. For additional information on quotation marks and punctuating dialogue, see pages 639–641.

Writing Activities *Drafting a Narrative*

A Read the following statements that tell what a character is like. Then rewrite them to *show* the same characteristics through action and dialogue.

1. Maria was angry, so she told Talia to leave immediately.
2. Jeong-Soo felt lonely at the new school.
3. Tony suddenly felt that nothing was impossible.
4. After the football game, Carlos was tired and discouraged.

B **Writing in Process** Using the scenario you developed in Activity B, page 192, and the suggestions in this lesson, write a first draft of your narrative. Save your draft in your writing folder. You will continue to work on it later.

5
Revising a Narrative

Before your narrative is ready for sharing, you need to ask
yourself whether it can be improved. A first draft is not the end
of the writing process. Go over your notes. Make sure you have
included all the information that is important to your story. Try
reading your narrative aloud. You might find that something that
sounded fine when you were drafting does not seem right the
next day. Finally, read your story to a friend, or ask a peer
editor to read it. Encourage listeners or readers to ask questions.
Here is how Rod revised the end of his first draft.

When Terry came into the farmhouse, Grandpa

In the dim light,

I want to
use the
senses.

was sitting at the kitchen table. ~~Somehow~~ Grandpa

"Were you wondering where I was?"

looked different to Terry. Terry sat at the table, and *Terry asked.*

"Don't matter, now that you're back," Grampa
replied.   *were talking*

for the first time ~~he could remember~~ they talked

Terry
sighed happily

being

together like friends without Grandpa pushy or

I want
to use
dialogue to
show what
happened.

snoopy and without Terry feeling angry or like a

kid. "Grandpa," Terry asked, "why didn't you ever

I want
to show
Grandpa's
friendliness.

tell me about your career?"

Then he grinned, "But I'm glad

"Don't like to brag," Grandpa shrugged. *you know about*
it now."

1. How does rewriting part of the scene as dialogue make the
   narrative more interesting?
2. How does appealing to the senses add interest to the
   narrative?
3. Is the revised ending more satisfying? Why?
4. What other changes would you make if this were your
   narrative?

Don't be afraid to revise your narrative. Ideas for improving your story can come at any time during the writing process. You also might get ideas for revision from friends who read your work. It may be hard to mark up a clean draft, but making the narrative better is worth it. The chart below shows questions you or a peer editor can ask when reading your narrative.

Revision and Peer-Editing Checklist

1. Does the beginning of the narrative interest readers and get them into the story?
2. Is the setting developed in a way that moves the narrative along? Are sensory details used?
3. Are readers *shown* characters instead of told about them?
4. Is dialogue used to reveal the characters and to develop the action of the narrative?
5. Do the events in the story make sense and seem complete? Is the ending satisfying?

Writing Activities *Revising a Narrative*

A The following three excerpts from a narrative need to be revised. Use the suggestions in parentheses to help you revise each excerpt.

1. This is a story about a boy named Juan who had to take care of his sick mother every day. One day, Juan had a problem at school. (Make the beginning more interesting and informative.)
2. Mr. Hyde, his English teacher, was trying to help Juan answer a question. But Juan didn't like getting help. He thought it made him look stupid in front of his classmates. (Show rather than tell. Use dialogue.)
3. Juan was a quiet boy, but he could be tough when the other students tried to push him. He never picked a fight but if he had to, he could defend himself. When this happened, he surprised everyone. (Show by using an incident.)

B **Writing in Process** Revise the first draft of your narrative. Use the checklist above to help you think about the changes that need to be made.

6
Proofreading and Presenting

Proofreading

A reader can be distracted from a good story if it is hard to read or understand. Before you send your narrative out into the world, make sure it is neat and correct. Carefully proofread it for errors in spelling, punctuation, and grammar. Make sure you have started a new paragraph for each change in speaker.

To fix minor mistakes, you can simply draw a line through the letter or word you need to change. Then neatly write the correction above. For a guide to proofreading marks, see the checklist on page 88.

Here is part of Rod's proofread narrative.

Student Model

As he saw Ms. Washington's car approaching, Terry waved. The Washington's wear old family friends.

"Hop in," she said "it can't be much fun walking in the rain."

"Thanks. I was beginning to think noone ever drived down this road anymore."

"I think I heard you were going to be visitting your grandfather," Ms. Washington said. You must be really proud of him. He was a reel wonder in the early days of baseball.

1. What errors in spelling did Rod correct?
2. What errors in punctuation did Rod correct?
3. What error in grammar did Rod correct?

Presenting and Publishing

Finally, your story is ready to be shared with an audience. There are several ways you can do this. You might want to read your story aloud to your classmates or to students in another class. Another method of sharing is to publish a class anthology. An **anthology** is a collection of stories or articles. All the stories written by the members of your class can be collected in one booklet. That anthology can then be kept in the classroom or in the school library.

Writing Activities *Proofreading and Presenting*

A Below is an unpunctuated passage of dialogue. Copy the passage onto a sheet of paper, adding quotation marks, question marks, commas, capital letters, and paragraph breaks where they are needed.

Did you just hear a moaning sound Sparky asked as he quietly closed the door.

It's only the wind Herb replied. Are you trying to scare me I'm the one who's scared. Listen. There it is again. And it isn't the wind, Sparky added.

Come on said Herb it was your idea for us to spend the night in this place.

I only wanted to show Joni how brave I am.

So why don't you show me asked Herb in a quivering whisper.

I'm not really sure that I want to. I don't feel brave quaked Sparky.

Herb said if Joni could see you now, she would be *very* disappointed. I sure am!

B **Writing in Process** Proofread the revised draft of your story and make a neat, final copy. Decide how you want to share the story. Here are some methods you might choose.

• Read it aloud.
• Assign people parts to read and have your story performed.
• Record it on tape.
• Publish it in a classroom anthology.
• Submit it to a magazine that publishes the type of story you wrote.
• Enter it in a writing contest.
• Start a writing club at school. Members can share and discuss their stories, plays, poems.

Speaking and Listening

Storytelling has been an important tradition in many cultures throughout time, especially in societies where reading and writing were not widespread. Families, organizations, religious groups, and even governments have used word of mouth to pass on their history, laws, culture, and important events from generation to generation. When the author,  Alex Haley, was writing his autobiographical epic *Roots*, he travelled to West Africa and found evidence of his family's beginnings by listening to the oral traditions of tribes still living there. Even today, when families gather for holiday celebrations, stories about great-aunts and great-great-grandfathers may be told to the children and grandchildren over and over again. Later, these youngsters will tell their children and grandchildren, and another family's oral history will continue.

In fact, some people have made storytelling a profession. These professional storytellers travel around, entertaining people by telling fanciful tales and interesting old legends. For them, storytelling is an art. Good storytellers know that no one likes to listen to a dull story, one without engaging characters, an interesting setting, or a convincing plot. Thus, the goal of a story is to narrate in an entertaining way.

Activity

Divide into small groups. Brainstorm together and develop a good story idea that can be told orally. You may choose to retell a familiar myth or legend, or you may make up a mythical tale or family history of your own. Assign each member of the group a section of the story. Entertain your class by telling the story.

Creative Writing

A Sometimes the most creative ideas for stories come from putting together unexpected combinations. Putting a familiar character into a strange, new setting can set your imagination free. Think of what would happen if Superman showed up in Philadelphia in 1776, if Elvis Presley showed up at a performance of the New York Philharmonic Orchestra, or if the Queen of England played second base for the New York Mets.

Now choose a character of your own, one you know from a story, a movie, a television program, or real life. Put this character in an unusual setting. Write a story about what happens.

B You've probably heard people say: "The plot thickens." This expression means that the series of events in a story are growing more and more complex. One event is building upon another and another and another, leading closer and closer to the final solution. Mysteries are a good example of this kind of writing. Pretend you are a mystery writer. Make a list of complex, related events for a story, then write the story.

Fragment, 1974.
Robert Amft.

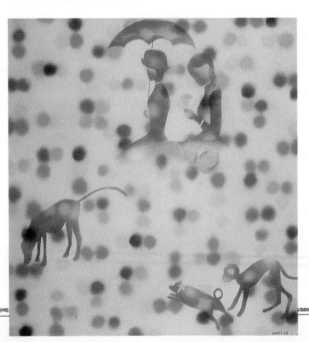

Application and Review

A Analyzing Narration Read the story beginning below.
Answer the questions that follow.

> "Eline! Where are you, Eline?" Anna stood in the
> middle of the small farmyard, cupping her hands
> around her mouth as she called her little sister's
> name. It was so cold that when she called Eline's
> name, her breath turned into billows of frosty
> smoke. It was midwinter in Norway and growing
> dark. The year 1865 was only two months old.
> Anna, the oldest girl in a family with seven
> children, was worried. It was her job to look after
> her four younger brothers and sisters while Mamma
> tended the farm—a big responsibility for a girl only
> thirteen years old.   —Sissel Keyn Lodding

1. What is the setting of this story and who is the main character?
2. What problem does the author introduce?

B Using Time Order Put these events of Anna's story in
chronological order.

- Mamma says she will take out the boat to find kelp.
- Anna goes out after her mother.
- Eline is in the barn crying that the animals have no food.
- Everyone had enough food that night.
- Mamma takes out the boat, but she doesn't return on time.
- Anna rescues Mamma, who has lost her oars.
- Anna tries to stop Mamma from going because of bad weather.
- When pulling in kelp, Mamma and Anna find a huge fish.

C Using Dialogue Rewrite the paragraph below as dialogue,
using the correct punctuation.

> Mamma said that she would take out the boat
> tomorrow and pick up as much kelp as she could.
> Anna said she should not go because the wind was
> too strong. She said that Mamma would drown.

11
Writing to Explain

You enter a cave, and instead of a big hollow space you find tremendous icicle-shaped rocks! You ask, "What *are* they?" but the only answer is the echo of your own voice.

You could get an answer from a geologist, who would explain how the rocks—called stalagmites and stalactites—are formed. You could look in a book or a pamphlet. In each case, you would be learning from someone's explanation. Explanatory writing is the means by which we share knowledge.

In this chapter you will learn the process of explanatory writing so you will be able to clearly explain the things you know.

1
What Is Exposition?

How does a bicycle pump work? What caused the Great Chicago Fire? When you write answers to questions like these, you are writing exposition. **Exposition** informs or explains.

Read and Think Mario is giving a program on special effects for a meeting of the Movie Club. First he will explain how special effects are added to movies. He did some research on this topic and here is one explanation he found.

Professional Model

Creatures, spaceships, and other objects are inserted into the action of the film by means of the blue-screen process. The figure is photographed against a blue background and then combined in an optical printer with the scene into which it will be placed. This must be repeated each time a new element is added to the scene. The pastry creatures that came to life in *Young Sherlock Holmes,* for example, were rod puppets, each shot individually and added one by one in as many as twelve layers. For a brief shot of a space battle in *Return of the Jedi,* sixty-three layers were required. This and other scenes are made possible by a computer-driven camera . . . that can repeat the same motion over and over so that new elements can be added with great precision.

From "Lights! Camera! Special Effects!" by Richard Zoglin

This explanation describes a **process**. It tells how something is done or how something works.

Next Mario will explain what has caused special effects to be so important in today's movies. Here is what he wrote.

Student Model

Special effects are used to add interest to a movie. Today, however, the effects themselves seem to be the stars of many movies. This is because the effects have become both spectacular and extremely realistic. One cause of the new importance of special effects is the advances in model making. Another is the computer. When highly realistic models are filmed by computer-controlled cameras, even bicycles can seem to fly, as they do in *E.T.*

This paragraph explains **causes and effects**. It tells why something has happened or is happening.

Finally, Mario will tell how special effects designer Carlo Rambaldi made the model E.T. seem so real. Here is an explanation he found in a magazine article.

Professional Model

What makes E.T. so remarkable is the number of points of movement possible. Rambaldi's heads for *King Kong* were capable of approximately a dozen individual movements, such as an eyebrow moving up and down. The E.T. model, on the other hand, can make thirty-five separate movements in the face alone. And the more movements possible, the more life-like the model.

From "The Making of E.T." by Kyle Counts

This paragraph tells how the models of King Kong and E.T. are different. It explains through **comparison and contrast**.

Think and Discuss Think about these questions. Discuss your answers with your classmates.

1. What examples of the blue-screen technique are given in the process paragraph? In what order are they given?
2. In the cause-and-effect paragraph, what two causes does Mario discuss? What is the effect, or result, of the causes?
3. How are the models of E.T. and King Kong different? What phrase signals a contrast of the two models?

Follow Up When you write to explain, you write to tell the reader how something is done, what something is, or why something is so. In this chapter, you will learn how to clearly describe a process, explain causes and effects, and explain through comparison and contrast. Keep these features of explanatory writing in mind as you read the following selection.

Exposition in Literature

Krakatoa: The Greatest of Them All

Margaret Poyton

*K*rakatoa was a small island made up of three
volcanoes—Perbuwatan, Danan, and Rakata—in the
Sunda Strait of Indonesia. . . . On August 26, 1883,
Krakatoa's three volcanoes began to erupt, the noise shaking
houses a hundred miles away. Steam rose to a height of
seven miles, and dust fell as far as three hundred miles from
the island.

By the end of the day, Krakatoa was hidden by clouds of
smoke and ash. Loud explosions occurred almost every ten
minutes, and stones were tossed high into the air as
lightning flashed through the inky black sky. The only other
light came from a shower of glowing mud that looked like
thousands of fireflies. It covered the ships in the area that
were trapped by the mass of floating volcanic rock.

Meanwhile, more openings appeared on the slopes of the
volcanoes, and hundreds of gallons of water rushed through
them. The plug in the main vent still held firm, and the
internal pressures grew. At dawn the next day, the sides of
the island started to burst open, and the first of four huge
explosions was heard. An hour later came a second; then
there was silence for over three hours.

A 10:02 that morning a gigantic explosion occurred,
making the loudest noise ever reported by human beings!
The sound waves cracked windows and walls for two
hundred miles around. In Burma, fifteen hundred miles
away, the noise sounded like gunfire at sea. A man on an
island in the Indian Ocean east of Africa heard the noise
from Krakatoa four hours later. The sound waves had
traveled three thousand miles!

The eruption caused a cloud of dust to rise fifty miles
into the air, and at least five cubic miles of rock and dirt

were blown out of the inside of the volcano. Since there

Effects on island

wasn't enough rock left to support it, the peak collapsed into the crater of the volcano, carrying two-thirds of the island with it. . . .

The ocean had been greatly disturbed by all the activity,

Ocean effects

and tidal waves, or *tsunamis* (tsoo-nah-mees), were formed. The largest, created by the 10:02 explosion and the island's collapse, rushed away from Krakatoa at a top speed of 350 miles per hour. As the huge wave approached land, it grew stronger and higher. A wall of water as high as a ten-story building crashed down on the coast of Java. Within minutes it destroyed three hundred villages, and parts of Sumatra were covered with eighty feet of water. . . .

For many months after the eruption, the Indonesian sea was full of floating rocks. The pillar of dust was caught up in

Conclusion

the winds of the upper atmosphere, where it orbited the earth. . . . Several years passed before the last of the dust fell back to earth. By that time, a bit of Krakatoa had been left in every part of the world.

Trying Out Expository Writing Now that you have read the article on Krakatoa, try some expository writing of your own. How will you choose a topic? What details will you include? How will you organize your information? After writing, think about your writing process. Which steps were easy? What skills could use improvement? What would you change next time?

2
Explaining a Process

When you explain a process, you tell how to make or do something, or you explain how something works. In industrial arts class you might be asked to explain how to build a bookcase. In science class you might be asked to explain how a tadpole turns into a frog. To explain a process you carefully select details describing each step in the process. Then you present the steps in order of occurrence, from first to last.

Read and Think Jenna's Scout troop was making jar terrariums. Here are the directions they used. As you read them, notice the specific details at each step of the process and how those steps are arranged.

Professional Model

A wide-mouthed gallon jar can easily be turned into the land version of an aquarium—a terrarium. With the jar firmly positioned on its side, put in a layer of sand mixed with potting charcoal. Over this place a layer of topsoil. The "ground" section should not be any higher than the mouth of the jar. . . .

Plants for the terrarium can be any of the smaller varieties, but those that are adapted to a humid environment will probably be more likely to thrive. Try striped wintergreen, rattlesnake plantain, partridge berry, mosses of various varieties, and lichens. Nurseries often have plants especially suited for a terrarium. You can also find them for yourself in your own neighborhood or on a trip to the woods.

Once you've positioned the plants in the soil, water them thoroughly, and screw on the top of the jar. Place it in the kind of light recommended for the plants you have selected. The plants will take root and continue to grow for as long as a year . . . without your ever having to open the jar!

From "Jar Terrarium" by Don Herbert

Think and Discuss Think about these questions. Discuss your ideas with your classmates.

1. Can you list the steps you need to make a jar terrarium?
2. Are the steps given in a logical order? Why?
3. What does the second paragraph in the directions tell about?
4. Why is there a list of plants in the second paragraph?
5. Are specific details important in explaining a process? Why?

Read and Think Another kind of process paragraph tells how something works. Dennis wrote this explanation of how a digital watch works for his science class.

Student Model

A digital watch shows the time in numbers. It has three main parts—a battery, a quartz crystal, and a microchip. Here is how the watch works. First the battery sends an electric current to the quartz crystal. This current makes the crystal vibrate an exact number of times every second. Every time the crystal vibrates, it produces an electrical signal. The microchip is like a tiny computer. It counts up the signals made by the quartz crystal. Then the chip tells the numbers on the face of the watch when to change. The microchip also counts up seconds, minutes, and hours. Then it tells the numbers to change to show the date and even to show which month it is.

Think and Discuss Read the paragraph again. Then discuss these questions in class.

1. What are the three main parts of a digital watch? What job does each of these parts do?
2. How would you describe the way the details in this paragraph are arranged?
3. Why does Dennis tell us that the microchip is like a tiny computer?
4. Can you identify any parts of the explanation that are unclear? How would you change them?

Follow Up You have read two examples of how to explain a process. One told how to make or do something, and the other told how something works. Each explanation used specific details to describe the steps of the process. These steps were arranged in a logical order. In each example, the writer understood the process being explained. This understanding allowed the writer to explain the process to the reader clearly and completely. You will now plan, write, and revise an explanation of a process.

Prewriting: Explaining a Process

You will write best about a process when you explain a subject that you know well and that interests you. Often you will need to explain how to do something you have done many times. For instance, you might need to write directions for a friend who has borrowed your VCR but has never used one. To test whether the topic you choose is suitable for a process explanation, see if it fits either of these patterns.

How to _____ . (explain how to make or do something)

How _____ works. (explain how something works)

Develop the Subject Next, gather information about your subject. If you are explaining how to do something, list the questions your audience is likely to ask, and then answer them. If you are explaining how something works, list the main parts of the subject and what each part does.

Organize the Information Most writing that explains how to make or do something uses an organization like this:

1. Why the process is important or useful
2. What preparations—supplies and equipment—are needed
3. What steps are needed to complete the process, in the order they are needed
4. What the results of the process are

Most writing that explains how something works uses an organization like this:

1. Why the process is important or worth understanding
2. What parts or elements are involved

3. How the process operates, in the order in which things happen
4. What the results of the process are

Notice that the details are arranged in **chronological order**. This means that the steps or parts of the process are explained in the order in which they should or did happen.

Drafting: Explaining a Process

There are many ways to draft an explanation of a process. Here is one method you might try.

Introduce the Subject Begin with a paragraph that interests the readers and identifies the subject. Also tell why the process is important or useful. Here is the opening paragraph of Kim's explanation of how to take interesting pictures of animals in zoos.

Student Model

Anyone can take a picture of a lazy lion dozing on a shelf in his cage. It takes effort to take interesting pictures of zoo animals, but the results are worth it.

Explain the Preparations If you are explaining how to do something, remember to tell what supplies and equipment are needed. Here is part of Kim's next paragraph.

Student Model

> A camera that allows you to change lenses is best. A telephoto or zoom lens, for example, can help you take a close-up of a baby giraffe at the back of its large, fenced enclosure.

Use Transitions As you tell the steps of the process in order, use transition words to help your reader. Some useful transition words are *first, next, then,* and *finally.* Notice the transitions Kim uses in this paragraph.

Student Model

> *First,* you should ask the zookeeper for the feeding schedule of the animal you want to photograph. Most caged animals are lively when they expect dinner. *Next* you should spend some time observing the animal to choose interesting behaviors to shoot.

Write a Conclusion Conclude by telling what has been produced or what value the process has. Here is part of Kim's ending.

Student Model

> With planning and patience, a trip to the zoo can yield pictures you will be proud to frame as decorations or gifts.

Revising: Explaining a Process

Answering these questions can help to guide your revision.

Revision and Peer-Editing Checklist

1. Is the introduction interesting? Does it identify the subject?
2. Are the steps organized from first to last? Are appropriate transition words used?
3. Is there an explanation of any preparations or supplies that are needed?
4. Are all special terms clearly explained?
5. Is the conclusion interesting and effective?

Grammar in Action

When explaining a process, be sure to use specific nouns and adjectives, not general ones. Specific nouns and adjectives clearly state the details of a process. General ones can lead to misunderstandings. Note these differences.

General: To make the bookcase, buy some lumber.

Specific: To make the bookcase, buy what is called "Number 2 white pine." Tell the dealer you want size 1″ × 10″ boards.

For additional information on nouns and adjectives, see pages 424 and 508.

Writing Activities *Explaining a Process*

A Listed below are the steps needed to give first aid for a minor injury. Rewrite them in order from first to last, numbering each step.

> Get medical attention if any redness develops.
>
> Wash the skin around the injury with soapy water.
>
> Cover the wound with a sterile bandage.
>
> Wash your hands to make sure you don't get dirt in the wound.
>
> Dry the wound.
>
> Be sure not to touch the sterile pad.

Then write the paragraph, using appropriate transitions.

B Writing in Process Explain some process you know well. You might look through Starting Points (pages 43–55) or Ideas for Writing in the Writer's Handbook (pages 653–654) for ideas. Identify an audience for your explanation. Then follow the method for prewriting, drafting, and revising introduced in this lesson. Share a final copy of the explanation with your audience.

3
Explaining Causes and Effects

Another kind of expository writing explains **causes and effects**. When you explain causes, you explain why an event happens or happened. For instance, you might explain why the Mt. St. Helens volcano erupted after hundreds of years of quiet or why the girls' volleyball team was undefeated this season. When you explain effects, you explain what happens or happened as a result of an event. For example, you might explain the effects of being an only child or the effects of the discovery of gold on the settling and growth of California.

Read and Think Carla was preparing an exhibit on dinosaurs for the science fair. She found this explanation of why dinosaurs may have become extinct.

Literary Model

About sixty-three million years ago, coinciding very closely with the disappearance of the dinosaurs, the world went through a great change of climate. It got colder. This may very well have killed the dinosaurs. While it is true that a big body keeps its heat for a long time, it is also true that it takes a very long time to regain it once it is lost. . . . A series of bitterly cold nights could have drained a big dinosaur of its heat beyond all recovery. With its body badly chilled, it might not be able to summon sufficient energy to move its huge bulk and browse. So a steady cooling of the climate . . . may well have led to the death of the large herbivores [plant-eating dinosaurs]. With them would go the carnivores [meat-eating dinosaurs] that hunted them and were therefore dependent on them.

From *The Living Planet* by David Attenborough

Think and Discuss Read the following questions. Think about how to answer them. Discuss your ideas with your classmates.

1. What two events occurred about sixty-three million years ago?

2. What relationship does the writer propose between the events?
3. Could you state in your own words why the writer thinks the herbivores (plant-eating dinosaurs) disappeared?
4. What facts or examples does the writer mention to support this theory?
5. Why do you think facts and examples are important in a cause-and-effect explanation?

Read and Think David was writing an editorial for his school newspaper about the effects of TV. Here is what he wrote.

> Some people think watching TV is bad for kids, but it's important to remember that TV has some good effects, too. For one thing, TV takes you to places and events all over the world. It gives you the best seats for important sports events like the Super Bowl and the Olympics, and it shows you how people live in such far away places as China and the Amazon jungle. Moreover, TV brings art, music, and plays into our living rooms. With a flip of the dial, you can watch a performance by the Dance Theater of Harlem, a concert by Alabama, or a play by Shakespeare. You can learn a lot from TV, too. Science programs like *Nova*, nature programs like *Living Wild*, and the evening news are great ways to learn about our world.

Think and Discuss Discuss your answers to these questions with your classmates.

1. What good effects does David think that TV has?
2. What organization does David use for his editorial?
3. Can you find the transition words David uses to link his ideas together? Why are these important?

Follow Up When you explain causes, you often answer the question *why?* by giving the reasons that an event occurred. When you explain effects, you often answer the question *what happened next?* by explaining the results or consequences of an event. In both kinds of writing, facts or specific examples are used to develop and support the main idea.

Prewriting: Explaining Causes and Effects

You will probably write about causes and effects many times in your classes. For instance, in English class, you might write a paper explaining what caused a character in a story to act a certain way, or on a health test you might explain the effects of exercise on the body.

Find a Subject To test whether a subject you are interested in is suitable for a cause-and-effect paper, see if it fits either of the following patterns.

> Why _____ happened. (main idea is to explain causes)
>
> What happened as a result of _____ . (main idea is to explain effects)

Gather and Organize Information Once you have gathered information, you will need to organize it. You might write down the effect you want to explain and then list its causes. You might write down the cause you want to explain and then list its various effects.

Sarah was writing a paper on the history of Chicago. Her main idea was to explain why Chicago grew so quickly. After reading some books and articles, she made these notes.

> **Effect:** Between 1830 and 1860 Chicago grew from a marshy village of 200 people to a large and important city.
>
> **Causes:**
>
> ③ In 1841, farmers in the Midwest produced a bumper crop of grain.
>
> ④ Wagons brought the grain to Chicago, and steamboats carried it to markets in New York and Europe.
>
> ① Chicago's location on the shore of Lake Michigan, surrounded by fertile farmland, was ideal.
>
> ② In 1833, a canal was dug connecting the Chicago River and Lake Michigan, creating a harbor.
>
> ⑤ By 1860, Chicago had become a hub for freight railroads that connected farmers and consumers.

State Street, Chicago, Illinois, 1869–71. Stereo photo by Carbutt.

Sarah's next step was arranging the details logically. The details can be organized in time order: first this cause or effect happened, then this one, and finally this one. Details can also be arranged in order of importance. Sarah decided to arrange her causes in a time sequence. The numbers show that order.

Drafting: Explaining Causes and Effect

The opening sentences of a cause-and-effect paper should state the main idea clearly. Here are Sarah's opening sentences.

Student Model

In 1830, Chicago was a marshy, uncivilized village of about 200 people. By 1860, it was a large and busy city humming with business and industry. There are many reasons why Chicago grew so quickly.

Use Examples and Transitions In the rest of your paper, explain each cause or effect in the order you selected. Use specific facts or examples to develop and support each cause or effect. Help your reader by using transition words such as *another important reason*, *as a result*, *in addition*, and *therefore*. Notice the specific examples and transition words Sarah used.

Student Model

Another important reason for Chicago's rapid growth was the coming of the freight train. By 1860, Chicago had become a rail hub linking farmers on the surrounding prairie with people who would eat the crops they produced. Trains carried wheat, corn, and cattle into Chicago from the farms and out to consumers in other areas.

Write a Conclusion The ending of a cause-and-effect paper should restate the main idea. Here is part of Sarah's conclusion.

For these reasons, it took Chicago only thirty years to grow from a tiny village on the prairie to a large and important city.

Revising: Explaining Causes and Effects

Answering these questions can help you revise a cause-and-effect explanation.

Revision and Peer-Editing Checklist
1. Does the introduction state the main idea?
2. Are details organized logically?
3. Is each point developed with facts and specific examples?
4. Are appropriate transition words used?
5. Is the main idea restated in the conclusion?

Writing Activities *Causes and Effects*

A Gene is writing an article for his school paper about the possible effects of the cancellation of the girls' and boys' basketball seasons. Here are his notes.

> **Cause**: The cancellation of the girls' and boys' basketball seasons
>
> **Effects:**
> School spirit will decrease.
>
> Supplies on hand such as uniforms and programs will be wasted.
>
> Athletes will be at a disadvantage when they go out for high school basketball.
>
> Parents will be disappointed.
>
> Girls' team will not be able to defend their championship.

Number the effects to arrange them in order from the most important to least important. Then write the article.

B **Writing in Process** Write a cause-and-effect explanation of a subject that interests you. You might look through *Starting Points: Ideas for Writing* (pages 43–54) for writing ideas. Then follow the method for prewriting, drafting, and revising in this in this lesson. Share a final copy with your audience.

4
Explaining Through Comparison and Contrast

How are schools in the United States different from schools in the Soviet Union? How is the heart like a pump? When you answer questions like these, you are explaining through **comparison and contrast**. When you compare and contrast, you tell about the important similarities and differences between two things so that your reader can understand each thing clearly.

Read and Think   Emily was giving a talk to her Skating Club about pair skating and ice dancing. Here is what she wrote.

Student Model

Pair skating and ice dancing look very similar. In both sports, a beautifully costumed man and woman glide around the ice to music. Both require strength, athletic ability, and gracefulness. Both are exciting to watch and difficult to do well. However, there are some important differences. Pair skating features many spectacular moves, such as double and triple jumps, overhead lifts, and dramatic spins. These moves are not allowed in ice dancing, which concentrates instead on interpreting music through dance steps on ice. The rules also allow the man and woman in pair skating to separate, so that they can skate and often jump side by side. In ice dancing, the man and woman are not allowed to separate, except to turn or to change positions. They must always seem to be dancing together. Knowing these differences can help you better appreciate these lovely and demanding sports.

Torvill and Dean, 1984 Olympics.

Think and Discuss These questions are about Emily's paragraph. Think about them. Then discuss your answers in class.

1. What sentence tells the reader that Emily is going to discuss similarities? What sentence tells the reader that she will discuss differences?
2. Can you list the similarities between pair skating and ice dancing? Can you list the differences?
3. How would you describe the way Emily organizes her explanation?
4. How does Emily end her comparison and contrast of the two types of skating?

Read and Think The following paragraph by a professional writer compares space voyages by robot explorers like the *Voyager* to the sea voyages of explorers like Columbus.

Professional Model

These voyages of exploration and discovery are the latest in a long series. . . . In the fifteenth and sixteenth centuries you could travel from Spain to the Azores in a few days, the same time it takes us now to cross the channel from the Earth to the Moon. It took then a few months to cross the Atlantic Ocean and reach what was called the New World, the Americas. Today it takes a few months to cross the ocean of the inner solar system and make planet-fall on Mars or Venus, which are truly new worlds awaiting us. In the seventeenth and eighteenth centuries you could travel from Holland to China in a year or two, the time it has taken *Voyager* to travel from Earth to Jupiter. . . . Our present spaceships, with their robot crews, are the harbingers, the vanguards of future human voyages to the planets. We have travelled this way before.

From *Cosmos* by Carl Sagan

Think and Discuss Read the comparison again. Then discuss your answers to these questions with your classmates.

1. How are sea voyages and space voyages alike? What point is the writer making with this comparison?
2. How would you describe the way the details in this comparison are arranged?

Above: Painting of the defeat of the Spanish Armada. Previous to this defeat in 1588, Spain explored and conquered much of South America and southern North America. Among its explorers were Columbus, Balboa, Cortés, and Pizarro.

Right: Launching of a space shuttle orbiter, 1980's.

3. Look up the word *harbinger* in a dictionary. Can you explain what the writer means when he calls spaceships *harbingers*?
4. What does the last sentence of the comparison mean? Why is this an appropriate ending for the paragraph?

Follow Up The most important thing about comparison is that the main idea of the comparison is clear to the reader. Arranging the details of a comparison in a logical order is one way you can help your reader understand the main idea. In the rest of this lesson, you will plan and write comparison-and-contrast explanations.

Prewriting: Comparison and Contrast

The prewriting steps for explaining through comparison and contrast will help you decide on a topic and the main idea of your comparison. They also help you organize the details.

Find a Topic and Identify a Main Idea A comparison explains how two related things are alike or different. It also says something important about the things being compared. For example, the main idea of a comparison between two kinds of touring bicycles might be to tell which bike would be better for a tour that your Bike Club is planning.

Paul's science class was studying the planet Mars. His assignment was to choose one other planet and write a report comparing Mars and the other planet. Based on the comparison, Paul was to tell which planet he would rather visit.

Paul remembered an article he had read about Venus. He decided to compare Mars and Venus. The main idea of his comparison would be to tell why he would rather visit Mars.

Choose Features to Compare A comparison paper can't possibly tell everything about a subject. The writer must choose several important features to compare. A feature is a significant point of comparison between two things.

As Paul read about Mars and Venus, he noticed several features that seemed important: order of planet from the sun, distance from the sun, temperature, atmosphere, and surface conditions. He made this comparison chart to help organize the information he found.

Features	Mars	Venus
Order from the sun	4th	2nd
Distance from sun	141 million miles	67 million miles
Temperature	Cold like Antarctica	Hotter than any oven
Atmosphere	Little oxygen, not poisonous	Thick acid clouds, poisonous
Surface conditions	Like Earth, rocky, sand dunes	Hostile, barren; softened rocks

Organize the Comparison There are two ways of organizing a comparison. One method is to discuss all the details about one subject and then all the details about the other subject. Another way is a feature-by-feature comparison in which, for example, you compare the atmospheres of Mars and Venus, and then compare their surface conditions.

Paul decided to use the first method of organization. "If I tell about Venus first," he thought, "I can show what an unpleasant place it is. Then I can tell about Mars and explain why I would rather visit there."

Grammar in Action

When you are comparing two things, use the comparative form. The comparative form adds *-r* or *-er* to the word or uses the word *more*, as in these examples:

Mars is colder than Venus.
Mars is more distant from the sun.

When you are comparing more than two things, use the superlative form. The superlative adds *-st* or *-est* to the word or uses the word *most*, as in these examples:

Of all the planets, Mercury is nearest to the sun.
Pluto is the most distant from the sun.

For additional information, see pages 513–514.

Drafting: Comparison and Contrast

The opening sentences of a comparison should interest the reader and identify the things being compared. Here is the beginning of Paul's report.

Student Model

There is a good chance that someday we might be able to travel to Venus and Mars. The two planets are very different, but I would have no trouble deciding which I would rather visit.

Follow Your Plan of Organization You should keep your plan of organization in mind as you write. Paul's report, for example, will have four sections: an introduction, a paragraph about the planet Venus, a paragraph about the planet Mars, and a conclusion. Use specific facts from your comparison chart to develop and support the comparisons you make.

Transition words and phrases are especially important in comparisons. Some useful transition words and phrases that show similarities are *also*, *in the same way*, *too*, and *like*. Some useful transitions to show differences are *on the other hand*, *however*, *unlike*, and *in contrast*.

Here is how Paul began his paragraph on Mars. Notice the transitions he used.

Student Model

> *Unlike* Venus, Mars is almost Earthlike. Although Mars has little breathable oxygen, at least its atmosphere is not poisonous *like* the acid clouds of Venus.

Conclude the Comparison The last paragraph of a comparison ties the details together and shows how they relate to the main idea. Here is the conclusion of Paul's report.

Student Model

> Neither Mars nor Venus would be a perfect vacation spot. But given a choice, I would rather visit Mars. Oxygen domes, heaters, and water tanks could easily make Mars a comfortable place for humans to live. I hope to go there someday.

Revising: Comparison and Contrast

Answering these questions can help you revise your comparison.

Revision and Peer-Editing Checklist

1. Is the main idea clear?
2. Does the introduction create interest and identify what is being compared?
3. Do the features that are being compared develop and support the main idea?
4. Is the plan or organization easy to follow?
5. Are appropriate transition words and phrases used?
6. Does the comparison end effectively?

Writing Activities *Comparison and Contrast*

A Tanya was reporting on which tent her Trail Guide group should buy for their summer backpack trip. Two Guides would share each tent. She found this comparison chart in a camping catalog. Use the information to write a comparison of the tents.

Features	Woodland Tent	Mountaineer Tent
Seasons	Warm weather	Year-round
Weight	4 lbs.	9 lbs.
Floor area	38 sq. ft.	52 sq. ft.
Capacity	2-3 people	3-4 people
Uses	Backpacking	Expeditions in snow or high mountains
Price	$75.00	$250.00

B Writing in Process Write a comparison-and-contrast explanation on a subject that interests you. For example, you might compare reading a book and seeing a movie, or compare soccer and football. *Starting Points: Ideas for Writing* (pages 43–55) may have more ideas. After selecting a topic, follow the steps for prewriting, drafting, and revising presented in this lesson.

Speaking and Listening

Think about the last face-to-face conversation you had with a friend. What types of messages were you sending back and forth? Of course, you were sending words, but didn't you also "speak" using the looks on your face (happy, mad, surprised), the tone of your voice (yelling, whispering), and the movement of your hands (touching, pointing)?

When writing, you don't have all of these ways to communicate. You only have your words, so you have to learn to make your words say as much as possible for you. You can do this by using descriptive words and strong adjectives, and by being as specific as possible. Think about telling a story or giving directions over the phone. When you give directions over the phone, for example, you know that pointing doesn't work, nor do phrases like "turn there." Your listener doesn't know where "there" is. Instead, you must choose specific buildings or landmarks that your listener can easily recognize and follow.

Activity

Find a partner. You will each need five to eight pencils, pens, sticks, or straws. (Each partner needs the same number.) Set up a barrier of notebooks or cardboard between the two of you on a table or desk, so that you can't see each other's desktop. Each person should take a turn and make a pattern with the pencils connecting in some way. Then, using only words, explain to the other person how to recreate the pattern with the other set of pencils. He or she should follow your directions.

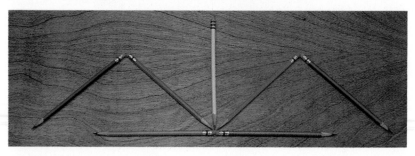

Application and Review

A Understanding the Explanation of a Process Read the following list of the steps involved in taking a double exposure photograph. Arrange them in a logical order; then write a paragraph using transitions.

- Use the manual film advance nob to roll the film back to the same picture frame.
- Find two interesting subjects that you want to appear in one picture.
- Take a picture of the subject you want in the background.
- Take a second picture of the subject you want in the foreground.
- Decide how you want the subjects to appear in the photo.

B Recognizing Cause and Effect Read this main idea: *Many small family farmers have gone bankrupt.* Identify which statements below are the causes of the farmer's trouble, and which are the effects.

1. Land once farmed is now being sold for housing.
2. Drought and bad weather have caused poor crops.
3. Farm equipment is expensive.
4. Small farmers can't compete with large corporate farms.
5. More food is grown by fewer farmers.
6. Market prices for food have been low.

C Identifying Types of Explanation Read the topic sentences below. Tell which type of explanation each one represents: *process, cause and effect,* or *comparison/contrast.*

1. The Country Store bakery, and not the Bake Shop, should make our cake because it has faster service and lower prices.
2. If our neighborhood theater closes, kids won't have a place nearby to meet friends, parents will have to drive kids to the movies, and the ice cream store next door will close.
3. The best way to make a stereo cabinet is to buy the wood at a lumberyard and assemble it using these directions.

12
Writing to Persuade

Have you ever heard a campaign speech? The words shine with glitter and promise. Politicians speak this way in order to persuade people to vote for them.

Public figures aren't the only ones who use persuasive language. You use it every time you try to convince someone to accept the same ideas or beliefs that you have. Sometimes you persuade during conversations. At other times you might persuade through writing.

How convincing you are depends on how well you understand the techniques of persuasion. This chapter will show you how to present and support your opinions successfully.

1
Understanding Persuasive Writing

You write to a friend, praising a movie you insist she must see. You work on a speech for your campaign for the class presidency. You draw up a list of reasons why your parents should buy a computer. You write to your school newspaper in support of uniforms for the pep squad. In each of these cases, you are writing to persuade. You are trying to persuade someone to adopt your opinion.

Read and Think Mona wrote this letter to her mayor in response to a story she read in the newspaper. The story reported that a local park might become a parking lot.

 Student Model

I read in this evening's *Times* that the city might turn Woodsfield Park into a parking lot. I think this is a bad idea. I know the city needs a place to park cars, but kids and birds and squirrels need a place of their own too.

My friends and I love every corner of Woodsfield Park. In summer, we play softball on the northeast diamond. In winter, we go sledding on the southeast hill. I walk with my grandfather in the garden on the other side of the park. He says, "This is the most peaceful spot in the whole city."

To make Woodsfield Park into a parking lot, you will have to cut down trees and destroy much of the area. If you did this, what would happen to the animals who live in those trees? Where would families go for relaxation?

Why not look for some other way to solve the parking problem? Perhaps you can ask people to take the bus downtown more often. Then you might not need a new parking lot. Another idea is to put the parking lot somewhere else.

Please think again before you cut down any trees and dig out any grass. Other alternatives exist for solving the parking problem. Choose one, and save the park for the people and animals.

Think and Discuss Discuss the following questions with your classmates.

1. Is Mona expressing a fact or an opinion about the proposed parking lot in Woodsfield Park?
2. What arguments does Mona use to support her point of view?
3. What alternatives does she suggest?

Read and Think Now read this movie review.

This is certain to be one of the more controversial films of the year. But as slimy and as grotesque as some of its special effects may be, *The Fly* is a far superior horror film to the top-grossing film in America of late, *Aliens.* Whereas *Aliens* simply throws spindly alien creatures at Sigourney Weaver for two hours, David Cronenberg's adaptation of *The Fly* is more appealing, because its creature is part human. Coat your stomach and give it a chance.

From a review of *The Fly* by **Gene Siskel**

Scene from *The Fly*, 1986.

Think and Discuss Read the following questions and discuss them with your classmates.

1. What opinion does Siskel express about *The Fly*?
2. Why does Siskel prefer *The Fly* over *Aliens*?
3. Does Siskel think everyone will have the same opinion about the movie? Why or why not?

Follow Up When you write to persuade, you must both express and support an opinion. Such opinions should be clearly stated and supported with facts, reasons, and examples. Keep these features of persuasive writing in mind as you read the literature selection on the next two pages.

Persuasion in Literature

from *My Wilderness*

William O. Douglas

*E*very trip to the Smokies leaves bright memories. Yet the most vivid of all was an October hike I made with Harvey and Anne. The Fall colors were more brilliant than any I had known. They fairly shouted, they were so gay. Orange, red, yellow, garnet, gold filled the hollows along the Middle Prong of the Little Pigeon River. The leaves had not yet fallen. There was no touch of breeze to disturb them. That night it snowed; and when we reached Ramsay Prong the next morning, the ground was covered with an inch of powder snow. A light breeze produced a shower of colored leaves. Soon the powder snow was transformed. There was a riot of color underfoot. The snow made every leaf a bright pastel.

Issue
identified The Smokies teach an important lesson to all who love the wildness of the forests and want it preserved. . . .

Its creation was difficult. Every acre of it was in big timber holdings, small farms, or private resort areas. Some 6,000 tracts had to be put together. Of these 5,000 were small holdings, many having only a twenty-five-foot frontage.

Much of what went into the Smokies was cutover land. Now that it is protected, it gets wilder every year. In time it will all be reclaimed by nature and restored to true wilderness.

This is the time in American history to follow that example in other areas. Our wilderness areas are being so fast destroyed that we must put even stump fields into sanctuaries, if those who follow us a century later are to have Author's
opinion a wilderness large enough to roam. The cause is desperate; the time is short. . . .

Civilization threatens many of our wilderness areas, even

Evidence supports opinion

though they are set aside as parks. The pressure for more roads, more lodges, more parking spaces within our national parks is changing their character. Some appear to be in competition with amusement parks. The purpose of the national parks was not only to attract tourists but to further the "outdoor education and exercise" of the people. The Park Service has in the main been faithful to that mandate. Yet at times it succumbs to pressures to turn parks into mass recreational areas. Road, roads, roads. Resorts, hotels, hostels. These encroach more and more, with Park Service

Call for action

approval. We must stop that trend. We must plan so that mass recreation is outside the parks, not within them. . . .

Of all our national parks, the Smokies is in most respects close to a model. Civilization centers mostly in towns like Gatlinburg, Tennessee. The hollows, streams, and ridges of the parks are largely unmolested. That should be the aim in all other parks, in all other wilderness areas. Today, the wilderness of America that is left is more and more shaped and designed for the conveniences of mass recreation. If that trend continues, we will become the victims of "civilization." Humankind will have no chance to escape. Wherever we go—unless we go by sea—the crowd will follow us by car.

Trying Out Persuasive Writing Think of an issue or problem that you feel strongly about. Then write to convince an audience to adopt your opinion. Use facts, reasons, and examples to support your point of view. In the rest of this chapter you will learn more about writing effective persuasion.

2
Prewriting

Before you write a persuasive paper, you need to go through several prewriting steps. First, choose an issue and decide how you feel about it. An **issue** is a topic about which people have strong opinions. Then learn more about the issue and make notes on the arguments for and against the issue. Next, consider your audience. Who will be reading your paper? The answer will help you decide what form your writing should take and what arguments you should use. Finally, look through your notes and plan the organization of your paper.

Identifying an Issue

Look for an issue that interests you. Begin by using the reflecting skills you learned in Chapter 2. What is happening in your school or neighborhood that you feel strongly about? Write down as many topics as you can. Another way to find an issue is to phrase a topic as a question. Mona's letter to the mayor, for example, was in answer to this question: "Should the city use Woodsfield Park for a parking lot?"

You should now have a list of possible issues or topics. Keep these points in mind when identifying your issue:

1. Choose an issue on which people disagree.
2. Focus on something that you care about.
3. Select a topic that you already know a great deal about or that you can find out about.

Here is an issue that interested Fred: "Should parents be fined if their children are caught creating graffiti?" Fred knew this was an issue, because some people in his community were opposed to the idea. He cared about it, and he knew he could get more information about it.

Supporting Your Opinion

Make sure you are fully informed about the issue you choose. Use the gleaning techniques explained in Chapter 2 to gather information. Talk with other people about the issue. Try to learn why some people are on one side of the issue while others are on the opposite side. Read books, magazines, and newspapers to find out what others have written about this question. As you glean information, make notes. Your notes may include facts, examples, comparisons, quotations, and reasons.

Make up your mind about the issue   Do you still have the same opinion that you did before you began gathering information? Sometimes you may change your mind when you are better informed. Ask yourself how you feel now about the issue. Then write a statement of opinion, your main idea, that you will be able to support with sound arguments.

Provide support for your opinion   Good persuasive writing does more than simply state your opinion that something is good, bad, or in need of change. Good persuasive writing provides evidence, such as facts, examples, or quotations from experts. Look over the notes you gathered. If you need more evidence, continue to ask questions or to read about the issue.

Determining Your Audience and Form

Before beginning to write, decide exactly whom you are trying to convince. Here are some matters to consider:

1. How much does the audience know about the issue? If your readers know a great deal, you will not have to provide background information. If they do not know much about the issue, you will have to give more explanation.
2. How much does the audience care about the issue? If readers care a great deal, you will not have to arouse their interest. If you think they might not care, you will have to find ways to make them interested.
3. What reasons will most appeal to your readers? What support will they find most convincing? You will also need to consider what arguments to use to win over an audience that is already opposed to your opinion.

Think about your audience   Fred decided his audience should include parents, property owners, court officials, and young people who might be tempted to make graffiti. All four groups would be interested in the topic and would probably already know something about it.

Decide on the form you should use   Persuasive writing can take several different forms: an editorial or review for a school paper, a letter, or an article. Fred decided to write a letter to the newspaper. The paper's readers include members of all four audience groups that he had identified.

Organizing Your Prewriting Notes

Writing to persuade is like making a sales presentation. To succeed you first need a plan. Do you present your evidence in the order of importance, giving the most important information first? Do you begin instead with a familiar example, then work in new information? You will choose the order to suit your audience. Once you have decided on the best order, use a questionnaire like the one on the next page to help you map out what you plan to do.

Writing Inside Out

In Chicago, WXRT radio station disk jockey Marty Lennartz is better known to his listeners as the Regular Guy. In 1984, Marty made up the character called the Regular Guy, a "guy who goes to the movies and just talks about what he saw." Three times a week, the Regular Guy does movie reviews for the radio station. As the Regular Guy, Marty tries to answer one basic question: "Is the movie worth paying five bucks for?" For the most part, Marty sees the Regular Guy as a comedy bit, but he knows that "a lot of people take it seriously and base what they see on what the Regular Guy says." At first, that fact surprised him. Now, he takes it in stride, saying:

Persuasion Questionnaire

1. What is the issue?
2. What is my opinion?
3. Whom am I trying to persuade?
4. What form will I use?
5. Does my audience need much background information on the issue?
6. Will I first have to catch my readers' interest?
7. What reasons will best persuade my audience?

Fred used the questionnaire to plan out what he would write about his topic, how to punish graffiti artists. His completed questionnaire looked like this:

Issue:　Should parents be fined if their children write graffiti on buildings and walls?

Opinion:　Fining the parents doesn't necessarily punish the ones who are guilty of making the graffiti.

"I'm not a film critic. I'm not someone who really knows a lot about movies, but I know what I like, what I want to pay to see, and I think a lot of people think the same way I do."

Marty talks about writing for radio:

"For a disk jockey, most of the stuff is not written down, but you're writing in your mind constantly. The movie review—I write down a script for it, a real conversational script and then I ad-lib off the script a lot."

"Radio writing should be very conversational. It's like talking on the phone. You have to make it personal. It's also important to keep it down-to-earth."

"Another thing, radio is great because you don't see it. People don't see what you're talking about but they visualize it. You can do anything on radio with voices and a sound-effects record. You can use your imagination. You can use other people's imagination. You can build any kind of world you want on radio."

Audience: This issue affects four groups of people: the graffiti writers, their parents, the people whose buildings or walls are written on, and those who punish the offenders.

Form: Everyone reads the *Evening Journal.* I will write a letter to the editor.

Need for background: Everyone knows about graffiti, but not everyone knows that some people have suggested fining the parents. I will need to go into detail about this.

Need to spark interest: Everyone thinks it's someone else's problem. I will have to show that it's their problem.

Order of major points of support:
1. Punishing the parents does not punish those who did wrong.
2. Fining the parents may help or it may not help. That leaves punishing the guilty up to the parents. Some will punish too little and some will punish too much.
3. Oakdale forced the young people to wash off or paint over the graffiti they made. Graffiti in Oakdale is down forty percent.

Writing Activities *Prewriting*

A Marie is leading a campaign to spend class funds on a computer strategy game based on early explorers. Her prewriting notes include the following reasons:

1. The game provides an interesting way to learn.
2. The kind of strategy the game calls for will make us apply math and geography lessons as well as history.
3. The whole class can get involved.
4. The game includes exciting action as well as text.
5. The game received high ratings in all its reviews.

Marie can make an informative poster promoting her idea, prepare a speech to deliver to her class, or write a letter to her teacher. Choose one of these forms and show how Marie might fill out the prewriting questionnaire.

B **Writing in Process** Look through Starting Points (pages 43–55) or Ideas for Writing in the Writer's Handbook (pages 653–654) for an issue that interests you. If you wish, use the brainstorming technique to find an issue you support. Reflect on and research your issue; then complete a prewriting question-naire. Save your notes in your writing folder for a later activity.

3
Drafting

Now that you have a plan, you are ready to draft your persuasive writing. Keep these points in mind as you prepare your draft.

Begin effectively   Think of persuasive writing as a form of salesmanship—you must "hook" your reader before you can sell your idea. Think about your particular audience and decide if the focus of the introduction should be on arousing interest, explaining the issue, or stating your opinion. In all cases, try to avoid a trite and boring sentence such as "The reason I like this is because . . . ." Use instead an opening question, a challenge, or some unusual phrasing. Look back at how Gene Siskel began his movie review: "This is certain to be one of the most controversial films of the year." His sentence makes you want to read on, to find out why.

Present your material in an organized way   Follow a plan, proceeding, for example, from the least persuasive to the most persuasive argument. Another way is to first attack opposing views, then present alternatives. Use transitions to move effectively from one point to another.

Provide support   Words such as *exciting, interesting, boring,* or *bad* all suggest how you feel about something, but they do not prove you are justified in feeling that way. Be sure to back up terms with clear definitions and examples. Include quotations and logical arguments also.

Conclude effectively   Use one of these techniques.

1. End with your strongest reason and its support.
2. Summarize your reasons with an appeal for support.
3. Suggest what your audience should do next.

Fred used his prewriting notes to develop the draft shown on the next page. Notice his thoughts as he worked on his draft.

Who is guilty when you find your storefront or your

∧ I think if there is a crime the guilty one is the one

wall smeared with graffiti? The graffiti artists, or their

who should be punished. Judge Michael Travis thinks *parents?*

the parents are the guilty ones. Judge Travis has

I don't think this punishes the right persons.

proposed fining the parents $50. ∧

→ I think this is a bad idea. Oakdale has a better idea.

In Oakdale the graffiti artists are the ones who are

punished. They have to wash off the graffiti they

made.

If Judge Travis thinks the parents will turn around

and punish their children for the courts, he may be

wrong. Some parents will and some won't. ↙

Writing Activities *Drafting*

A Marie worked on drafting a speech to convince her classmates to buy the computer game on early explorers.

1. Discuss which of the following openings are most effective and why.

a. Would you like to have stepped ashore at San Salvador with Columbus? Do you wish you could have battled your way through the storms alongside Magellan? Well, now you can with a new computer program.

b. I think we should buy this computer program because it has gotten excellent reviews.

c. Here is a way to make sure students spend more time at the computer. This game makes learning fun.

d. "Journeys Through Time" is a good computer program. I like it, and it has become very popular in recent months. We should buy it.

2. Discuss which of the following conclusions Marie could use effectively and why.

a. So those are the reasons I think we should buy this game.
b. If you vote for this game, you vote for learning and fun.
c. You've heard my reasons. Now mark your ballot "yes" for the computer game.
d. In conclusion, you know my opinion, and I hope that you will agree with me.

B Writing in Process Look over the prewriting questionnaire you completed in Activity B on page 240. Use those notes to help you draft a letter, editorial, or other form of persuasive writing.

Grammar in Action

You can get different effects in persuasive writing by emphasizing either the first-person, second-person, or third-person pronouns. (See pages 446 and 448.)

Use the first person (*I, me, we,* and *us*) to stress your own beliefs. Look at this sentence:

> EXAMPLE   I know one thing—I don't want to see this movie again.

Use the second person (*you*) to speak directly to your readers:

> EXAMPLE   If you like adventure, you will love this book.

Use the third person (*he, him, she, her, they, them, it*) to emphasize the issue and to refer to authorities:

> EXAMPLE   Reviewers agree that they find the sound of this new musical group really unique.

Writing Activity Write a one-line review of your favorite TV program, using the first-person pronoun. Rewrite your sentence, using the second-person pronoun instead of the first-person. Repeat the process, using the third-person pronoun.

4
Revising and Presenting

Before you share your persuasive writing with your audience, you will want to make revisions. Arrange your time so that you can put your draft aside for a while before revising it.

Read the draft to yourself at least three times, making changes as you read. First, study your overall reasoning and organization. Then, look for problem spots such as unclear sentences or grammatical errors. Finally, proofread for errors. You may also want to ask a classmate to serve as a peer editor. Use the following checklist as a guide.

Revision and Peer-Editing Checklist

1. Does the opening "hook" the reader by creating interest, providing necessary background, or stating an opinion in an effective way?
2. Is the writing well organized? Are transitions used to link one point to another?
3. Are the author's reasons convincingly supported with evidence? Are the reasons likely to appeal to the audience?
4. Does the paper effectively conclude with the strongest reason and its support, a summary, or a call to action?

Fred read the draft of his letter aloud several times. He continued to make changes. His thoughts as he worked are shown in the blue bubbles.

> **Oops, I've switched from singular to plural.**

Who are the

~~Who's~~ guilty when you find your storefront smeared

with graffiti? The graffiti artists or their parents? Judge

Michael Travis thinks the parents are the guilty ones.

Judge Travis proposed fining the parents $50. I don't

think this punishes the right party. Also, if Judge

I wonder if everyone will understand my point.

Travis thinks the parents will turn around and punish

their children, he may be wrong. Some parents will

and some won't. *Unless the graffiti artists themselves feel some pain, they may continue to smear other people's property.*

Oakdale has a better idea. In Oakdale, the graffiti

The court forces them

artists are the ones who are punished. ~~They have to~~

"Have" is a weak word. I can do better.

wash off the graffiti that they made. *The Oakdale plan pays off. Last year graffiti in Oakdale dropped forty percent.*

I forgot this fact. It will make my ending stronger.

Fred could have used a peer editor to identify the parts of his draft that needed changing. A peer editor's comments can help you to evaluate the effectiveness of your work. When you act as a peer editor, use the following guidelines.

1. Use the Revision Checklist on page 244 to judge the strengths and weaknesses of the writing.
2. Always begin with the positive. Point out what you liked and explain why you liked it.
3. Ask questions if there is something that you do not understand or that you wish to know more about.
4. Make specific suggestions for improvement. If you find a weak spot, suggest a way of improving it.

Writing Activity *Peer Editing*

Writing in Process Take out the persuasive writing that you drafted in Activity B on page 243. Find a peer-editing partner and read one another's drafts. Respond to each other's work, using the Revision Checklist on page 244 and the peer-editing guidelines on this page.

Then make a final revision of your draft. Consider the responses of your peer editor, but remember that you must use your own judgment in deciding what needs to be changed. Don't forget to proofread for grammar, spelling, and punctuation.

Speaking and Listening

Commercials on television or radio try to persuade you to buy products. They tell you that a certain cereal has the most vitamins, or that a particular toothpaste will give you a brighter smile. With so many ads, how can you decide which ones to believe? Perhaps, you could decide if you knew more about how commercials are developed. Commercials use five main ad strategies. See if you can recognize products that use these strategies.

1. They claim that the product is the best, or better, than the competition.
2. They suggest that you will be happier if you use the product.
3. They create a problem—then solve it.
4. They suggest that the product will give you the look or image that you want.
5. They get famous and well-known people to say how much they like the product.

Activities

A You've been hired by a company to create a radio or television commercial for a product of your choice. Work alone or with one or two classmates to plan out the ad, using one or more of the strategies above. Present the commercial to your class as a rehearsal for the actual writing.

B Select five different commercials from television, radio, newspapers, or magazines. Analyze the commercials and identify which strategy each one uses. Discuss them with your classmates.

Application and Review

A Identifying Fact and Opinion Tell whether each statement below is a fact or an opinion.

1. An orange contains both vitamin C and potassium.
2. Oranges are the most delicious fruit.
3. Florida and California grow the most oranges.
4. You should eat an orange every day.

B Supporting an Opinion Read the opinion below and the statements that follow it. On your paper, write down all of the statements that can be used as evidence to support the opinion.

OPINION: Everyone should practice *EDITH*, or *Exit Drills in the Home*.

1. Sixty percent of all deaths by fire happen in the home.
2. Most deaths in home fires could have been prevented very easily.
3. Home fires are tragic.
4. Fatalities in home fires in a neighboring town have decreased since the fire department started its *EDITH* educational program.
5. I think that people are crazy if they do not practice *EDITH*.
6. Preparing an *EDITH* program for your home costs little or no money.
7. Preparing an *EDITH* program takes only a short amount of time.
8. There is no reason to be without an *EDITH* program.
9. Fire Chief Edwin Miller predicts that *EDITH* can save the lives of dozens of children in our city every year.
10. I think that *EDITH* is a wonderful idea.

C Writing Effective Openings and Closings Based on the statements you selected as evidence above, write an effective introduction and conclusion in support of the *EDITH* fire prevention program.

13
Writing Reports

If a television reporter were doing a documentary on African culture, how do you think she would go about writing her report?

She would not just sit down and begin writing. Instead, she would follow a series of steps. She would focus her topic, research it thoroughly, make an outline, and then write the report.

Reports, whether they are for television, business, or school, require an organized approach. This chapter explains the process that will help you prepare effective reports.

1

Prewriting: Selecting a Subject

The first step in writing a report is to choose and limit a subject. Begin by making a list of subjects that interest you, or about which you would like to learn more. Then choose the subject that interests you most. Remember, however, that the details of a report must be gathered from outside sources of information. You may find that the subject you choose is so personal that you are the main source of information. If so, the subject is not suitable for a report. Discard the idea and try to think of a different subject.

Writing Activities Finding a Subject

A Look over the following list of subjects for reports. Write down four that interest you. Then add four or more subjects of your own. Save this list. You may add to it at any time.

1. How bats use radar
2. Food from the ocean
3. Japanese festivals
4. Computers
5. How dolphins communicate
6. Skiing for the blind
7. Homes of the future
8. Weather satellites
9. The Cherokees and the Trail of Tears
10. Early bicycles

B **Writing in Process** Turn to *Starting Points: Ideas for Writing* on pages 43–55. Look through the pages for report ideas. Write down any ideas that appeal to you and add them to the list from Part A. Study your list and decide on a subject for a report. Then write a brief paragraph describing the subject. If necessary, do some reading about your subject in an encyclopedia. Save your notes and paragraph in your writing folder.

Narrowing the Subject

Once you have chosen a general subject, your next step is to limit it until you have a topic that is the right size for your report. How much you limit it depends on the amount of information available and on the length of your report.

If you are unfamiliar with your subject, begin the narrowing process by reading a general article about it in a magazine or encyclopedia. Such an article will give you an idea of just how large your subject is. It may also suggest possibilities for limiting your subject.

Nancy, for example, chose the subject "Chinese Holidays" and read an encyclopedia article on the subject. She found that, like people throughout the world, the Chinese have many holidays. To describe them in detail would require a very long report. Because Nancy knew that her report was to be only one or two pages long, she scanned the article looking for ways to make her subject more specific.

Within the general subject "Chinese Holidays" was the specific subject "The Chinese New Year." This narrowed subject can be adequately developed in a short report. After checking to see that there was no other topic that interested her more, Nancy chose "The Chinese New Year" as her report subject.

Writing Activities *Narrowing the Subject*

A The subjects below are too broad to be covered in a short report. Narrow each subject to make it suitable for a one- or two-page report. You may have to do some reading first.

> EXAMPLE General subject—Dogs
> Narrowed—How to Train a Dog

1. Computers
2. Solar energy
3. Dance in America
4. Vanishing species
5. The space program
6. Caves
7. Archaeology
8. Cars
9. England's royal family
10. Myths

B **Writing in Process** Review your report subject and the paragraph you wrote about it in Activity B, page 250. Do some general reading on the subject. If necessary, narrow it to a size suitable for a short report.

2
Prewriting:
Preparing to Do Research

Before you begin gathering facts for a report, make a list of questions that someone unfamiliar with your subject would want answered. Such questions will help you make sure that all necessary information is included in the report.

The writer of the report on the Chinese New Year listed four questions that her readers might wonder about:

1. What and when is the Chinese New Year?
2. How is the Chinese New Year celebrated?
3. Why is the Chinese New Year an important holiday?
4. What traditions are involved?

By preparing similar questions and keeping them in mind as you select your facts, you will be certain not to leave any important information out of your report. Of course, you may think of other questions as you continue to read about your subject. These questions and their answers can also be included in your notes.

Writing Activities *Planning Questions*

A Write five questions about each of these report topics. You may have to read a bit about each subject first.

1. The legend of the Bermuda Triangle
2. The job of an air traffic controller
3. The sign language of the deaf
4. Common superstitions
5. Noise pollution

B Writing in Process Using the final subject you chose for your report, write five questions that you think need to be answered. Save them in your folder.

3
Prewriting:
Gathering Information

To write a thorough report, you must first read as much as you can about your subject. Begin your search for information in the library. Check the card catalog and the *Readers' Guide to Periodical Literature*. These sources will lead you to books and magazine articles on your subject. Also consult encyclopedias and other reference books. They too might contain useful information. See Chapter 16 for more reference information.

Working with Facts

As you read, remember that the purpose of a report is to present information clearly and accurately. Because reports are based on facts, it is important for you to learn exactly what facts are and how to record them.

In the articles you read, you will find many kinds of statements. Some will be facts suitable for a report. Others may simply be statements of opinion. Because the information in a report must be factual, it is important that you be able to separate facts from opinions. Remember that a fact is a statement that can be proved. An opinion cannot be proved.

Fact: Florida is a Southern state.
Opinion: Florida is a good place to vacation.

Fact: Jeans are washable.
Opinion: Jeans are comfortable.

Fact: The train from Aurora is late.
Opinion: Railroads are too noisy and slow for me.

Fact: Mr. Marsh teaches English.
Opinion: Mr. Marsh is a wonderful teacher.

Once you have found a fact, make sure that you record it clearly and specifically. Look at these statements:

Computers are selling fast.
The Wizards Company has sold 200,000 computers.

Readers may have different ideas of what it means for computers to be "selling fast." The second, more specific statement prevents any confusion.

To make sure that the facts in a report are correct, check them carefully. Make sure they are from a reliable source. A reliable source is one that is qualified, unbiased, recent, and widely recognized.

Writing Activity *Working with Facts*

Study the following statements. Label each one as *Fact* or *Opinion*. Then make each fact more specific. Use a dictionary or encyclopedia to help you rewrite the facts.

EXAMPLE: The whale is a mammal. (Fact)
The whale is the largest mammal in existence. (More specific)

1. The American Revolution occurred in the 1700's.
2. Morocco is in Africa.
3. The trumpet is a terribly noisy instrument.
4. Boise is the capital of Idaho.
5. Democracy is a kind of government.
6. The tax system is unfair.
7. Handsprings are more fun to do than cartwheels.
8. Lake Huron is partly in the United States.
9. Coral comes from animals.
10. A conch is a small mollusk.
11. Handel composed magnificent music.
12. Lemurs are odd-looking animals.
13. Carl Sandburg was a writer.
14. Cactus plants grow in warm places.
15. Navajo sand-painting is an art.

Taking Notes

When you find information that you want to include in your report, write it on a 3″ x 5″ card. Write only one piece of information on each card. This will help you organize your information. At the top of the card, record the title of the book or article. Also write the page number of the information.

Book

Title	*The First Book of Holidays*
Pages	pages 7 - 8
Information	People in the Chinese New Year's parade blow whistles, play instruments, and crash cymbals together.

Magazine Article

Title	"Welcoming the Year of the Monkey"
Pages	pages 60 - 63
Information	The Chinese give each year the name of an animal.

Reference Book Article

Title	"Feasts and Festivals"
Pages	pages 62 - 63
Information	A colorful dragon is part of the New Year's parade.

As you take notes, always use your own words and not those of the source. Then the report that you write from your note cards will also be in your own words. Notice how this writer summarized information from an encyclopedia article:

Encyclopedia Excerpt The Chinese used the lunar calendar for about 4,000 years. This calendar is based on the waxing and waning of the moon. Today the Chinese New Year's Day falls between January 21 and February 19 each year.

Student Note Card

> "New Year's Day"
> page 237
> The Chinese New Year is celebrated sometime between January 21 and February 19. The date is based on the lunar calendar.

On a separate sheet of paper, list every source that you use. Follow the guidelines below when preparing this list. Notice that the names of authors are given last name first.

Guidelines for Listing Sources

1. For books, give the author, the title, the city of publication, the publisher, and the copyright date.
   Burnett, Bernice. *Holidays*. New York: Franklin Watts, 1974.
2. For magazines, give the name of the author of the article, the title of the article, the name and date of the magazine, and the page numbers.
   Cure, K. "Welcoming the Year of the Monkey." *Travel* Jan. 1980: 60–63.
3. For encyclopedias, give the title of the encyclopedia article and the set's name and year.
   "Feasts and Festivals." *The World Book Encyclopedia*. 1988 ed.

Writing Activities *Taking Notes on a Subject*

A Assume that you are writing a report on guide dogs. Write five note cards based on this article from the 1986 edition of *The World Book Encyclopedia*. Put the information into your own words.

GUIDE DOG is a dog specially trained to guide a blind person. Dogs chosen for such training must show qualities of good disposition, intelligence, physical fitness, and responsibility. Breeds best suited for guide dog work include, in order of importance, German shepherds, Labrador retrievers, golden retrievers, and boxers.

At the age of about 14 months, a guide dog begins an intensive course that lasts from three to five months. It becomes accustomed to the leather harness and the stiff leather handle it will wear when guiding its blind owner. The dog learns to watch traffic and to cross streets safely. It also learns to obey such commands as "forward," "left," "right," and "sit," and to disobey any command that might lead its owner into danger. For example, a guide dog will refuse to cross a busy street unless the traffic has stopped.

The most important part of the training course is a four-week program in which the guide dog and its future owner learn to work together. However, many blind people are unsuited by temperament to work with dogs. Only about a tenth of the blind find a guide dog useful.

The organized training of dogs to guide the blind began in Germany during World War I (1914–1918). The first guide dog school in the United States, The Seeing Eye, Incorporated, was founded in 1929. Other U.S. schools include Guide Dogs for the Blind, Incorporated; and Leader Dogs for the Blind.

Kenneth A. Stuckey

B **Writing in Process** Use the questions you wrote for Activity B, page 252, to research your subject. Take notes for your report, using 3″ × 5″ cards (or pieces of paper cut into 3″ × 5″ rectangles). Also prepare a separate, complete list of your sources. Save your note cards in your writer's folder. You will use them in the next activity.

4
Prewriting: Organizing Information

Once you have gathered all the information you need, you are ready to organize your notes. You will probably notice that most of your information seems to fall under certain key ideas. One good organizational technique is to divide your note cards into groups. Each group should contain only the cards related to one of the key ideas. You may want to begin separating your cards this way while you are still taking notes.

Nancy found that her information on the topic "The Chinese New Year" fell into these groups.

1. A new beginning
2. Home decorations
3. The New Year's parade

As you sort through your note cards, you may discover that some facts are unrelated to the key ideas. On the other hand, you may find that you need more information to develop some of the ideas well. Do not be afraid to discard or add information at any point in the writing process.

After you have grouped your cards, put the groups and then the facts within them in some sort of logical order. You will then be ready to write your outline.

Outlining a Report

Making an outline will give you a blueprint, or plan, for your report. An outline shows how the facts logically fit together, forming a well-structured whole.

Each group of note cards becomes a major part in an outline. The key idea of each group becomes the part's main heading. The important facts from the note cards then become subheadings under each key idea.

Nancy made the outline on the following page, using a standard outline form.

The Chinese New Year

I. A time for a new beginning
    A. Houses cleaned
    B. Windows washed
    C. Curtains cleaned
    D. Silver polished
    E. New clothes bought
    F. Banquets and reunions attended

II. Homes decorated with flowers, fruit, and colorful hangings
    A. Branches of peaches, pears, almonds, or apricots
    B. Paper hangings with inscriptions
    C. Azaleas and camellia plants
    D. Dishes of narcissus and daffodil bulbs
    E. Arrangements of oranges, kumquats, and tangerines

III. The big New Year's parade
    A. Firecrackers
    B. Cymbals, drums, and metal gongs
    C. Floats
    D. Bands
    E. Lion dancers
        1. Head of papier-mâché
        2. Head painted red, yellow, green, and orange
    F. Dragon
        1. Breathes fire and smoke
        2. Twists and writhes down the street
        3. Brings rainfall
        4. Symbolizes the Emperor
        5. Appears at the New Year

IV. Importance of New Year celebrations

When you have completed your outline, look it over carefully. Does it contain any unrelated ideas? Should the order of details be changed? You may want to rework the outline until you feel it is a satisfactory guide for writing your paper.

For more information on outlining and other graphic organizers, see the Writer's Handbook, pages 652–681.

Writing Activities *Making a Report Outline*

A Below is a partial outline for a report. Copy it on your paper. Then add the following headings where they belong.

In Germany   Texture of coat
Awards   Best of breed
On platforms   Shape of head
Champion

Dog Shows

I. Popularity of dog shows
   A. In Great Britain
   B.
   C. In the United States

II. How dogs are shown
   A.
   B. In judging rings

III. Standards for judging
   A.
   B. Color
   C. Walk
   D.
   E. Placement of ears

IV.
   A.
   B.
   C. Best of show

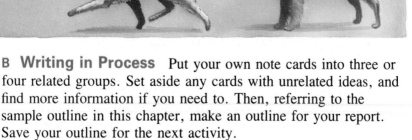

B Writing in Process Put your own note cards into three or four related groups. Set aside any cards with unrelated ideas, and find more information if you need to. Then, referring to the sample outline in this chapter, make an outline for your report. Save your outline for the next activity.

5
Drafting:
Writing from an Outline

A report has three main parts. They are the introduction, the body, and the conclusion. Use the sections of your outline as guidelines for writing these parts.

The Introduction

The introduction of a report should serve two purposes. First, it should be interesting enough to make the reader want to go on. Second, it should give the reader an idea of the report's topic.

When you studied the parts of a composition in Chapter 7, you learned some ways to make an introductory paragraph interesting. You might, for example, ask a question, state an unusual fact, or tell an amusing anecdote. You might use a quotation that helps to introduce your topic.

How well do you think the following paragraph introduces the report about the Chinese New Year? Would it interest a reader and make him or her want to continue reading?

> In this composition, I am going to tell you about the Chinese New Year. I have studied this holiday for quite a while. It is an interesting topic, and I am sure you will learn something from this report. For example, the holiday takes place in either January or February.

Although the paragraph gives an idea of the report topic, it does not attract a reader's attention. The following introduction fulfills both purposes:

Student Model

> To the Chinese in the United States, as well as elsewhere in the world, the most important festival of the year is that of the New Year. This holiday can fall any time between January 21 and February 19. It is believed that at this time the forces of Yang—warmth and light—are ready to overcome the forces of Yin—cold, dark winter.

Grammar in Action

There are many ways to write an interesting introductory paragraph. You might use different types of sentences: declarative, interrogative, imperative, or exclamatory. (See pages 404–406.) Another possibility is to vary the length or complexity of the sentences. (See Chapter 28, pages 560–575.)

What types of sentences does the writer of the following paragraph use to make the introductory paragraph more appealing?

> What do a *hogan* and a *wickiup* have in common? Both are American Indian dwellings. The *hogan* is made of earth, and the *wickiup* is made of brush. The *hogan* is a Navajo house. Its one room is big enough for the entire family!

Notice that the writer began with an interrogative sentence, then used a compound sentence that was longer than the sentence before it. The writer ended with two short sentences, one of which was exclamatory.

Writing Activity Write an introductory paragraph about a house or building in your neighborhood. Experiment with a variety of sentence types. Vary the lengths of the sentences.

Writing Activities *Writing Introductions*

A Decide which of the following are strong introductory paragraphs. Then rewrite the other paragraphs to make them more appealing introductions to the topic.

1. The Rocky Mountains have craggy peaks. The Appalachians have rolling slopes, and Mount Everest is a rounded dome. Why do these mountains look so different? Scientists tell us it is due to the three different ways that mountains can be formed.

2. I am going to write a report about the Loch Ness monster. It lives in a lake in Scotland. The lake is also called Loch Ness.

3.   This report is about fossils, which are records of plants and animals. There are four main kinds of fossils. Some are petrified remains. Later I will explain what petrified fossils are. The other fossils are molds and casts, prints, and whole animals and plants. Scientists study fossils. Fossils can tell them what life was like before written records. In my opinion, the most interesting are the petrified fossils.

B   Writing in Process   Using the outline you developed, write the introductory paragraph of your report. Make sure that your introduction is both interesting and informative. Save your introduction. You will add to it in the next two activities.

The Body

The body of a report presents most of the information. It is organized into paragraphs, each with a topic sentence. As in any paragraph, facts or details develop the paragraph's topic sentence.

Once you have written an outline, the body paragraphs are already laid out. As you write your first draft, each main part of the outline becomes a paragraph in the body of the report. The heading of each part can be developed into a topic sentence, and the subheadings become the supporting facts or details.

Once Nancy had written the introduction to "The Chinese New Year," she had these main headings to cover in the body paragraphs of her report:

II.   A time for a new beginning
III. Homes decorated with flowers, fruit, and colorful hangings
IV.   The big New Year's parade

Nancy followed her outline as she wrote the body paragraphs. Notice how the sentences flow together smoothly:

The Chinese New Year

Student Model

To the Chinese in the United States, as well as elsewhere in the world, the most important festival of all is that of the New Year. This holiday can fall any time between January 21 and February 19. It is believed that at this time the forces of Yang—warmth and light—are ready to overcome the forces of Yin—cold, dark winter.

Camillia, Shodo.

The New Year is a welcome to spring and a new beginning, a time to make a fresh start. Before the holiday, families are busy giving their houses a thorough cleaning. Windows are washed and curtains cleaned; silver is polished and everything is made spotless. If possible, each person gets new clothes. It is the season to celebrate with families and friends and to attend banquets and reunions.

Flowers, fruits, and colorful hangings brighten the Chinese home. Flowering branches of peaches, pears, almonds, or apricots, as well as red paper hangings with good luck inscriptions, are everywhere. Azalea and camellia plants and dishes of flowering narcissus and daffodil bulbs foretell spring. Arrangements of oranges, kumquats, and tangerines are placed throughout the home and add to the color.

The highlight of the New Year is the big parade in Chinatown. To scare away evil demons, people set off firecrackers and strike cymbals, drums, and metal gongs. Decorated floats and performing bands go by. Groups of lion dancers perform. The lion's head is made of papier-mâché and is painted red, yellow, green, and orange. One dancer holds the head while others hold up the rest of the silk body.

A huge dragon nearly a block long breathes out fire and smoke. Dozens of dancers inside make him twist and writhe down the street. To the Chinese the dragon is not a monster, but a kind, supernatural being who brings rain, which is a symbol of life and rebirth. He is also a symbol of the Emperor. According to legend, the dragon awakens from his sleep and appears on earth at the New Year.

As you write your report, you may find yourself wanting to add, delete, or reorganize information. Do not be afraid to depart somewhat from your outline. Notice, for example, that Nancy needed two paragraphs instead of one to cover material in her main heading about the New Year parade. When you depart from your outline, just make certain that the ideas are all related to your subject and that the order makes sense.

Remember that you will be making one or more rough drafts of your report. As you write the first draft, concentrate mainly on including all the information that you feel is important.

Writing Activity *Writing the Body Paragraphs*

Writing in Process Following your outline, write the body paragraphs of your report. Make sure that each paragraph has a topic sentence. Try to make your ideas flow smoothly.

The Conclusion

To end a report, you must have a concluding paragraph. Even though it may not add new information, a conclusion is necessary. It not only ties the report together, but it also tells the reader "The End."

Often the conclusion of a report summarizes the ideas of the report in a new way. Because it often leaves an impression in the reader's mind, the conclusion should be bright and fresh. One way to make the conclusion interesting is to use a vivid quotation. The writer of "The Chinese New Year" ended her report with a quotation that relates to the topic. Notice also how her conclusion ties together and summarizes the report's main idea.

Student Model

An old Chinese proverb says: "A phoenix begets a phoenix, a dragon begets a dragon." Perhaps the most important reason the Chinese celebrate the New Year is that by doing so they will help beget a happy, prosperous New Year.

Writing Activity *Concluding Your Report*

Writing in Process Write the concluding paragraph of your report. Make sure it ties the report together and provides a definite finish. Save your report draft in your folder.

6
Naming Sources

In a report, you use information from outside sources. You must give credit to those sources. The usual method is to name the sources at the end of the report in a special section called the **bibliography**.

In addition to naming sources, a bibliography serves several other purposes. It lets the reader know where he or she can find more information on the subject. It also shows the amount of research that went into the report. The dates that the books or articles were written tell how up-to-date the report itself is.

Look at the bibliography that was prepared by Nancy for her report, "The Chinese New Year."

Bibliography

Burnett, Bernice. *Holidays*. New York: Franklin Watts, 1974.

Cure, K. "Welcoming the Year of the Monkey." *Travel* Jan. 1980: 60–63.

"Feasts and Festivals." *The World Book Encyclopedia*. 1988 ed.

The examples above show the form for a book, a magazine article, and an encyclopedia article. Notice that they are alphabetized according to the authors' names. Where no author is given, the material is alphabetized according to the title of the article itself.

Writing Activity **Naming Sources**

Writing in Process Make a bibliography by listing the sources used in your report. Be sure to underline the titles of books and magazines. Also underline the names of encyclopedias. Follow the examples given above. The list of complete sources you made earlier has the information you need to prepare your bibliography.

7
Revising, Proofreading, and Presenting a Report

Once all three parts of your report are written, study your work carefully. Use the guidelines for revising and proofreading on pages 86–87 to help you improve your report. Make sure that the report covers your topic thoroughly and presents the information in a clear and lively manner. Rewrite sections that need work.

Because this is a report, you must add one more step to the revision process. *Check your facts*. Make sure all dates, statistics, and other information are correct. Check to see that you have listed your sources accurately. One error of fact could make a reader question your whole report.

Once you are finished revising, make your final clean copy. Follow the form your teacher gives you. Proofread this copy. Use correct grammar, capitalization, punctuation, and spelling.

Your report is now ready to be shared. Perhaps your report can be published as a part of a larger booklet. You may wish to present it to your class or to a group of students who have a particular interest in your topic.

Writing Activities *Revising and Presenting*

A Read, revise, and proofread the following paragraphs on the discovery of the *Titanic*.

> The *Titanic* suffered obious damage. The hull may have been fractured when it first hit the ice berg. Robert Ballard, who helped discover the ship, thinks it was damaged when the great ship twisted to the bottom. Some authorities think the ship hit bottom at one hundred miles per hour. ballard thinks the hull landed gently. Some authorities think the hull was probably fracture on the surface of the water.

B **Writing in Process** Read, revise, and proofread your report. Make a final copy. Find ways to share your report with others.

English and Physical Education

Sports writers have always used their own special language in their reports, whether they're writing from the baseball diamond, tennis court, or swimming pool. Their words bring us inside the exciting world of sports, showing both the action and the emotions. We share the struggle, the pain, the thrill, the disappointment, the victory, and the defeat. Sportswriters show us what it would be like to be the quarterback who threw for a touchdown in the last seconds of the game, or the gymnast who scored a "10" in the Olympic games, or the outfielder who dropped the winning hit in the World Series. All of this they do through their words alone: rich, powerful, action-packed words like *clinch, pounce, trounce, rush, launch, capture,* and *plunge.*

Activity

You are the new sports writer for the school newspaper. For the next issue of the paper, your editor has asked you to choose a sporting event to cover. It can either be a school or community game (even a game in gym class will work), or a professional game on television. Write an article that will make your readers feel like they were there with you. Remember that action verbs and vivid adjectives will help make your story come alive.

Application and Review

A Using Note Cards Make a note card for this paragraph taken from page 8 of the article, "Nature's Violent Side," by Craig E. Blohm in the April, 1986, issue of *Cobblestone* magazine.

> Uncontrolled wind can be as devastating as earthquakes or floods. Spanish explorers, en route to the West Indies after Columbus, encountered storms of incredible violence. Called *huracan*, or "evil wind," by the local Indians, these storms are now known as hurricanes.

B Preparing an Outline Sort the following facts into three groups under the key ideas: *value, history,* and *beginning a collection*. Put the groups and the facts within them in some logical order. Omit irrelevant facts. Make a report outline.

Collecting Baseball Cards

1. The Honus Wagner baseball card, worth about $20,000, is the most valuable.
2. About a hundred years ago, the first baseball cards were developed to help companies sell certain products.
3. You can check the value of the baseball cards you get in *The Sport Americana Baseball Card Price Guide*.
4. Keep your cards in good shape to increase their value.
5. To trade cards, some people flip them like cards, with the "head" winning and the "tail" losing.
6. Baseball is based on the games of rounders and cricket.
7. In the 1930's, candy and chewing gum companies first started to issue baseball cards with their products.
8. Do not throw away duplicate cards, because you can trade them with friends to get the cards you don't have.
9. Over the years, the cards have become more important than the candy or gum. Today some companies sell them alone.
10. A 1960 Carl Yastrzemski rookie card is already worth $60.
11. Many of the oldest and most valuable cards can be seen at the Baseball Hall of Fame in Cooperstown, New York.

Resources and Skills

Writers, like artists, need tools to help them create finished works. Just as an artist needs brushes and pigments to create a painting, a writer needs tools such as a good vocabulary and sound research skills. When a writer, like an artist, knows how to find and use the tools that are available, the result can be as alive and appealing as this painting.

14
Studying Language and Vocabulary

The English language contains many Arabic words. *Algebra* and *sheik* are just two examples. Luckily you don't need a translator to understand them or the thousands of other English words that are borrowed from other languages.

In Chapter 14 you will learn how words entered our language, developed, and changed. You will also learn how to make sense of unfamiliar words by using prefixes, suffixes, synonyms, antonyms, and context clues.

1
The History of English

The English language is made up of over one-half million words. A small percentage of these words—about 15 percent—are native English, or Anglo-Saxon, words. The rest have been borrowed from other languages.

It is easy to see why word borrowing occurred. Northern Europe was constantly being conquered and ruled by other groups. These rulers, especially the Romans, Scandinavians, and French, left their mark on the English language. For example, the words *camp, skull, mountain, cap, govern, scowl,* and *prison* all came from languages other than English.

As they began to explore and settle other parts of the world, the English-speaking peoples continued to borrow words from the groups they met or conquered. Our language is full of words taken from the native American Indians. For example, the words *coyote, skunk, squash,* and *tomahawk* come from Indian languages. Every word you use has a history. You may want to keep a notebook of interesting word origins.

Linguists—people who study language—believe that many modern languages have a common ancestry. This original language, called Indo-European, was spoken by the peoples who once lived in northern Europe and India. Let's follow the changes in the word *wedi*, which linguists believe was the Indo-European verb meaning "to see." In time, *wedi* found its way into the language of the ancient Romans and became *vidēre* which also means "to see." The English words *video, advise, preview,* and *evident* come from *vidēre*.

Wedi entered our language by other paths as well. In an old form of German, *wedi* became *wisan* meaning "to know." This word made its way into Old English and became *wītan*. Some modern words that come from *wītan* are *wit, wise,* and *witness*.

More than one hundred English words have come from the one Indo-European word *wedi*. Some of these are shown in the chart on the following page. Can you see how the idea of "seeing" is contained in the meaning of each of the modern English words that come from *wedi*?

Indo-European

wedi

Greek	Latin	Anglo-Saxon	Old High German
ideia	video	wītan	wisan
eidolon	visus	wīse	witan

English

idea	video	wit	disguise
ideal	evidence	witty	guide
idealism	envy	witness	guidance
idol	survey	wise	
	clairvoyant	wisdom	
	view		
	review		
	visible		
	television		
	visual		
	supervise		
	advise		
	vista		

Native English and Borrowed Words

About A.D. 500, three tribes of people were living in northern Europe. They were the Angles, the Saxons, and the Jutes. Linguists call their language Anglo-Saxon. We can think of Anglo-Saxon as the beginning of the English we speak today. In fact, some Anglo-Saxon words are still used. We can call them native English words.

The ten most frequently used English words are all native English words. They are:

the   of   and   a   to   in   is   you   that   it

While these frequently used words are native to English, remember that the great majority of English words have been borrowed from other languages. The chart on the following page gives examples.

Some Words Borrowed from Other Languages

American Indian

> **Animals** chipmunk opossum moose skunk
> **Culture** totem moccasin tomahawk mackinaw
> **Food** hominy pone succotash

Spanish

> **Plants and Animals** mustang alfalfa coyote
> **Geography** canyon key mesa sierra
> **Structures** adobe cafeteria patio plaza
> **Food** chile tortilla taco tuna

French

> **Plants and Animals** caribou gopher pumpkin
> **Geography** bayou prairie butte rapids
> **Food** chowder à la mode jambalaya

Dutch

> **Transportation** caboose sleigh
> **Social Classification** boss patroon Yankee
> **Food** cole slaw cookie waffle

German

> **Education** semester seminar kindergarten
> **Miscellaneous** house nickel poodle waltz
> **Food** noodle pretzel hamburger frankfurter

Each group that conquered England left its mark on the English language. The Romans ruled a large area, including what is now England, for hundreds of years. The Romans spoke Latin, and the Anglo-Saxons began borrowing Latin words from their rulers. They took from them political and military terms such as *senate* and *legion*, and words for structures, such as *aqueduct, viaduct, porch,* and *column.*

The Roman Empire fell, and the French-speaking Normans invaded and conquered England in 1066. French then became the official language of England, and the Anglo-Saxons continued their practice of borrowing words. Among those adopted were such French words as *dinner, jelly, army,* and *flower.*

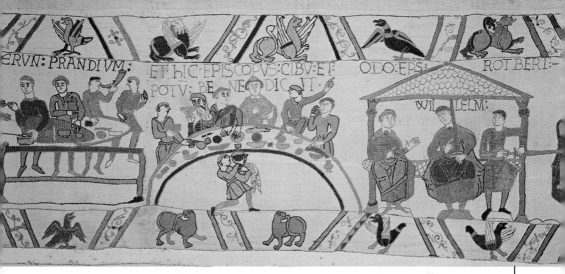

Bayeux Tapestry. This 11th c. piece shows the Norman invasion of England.

The history of a word, or its **etymology**, is part of the information you can find in your dictionary. The etymology is given in brackets before the definition of the entry word. Names of languages from which words come are almost always abbreviated. However, you can find a list of these languages and their abbreviations in the beginning of your dictionary.

Exercise

Use a dictionary to find the origin of each word below. Write the word and the language from which it was borrowed.

1. chowder	6. chow mein	11. tornado	16. moose
2. psyche	7. raccoon	12. prairie	17. filibuster
3. skin	8. succotash	13. hickory	18. kaleidoscope
4. ouch	9. cole slaw	14. noodle	19. spaghetti
5. kettle	10. scrap	15. gopher	20. shampoo

Adopting New Words into English

In addition to borrowing, there are many other ways by which new words enter our language. New words can come from sounds, they can be made from names, and they can be formed by combining and shortening.

Words Made from Sounds Sometimes a word "echoes" or imitates the thing it names. For this reason, it is called an **echoic** word. The word *boom*, for example, almost sounds like a distant clap of thunder or an explosion.

Words Made from the Names of Persons or Places The *saxophone* was named for Adolphe Sax, the Belgian instrument maker who invented it. *Bloomers*, the loose trousers women once wore under their dresses, were named for Amelia Bloomer, who made them popular. Many other words in English have come from interesting persons or places.

Words Made by Combining A new word may be made by combining existing words in either of two ways. In a **compound word**, two complete words are joined.

ant + eater = anteater   over + haul = overhaul

In a **word blend**, only parts of two words are combined.

laundry + automat = laundromat
helicopter + airport = heliport

Words Made by Shortening People who speak English like to shorten long words. For example, *omnibus* became *bus* and *photograph* became *photo*. These words are called **clipped words**. When we want to shorten a long string of words, we sometimes use the initials of the words. *Light amplification by stimulated emission of radiation* became *laser*. The initials are pronounced as a word. *Citizen's Band radio* became *CB*. The initials are pronounced as the two letters. *Laser* and *CB* are examples of **acronyms**, meaning literally "the tips of words." Do you see why?

SCUBA
SELF
CONTAINED
UNDERWATER
BREATHING
APPARATUS

Exercises

A Write the word that comes from each of these names.

1. What do you call the engine invented by Rudolph Diesel?
2. Louis Pasteur invented a way to kill germs in milk. What do we call milk that has been treated in this way?
3. In the eighteenth century, the Irish poets of Limerick made a certain poetic form popular. What do we call this kind of poem today?
4. This blue cloth came originally from the French town of Nimes so the French said it was cloth "de Nimes." What do we call this cloth?
5. General A. E. Burnside wore whiskers on his cheeks in front of his ears. What do we call such whiskers now?
6. J. T. Brudnell, the Earl of Cardigan, wore a sweater that was open in front. What do we call that kind of sweater?
7. The German city of Hamburg gave its name to a favorite dish enjoyed by many people today. What is it?
8. James Watt was a Scottish engineer and inventor. What measure of electrical power is named after him?
9. What do we call the kind of wool cloth first made in Scotland near the Tweed River?
10. British sailors on the ship *Blazer* wore a new kind of coat. What do we call it today?

B Write the following words on your paper. Tell which ones are word blends and which are compound words.

1. motorcycle
2. smog
3. sunbeam
4. brunch
5. stagehand
6. videodisc
7. motel
8. telethon
9. flashback
10. outfield

C Write the following words on your paper. Explain how each word entered the language. Then identify the word as an *Echoic Word, Person's Name, Place Name, Compound Word, Word Blend, Clipped Word, Borrowed Word,* or *Acronym.* Use a dictionary for help.

1. NOW
2. sputter
3. Celsius
4. limousine
5. harass
6. fan
7. boatel
8. handball
9. blip
10. moose

2
Base Words, Prefixes, and Suffixes

You have already learned ways in which the English language has grown and developed. It is still developing today. New words are continually added to the language. However, these new words are often built from words and word parts that have been used for many years. Knowing these words and word parts will help you unlock the meaning of new words.

In Part 1, you learned that new words can be made by combining smaller words. You can also form new words from other types of combinations. Simple words can be combined with certain word beginnings and word endings, called **prefixes** and **suffixes**, to produce new words. Prefixes and suffixes are word parts that cannot stand alone. They must always be combined with a base word. A **base word** is a word that can stand alone. The word *secure* is a base word: it can stand alone. If the prefix *in-*, meaning "not," is added, we get the word *insecure*, with the opposite meaning. If the suffix *-ly*, meaning "in a certain manner," is added, we get the adverb *securely*. Remember that a prefix or a suffix must be used with a base word.

Exercise

Write the following words on your paper. Identify the base word in each and write it after the word. Remember, a base word can stand alone; a prefix or suffix cannot.

1. illegal	4. useful	7. helper	9. artist
2. preheat	5. unable	8. disassemble	10. refill
3. clearly	6. contentment		

Prefixes

A **prefix** is a word part that may be added to the beginning of a base word. This creates a new word that has a new meaning. If, for example, the prefix *re-*, meaning "again," is placed before the verb *read*, the new verb *reread* is formed.

Common Prefixes	
non- in- im- il- ir-	These prefixes mean "not." (A *nonswimmer* cannot swim. An *informal* dance is not formal. Something *improper* or *illegal* is not proper or legal. An *irregular* design is not regular.)
un-	This prefix may mean either "not" or "the opposite of." (A person who is *unsettled* is not settled. The opposite of *tie* is *untie*.)
de- dis-	These prefixes mean "away from" or "the opposite of." (A train *derails* when it pulls away from the tracks. To *displace* something is to move it away from where it was. The opposite of *code* and *approve* are *decode* and *disapprove*.
mis-	This prefix means "wrong." (To *misspell* a word is to give a wrong spelling.)
re-	This prefix may mean either "back" or "again." (If the factory *recalls* your car, it calls the car back for repairs. If you have to *restart* your car, you start it again.)
pre- fore-	These prefixes mean either "before" or "ahead of time." (To *precook* means to cook before. To *forewarn* means to warn ahead of time.)
sub-	This prefix may mean either "under" or "less than." (Something *subsurface* is under a surface. A *subzero* number is a number less than zero.)
super-	This prefix may mean either "above" or "more than." (The *superstructure* of a ship is the structure above the deck. A *superstar* is more successful than most other stars.)
trans-	This prefix means "across" or "to the other side of." A *transatlantic* flight crosses the Atlantic.

Suffixes

A **suffix** is a word part that may be added to the end of a base word. Like a prefix, a suffix helps create a new word with a new meaning. For example, adding the suffix *-less,* meaning "without," to the noun *care,* forms the adjective *careless.* Suffixes can often be grouped according to meaning.

Here are some more examples of base words and suffixes:

harm + -less = harmless   cheer + -ful = cheerful
up + -ward = upward   kind + -ness = kindness

Common Suffixes
-less   This suffix means "without." (Something *useless* is without use.)
-ful **-ous**   These suffixes mean "full of." (Something *harmful* is full of harm. A *dangerous* adventure is full of danger.)
-er **-or** **-ist**   These suffixes mean "someone or something who does something." (A *painter* paints, an *actor* acts, a *reflector* reflects. A *violinist* plays the violin; a *tourist* tours.)
-able **-ible**   These suffixes mean "can" or "able to be." (An *adaptable* person is able to adapt quickly. A *reversible* coat can be reversed and worn on either side.)
-ship **-ment** **-ness** **-hood**   These suffixes mean "the state or condition of" or "the act or process of." (*Friendship* is the state of being a friend. The state of being content is *contentment*. The condition of being dry is *dryness*, and the state of being a child is *childhood*.)
-ward   This suffix means "in the direction of." (*Homeward* is in the direction of home.)

In some cases, when a suffix is added to a base word a letter is changed, dropped, or doubled.

fancy + -ful = fanciful
create + -or = creator
spin + -er = spinner

Exercises

A Make three columns on your paper. Label them *Words, Prefixes,* and *Suffixes.* In the first column, write on your paper the following words. Then write their prefixes and/or suffixes in the correct column.

1. foresee
2. decode
3. curable
4. witless
5. falsehood
6. preshrunk
7. recycle
8. impatient
9. ecologist
10. biannual
11. leftward
12. illiterate
13. nonpoisonous
14. irreplaceable
15. disagreement

B Write on your paper the words given in parentheses, adding appropriate prefixes to the words in the first five sentences and appropriate suffixes to the words in the last five sentences. The new word you form by adding a prefix or a suffix should make sense in the sentence.

1. This new (abrasive) bathroom cleaner will not scratch the paint in the bathtub.
2. The flood (placed) many families from their homes.
3. We will (heat) the dinner leftovers for lunch tomorrow.
4. The runner started to sprint too early because he (calculated) the distance to the finish line.
5. A (marine) is a vessel that operates under the sea.
6. The weight lifter's (weak) made it impossible for him to continue in the competition.
7. The writer was seeking a talented (illustrate) to do the art for his new book.
8. The spy gave his captor a (murder) look and then made his escape.
9. I have an entire room full of (collect) items, such as baseball cards and stamps.
10. What is the (likely) that we will get to the game in time for the kickoff?

3
Clues to Meaning Through Context

You can unlock the meaning of an unfamiliar word in many different ways. You have already learned how to unlock the meaning of a word from its base word, prefix, and suffix. You can also discover the meaning of a word from the context, or sentence, in which it is used.

You may have guessed that there is a connection between the words *context* and *text*. Both words come from the Latin word meaning "to weave." The prefix *con-*, meaning "together," has been added to the base word *text* to form *context*.

To see how a new word fits into an entire sentence, you must look for clues to its meaning in the text around it. Words are woven into sentences and paragraphs the way thread is woven into cloth. In this part you will learn how to use different kinds of context clues to determine word meaning.

Meaning Through Definition and Restatement

Two similar types of context clues are **definition** and **restatement.** Writers often define a new or unfamiliar word within the sentence where they first use it. Definitions are often introduced with key words and phrases such as *is, which is, that is, is called,* and *in other words.* Sometimes, however, key words are not used to signal the presence of a definition. When a definition is presented without key words to introduce it, the writer is simply restating the meaning of the word. A restatement tells you almost as much as a definition, but it is more difficult to spot. Writers often set off restatements with commas, dashes, or the word *or.*

Definition   *Poaching*, which is the taking of game or fish in a forbidden area, was once punishable by death.

Restatement   *Hieroglyphics*, the symbols used in the ancient Egyptian system of writing, were all over the walls of the tomb.

In the first sentence, you are told directly that *poaching* is the taking of game or fish in a forbidden area. In the second sentence, commas alert you to the fact that *hieroglyphics* are the symbols used in the ancient Egyptian system of writing.

The use of a synonym that is familiar to readers is another good way to give a brief definition or restatement. **Synonyms** are words with the same or almost the same meaning.

> I want your *candid,* that is, your honest opinion.
> The *salutation,* or greeting, begins at the left margin.

Meaning Through Example

Examples are sometimes used to convey the meanings of words. Writers usually introduce examples with phrases such as *for instance, for example, and other, like,* and *such as.*

> *Kelp* and other kinds of seaweed can be made into food.
> Some kinds of seaweed, like *kelp*, can be made into food.

Neither sentence tells you just what kelp is, but both sentences tell you that kelp is one example of seaweed.

Exercises

A Write the meanings of the italicized words in the following sentences. Look for definition and restatement clues.

1. *Ecology*—the science that studies living things within their environment—is very popular at our school.
2. All non-Romans were called *barbarians* by the Romans.
3. Work as *scrupulously*, that is, as carefully, as you can.
4. My mom teaches *geometry*, or the measuring of angles.
5. The *stylus* was an early writing instrument.

B Write the meaning of the italicized word in each of the following sentences. Look for example clues.

1. *Ozone* and other strong smelling gases form smog.
2. The forest was made up of pine, fir, and other *conifers.*
3. Many scientists study *malaria* and other tropical diseases.
4. The *novice* violinist, like any new and inexperienced musician, made many mistakes.

5. Many types of hawks, such as the *peregrine*, are hunters.
6. The *continuous* pattering of the rain combined with other ongoing sounds to keep me awake.
7. Oil, a *lubricant*, lessens the friction between moving parts.
8. *Legislators* and other members of government complain about the many meetings they must attend.
9. Exotic fruits, like papayas and *kiwis*, are my favorites.
10. Chinese food is often spicy, especially if it is cooked *Szechwan* style.

Meaning Through Comparison and Contrast

You have already learned that synonyms are used to restate the meaning of a word. Writers also use synonyms to form comparisons. You can discover the meaning of an unfamiliar word from a comparison.

> Sandra was *tardy*, and her sister was late too.

The more familiar word, *late*, is a synonym for *tardy*. By using *late* in the comparison, the author has conveyed the meaning of *tardy*.

Writers usually introduce comparisons with one of the following words or phrases: *like, as,* and *similar to.*

> The hot-air balloon tugged at its *tether* like a dog tugging at its leash.

In this sentence, the writer compares a balloon on a tether to a dog on a leash. Both the balloon and the dog are tugging; they are similar parts of the comparison. Tether and leash are being tugged. These, too, are similar parts of the comparison. From the comparison, then, you should be able to understand that a tether must be something like a leash.

Word meaning can also be conveyed by contrasting an unfamiliar word with a more familiar one. The easiest way to form a contrast is to use an antonym. **Antonyms** are words with the opposite or very nearly the opposite meaning. A writer usually uses an antonym not just to make the meaning of a word clear but to stress that particular meaning.

The coach was *adamant* about the rules, not relaxed.

Writers usually introduce contrasts with one of the following words or phrases: *unlike, but, on the contrary,* and *on the other hand*. A writer who uses one of these introductions contrasts things that are basically similar in order to point out a way in which they differ.

Unlike other mammals, the *platypus* lays eggs.

In this sentence, the writer contrasts the platypus with "other mammals." A platypus, then, must be a kind of mammal. You can also be reasonably sure that except for the way it bears its young, the platypus is like other mammals.

Tony was *reticent*, but Phyllis was outspoken.

In this instance, the word *but* signals that the phrase "Tony was reticent" differs from "Phyllis was outspoken." Therefore, being reticent probably means "not being outspoken."

Exercise

Write the meanings of the italicized words. Look for context clues to help you.

1. I was *anxious*, but everyone else was calm and relaxed.
2. *Stalactites* hung like icicles from the roof of the cave.
3. Amy, unlike most *entymologists*, does not collect insects; she only observes them.
4. Pull the taffy until it is as *elastic* as a rubberband.
5. Most of us agreed, but Cheryl *dissented*.

Crossroads

English and Health

What do you take for a cold? There are many medications for the many different cold symptoms. There are decongestants for chest colds, nasal sprays for sinusitis, antiseptic lozenges for sore throats, and many more. But what do all these terms really mean? Medical words may seem difficult to understand, but once they are broken down into their prefixes, suffixes, and base words, their meanings become clear. For example, a decongestant lessens congestion (the prefix *de-* means "the opposite of"; the suffix *-ant* means "a person or thing that"). Sinusitis is an inflammation of the sinuses (the suffix *-itis* means "the inflammation of").

Common prefixes and suffixes used in medicine include *pre-* ("before," or "ahead of"), *post-* ("after," or "following"), *anti-* ("against"), *hyper-* ("above," or "more than normal"), *hypo-* ("under," or "less than"), *-itis* ("the inflammation of"), *-ology* ("the study of"), and *-gram* ("something written or recorded").

Activity Using your knowledge of prefixes, suffixes, and base words, write the meanings of the following medical terms.

1. premature
2. postoperative
3. antibodies
4. anti-inflammatory
5. hyperextend
6. prescribe
7. tonsillitis
8. immunology

Now write a list of five more medical terms using the prefixes and suffixes discussed in this lesson.

Computer-generated model of a plant virus besieged by antibodies.

Application and Review

A Identifying Word Origins Identify each of the following words as a *Borrowed Word, Person's Name, Place Name, Clipped Word, Word Blend, Compound Word, Echoic Word,* or *Acronym.*

1. injury
2. mainstream
3. radar
4. disco
5. ohm
6. babble
7. magnet
8. motel
9. decal
10. tuxedo

B Recognizing the Parts of Words Make three columns labeled *Base Words, Prefixes,* and *Suffixes.* Write each part of the italicized words in the correct column.

1. Annie's first day at *preschool* was *wonderful*.
2. I am *unwilling* to give up her *friendship*.
3. Corazon is not *likely* to *prejudge* someone.
4. As an *artist*, Alex gets *impatient* with *misguided* criticism.
5. We will need to *reorder* the *computer*.
6. The *nonsense* verse was *ridiculous*.
7. Help! The blue dragon is about to *return*.
8. *Nonfiction* books are my favorites.
9. *Immovable* linebackers are assets to football teams.
10. These jeans are *preshrunk* and *washable*.

C Understanding Words from Context Write on your paper the meanings of the italicized words from the following sentences.

1. Alfredo enjoys playing stringed instruments like the *lute*.
2. Florida is a *peninsula*, which is a piece of land almost entirely surrounded by water.
3. I have been *hoarding* my pennies; my sister, on the other hand, never saves any of her money.
4. The *tortilla*—a pancake made from cornmeal or wheat flour—was a staple of the Aztec diet.
5. My throat felt as *arid* as the Sahara Desert.

15
Speaking and Listening Skills

It is not only in writing that you use your language skills. When you interview someone, when you tell friends about something you have witnessed, and when you give or listen to a speech, you are using language skills.

Just as there are steps to writing effectively, there are steps that will help you speak and listen effectively. In this chapter you will learn skills for speaking in formal and informal situations. You also will learn how to listen carefully and evaluate what you hear.

1
Speaking Informally

The most important skills in speaking informally are those required for preparation and presentation.

Preparation

Even though informal talks are short, you may need to do some background work to be sure you have all the information you need. You may interview the person sponsoring the event at which you will be speaking, or you may need to go to the library to check a reference book for any facts you need. When doing background work, always take accurate notes. Accurate notes give you confidence and help you to organize your talk.

It is a good idea to practice giving your talk, preferably in front of a mirror, so you can watch yourself and correct any movements you might not like. Once you are satisfied with your talk, you are ready for the presentation. The following guidelines can be applied to various kinds of informal speaking.

Guidelines to Effective Speaking

1. **Look directly at your audience.** Good eye contact helps to keep the audience interested.
2. **Stand in a relaxed position.** Stand tall but comfortably, with your legs slightly apart for good balance. This will help your voice project, and your audience will think you are at ease—even if you are a bit nervous at first.
3. **Speak so you can be heard.** Keep your head up and speak slowly enough to be understood. Project your voice so that everyone can hear you and vary the tone of your voice to keep your audience interested.
4. **Use natural, relaxed gestures for emphasis.** Gestures are facial expressions and hand movements that help emphasize what you are saying. Gestures should be natural, for example, pointing to an illustration, but too many gestures can distract your audience.

Presentation

When you finally give your talk, you want to be as relaxed and confident as possible. Naturally, you are going to be a bit nervous. Good preparation and practice, however, will give you confidence.

The way you present your information and yourself affects the interest of your audience and determines the success of your talk. In the sections that follow, notice the differences between making announcements and giving a demonstration talk.

Making Announcements

In school you hear announcements several times a day. Some of them you remember, but others never seem to catch your attention. Announcements are short and simple, but the information should be clear and include the following details:

Who's involved
What's happening
Where the event will take place
When it will happen
Why should listeners be interested

Get your listeners' attention first by mentioning something you know will interest them. Repeat the most important facts, especially the *where* and *when*, as in the following example:

Are you up to date on the latest news? Here's your chance to find out. Tomorrow, Wednesday, October 15, the first issue of the school paper, *The Eagle's Eye*, will be sold in the school cafeteria during all lunch periods. The cost is only ten cents. Don't forget—tomorrow, Wednesday, the school paper will be sold in the cafeteria.

Giving a Demonstration Talk

How do you ride a bike?
Just hold on to the handlebars, push the pedals with your
    feet, and go.

It sounds easy enough, but if you explain it that way to a child who has never done it, he or she will fall right over.

When you demonstrate how to do something, you have to be as exact as when you are giving directions. The following steps will help you to give an informative demonstration talk.

> **Steps for a Demonstration Talk**
> 1. **Know your subject.** The best demonstration will be about something you know how to do well. Also, choose a subject that you know will interest your audience.
> 2. **Organize your material.** Your audience will understand your demonstration best if the information is presented in the proper order. If you present each step in the order it occurs, your demonstration will make sense.
> 3. **Check your equipment.** Most demonstrations involve some kind of equipment. Some require many utensils or tools. To keep yourself organized, make a list of the equipment you will need for each step. However, try to choose a subject that is not too complicated.
> 4. **Be interesting.** Start with an attention-grabbing positive statement that gets your audience immediately involved. The people in your audience need you to tell them why they should be interested in your subject. Then, stop briefly after each step to make sure your listeners understand.

Exercises

A Make an announcement to the class. Use one of the following events or an event that is going to take place in your school. If you wish, make up an event, but be sure to include the specific information that is required.

a student council event	tryouts for a play
a club meeting	an assembly
a bake sale	a talent show competition
an athletic event	a field trip

B Plan a demonstration on making guacamole dip or some other cold food that you know how to prepare or can look up in a cookbook. Outline the steps of the demonstration, so that you know exactly what you'll say and do. Make a list of materials you will need.

2
Speaking Formally

When you are asked to speak about a specific topic, to a specific group, for a specific purpose, you will be presenting a formal talk. A formal talk is longer and requires more preparation than an informal talk.

Preparation for your talk is the same as preparing to write something. The same process of thinking, writing, and revising applies. You might think that speaking formally is harder and more complicated than speaking informally, but if you follow the step-by-step procedures in this chapter, you will soon learn the routine.

Step 1: Know Your Audience

Suppose that your teacher has asked you to give a talk, first to your classmates, next to a fifth-grade class, and then to the PTA. You want to be sure that each group will understand and be interested in what you are saying. This may involve adapting your content, word choice, and formality of language to fit each new audience. To determine how you should rework your material, consider all of the following facts about your audience.

1. **The purpose of the group.** Is this group meeting to learn something new, or merely to relax and have fun? If you know the purpose of the group, you can include in your talk the ideas and information that will help the group achieve its purpose.
2. **The composition of the group.** How many people are there in the group? Are they alike or different in age, sex, education, and occupation? The more differences a group has, the more you will have to think about what kinds of information to include in your talk and how formal your language should be.
3. **The experience of the group.** How well will the group listen? Is the group used to hearing speakers? Are you one of a series of speakers? How can you relate your material to the experiences of the group?

4. **The occasion.** Is the group meeting for a social occasion, such as the Fourth of July or an awards presentation? If so, you should try to relate your material to the occasion in such a way that it will be both relevant and interesting.

Step 2: Select a Topic

Often, the topic for a formal talk is assigned, but there may be occasions when you will choose your own topic for a formal talk. You are likely to select a topic that you know well, but don't be afraid to choose a new topic that interests you.

Following are suggestions that will help you to select a topic:

1. **The unusual** appeals to everyone. Consider a new topic or one seldom discussed that would be of interest.
2. **A familiar topic** is one about which your audience already has general information. Look for new details to interest your audience. A familiar topic can sometimes be dull.
3. **A factual topic** is informative. To keep the details interesting, look for new sources that might supply you with unexpected highlights.
4. **Contrasts** are also interesting, for example, a talk showing the differences between American and British television.

Step 3: Define Your Purpose

Once you have chosen an appropriate topic for the group, you need to define exactly what you wish to achieve with your talk. Formal talks generally fall into one of the following categories. Decide which of these three purposes your talk has.

To inform   In most formal talks, your purpose is to help your audience understand or appreciate what you are telling them. Talks to inform might include a report on a book, an explanation of voting procedures, or an explanation of how the heart works.

To persuade   When the purpose of your talk is to persuade, you have chosen a topic that has two sides to it. Make sure that your information is accurate and that you have strong points to support your opinion. Your main purpose will be to persuade listeners to accept your point of view. The following are examples of topics: the election of a candidate, the dangers of drugs, or city living versus suburban living.

To entertain A talk for the purpose of entertainment might be about a humorous or unusual personal experience, a visit to an unusual place, or life with your pet.

Step 4: Select a Theme

The theme is the main idea you want to get across to your audience. To make sure that the theme is clear in your mind, write it out in a full sentence. The following sentence states a theme:

> John Steinbeck's novel *The Pearl* is an excellent example of how greed can destroy a person.

All of the information that you gather and present should support your theme in some way. You may even want to use your theme sentence as part of your speech to make sure that the theme is clear to your audience.

Step 5: Gather Your Material

Once you have decided on your theme, you can begin to gather material to support your main idea. A variety of information, such as illustrations, facts, quotations, and charts, will make your talk more interesting. Most of your material will come from these three main sources:

1. **Firsthand experience.** Personal experience adds life to your talk. Be careful, though, that you separate fact from opinion in presenting your material.
2. **Experience of others.** If you have not had a personal experience related to your subject, it is a good idea to interview someone who has. When you do interview someone, be sure to use a tape recorder or to take very good notes.
3. **Research in the library.** The library offers you the largest variety of information. Refer to Chapter 16 to learn more about the resources of your library.

Step 6: Organize Your Material

Once you have gathered all of your information, you need to organize it so it will make sense. Divide your material into three parts: the introduction, the body, and the conclusion.

Introduction The purpose of the introduction is to get the attention of the audience. You can accomplish this with a humorous anecdote, an explanation of the title, a statement of your theme, or an unusual fact. You will need to judge which kind of introduction is appropriate for your presentation.

Body The body is the major part of your talk. It must inform, entertain, or persuade your audience. After getting the attention of your audience with your introduction, provide facts and details to support your theme. Here are two guidelines:

1. **Determine your main points.** How much time you are given to speak will determine how many main points you will be able to use. The points you use must also have details to support them. To organize your main points, arrange them in logical order in outline form.

How Creatures Protect Themselves

   I. Speed
  II. Protective coloring
 III. Protective resemblance
 IV. Armor
  V. Weapons
 VI. Habits

2. **Develop your main points.** Use details from your notes, charts, graphs, illustrations, personal experience, or quotations from your sources.

How Creatures Protect Themselves

  V. Some creatures carry weapons for protection.
    A. The porcupine has spines. (Show actual quill.)
    B. Lions, tigers, and leopards have claws.
    C. Some creatures use poison.
      1. The sea anemone shoots out poison darts.
      2. Bees and wasps inject poison with their stings.
    D. Some animals, like skunks, give out a bad odor.

Conclusion The conclusion of your talk is a summary of the main points. It should be brief. Do not introduce any new information. Repeat your theme for emphasis.

> Some creatures may not be our favorite friends. In fact, we humans seem to be the enemy of some. However, creatures must be able to protect themselves. They do this effectively, and in varying ways, by speed, coloring, resemblance to other things in nature, armor, weapons, and habits.

By organizing your ideas in a logical order, you can help the listener follow them and understand your talk.

Step 7: Practice Your Presentation

After you have organized your material, practice giving your talk out loud. You want to be familiar with the material and at ease in front of your audience. Begin by reading through the material several times. Then, underline the points you want to emphasize. Next, memorize as much of the talk as possible so you can speak directly to your audience. Then practice in front of a mirror to be sure your gestures seem natural. Finally, present your talk to a group of family or friends to get reactions and suggestions.

Step 8: Deliver the Talk

When you present a formal talk, use the guidelines on page 292 for presenting an informal talk.

Exercises

A Suggest a possible theme for each of the following subjects. Write out the theme in a full sentence.

astronomy   olympic medal winners   pro quarterbacks

B Choose one of the topics above or one of your own. Find four different sources of information about the topic. Write down the name of each source, the page number, and the sample information. The sources of information may include interviews and personal experience. Using the information you have gathered, write out and deliver a talk on your subject.

3
Listening

Listening involves more than just using your ears. What would happen, for example, if you were listening to the band rehearsing outside your classroom window while your teacher was giving tomorrow's assignment? You would not be in as much trouble as this duck, but missing an assignment can be serious, too.

Listening in Conversations

In conversations, listening is as important as talking. You are constantly changing roles from speaker to listener to speaker again. At times you may want to focus on what you will say next, instead of listening to what the other person is saying. However, if you do not listen, you might as well be talking to yourself.

Janet So, I hear you're on the school newspaper. How can I get on it?

Eddie Yes, I'm on the paper. I'm the sports reporter.

Janet I'd like to write about the Academic Olympics.

Eddie I was in the Academic Olympics last year. I almost won.

Eddie may have discouraged Janet from joining the newspaper staff. He also probably gave her the idea that he is quite self-centered. Listen closely in conversations. Ask questions; pursue the other person's points as well as your own.

Taking Directions

You need to listen attentively and thoughtfully when you get directions, also. Often, you may want to repeat directions aloud or take notes to make sure you are listening well. Common kinds of directions might tell you about a class assignment or explain how to get somewhere.

Assignments Sometimes assignments are made at the end of a class period. There may be the confusion of students gathering books and preparing to go to another classroom. If you are not clear on any point, ask questions. Jot down the details of the assignment immediately and be sure you know what you are to do and when the assignment must be completed.

How to Get Somewhere When someone is directing you somewhere, repeat what is being said to be sure you are clear about the directions. Use compass points, even if the person directing you is not using them. Repeating and clarifying directions will also help you remember them.

Sam Go to the corner and turn right on Deer Road.

You Go to the corner and turn south on Deer Road.

Listening to a Speech

Conversations and directions can be considered informal listening. Often, however, you will be called upon to be an attentive listener in a more formal setting.

Try to remember the last time you were in the school auditorium, listening to a prepared speech. Who was the speaker? How attentive were you? Keep in mind that being a member of the audience requires as much responsibility as being the speaker. Following these guides to good listening will also help you to evaluate the speech fairly:

1. **Be ready.** First, make sure that you are located in a position to hear the speaker well. Second, know why you are listening to the speaker. Is the speaker's purpose for speaking to inform, to persuade, or to entertain? The speaker's purpose will relate to your reason for listening. Only a good listener can intelligently evaluate a speaker.
2. **Be attentive.** To be a good listener, you have to give strict attention to the speaker. To evaluate the speaker fairly, you can't miss any information, overall organization, or any other aspects of preparation and presentation that add meaning to the talk.

3. **Be open-minded.** Sometimes a speaker's subject will not interest you, or you may not have the same opinion as the speaker does. In either case, you should still listen carefully to everything the speaker has to say.

Once you have learned to follow the guides to being a good listener, you will be better able to evaluate the speaker fairly. When it is your turn to speak, you can expect to be evaluated fairly if the audience has followed these guidelines.

Guidelines to Fair Evaluating

1. **Topic.** Was the topic interesting to the majority of the group? Do not judge the topic by your personal interests. Watch the response of the group before you decide whether the topic was appropriate.
2. **Purpose.** Was the speaker's purpose to inform, to persuade, or to entertain? Was the purpose achieved?
3. **Preparation.** Did the speaker have enough information about the subject? Was there unneeded information?
4. **Organization.** Did the speaker present the information in a logical order? If the information was well organized, you should not have had any trouble understanding it. Was the speaker ready with any equipment that was needed, such as tools for a demonstration or an illustration to help explain? If the speaker forgot such materials, the information was not as well organized as it should have been.
5. **Presentation.** Several aspects should be considered in evaluating the presentation:
   a. **Eye contact.** Did the speaker look at the people in the audience in order to keep their interest?
   b. **Posture.** Did the speaker appear relaxed, or did nervous habits distract the audience?
   c. **Voice.** Could you hear the speaker? Was there good expression in what was said?
   d. **Gestures.** Were gestures used when they were needed, especially facial expressions? Were the gestures too distracting to the audience?
   e. **Practice.** Was the speaker familiar with the material, or was more practice needed?

The United States Congress, Capitol Building, Washington, D.C.

The most important point to remember in evaluating a speaker is to be fair. Speaking to a group is not a contest; it is a skill that you are learning to develop. Try to be as constructive as possible in your criticism. As an evaluator, you can help other people to become better speakers, and you can also help yourself to become both a better listener and a better speaker.

Exercises

A Break up into groups of four or five and choose a topic for a group discussion. Spend about twenty minutes discussing the topic. Then evaluate the discussion. Did anyone monopolize the conversation? Did everyone get a chance to express his or her ideas? What was each person's opinion? Did anyone's opinion change during the discussion?

B Listen as your teacher reads a magazine article to the class. Take complete notes on the presentation. Use your notes to make up a ten-item quiz on some important facts from the article. Exchange quizzes with another student and try to answer his or her questions. Correct each other's papers. Then go over your answers together and see how helpful your notes were. Did you leave out any important points?

C Listen to a speech on television, at school, at a political rally, or some other situation. Evaluate the speech using the five guidelines to fair evaluating on page 302. What were the good and bad points of the speech?

Crossroads

English and Music

You probably hear all kinds of music every day. Besides the music you choose to play, you hear music on television, in waiting rooms, and even on the street.

Often, we barely hear the music around us because we are concentrating on other things. To really "hear" music requires careful attention to detail. For example, imagine that you are listening to jazz fusion. If you listen carefully to the melody, you will notice that the musicians improvise, that is, they create variations in the melody as they play. Improvisation is a special feature of jazz. If you listen to the rhythm of jazz fusion, you will hear that the musicians use rock 'n roll rhythms. You may also note that they use rock instruments. Which ones do you hear? Synthesizers? Drum machines? Electric guitars? As you learn more about jazz fusion, you find that this music combines elements of both jazz and rock.

Activity Practice your speaking and listening skills by presenting a short oral report on one of the types of music listed below. Play a short example of the music in class. You will most likely be able to borrow records from your library, and you can find explanations of the types of music in a dictionary such as *The Harvard Dictionary of Music*. Listen carefully to the music several times so that you can describe its basic elements and special features.

1. blues
2. opera
3. sonata
4. madrigal
5. concerto
6. bluegrass
7. bebop
8. symphony
9. third-stream
10. swing

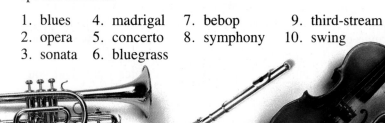

Application and Review

A Speaking Skills Write on your paper the correct word from those given in parentheses.

1. When you give an announcement, look directly at your (notes, audience).
2. While giving a talk, stand in a (stiff, relaxed) position.
3. Movements you make with your hands as you speak are known as (gestures, directions).
4. Announcements are usually (short, long).
5. Giving directions is (informal, formal) speaking.
6. The first step in preparing a formal talk is to know your (purpose, audience).
7. The purpose of a formal talk is usually to inform, to persuade, or to (memorize, entertain).
8. When you evaluate a speaker, the most important thing to remember is that you must be (critical, fair).
9. The major part of your talk is the (body, conclusion).
10. To evaluate a speech fairly, you must be (attentive, an expert).

B Listening Skills Each statement below is followed by two possible responses. Write on your paper the letter of the response that a good listener would give in a conversation.

1. I saved my money from work and bought a new bicycle.
   a. I have a job, too.   b. What kind of bicycle is it?
2. Our yearly show is going to have popular and classical music.
   a. What will you do in the show?   b. I like jazz.
3. I tried out for the All-City High School Ballet.
   a. I hope you make it.   b. Modern dance is better.
4. I'm going to San Diego with my family on vacation.
   a. Do you know anyone there?
   b. We're not taking a vacation this year.
5. I think Woodrow Wilson was one of our greatest Presidents.
   a. I think Jefferson was the best.   b. Why do you say that?

16

Using the Library and Reference Works

You probably have been going to the library since you learned to read and maybe even earlier. Like many people, you might think of it as a storehouse of books and encyclopedias, but the library is much more than that. In the library you can find the latest magazines on sports, fashion, and other subjects that may interest you. You can find records, tapes, and maybe a personal computer. Some libraries even present concerts and show movies.

In this chapter you will learn how to use your library—a skill that will make your life easier and more fun.

1
The Library

If someone always answers your questions, you will not learn how to answer them yourself. Other people are good resources, but they are not always around when you need them. If you always depend on others, you will never develop your own skills. If, however, you learn how to use the resources in the library, you will be able to answer most questions that occur to you during your life.

Library Resources

You may not realize all the different kinds of things you can research in a library. You may only be familiar with the encyclopedias, books, and magazines your library keeps. However, libraries are storehouses of other materials such as pamphlets, newspapers, sound recordings, art reproductions, films, filmstrips, videos, games, and even computers. At the library, you can discover the best places to stay and the best restaurants to eat at when you and your family are on vacation. You can find out if a glacier ever covered the land where you now live. Did you know that the first cowboys were actually British patriots who hid in the woods ringing cow bells during the American Revolution? They did this to lure American patriots into an ambush. This and many other interesting facts can be discovered in your library.

Sections of the Library

The library is designed to make your search for materials as easy as possible. First, all the materials housed in the library are carefully organized. For instance, books are shelved in one of three sections: fiction, nonfiction, or reference. Second, in one or more of the library catalogs, each item in the library is listed along with its location. Third, librarians are available to assist you in finding the information and materials you need.

All library book collections are organized into the same basic sections. Only the location of these sections varies among libraries. Following are descriptions of five important areas of a library.

Catalog Section "Who wrote *Flowers for Algernon*?" "What is a good book about pioneer women of the 1800's?" You can answer these questions in the catalog section. In the catalog, information about books and their locations is stored on cards that contain authors' names, book titles, and subjects. Today, however, some libraries store this information on computer catalogs. In addition to the information contained in card catalogs, computer catalogs usually tell if the book you want has been checked out and when it is due back in the library. You may need to ask a librarian how to use a computer catalog. You will learn how to use the card catalog in Part 3 of this chapter.

Stacks "Now that I know which book on pioneer women I want, where do I find it?" You can find it in the stacks. The **stacks** is a term used to describe the large group of bookcases where the library's main collection of books is kept. Nonfiction books not kept in the reference section and all fiction books are shelved in the stacks.

Periodical Section This section is usually near the reference section. Current magazines and newspapers are shelved here. Old issues are kept in a private storage area or sometimes transferred to microfilm. You can get one of these older issues by asking a librarian.

Reference Section "How many records has Bruce Springsteen made?" "According to the United States Census Bureau, which states have had the greatest population growth over the past five years?" These are questions you can answer in the reference section.

The reference section is usually contained within one large room. Tables and chairs at which you may do your research are usually provided in the reference room because most libraries do not allow reference books to be checked out. This ensures that the information in these materials will always be available to anyone who might need it. Also in the reference section you will find a librarian. The reference librarian is another resource. He or she may assist you in your research by helping you locate the information you need. You will learn more about the reference section in Part 4 of this chapter.

Children's Section You usually find this section only in public libraries where it is often contained in a single room with its own card catalog. The entire section is devoted only to children's materials. Here you can find stories to read to younger brothers, sisters, or cousins. Nonfiction books are also available and some children's sections may have magazines, records, and cassettes.

The floor plan of a typical library is shown below. Remember though, not all libraries are arranged this way. You will need to become familiar with the arrangement of your particular library so you can use it with ease.

Library Floor Plan

Records / Tapes / Movies / Nonprint Materials / Computers / Children's Area

Stacks Area / Nonfiction / Fiction / Mystery / Biography / Story Collections / Science Fiction

Periodicals / Microfiche Readers / Reference

Circulation Desk / Catalog Area

A Special Section: Nonprint Materials

In the nonprint section, you can get a recording of sound effects or rent reproductions of famous paintings. Recordings, art reproductions, films, filmstrips, projectors, and sometimes even videos are stored here. You may also find computers in this section.

All these items, except the projectors and computers, are listed along with their locations on cards. These cards are usually stored in specific catalogs rather than in the card catalog for books. One catalog will contain the cards for recordings while another lists art reproductions, and so on.

Nonprint materials are especially good for improving classroom presentations. For example, you could make a report on Louis Armstrong much more interesting and meaningful by actually playing a recording of Louis Armstrong performing a jazz trumpet solo.

Computers may be useful to you in a variety of ways. You might use a computer program to increase your typing speed and accuracy, to study math, or to write an essay or report. Or, you might challenge a computer to a game of chess.

Exercises

A Write on your paper the section of the library where you are able to do the things described.

1. Find a video to watch on Saturday night.
2. Glance through a book by James Thurber.
3. Look at the current issue of *Newsweek*.
4. Find out how many books the library has about Mother Teresa.
5. Locate a book about Mother Teresa.
6. Do quiet studying.
7. Use a computer to type up a report.
8. Find a recording of songs from the 1950's.
9. Find the definition of a scientific term.
10. Find the address of the American Kennel Club.

B Draw the floor plan of the library you usually use. If the library is a large one, draw the floor plan of the section you use most often.

2
The Classification and Arrangement of Books

Fiction books are shelved alphabetically by the authors' last names and separated from the nonfiction books. To begin a search in the stacks for a work of fiction—a novel or a short story collection—you would look for the letter that begins the author's last name. Books by one author are placed together on the shelf and arranged alphabetically according to title. If a title begins with *A*, *An*, or *The*, it is alphabetized by the second word in the title. If two authors have the same last name, their books are alphabetized by the authors' first names.

Nonfiction books—factual works not based on imagined events—are grouped according to their subject matter and then shelved alphabetically in these groups. Some libraries organize nonfiction books according to the Library of Congress system, but most school libraries use the Dewey Decimal system.

The Dewey Decimal System

The **Dewey Decimal System**, originated by Melvil Dewey, is a method of arranging nonfiction books. This system divides nonfiction books into ten major categories.

Dewey Decimal System	
000–099	General Works (encyclopedias, bibliographies)
100–199	Philosophy (conduct, psychology)
200–299	Religion (the Bible, mythology, theology)
300–399	Social Science (law, education, economics)
400–499	Language (grammars, dictionaries)
500–599	Science (mathematics, biology, chemistry)
600–699	Technology (medicine, inventions, cooking)
700–799	The Arts (painting, music, theater, sports)
800–899	Literature (poetry, plays, essays)—not fiction
900–999	History (biography, geography, travel)

Each of the ten categories are divided into still smaller categories. For example, look at the list below.

700 The Arts
710 Civic and Landscape Art
720 Architecture
730 Sculpture, Plastic Arts
740 Drawing, Decorative Arts
750 Painting
760 Graphic Arts, Prints
770 Photography
780 Music
790 Recreational and Performing Arts

In this system, you would find a book on rock music in the category of arts (700–799), the subdivision of music (780–789), and a further subdivision for rock music (781).

According to the chart of ten categories, biography is located somewhere between 900 and 999. The actual Dewey number for biography is 920. Some libraries have a special section for biography and autobiography. Books in this section are arranged by the last name of the person about whom the book was written.

Exercises

A Write the following fiction titles and authors in the order in which they should appear on the library shelves.

1. Richter, Conrad. *The Light in the Forest*
2. Lee, Mildred. *Fog*
3. Neville, Emily C. *Berries Goodman*
4. Hinton, S.E. *Rumblefish*
5. Neville, Emily C. *It's Like This, Cat*

B Write the correct Dewey classification number for each of the following books. You may refer to the chart at the bottom of page 312.

1. *School Effectiveness*
2. *The World Book Encyclopedia*
3. *Chinese Mythology*
4. *You and Your Feelings*
5. *Tales from Shakespeare*

3
The Card Catalog

The names and locations of all library books and often nonprint materials as well are recorded on the cards stored in the card catalog. Other information is also provided, such as the author, publisher, number of pages, and whether the book is illustrated. A catalog card may even include a brief summary of what the book is about.

As you may recall, cards are filed by author, title, and subject. These cards are arranged alphabetically in small drawers that are labeled on the front with the letters of the alphabet.

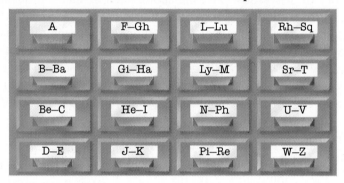

Call Numbers

A **call number** tells you where a book is located in the stacks. These numbers are printed on the upper left corner of a catalog card. For nonfiction listings, the call numbers begin with the Dewey decimal numbers by which books are arranged in the stacks. If a library uses the Library of Congress classification system, then a Library of Congress letter-number code appears on the card. Underneath the Dewey number—or Library of Congress code—is a letter-number code called the **cutter number**. Many books have the same Dewey number, but very few have the same cutter number. The cutter number helps you locate a specific book within all the books in the stacks that have the same Dewey number. You will find that books are arranged alphabetically according to the first one or more letters of the cutter code.

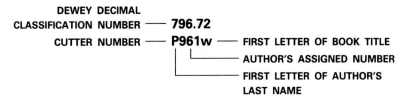

DEWEY DECIMAL
CLASSIFICATION NUMBER —— **796.72**
CUTTER NUMBER —— **P961w** —— FIRST LETTER OF BOOK TITLE
                                └——— AUTHOR'S ASSIGNED NUMBER
                         └——————— FIRST LETTER OF AUTHOR'S
                                   LAST NAME

Above the Dewey call number, you may see a letter code. This letter code identifies the section of the library in which the book is located. For example, the letters *R* or *REF* above a call number tell you that the book is in the reference section. The letters *B* or *BIO* tell you the book is shelved in the biography section. If the book is in the children's section, you will see the letters *J* or *JUV*, which stand for *juvenile*.

Since works of fiction are usually arranged alphabetically by the authors' last names, these books do not need call numbers. Cards that give information about a work of fiction usually have an *F* or *FIC* printed where the call number would be.

JUV

BIO

FIC   McCaffrey, Anne
       The White Dragon

Guide Cards

Inside each drawer of the card catalog are **guide cards**. These extend higher than the other cards in the drawer. They may have letters of the alphabet, complete words, or subject headings printed on them. If you remember that cards are filed alphabetically, the letters or words on these cards will help you narrow your search for a particular word.

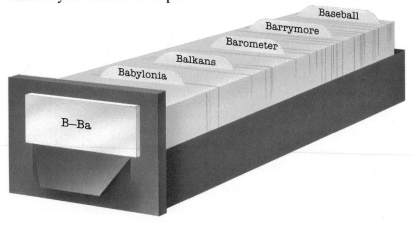

Baseball
Barrymore
Barometer
Balkans
Babylonia

B—Ba

Author Cards

Imagine you have read a fiction book by Isaac Asimov and liked it so well that you want to read another book by the same author. You could go to the stacks and look through each of the books you found under *Asimov*. However, he has written nonfiction books too. How would you find these? Furthermore, some of the books by Asimov that are part of the permanent collection at your library may be checked out. A better way to find out about this author's books would be to look up *Asimov, Isaac* in the card catalog. Here you would find all the books by Asimov your library carries.

There is one rule to keep in mind when looking up authors' names in the card catalog. Names that begin with *Mc* and *Mac* are filed as though they were spelled as one word that begins with *Mac*.

The following is an example of an author card for the book *The NOVA Space Explorers' Guide*.

Author Card

Call Number ——— 629.4	Maurer, Richard ——————————— Author
Cutter Number ——— M143	The NOVA space explorers' guide —— Title
	Richard Maurer. —New York: ——— Publisher
Publisher ————————— Clarkson N. Potter, 1985. ——————— Copyright Date
Length ————————— 181 p.: ill.; 24 cm. ——————— Height
Illustrated ———	
	1. Space. I. Title ——————— Other Ways Book Is Listed

Title Cards

Suppose that someone recommended you read *The NOVA Space Explorers' Guide*, but all you know of the book is its title. You can actually find the listing for the book just by looking up this title. However, remember the following filing rules:

1. If the title begins with an *A, An,* or *The,* the card is alphabetized by the next word in the title. Articles within

titles, however, follow the word-by-word alphabetizing rules listed below, so *Acting on a Stage* comes before *Acting on the Stage*.

2. Abbreviated words are alphabetized as they would be if the words were spelled out in full. This means that *Mr.* is filed as if it were spelled *Mister*.

3. Numerals are alphabetized as if they were spelled out.

4. Use word-by-word alphabetizing to find entries in most library card catalogs. In this system, *book review* comes before *bookmark* because the word *book* comes before the word *bookmark*. In letter-by-letter alphabetizing spaces are ignored as if all the words in a title were a single word. In this system, *bookmark* is listed before *book review*. You need to learn which system your library uses.

The following is an example title card.

Title Card

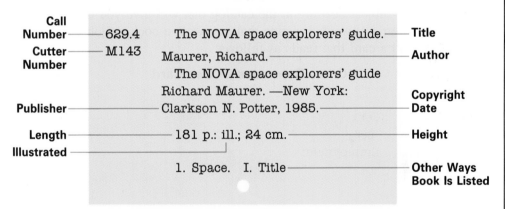

Subject Cards

Maybe you have just received a telescope and want to learn more about the stars you are viewing, or you are interested in becoming an astronaut. The best way to pursue your interest in space is to look for books on the subject, *Space*, in the card catalog. When you look up a subject in the card catalog, you will find all of the books on that subject filed alphabetically by the authors' last names. One subject card on *Space* would look like the one at the top of page 318.

Subject Card

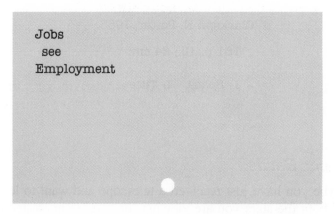

SPACE ———————————————————— **Subject**

Call Number — 629.4   Maurer, Richard. ———————— **Author**

Cutter Number — M143   The NOVA space explorers' guide — **Title**
    Richard Maurer. —New York: **Copyright**
Publisher ———————— Clarkson N. Potter, 1985. ———— **Date**

Length ———————— 181 p.; ill.; 24 cm. ———— **Height**
Illustrated ————————————————

    1. Space.   I. Title. ———————— **Other Ways Book Is Listed**

Cross-Reference Cards

Sometimes when you look up a subject, you will find a card that is printed with *See* or *See also*. The "See" card refers you to another subject heading in the catalog that will give you the information you want. Imagine that you want a book on jobs, and you find a card that reads as follows:

Cross-Reference or *See* Card

Jobs
  see
Employment

This "See" card shows that the library lists all books on the subject *Jobs* under the subject heading *Employment*.

"See also" cards refer you to other subjects closely related to the one you are interested in. Under these other subjects you may find listings of books that contain information useful to you. Look at the example at the top of the next page.

See Also Card

> Animals
>
>   see also
>
> Desert animals   Marine animals
> Domestic animals   Pets
> Fresh-water animals
>
>   also names of individual animals, e.g., Dogs

Exercises

A For each group below, write the entries in the order in which they would appear in the card catalog. Use the word-by-word system of alphabetizing.

1. a. LAW
   b. The last frontier
   c. Last race
   d. The law of life
   e. The last out
   f. Law enforcement

2. a. The new math
   b. Newman, James R.
   c. NEWSPAPERS
   d. NEW YEAR
   e. New tall tales of Pecos Bill
   f. Newton, Isaac

B Use the card catalog to find the title, author, call number, and publication date of a book for three of the following subjects.

1. Metrics
2. Alligators
3. Tahiti
4. Country and western music
5. Home Repair
6. Greek Drama

C Imagine you are a librarian who has been assigned the job of writing the "See also" cards for the card catalog. Write one "See also" card for each of these general headings: *Sports, Dance, U.S. History*, and *Cooking*.

4

The Reference Section

Every library has either a reference room or a reference section. The resource materials shelved in this section may be the most valuable resources the library has to offer you. However, to take advantage of these materials you must know what they are and how to use them.

Basic Resources

The basic resource materials available to you are these:

dictionaries
encyclopedias
almanacs and yearbooks
atlases
biographical references

pamphlets, booklets, and
    catalogs
*Readers' Guide to Periodical
    Literature*
periodicals

Following are descriptions of each of these resources.

Dictionaries Dictionaries are among the best general references. They tell you the spelling, pronunciation, and meaning of a word. They also give you brief information about many subjects, including people, places, abbreviations, and foreign terms.

Dictionaries on special subjects—science, economics, history, music, art—define terms that are used in a particular subject area. The following are some special subject dictionaries: *Dictionary of Costume*, *Oxford Dictionary of Music*, *Dictionary of Architecture*, and *A New Dictionary of Physics*.

One group of dictionaries deals with specific aspects of the English language, such as synonyms and antonyms, rhymes, slang, Americanisms, and etymology. A **thesaurus**, for example, is a dictionary of words that have similar meanings. Other dictionaries of language include *Abbreviations Dictionary*, *A Dictionary of Slang and Unconventional English*, *A Dictionary of Word and Phrase Origins*, *Mathew's Dictionary of Americanisms*, *The New Roget's Thesaurus in Dictionary Form*, and *Wood's Unabridged Rhyming Dictionary*.

Encyclopedias These are collections of articles on nearly every known subject. These articles are arranged alphabetically by subject into volumes. The volumes are shelved as sets. The last volume of each set is the index. You would use this index to find all the articles in the encyclopedia that are on or related to the subject you are researching. A few of the most commonly used encyclopedias are *Collier's Encyclopedia*, *The World Book Encyclopedia*, and *Encyclopaedia Britannica*.

Many special encyclopedias are devoted entirely to one subject. These encyclopedias provide more detailed information than a general encyclopcdia. Take note of the many special encyclopedias shelved in your library. You may find them useful the next time you need to do research. A few special encyclopedias are the following: *Encyclopedia of Jazz*, *Encyclopedia of Sports*, *Reader's Encyclopedia of American Literature*, *McGraw-Hill Encyclopedia of Science and Technology*, *Encyclopedia of World Art*, and *Encyclopedia of Animal Care*.

Almanacs and Yearbooks Almanacs and yearbooks are packed with facts and statistics. Since these books are published every year, they are an excellent resource when you need up-to-date information. From an almanac or yearbook, for example, you can find out how much rain fell on Seattle last year and who were the longest-lived triplets on record. The best-known books of this kind are *World Almanac and Book of Facts*; *Information Please Almanac, Atlas, and Yearbook*; *Guinness Book of World Records*; and *Guinness Book of Sports Records*.

Atlases An atlas is a reference book that contains large, detailed maps of various parts of the world. Many atlases also provide other types of geographical information. This information may be statistics about populations, temperatures, oceans, and/or deserts. No two atlases publish exactly the same type of information.

Biographical References Both a dictionary and an encyclopedia will give you information about people. However, the best references to use when you need detailed information about a person are biographical references. They are specific subject books that deal only with information about people. These are a few commonly used biographical reference books: *Current*

Biography, *Who's Who in America*, *Webster's Biographical Dictionary*, *Contemporary Authors*, and *International Who's Who*.

Vertical File Many libraries have file cabinets where they keep pamphlets, booklets, catalogs, handbooks, and clippings about a variety of subjects. Often these subjects are of particular interest to the people who use that library. The file may also contain useful information on careers or even illustrations that would be useful for a report.

Readers' Guide to Periodical Literature This is a special index that can help you track down articles in magazines and newspapers. You can use this guide in much the same way as you use the card catalog. The information is listed alphabetically by author and by subject. The following is an excerpt from the *Readers' Guide*.

Video discs *See* Videodiscs
Video festivals
        California
  National Video Festival: fast-forward. M. Brody.
    il *Film Comment* 22:73-4 Ja/F '86
Video games
  Armageddon under the Christmas tree [Nuclear
    War board game and Balance of Power
    computer game] A. Gross. il *Technol Rev*
    89:73-4 F/Mr '86
  Computer gaming. *Futurist* 20:34 Ja/F '86
  Eddie and the Cruisers [Cycle staff challenges
    E. Lawson on Grand Prix racing video game,
    Hang-on] K. Vreeke. il pors *Cycle* 37:75-7+ F
    '86
  That's entertainment [computer games] il *Sci Dig*
    94:77 Ja '86
        Educational use
  The Halley Project: a mission in our solar
    system. J. E. Mosley. *Sky Telesc* 71:295 Mr '86
        Psychological aspects
  Who plays adventure games . . . and why. J.
    Hayes. il *Pers Comput* 10:95-9+ Mr '86
        Testing
  A murder mystery [Deja Vu] P. Honan. il *Pers
    Comput* 10:158 Mr '86
  Winter league [baseball programs] R. Scibilia. il
    Pop Mech 163:36 F '86

Notice that much of the information in the *Readers' Guide* is abbreviated. You will find explanations of these abbreviations in the front pages of the guide. The following diagram shows the parts of an entry. Study this diagram for a better understanding of what the abbreviations stand for.

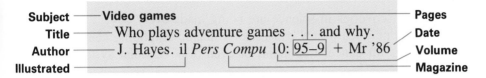

Periodicals These are magazines and newspapers that are issued at various times throughout the year, or periodically. Magazines are usually shelved alphabetically by title and then arranged chronologically—according to the date they were issued. Newspapers are generally grouped together in their own section and arranged in the same way as magazines. If you don't find the issue you need on the shelves, ask a librarian for help. Older copies of periodicals may be kept in storage or recorded on microfilm.

Exercise

What is the best reference source to use to find answers to the following questions? Write one of the following: *Dictionary, General Encyclopedia, Subject Encyclopedia, Almanac or Yearbook, Atlas, Biographical Reference, Vertical File, Readers' Guide to Periodical Literature*, or *Periodical*.

1. What does the abbreviation ALDS stand for?
2. What historical event happened in the Middle East on November 19, 1977?
3. Who was Alexandre Dumas?
4. Which magazine contains the most recent article on holograms?
5. What new information does the magazine article on holograms give you?
6. What is meant by "sweet jazz"?
7. What careers are available in hotel management?
8. What is the best route from Chicago to New York City?
9. What are some general facts about horses?
10. What does the term *belabor* mean?

Crossroads

English and Science

New discoveries in science are being made every day. Scientists may learn new causes for volcanic eruptions, identify new drugs for cancer treatment, or even discover solar systems.

The most important of these discoveries eventually are presented in textbooks and other books. However, when you need to find the latest information, perhaps for a science class report, you need to consult more timely sources. You can consult specialized reference books that are updated yearly, such as *Science Year: The World Book Science Annual.* You also can consult periodicals—magazines and newspapers.

Your library has issues of many different magazines and newspapers. Several of these periodicals are devoted strictly to science. Some may contain articles on just one kind of science, such as medicine or ecology. Others may contain articles on a broad range of scientific topics.

Activity What science resources are available at your library? How useful and interesting are they to you? Make a list of as many science periodicals and science reference books as you can find. Beside the name of each source, write the particular science to which it is devoted. If it contains articles related to many sciences, write *general.* Choose two periodicals or current reference books from your list and make a brief summary of them. Answer the following questions: (1.) Can a general reader understand the articles, or does the reader need specialized information? (2.) Do the articles make their subjects sound exciting? You will need to skim at least one issue of each periodical to evaluate it.

Application and Review

A **Finding Library Materials** Imagine that you are a librarian who is asked the following questions. Write the answers.

1. Where can I find listings of all the Kurt Vonnegut books this library carries?
2. Now I know which Vonnegut book I want, but where should I go to get it?
3. I want to find a book that has *JUV* printed above its call number. Where should I look?
4. Where in the library will I find the atlases?
5. Where can I find the latest copy of *National Geographic* magazine?
6. Where can I find out what magazine articles have recently been written on volcanoes in the Hawaiian islands?
7. Where can I find an illustration for my report on our town?
8. Which reference work would give me general information about Egypt and its history?
9. In what type of reference work should I look to find a list of synonyms for *greedy*?
10. What type of book would tell me the world's record for high jumping?

B **Using Library Materials** Suppose that you must explain to another student how to read an entry from the *Readers' Guide to Periodical Literature*. This entry is given below. Copy it on your paper and label the following parts: *Subject, Title, Author, Magazine, Volume, Pages,* and *Date*. Then, tell whether the article listed is illustrated.

Video jockeys
    The MTV VJs: airheads of the air? D. Maychick.
        Mademoiselle 92 : 58 Ja '86

17
Dictionary and Spelling Skills

Looking at these photos, it's plain that a plane is not always the same thing as a plane. The word refers to a tool, if you're a carpenter; to an aircraft, if you're a pilot; and to a flat surface, if you're a mathematician.

A dictionary and a knowledge of spelling rules are two tools you can use to gain a better understanding of words and therefore improve your writing. In this chapter you will learn how they can help you find the best words for the job and then spell those words correctly.

Finding a Dictionary Entry

In order to use a dictionary effectively, you need to know how it is organized. Dictionary entries are easy to find. All entries are listed in alphabetical order. In addition, guide words at the top of each page tell you the first and last words on that page.

Alphabetical Order

Alphabetical order is the usual order of the letters of the alphabet. The words found in the dictionary, called **entry words**, are listed in alphabetical order.

Words that begin with the same letter are alphabetized according to the second letter. Words that begin with the same first two letters are alphabetized according to the third letter, and so on. The words in each of the columns below are in alphabetical order.

anteater	**aa**rdvark	grass**h**opper
groundhog	**al**batross	gre**y**hound
hedgehog	**an**teater	gri**ff**in

Guide Words

Guide words are the two words printed in heavy black type at the top of a dictionary page. They give the first and last entry words that appear on the page. The guide word on the left tells you the first word on the page. The guide word on the right tells you the last word. Entry words that fall alphabetically between these two words will be found on that page.

Alma   25   **alter**

Al·ma (al′mə) [L. fem. of *almus*, nourishing] a feminine name
al·ma ma·ter (al′mə mät′ər, mät′ər) [L., fostering mother] **1.** the college or school that one attended **2.** its anthem, or hymn
al·ma·nac (ôl′mə nak′, al′-) *n.* [< ML. < LGr. *almenichiaka*, calendar] **1.** a calendar with astronomical data, weather forecasts, etc. **2.** a book published annually, containing information, usually statistical, on many subjects
al·might·y (ôl mit′ē) *adj.* [< OE. < *eal*, all + *mihtig*, mighty] **1.** having unlimited power; all-powerful **2.** [Slang] great; extreme —*adv.* [Slang] extremely —**the Almighty** God —**al·might′i·ly** *adv.* —**al·might′i·ness** *n.*
al·mond (ä′mənd, am′ənd, al′mənd) *n.* [< OFr. < L. < Gr. *amygdalē*] **1.** the edible, nutlike kernel of a small, dry, peachlike fruit **2.** the tree bearing this fruit **3.** anything shaped like an almond, oval and pointed at one or both ends —**al′mond·like′** *adj.*
al·mon·er (al′mən ər, ä′mən-) *n.* one who distributes alms, as for a church, etc.
al·most (ôl′mōst, ôl′mōst) *adv.* [OE. *eallmæst*: see ALL & MOST] very nearly but not completely
alms (ämz) *n., pl.* **alms** [< OE. < LL. < Gr. *eleēmosynē*, alms < *eleos*, pity] money, food, etc. given to poor people —**alms′giv′er** *n.*
alms·house (-hous′) *n.* formerly, a home for people too poor to support themselves; poorhouse
al·oe (al′ō) *n., pl.* **-oes** [< L. < Gr. *aloē* < ? Heb.] **1.** a South

al·pac·a (al pak′ə) *n., pl.* **-pac′as, -pac′a:** see PLURAL, II, D, 1 [Sp. < SAmInd. *allpaca*] **1.** a domesticated S. American mammal related to the llama, with brown or black fleecy wool **2.** this wool **3.** a cloth woven from this wool, often mixed with other fibers **4.** a glossy cloth of cotton and wool, used for linings, suits, etc.
al·pen·horn (al′pən hôrn′) *n.* [G., Alpine horn] a curved, wooden, powerful-sounding horn, from five to twelve feet long, used by Swiss Alpine herdsmen for signaling: also **alp′horn′**
al·pen·stock (-stäk′) *n.* [G., Alpine staff] an iron-pointed staff used by mountain climbers
al·pha (al′fə) *n.* [Gr. < Phoen. name whence Heb. *aleph*: see ALEPH] **1.** the first letter of the Greek alphabet (A, α) **2.** the beginning of anything **3.** the brightest star in a constellation
al·pha·bet (al′fə bet′) *n.* [< LL. < LGr. < Gr.: see ALPHA & BETA] **1.** the letters of a language, arranged in a traditional order **2.** a system of signs or symbols used to indicate letters or speech sounds **3.** the first elements, or a subject
al·pha·bet·i·cal (al′fə bet′i k′l) *adj.* **1.** of or using an alphabet **2.** in the usual order of the alphabet Also **al′pha·bet′ic** —**al′pha·bet′i·cal·ly** *adv.*
al·pha·bet·ize (al′fə bə tīz′) *vt.* **-ized′, -iz′ing** **1.** to arrange

ALPENHORN

ALMOND (shell & kernel)

328

Exercises

A Write the words in each of the following columns in alphabetical order:

1	2	3	4
franc	elm	Mercury	heel
dollar	beech	Earth	head
krone	birch	Mars	hand
lira	apple	Neptune	heart
mark	aspen	Jupiter	hose

B After each set of guide words in the following list, an entry word is given. Write *Before, With,* or *After* to indicate whether the word would come on a page before, with, or after the one on which the guide words appear.

EXAMPLE **Guide Words**   **Entry Word**
        composition comrade   computer

Because it falls alphabetically between *composition* and *comrade*, *computer* would be found on the page with these guide words. Therefore, *With* is the correct answer.

	Guide Words		**Entry Word**
1.	**career**	**carnivorous**	cargo
2.	**drill**	**drop**	drowsy
3.	**enlist**	**enter**	enormous
4.	**gear**	**general**	generic
5.	**titled**	**toboggan**	together

Finding a Word

Sometimes you want to look up a word, but you aren't sure how to spell it. If your dictionary has a word-finder table, this feature can help you find the entry word. A word-finder lists the different spellings for the various sounds that form the word. To use the table, find the spellings for the sounds in the word you want. Then look for the word under these different spellings until you find it.

A word-finder table appears at the front of many dictionaries. The table at the top of the next page is a simplified word-finder table.

Word-Finder Table

If the word begins with a sound like. . .	then also try the spellings. . .	as in the words. . .
a in care	ai	air
e in get	a	any
e in here	ea, ee	ear, eerie
f in fine	ph	phrase
g in go	gh, gu	ghoul, guard
h in hat	wh	who
j in jam	g	gym
k in keep	c, ch, q	can, chorus, quick
n in no	gn, kn	gnaw, kneel
o in long	a, ou	all, ought
r in red	rh	rhyme
s in sew	c, ps, sc	cent, psychology, scene
sh in ship	s	sure
t in top	th	thyme
u in under	a, o	ago, onion
u in use	you, yu	youth, yule
ur in fur	ear	earn
w in will	wh	wheat
z in zero	x	xylophone

Exercise

Use the word-finder table and your dictionary to identify each of the words described below. Then write the correct spelling of each word.

1. the word that sounds like *foto* and means a picture taken with a camera
2. the word that sounds like *Tieland* and names a country in Southeast Asia
3. the word that sounds like the name *Kay* and is the name for a wharf or dock
4. the word that sounds like *new* and is the name of an African antelope
5. a word that sounds like *cent* and means an odor

2
Using a Dictionary Entry

A dictionary entry provides a great deal of information about each of thousands of words. That is why dictionary entries are written in a standard sort of shorthand. To make use of your dictionary, you must be able to decode this shorthand.

Word Division

The way each entry word is printed shows you how to divide the word into its syllables. Either a space is left between the syllables or a dot is placed between them.

> bar gain   bar•gain

Sometimes an entire word will not fit at the end of the line you are writing or typing. Part of the word will have to run onto the next line. When that happens, you must divide the word between syllables and use a hyphen to show that the word continues on the next line.

Pronunciation

A dictionary entry also tells you how to pronounce a word. This pronunciation appears immediately after each entry word, and it is respelled with symbols. The key for deciphering the code is called a **pronunciation key**. It appears in the front of the dictionary. A shortened form of this key is also at the bottom of each of the dictionary's entry pages. How might such a key have helped the caveman in the cartoon?

"Look out, Thak! It's a ... a ... Dang! Never can pronounce those things!"

Sample Pronunciation Key

a	ask	o͞o	ooze	ch	chin	ə	a in ago
ā	ape	oo	look	sh	she		e in agent
ä	ah	yo͞o	use	th	thin		i in sanity
e	elf	yoo	united	*th*	then		o in comply
ē	even	oi	oil	zh	azure		u in focus
i	is	ou	out	ŋ	ring		
ī	ice	u	up	'	able (ā'b'l)	ər	perhaps
ō	open	ur	urn				
ô	all						

When pronouncing a word of more than one syllable, you need to know which syllable to say more strongly. Accent marks in the respelling show you where to put this heavier emphasis. An accent mark looks like this: ('). Some words have two accent marks. The darker one tells you which syllable gets more emphasis.

rid•ing (rīd'ing)
hast•y (hās'tē)
bas•ket•ball (bas'kit bôl')

Exercises

A Rewrite the following words, placing a dot between the syllables. Use your dictionary for help.

1. jellyfish
2. complete
3. narrow
4. lawyer
5. preserve
6. brainstorm
7. sushi
8. reading
9. unable
10. thirteenth

B Write on your paper the following groups of words. Next to each word, write the way it is pronounced. Then note the words within each group that rhyme. Use your dictionary.

1	2	3	4	5
daughter	cuff	creator	knight	dough
laughter	rough	greater	height	tow
water	through	grater	weight	sew

Definitions and Parts of Speech

The **definition** is the meaning given for an entry word.
Because most words have more than one meaning, definitions are
usually numbered.

When a word can function as more than one part of speech,
the dictionary will indicate the parts of speech with abbreviations
before the various definitions. As you will see in the example
below, the numbering starts again after each part of speech.
These are the most common abbreviations for the parts of
speech:

n.	noun	**adj.**	adjective
pron.	pronoun	**adv.**	adverb
v.	verb		

A definition may be followed by an example of the way the
word is used. This example will be a short phrase or sentence
printed in italics or enclosed in brackets.

Examine the entry for *country* below. Seven different
meanings are given. Five are definitions for *country* used as a
noun and two are for *country* used as an adjective. After the first
definition, there is an example in brackets of the word used as a
noun. Other examples are given in later definitions.

coun•try (kun' trē) **n.,** *pl.* **-trles** [< OFr. < VL. *contrata,* that
which is beyond < L. *contra,* opposite] **1.** an area of land;
region [wooded *country*] **2.** the whole territory of a
nation **3.** the people of a nation [a broadcast to the whole
country] **4.** the land where one was born or is a citizen
["my *country,* 'tis of thee"] **5.** land with farms and small
towns; rural region —*adj.* **1.** of, in, or from a rural
district **2.** like that of the country; rustic [*country* music]

Exercises

A Write the words printed in italics in the following sentences.
For each, give the dictionary meaning that best fits the word as it
is used in the sentence.

1. These *candid* photographs of the children really capture the
   festival spirit.
2. I want a skirt with a lot of *frills* for the dance.

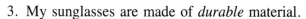

3. My sunglasses are made of *durable* material.
4. My parents *enclosed* our yard with a wooden fence.
5. My father is a *modest* and dependable person.
6. I sell newspapers from a *kiosk* downtown.
7. Bonita and I both *prefer* rainy afternoons.
8. The dog created a *flurry* in our math class.
9. That trip to the beach was a *lark*.
10. The *ponderous* movie put us to sleep.

B Look up the following words in your dictionary. Write two sentences for each word. In each sentence, use the word as a different part of speech. Underline the words in the sentences and write their parts of speech.

1. chestnut   2. bridge   3. correspondent   4. loft   5. farm

Synonyms

Synonyms are words that have similar meanings. For example, the words *big* and *large* are synonyms. *Happy* and *glad* are synonyms.

Look at the dictionary entry for *story* that appears below. The abbreviation *SYN.* appears after the definitions. This abbreviation introduces a list of synonyms.

> **sto·ry**[1] (stôr′ē) **n.,** *pl.* **-ries** [<OFr. < L. < Gr. *historia*: see HISTORY] **1.** the telling of an event or series of events, whether true or made-up; account; narration **2.** an anecdote or joke **3.** a piece of fictional writing shorter than a novel; narrative; tale; specif., *same as* SHORT STORY **4.** the plot of a novel, play, etc. **5.** *a)* a report or rumor *b)* [Colloq.] a falsehood or fib **6.** romantic legend or history ☆**7.** a news event or a report of it, as in the newspapers **–vt. -ried, -ry·ing** to decorate with paintings, etc. of scenes from history or legend
> **SYN.–story** is a general term for any informative or entertaining account, either oral or written, of something that really happened or that is partly or wholly made-up; **narrative,** a more formal term, is typically a prose account of a happening or series of happenings, either real or fictional; **tale** usually means a simple, leisurely story, more or less loosely organized, esp. one that is made-up or legendary; **anecdote** is a term applied to a short, entertaining, often instructive account of a single incident, usually personal or biographical

The list of synonyms that follows the abbreviation *SYN.* is called a synonymy. The **synonymy** explains the special meaning and use of each synonym. Sometimes a synonymy will also give phrases or sentences showing how each synonym is used. A synonymy can help you choose the best word for what you want to say or write.

The dictionary entry for *story* lists three words with meanings similar to *story: narrative, tale,* and *anecdote.* The special meaning and use of each synonym is provided. Can you see how each word means something slightly different?

Exercises

A Write an appropriate synonym for the word *story* in each of the following sentences, using the synonymy given on page 334.

1. I am reading a fascinating *story* about the French Revolution.
2. The guests on a talk show usually tell lots of funny *stories*.
3. We have to write a *story* about something important that has happened in our lives.
4. I could sit for hours listening to my grandmother's wonderful *stories* of talking fish and enchanted forests.
5. I like Ms. Kaplan's class best because she teaches us with short, funny *stories*.
6. Let's sit around the campfire and make up *stories*.
7. Did you read the *story* about the young boy who was lost in the Amazon?
8. This *story* is legendary.
9. My uncles love to swap *stories* about growing up during the Great Depression.
10. Many *stories* come from ancient folklore.

B Use a dictionary to find two synonyms for each of the following words. Write a sentence for each synonym. Underline the synonym.

1. comfort	3. information	5. flash	7. agree	9. soft
2. funny	4. noticeable	6. eject	8. fair	10. false

3
Spelling and Writing with the Aid of a Dictionary

A dictionary is one of the most useful reference books you can have. It can help you spell, divide, and use words correctly. It can also help you find the right words to express yourself clearly. You will refer to a dictionary most frequently, however, when you're proofreading and revising your writing. (See Chapter 5 for more information on proofreading.)

Exercise

Rewrite the following paragraph according to the directions below it. Refer to a dictionary as needed.

> (1) People react to the colours that surround them. (2) A red room tends to make people feel jumpey and unsetled. (3) It can even lift a person's blood pressure. (4) Restaraunt owners who want their customers to eat fast and leave quick might decorate their restaurants in red. (5) Dark blue is a calming and relaxing colour. (6) It can lower a purson's blood pressure. (7) The dark blue seats and carpeting found on some air planes probly help relax passengers. (8) What is the colour of the roome in which you feel most happy?

1. Use the American spelling of *colour* in sentences 1, 5, and 8.
2. Correct the two misspellings in sentence 2.
3. Replace *lift* in sentence 3 with a more appropriate word.
4. Correct the misspelling in sentence 4.
5. Use the adverb form of *quick* in sentence 4.
6. Correct the hyphen error in sentence 5.
7. Correct the spelling error in sentence 6.
8. Combine the two parts of a compound word in sentence 7.
9. Correct the misspelling in sentence 7.
10. Correct the misspelling in sentence 8.

4
Spelling Tips and Rules

The dictionary is a useful tool for writing. However, you have another tool as well—your own understanding of how words are spelled. By knowing how to spell correctly, you will save yourself many hours of flipping through dictionary pages looking for words. You will also be better able to spell difficult words when a dictionary is not nearby. Learn to be a better speller by studying the following rules and methods for improving your spelling.

How to Become a Better Speller

1. **Find out what your personal spelling demons are and conquer them.** Do this by listing and studying the words you misspelled in old compositions and other homework.
2. **Pronounce words carefully.** Pronouncing words correctly helps you to write them correctly. If you write *probly* for *probably*, you could be mispronouncing the word.
3. **Get into the habit of seeing the letters in a word.** Take a careful good look at new or difficult words. Look at a word like *mirror*, for example, and spell it to yourself: m-i-r-r-o-r.
4. **Think up a memory device for difficult words.** The following examples show memory devices that have worked for others.

> a**cq**uaint (*cq*) To get a**cq**uainted, I will *seek* you.
> princi**pal** (*pal*) The princi**pal** is my *pal*.
> princi**ple** (*ple*) Follow this princi**ple**, *please*.
> bus**i**ness (*i*) **I** was involved in big business.

How to Master the Spelling of Particular Words
1. Look at the word and say it one syllable at a time.
2. Look at the letters and say each one.
3. Write the word without looking at your list.
4. Now look at your list and see whether you spelled the word correctly. If you did, repeat steps 3 and 4.
5. If you made a mistake, note exactly what it was. Then repeat steps 3 and 4 several times.

Spelling Rules

One of the best ways to become a better speller is to learn the following spelling rules. Once you have learned them, you will become a better speller.

Words Ending in a Silent e

When a suffix beginning with a vowel is added to a word ending in a silent *e*, the *e* is usually dropped.

relate + -ion = relation   create + -ive = creative
amaze + -ing = amazing   fame + -ous = famous

When a suffix beginning with a consonant is added to a word ending in a silent *e*, the *e* is usually retained.

hope + -ful = hopeful   noise + -less = noiseless
state + -ment = statement   wide + -ly = widely

The following words are exceptions.

truly   argument   ninth   wholly

Words Ending in y

When a suffix is added to a word ending in *y* preceded by a consonant, the *y* is usually changed to *i*.

easy + -ly = easily   sixty + -eth = sixtieth

When *-ing* is added, however, the *y* does not change.

hurry + -ed = hurried   *but*   hurry + -ing = hurrying
study + -ed = studied   *but*   study + -ing = studying

When a suffix is added to a word ending in *y* preceded by a vowel, the *y* usually does not change.

employ + -er = employer   play + -ing = playing

Exercise

Proofread the following sentences. Rewrite each misspelled word correctly.

1. Our class is competeing in the state science fair.
2. The gymnast's performance was truely amazeing.

3. My brother and I spent the afternoon rakeing leaves.
4. The nurse placed the baby carfully on her shoulder and patted her back.
5. I have enjoied playing these duets with you.
6. I carryed the heavy platter quite easyly.
7. It was truly exciteing to meet the professional football playiers.
8. My sister's wedding was planned to be on her twentyeth birthday.
9. I have been lazyer than ever on this beautyful day.
10. The operator hasteily relayed the message.

Words Ending in a Consonant

In words of one syllable that end in one consonant preceded by one vowel, double the final consonant before adding *-ing, -ed,* or *-er*.

> bat + -ed = batted   bed + -ing = bedding
> run + -er = runner   grab + -ed = grabbed

The rule does not apply to words of one syllable that end in one consonant preceded by two vowels.

> treat + -ing = treating   loot + -ed = looted
> near + -er = nearer   feel + -ing = feeling

Exercise

Add the suffixes to the following words.

1. dig + -ing	6. win + -er	11. hop + -ing
2. fear + -ing	7. split + -ing	12. big + -er
3. fat + -er	8. drop + -ed	13. creep + -ing
4. slap + -ed	9. roar + -ed	14. swim + -er
5. pat + -ing	10. let + -ing	15. pair + -ed

The Suffixes -ness and -ly

When the suffix *-ly* is added to a word ending in *l*, both *l*'s are retained. When *-ness* is added to a word ending in *n*, retain both *n*'s.

> actual + -ly = actually   thin + -ness = thinness

Prefixes

When a prefix is added to a word, do not change the spelling of the base word.

mis- + spell = misspell   re- + place = replace
il- + legal = illegal   im- + perfect = imperfect
un- + even = uneven   dis- + approve = disapprove
pre- + record = prerecord ir- + regular = irregular

Exercise

Proofread the following sentences. Rewrite each misspelled word correctly.

1. The landlord is disatisfied with the people who live upstairs.
2. We received a thoughtfuly written thank-you note.
3. What might happen if an iresistible force met an imovable object?
4. If I am not mistaken, we are practicaly neighbors.
5. Our car is parked legally, but yours is in an ilegal space.
6. My ceramic vase is slightly mishapen.
7. Scrooge's meaness gave way to kindness and charity.
8. If you don't write carefuly, your handwriting may be ilegible.
9. They are actualy working to elect our former governor.
10. Unoticed, I left the theater and rentered the street.

Words with the "Seed" Sound

Only one English word ends in -*sede: supersede*. Three words end in *ceed: exceed, proceed,* and *succeed*.
All other words ending in the sound *seed* are spelled with *cede*.

concede   precede   recede   secede

Words with ie *and* ei

When the sound is long *e* (ē) the word is spelled *ie* except after *c*.

I BEFORE *E*			EXCEPT AFTER *C*		
believe	shield	yield	receive	ceiling	deceive
niece	brief	field	conceive	conceit	receipt

The following words are exceptions to this rule:

either   weird   species
neither   seize   leisure

The Red Horses. Franz Marc.

Exercise

Proofread the following sentences. Rewrite each misspelled word correctly.

1. Red horses don't seem so wierd when you know why the artist painted them that way.
2. Artist Franz Marc concieved a color code to use in his paintings.
3. He used red to reppresent matter.
4. He succeded in finding new ways to use color.
5. Marc also used horses intentionaly.
6. He intendded them to be symbols of purity and harmony.
7. Have you noticed that the curves of the horses and the hills are simillar?
8. Marc beleived that successfuly unifying these would get across a sense of harmony in nature.
9. The career of this talented German artist was sadly breif.
10. It spanned just the eleven years preceeding World War I.

5
Words Commonly Confused

The following words are often misused and misspelled. Many of these words are homonyms. **Homonyms** are words that have the same sound or the same spelling but different meanings.

As you look at these words, notice how their meanings differ. Try to think of memory devices to help you recall which meaning belongs with which word.

accept means "to agree to something" or "to receive something willingly."

except means "to exclude" or "to omit." As a preposition, *except* means "but" or "excluding."

> Kay did *accept* the Hansens' invitation to go camping.
> The class will be *excepted* from locker inspection this week.
> Everyone *except* the team will sit in the bleachers.

all ready expresses a "complete readiness or preparedness."
already means "previously" or "before."

> The pilots and their crew were *all ready* for the landing.
> We had *already* made arrangements to take the early train.

capital means "excellent, most serious, or most important; seat of government." In law it refers to a "very serious" crime.
capitol is a "building in which a state legislature meets."
the Capitol is "the building in Washington, D.C., in which the United States Congress meets."

> The man had been arrested for a *capital* offense.
> The committee held a meeting at the *capitol* building.
> We visited the *Capitol* in Washington, D.C., last summer.

des′ert means "a wilderness" or "dry, sandy, barren region."
de•sert′ means "to abandon."
dessert (note different spelling) is a sweet, such as cake or pie.

> The Mojave *Desert* is part of the Great American *Desert*.
> When we ran out of fuel, we *deserted* our car.
> Jon and Sue baked a strawberry pie for *dessert*.

hear means "to listen to," or "take notice of."
here means "in this place."

> Because of poor acoustics, we couldn't *hear* the speaker.
> We finally arrived *here* in Seattle after a delay in Denver.

its is a word that indicates ownership.
it's is a contraction for *it is* or *it has*.

> The city lost *its* power during the thunderstorm.
> *It's* almost noon and I haven't finished my work.

lose means "to mislay or suffer the loss of something."
loose means "free," or "not fastened."

> Our car began to *lose* its power as we neared the summit.
> The hinges on the back gate are quite *loose*.

past means "that which has ended or gone by."
passed is the past tense of *pass* and means "went by."

> Our *past* experience has taught us we can win.
> We *passed* through the Grand Tetons on our vacation.

piece refers to a "section or part of something."
peace means "calm or quiet," and "freedom from disagreements or quarrels."

> We cut the firewood into smaller *pieces*.
> There was a certain *peace* as I sat and watched the sunrise.

principal describes something "of chief or central importance."
It also refers to the head of an elementary or high school.
principle is a "basic truth, standard, or rule of behavior."

> The *principal* cities of France include Paris, Marseilles,
>   Lyons, and Nice.
> The *principal* of our school presented the awards.
> We will study the *principles* of democracy.

quiet refers to "no noise" or to something rather "peaceful or motionless."
quite means "really or truly," and it can also refer to "a considerable degree or extent."

> Everyone was absolutely *quiet* during the ceremony.
> We were *quite* sure that the school bus would be late.

stationary means "fixed or unmoving."
stationery refers to "paper and envelopes used for writing letters."

> The new digital scoreboard will be *stationary* in the large gym.
> Two students in my art class designed the school *stationery*.

there means "in that place."
their means "belonging to them."
they're is a contraction for *they are*.

> Please put the groceries over *there* on the counter.
> In 1803, Lewis and Clark led *their* expedition west.
> Sue and Pam are skiing, and *they're* going snowmobiling, too.

to means "toward," or "in the direction of."
too means "also" or "very."
two is the number *2*.

> We all went *to* the zoo last weekend.
> It was much *too* cold to go cross-country skiing.
> *Two* television stations carried the President's speech.

weather refers to "atmospheric conditions such as temperature or cloudiness."
whether helps to express choice or alternative.

> Daily *weather* reports are studied by meteorologists.
> *Whether* we call or write for reservations, we must do it soon.

whose is the possessive form of *who*.
who's is a contraction for *who is* or *who has*.

> Do you know *whose* bicycle is chained to the parking meter?
> *Who's* going to volunteer to help?

your is the possessive form of *you*.
you're is a contraction of *you are*.

> Please take *your* books back to the library today.
> *You're* going there right after school, aren't you?

Exercise

Write the correct word given in parentheses in each of the following sentences.

1. Besides bananas and eggs, please buy a paper (to, too).
2. Is Beth (all ready, already) for her flute recital?
3. Be sure you use (capital, capitol) letters correctly.
4. Do you know (who's, whose) scarf this is?
5. Naturally, (they're, their, there) going to eat breakfast before the game.
6. The weather (hear, here) has been extremely cold.
7. (Its, It's) hard to remember certain dates in history.
8. This button has gotten so (lose, loose) I'm afraid it will fall off.
9. This (past, passed) year I had a special tutor in math.
10. The Treaty of Versailles established (piece, peace).
11. The (principal, principle) actors took their bows.
12. I am (quiet, quite) nervous about going to high school.
13. I received a note of thanks on the mayor's official (stationary, stationery).
14. Our neighbors never let (there, their) cat out at night.
15. (Their, They're) widening Main Street to add a turn lane.
16. All the players (accept, except) the goalie were arguing.
17. Does your family own (too, two) cars?
18. The sportscaster cannot predict (weather, whether) the Bears or the Eagles will win.
19. (Whose, Who's) coming up to bat next?
20. Call us when (your, you're) ready for dinner.

English and Physical Education

What sport is described here?

> "The players are all in place on the *cancha*. Now the server smashes the *pelota* off the far wall. Will his opponent catch it in his *cesta* before or after the first bounce? If he misses, the server scores."

You probably are familiar with terms like *court, dribble, glove,* and *offside* from the popular sports of basketball, baseball, and football. However, the terms in a sport like jai alai, described above, may sound strange. Even the name jai alai (hī´ lī´), which comes from a Basque word meaning "merry festival," may be difficult to spell and to pronounce.

Sports like jai alai, polo, and rugby are becoming more popular. When you read about them in the newspaper or watch them on television, you'll enjoy them more if you understand the "language" of the sport. Some of these special terms may be in your own dictionary or an encyclopedia. Others will require a special dictionary of sports terms. Specialized dictionaries can help you make the terms of many games and sports as understandable as *touchdown* and *home run.*

Activity Choose one of the sports listed below. Using at least five terms from the sport you choose, write a paragraph describing how it is played. Then, use a dictionary of sports terms to define the terms and provide their pronunciations.

1. lacrosse 3. polo 5. curling 7. rugby 9. cricket
2. discus 4. billiards 6. fencing 8. horseshoes 10. croquet

Application and Review

A Using the Dictionary Follow the directions for each item below. Use a dictionary when necessary. If your dictionary does not have a word-finder, use the one on page 330.

1. Arrange the following words in alphabetical order: *enigmatic, energy, energize, excite,* and *dance.*
2. Write two words that you would find on a dictionary page with the guide words **glower-----go**.
3. Write the correct spelling of the name for ancient Egyptian kings which sounds like *fairrow.*
4. Divide the word *glorious* into syllables. Then write the pronunciation of the word, showing the accented syllable.
5. Write the meaning of the word *frog* in the following sentence: The jacket is fastened with *frogs.*
6. Use *motor* as different parts of speech in two sentences.
7. Write a synonym for *curious.*
8. Write the first, or preferred, spelling of the word *theatre.*
9. Write the adverb form of *bad.*
10. Look up *Pin Wheel* in your dictionary and write it correctly.

B Spelling and Using Words Correct the misspelled words in each of the following sentences.

1. We are rewriteing our skit for the talent show.
2. They keep an old-fashioned carryage in their garage.
3. Shelagh has been runing all day.
4. I have been hearring the waterfall from here.
5. The barreness of the desert amazed me.
6. Your truly welcome at our house any time.
7. It's all ready impossible to see anything but clouds.
8. Neither driver exseeded the speed limit.
9. I believe the missing puzzle peace is under the table.
10. The children must remain stationery while I take a picture.

18
Mastering
Study Skills

"Seventy-six trombones led the big parade,
With a hundred and ten cornets close at hand . . ."
Meredith Willson

How does a marching band manage to keep the trumpets from trampling the trombones and the baritones from bumping into the saxophones? The band members learn a routine and practice it.

Studying requires practice, too. Whether you are preparing a school report or gathering information on your own, a good study routine will help your efforts. This chapter explains the SQ3R study method and other study skills.

1
Getting Started

In order to complete any assignment, you must first understand exactly what is expected of you:

1. What should my final product be?
2. What will I need to do?
3. What resources will I need?
4. When is the assignment due?

Listening to Directions

You can usually get answers to the above questions from the directions for the assignment. To take directions well, you may want to follow the guidelines below.

1. Focus your attention on only the directions being given.
2. Notice how many steps are involved.
3. Associate a key word—*Read, Answer,* or *Write,* for example—with each step.
4. Ask questions to clarify any step you do not understand.
5. Repeat the directions to yourself.
6. Write down the directions.

Using an Assignment Book

No one can remember everything that is said or assigned. Therefore, you should write down each assignment in an assignment book as soon as it is given. Include the subject, the assignment itself, the date it was assigned, and the date it is due. An example page from an assignment book is shown below.

	Subject	Assignment	Date Given	Date Due
O	Science	1. Read pp. 86-94	11-6	11-7
		2. Write answers to questions on p. 94		
	Math	1. Work even-numbered problems, Ex. A, p. 62	11-6	11-7

Setting Goals

Next, you will need to determine which assignments you can and must complete by the next day and which ones you will need several days to complete. This is the first step in goal-setting. By doing this, you get an idea of what your short-term and long-term goals should be.

Your **short-term goals** are to complete those assignments due the next day. To regularly achieve your short-term goals, set aside a block of time each day. During that time, complete the assignments due the next day.

Your **long-term goals** are to complete those assignments that involve several steps and may take days or weeks to complete. To achieve your long-term goals, break the long assignment into smaller tasks. Then handle each task as a short-term goal. Decide how much time each task will take to complete. Finally, organize your time with a study plan.

Making a Study Plan

Your study plan is a schedule that shows when you will actually work on each task. This schedule will help you juggle all of your responsibilities and complete each step of a long assignment. Since each step of any assignment must be scheduled around your other daily homework and your usual activities, a study plan is very useful. The sample study plan below is for completing a book report.

Monday	Tuesday	Wednesday	Thursday	Friday	Saturday	Sunday
Library- Read			Read extra-		→	All day trip to State park
		Drum Lesson 4:30-5:30	no time on Friday	Dinner at Uncle Ron's		
Prepare and organize notes	Write rough draft	Drum Lesson 4:30-5:30		Revise draft	Help paint garage	Make final copy
		Study for math test	Youth Group 7:00-9:30		Movie with Jason and Sue	Proofread

What is wrong with Luann's study plan?

LUANN by Greg Evans
©by and permission of News America Syndicate, 1987.

Exercise

Follow the directions that are numbered and given below.

1. Record the important parts of the following assignment. Be sure to include the subject, the assignment itself, the date it was assigned, and the date it is due.

> For your science project, you are to collect at least twenty local varieties of tree leaves. Then mount the leaves on pages and label them. Write the scientific and common name beside each leaf. Today is Monday, the first. Your project will be due on Friday, the nineteenth.

2. Make a daily schedule that shows each of the following activities:

> Flute lessons—Wednesdays, 7:00–8:30 P.M.
> Orthodontist appointments—Thursdays, 4–4:30 P.M.
> Swim team—Fridays, 4:00–6:00 P.M.
> A swim meet on the 6th from 9:00 A.M.–12:00 P.M.
> A movie with friends on the 6th at 8 P.M.
> A party on the 14th from 1:00 to 5:00 P.M.
> A family vacation on the last weekend of the month.

3. Now, set up a study plan for the science assignment in question number 1. Write all the tasks in the daily schedule you have already created.

2
Using the SQ3R Study Method

SQ3R is the name of a study method. The letters stand for the following steps: **S**urvey, **Q**uestion, **R**ead, **R**ecord, and **R**eview. These five steps can help you organize your thoughts as you study and take notes. Here is a detailed explanation of how to follow the SQ3R study method:

SQ3R

Survey	Look over the material to get a general idea of what it is about. Read the titles and subtitles; notice the illustrations; read the introduction and summary.
Question	Find out what questions you should be able to answer after your reading. Preview any study questions presented at the end of the chapter or provided by your teacher. Make up your own questions by turning titles and topic headings into questions. Any illustrations, maps, tables, or graphs can also be used for questions.
Read	Read the selection to find the answers to the questions. Identify the central thoughts in each section.
Record	After reading, write your answers to the questions in your own words. Also record any other important points from the material.
Review	Try to answer each of the original questions without consulting your notes. If you can't, review the selection to find the answer. Then look over your notes to impress the material on your mind so that you will be able to recall it at a later date.

Exercise

Use the SQ3R method to study the following article. Answer the questions and follow the directions below.

1. Survey the article. Where should you look for clues about the content? What kind of clues do you have?
2. Are you given any study questions? Use the titles and subtitles to make up two additional study questions.
3. Read the selection to find the answers to all the questions.
4. Record the answers to the questions.
5. Review the article to confirm your answers. Make sure you have identified the main points. Write down the main points.

Grandma Moses

Taking Leg Bale for Security, 1975. Grandma Moses.

Grandma Moses (1860–1961) was an American painter born in Washington County, New York. Her real name was Anna May Robertson Moses. She was a farmer, a painter and the mother of ten. She began by embroidering pictures on canvas. It was not until she was in her seventies and her fingers were stiff with arthritis that she began painting. After an art collector discovered her paintings in 1938, she began to show them in museums. She became famous in her lifetime.

Her Style Grandma Moses has been called a "primitive painter"; that is, an artist with no professional training. However, she created a distinctive, unique style. The major theme of her work is life on the farm and in the country.

Her Subjects Most of Grandma Moses's paintings are landscapes of the upstate New York countryside. Towns, villages, and buildings in that area were part of her life and became the subjects of her paintings. The landscape of Virginia, especially the Shenandoah Valley, was also depicted.

For Review
What were Grandma Moses's occupations?
Why is she called a "primitive" artist?
What is the subject of most of her paintings?

3
Taking Notes

Whether you are in class, researching, or studying, it's a good idea to take notes. Taking notes will help you gather and organize the important facts, understand and remember the material, and focus your concentration on the new ideas. Your notes will later provide you with a study guide.

Using a Notebook

Keep a notebook for your notes. Divide your notebook into sections for each subject, and date each page. Your notes should consist of the key words or phrases you hear in class or read for class. Take notes clearly and in your own words.

Skimming and Scanning

Different types of reading will help you in different situations. Two important types are skimming and scanning.

The purpose of **skimming** is to get a general overview of reading material. Move your eyes over the page, looking for titles and charts that will give you an overall impression of the material. The purpose of **scanning** is to locate a specific piece of information. Move your eyes rapidly over the page. Look for key words that signal the information you want. Then read closely to find the specific details.

If you want a general overview, skimming is best. For particular information on a subject, scanning would be better.

Exercise

Read the following statements about reading activities. Decide whether each is true or false.

1. You skim through a magazine to see if you would enjoy any of the articles.
2. You skim an article on the state of Massachusetts to find out how it got its name.
3. You scan to survey a chapter of your health book.

4
Using Graphic Aids

A **graphic aid** is any type of visual aid that is used to present information. You are probably already familiar with many types of graphic aids.

Pictures, along with the captions beneath them, can be valuable keys to understanding.

Maps are drawings of all or part of the earth's surface. They are used to show the physical characteristics of the land as well as features such as population or rainfall.

Diagrams are drawings, usually with labels, that show the parts or workings of something.

Charts are groups of facts displayed in a way that shows a specific type of organization. Information is often presented in labeled columns.

Graphs are special charts that show the relationship between sets of facts. There are several different types of graphs, but one basic set of guidelines can help you understand them all.

How to Read Graphs
1. Read the title or caption of the graph.
2. Read the key to the symbols or abbreviations.
3. Read the information along the sides and across the top and bottom of the graph.
4. Find specific information by locating the point where the bar, line, or symbol in an up-and-down column meets the one in the column going across.

Look at the graph below. Read the information given outside the graph. What information does this graph provide? If you were the station manager of WZZZ, what kind of music would you play most often? Least often?

Music Preference of WZZZ Listeners

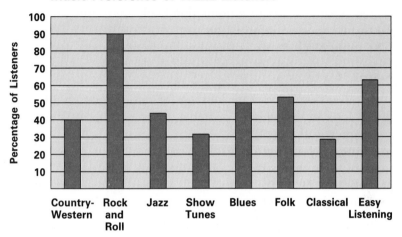

Exercise

Read the information around the outside of the graph below. Then use the graph to answer the questions.

Participation in After-School Activities

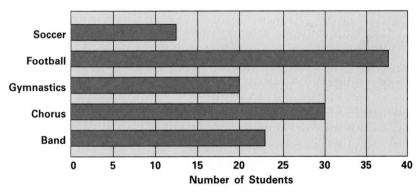

1. What is the subject matter of the graph?
2. How many students participated in gymnastics?
3. Which activity had the largest number of participants?
4. Which activity had the smallest number of participants?
5. How many students took part in chorus?

5
Using the Parts of a Book

Three separate parts of a nonfiction book are useful when you need to find specific information.

The **table of contents** is found at the front of most nonfiction books. It lists the title of each chapter in the book and the page on which it begins. It may also list the main topics that each chapter discusses. If you are looking for information on a topic, you can look in the table of contents to see whether it is covered by a chapter in the book.

An **index** is found at the back of most nonfiction books. Every important topic that is discussed in the book is listed in alphabetical order in the index. Each topic is followed by the page numbers on which it is discussed.

The index is a good place to look for specific terms. Look for broader topics in the table of contents.

Some nonfiction books also contain a glossary. A **glossary** lists difficult words in alphabetical order. Often their pronunciations are given. Then they are defined according to the way they are used in that book. A glossary is especially helpful in books that use technical terms.

Exercise

Write whether you would first look in the table of contents, the index, or in the glossary of a book on plants to answer each of the following questions.

1. Does the book have a chapter about photosynthesis?
2. On what page is poison ivy described?
3. How is *epidermis* pronounced?
4. What is the definition of *monocot*?
5. Is the broad topic of poisonous plants covered?
6. How many chapters does the book have?
7. On how many pages does the term *Venus' flytrap* appear?
8. In which chapter are trees discussed?
9. What is the meaning of the term *organic*?
10. What is the shortest chapter in the book?

6
Memorizing

Memorizing is an important study aid. Certain information must be memorized so that you can use it. For example, if you are writing answers to essay questions, you must have some knowledge on which to base your answer.

Following are several different ways to memorize information. People learn in different ways—choose your own method.

1. **Recite the information.** The sound of your own voice often helps you remember.
2. **Write the information.** The action of moving a pencil on paper helps imprint things in your memory. Seeing what you have written also helps the material stay in your mind.
3. **Connect ideas.** Connect, or associate, the facts in some way. When you associate things, you think of some way they fit together. You might put a list of science words in alphabetical order. A shopping list could be divided into categories.
4. **Use memory games.** Try visualizing what you want to remember. Close your eyes and picture the items on a list.
   Try making up a sentence whose words start with the first letters of the words you want to memorize. Many music students recall the notes of a musical staff—EGBDF—with the sentence "Every Good Boy Does Fine."
5. **Repeat the information often.** Repeat your list or memory game until the material comes easily to mind.

Exercise

The following names are the ten Canadian provinces. Try to memorize them by making up a sentence with words that begin with the first letter of each province's name. Then close your book and write as many provinces as you can.

Alberta	Nova Scotia
British Columbia	Ontario
Manitoba	Prince Edward Island
New Brunswick	Quebec
Newfoundland	Saskatchewan

English and Drama

What do you think happens when an actor first wins a part in a play or movie? Of course, there will be some excited cries and broad smiles, but what comes next? Because a good actor knows how important it is to understand the character being played, his or her next step is to study the person being portrayed.

Think about it: you've just been offered the role of someone like Queen Elizabeth I or Dr. Martin Luther King, Jr. To study Dr. King, for example, you would need books to read (Who was he? What was the civil rights movement about?), pictures to study (How did he look? What were his gestures and facial expressions?), and a script to memorize. The study skills that you've learned will help you when you start to take notes and skim material.

Activity Each of the following plays is about one or more well-known characters shown in parentheses. Choose one character. Find out as much as possible about that character's life, home, time period, and life style from sources other than the play itself. Organize the information you find into a chart and draw a picture of the character in costume.

1. *Sunrise at Campobello*   (Franklin Delano Roosevelt)
2. *The Miracle Worker*   (Helen Keller, Annie Sullivan)
3. *Camelot*   (King Arthur)
4. *The Diary of Anne Frank*   (Anne Frank)

Application and Review

A Understanding Study Skills Write the answer to each of the following questions.

1. What information should you include when writing down an assignment?
2. What is the purpose of SQ3R?
3. What are at least three purposes for taking notes?
4. Which part of a book lists page numbers of every important topic in the book?
5. What is one way to connect ideas in order to memorize them?
6. What kind of goal is tomorrow's spelling assignment?
7. What kind of goal makes you create a study plan?
8. What is the purpose of skimming?
9. What is the purpose of scanning?
10. What graphic aid is a drawing of the earth's surface?

B Reading Graphs Read the information around the outside of the graph below. Then answer the questions below the graph.

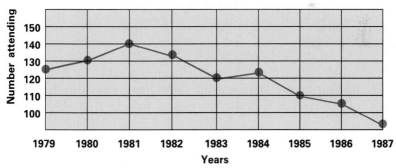

Attendance at the Sports Banquet

1. In what year was attendance at the banquet lowest?
2. In what year was attendance highest?
3. Overall, has the banquet gained popularity over the years?
4. In which years did attendance increase over the 1979 level?
5. How many people attended in 1985?

19
Test-Taking Skills

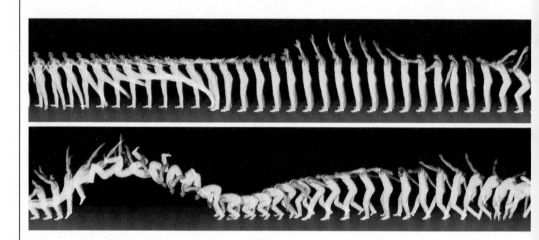

You have practiced your flips and your vaults, your mounts and your dismounts. Now the judges are watching, and it is time to show your stuff. Are you ready?

You probably ask yourself this same question before a test. To answer "yes," you need to do more than just learn the material. You also must be aware of the type of test you are taking and the type of answers you need to provide. In Chapter 18 you learned the study skills that will get you started. Now you will learn to apply those skills to various types of tests.

1
Preparing for Tests

To master a test you must master more than just the material covered in the test. You should know what type of test you will be taking and the features of that type of test. There are two main types of tests: course or textbook tests and standardized tests. You should prepare in a particular way for each type of test.

Course or Textbook Tests

Course or textbook tests measure how well you understand the material in a course in school or a chapter in a textbook. These tests are based on specific subject areas. For example, you might be studying the countries of Africa in geography class. The test would then cover only information that you have been learning about African countries.

To prepare for this test, you would study the materials you have been using to learn about African countries. These materials might include notes you took during class sessions, a chapter or several chapters in a textbook, or any material provided by your teacher.

If you have used the SQ3R method to study and have used your note-taking skills to keep an organized notebook, you will be well prepared to review for a written test. Review by going over your class notes and the questions and answers you used as you read your textbook.

Follow these study steps:

1. **Find out what the test will cover.** This will tell you what to study.
2. **Make a study plan to organize your time.** This will allow you to spread out your study times and avoid last-minute cramming.
3. **Gather your materials.** Study by reviewing your class notes, skimming the chapters you have already read, and going over questions and answers you developed as part of the SQ3R study method.

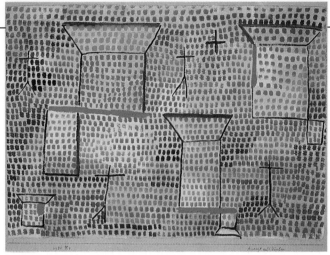

Croci e Colonne, 1931. Paul Klee.

4. **Memorize important facts.** You should then be able to remember names, dates, events, or vocabulary terms.
5. **Rest and relax.** Get plenty of sleep the night before a test.

Standardized Tests

Standardized tests measure your understanding of a variety of subjects. They are sometimes called **achievement tests** because they try to find out what you have achieved, or learned, in all your years at school. For example, many standardized tests have sections on mathematics, vocabulary, reading comprehension, grammar and language skills, science, and social studies.

You do not have to study for standardized tests. You have been in school most of your life, and you have learned a great deal. In fact, you have already studied for this kind of test every day that you have been in school.

To prepare for a standardized test, however, you need to do one important thing: relax. It is important to be relaxed during the test because your mind works better when you are relaxed.

One good way to relax is to get a good night's sleep the night before the test. Another way to relax is to remember that you are already prepared for this test because you have been in school most of your life.

Exercise

Think about how you actually prepare for a test. Then, in a paragraph, compare your study habits with those listed on these two pages. What improvements could you make in your test preparation?

2
Types of Test Questions

The main types of test questions are true-false, multiple-choice, matching, fill-in-the-blanks, analogies, short-answer, and essay questions.

Learn to recognize the different kinds of test questions and the best way to approach them. The following may help you.

True-False Questions

True-false questions are really statements. You are asked to decide whether each statement is true or false.

Ⓣ F 1. Columbus sailed to America in 1492.
Ⓣ F 2. The earth has seven continents.
T Ⓕ 3. A seed plant can be identified by its leaves.

Watch for the words *all, always, never,* and *none* in true-false statements. These words often signal that the statement is false.

T Ⓕ *All* planets have moons.
T Ⓕ The people of India *never* eat beef.

Other words often signal that a statement is true: *most, many, some,* and *usually.*

Ⓣ F *Some* planets have moons.
T Ⓕ The people of India *usually* eat beef.

However, as you can see from the last example, this does not happen in every case. You should read each true-false statement to get *all* the information it contains. If *any part* of the statement is false, then the statement is false.

Multiple-Choice Questions

Multiple-choice questions provide three or more possible answers for one question. You are to choose the *best* answer from these choices.

A noun is the name of

    a. an action.
    ⓑ a person, place, thing, or idea.
    c. a connector.

Sometimes one possible answer is partly correct, but another one is more completely correct. Be sure to read *all* the possible answers, even though one may already seem correct.

A noun is the name of

    a. a person.
    b. a person or place.
    ⓒ a person, place, thing, or idea.

The first possible answer, *a. a person*, is partly correct, but so is the second possible answer, *b. a person or place*. The third possible answer, *c. a person, place, thing, or idea* is the most correct because it is the most complete answer. If you had not read all three possible answers, you might have chosen the first or second one as your answer.

Sometimes you are unsure which possible answer is correct. In that case, first eliminate the possible answers that you know are incorrect. Often you can eliminate one or two right away. Then you will have fewer possible answers to consider. Think carefully about each one and choose the one that makes the most sense.

What is the meaning of *hearty*?

    ⓐ expressed with warmth of feeling
    b. shown to be false
    c. covered with hair
    d. made of metal

In the above question, you can eliminate choice *c. covered with hair* because you know that the root word *heart* has nothing to do with hair. You can eliminate *d. made of metal* because the root word *heart* also has nothing to do with metal. Now consider the two remaining choices. Is it more likely that the root word *heart* is related to *warmth of feeling* or to *false*? You know that people express emotion with the word *heart,* as when they say "with all my heart" or "I feel this way in my heart." Therefore, the best answer is *a. expressed with warmth of feeling.*

Matching Questions

In matching questions you match items from one list with items from the other list. For example:

Match the inventors with their inventions:

telephone ——————— Benjamin Franklin
phonograph ——————— Alexander Graham Bell
steam engine ——————— Thomas Alva Edison
cotton gin ——————— Robert Fulton
lightning rod ——————— Eli Whitney

To answer matching questions, first match all the items of which you are certain. This will leave fewer choices.

Write the letter of each body part next to its body system.

_d_ 1. circulatory system   a. bone
_c_ 2. respiratory system   b. stomach
_b_ 3. digestive system   c. lungs
_a_ 4. skeletal system   d. heart

You may know that the heart is part of the circulatory system, and the lungs are part of the respiratory system. You would first fill in the letter *d* next to item number 1 and the letter *c* next to item number 2. That leaves you with two body parts and systems to match. You may then study the phrase *digestive system* and realize that it contains the root word *digest*. You might then suppose that the stomach *digests* food, since food goes directly to the stomach. You would then fill in *b* for stomach next to item number 3. This leaves you with bone as the only remaining choice. You would then fill in *a* for bone next to item number 4.

Fill-in-the-Blanks Questions

Fill-in-the-blanks questions are sometimes called *completion* questions. They consist of statements with missing words or phrases. You are to fill in the missing word or phrase:

A _triangle_ is a geometric figure with three sides.

The country that is also a continent

is _Australia_ .

Do not spend too much time on questions for which you do not know the answers. First, fill in the answers of which you are certain. Make sure that your answers fit the questions grammatically. For example, you should not fill in the blank with a verb when the blank is in the subject position of the sentence. Then go back and reread the sentences in which you have left answers blank. You will probably be able to fill in more answers each time you go back over the questions.

Analogy Questions

Analogy questions look like fill-in-the-blanks questions, but analogy questions ask you to think about how items are related:

Hot is to *summer* as *cold* is to _____ .

This analogy compares two pairs of things. The first pair is *hot* and *summer*. The second pair is *cold* and an unknown item. You are to decide how the items in the first pair are related. The items in the second pair should be related in the same way as the items in the first pair. Try to make a sentence out of the first pair of words (*hot* and *summer*) that explains their relationship.

Hot describes the temperature in the *summer*.

Now take your sentence and substitute the incomplete pair (*cold* and _____) for the first pair.

Cold describes the temperature in the _____ .

What word should be put in the blank to make the second sentence correct? The answer is *winter* because *cold* describes the temperature in *winter* just as *hot* describes the temperature in *summer*.

Many analogy questions provide answer choices:

Puppy is to *dog* as *kitten* is to _____ .
a. claws   b. purr   c. cat   d. animal

Again, try to make a sentence out of the first pair of words that explains the relationship between them.

A *puppy* is a young *dog*.

A *kitten* is a young *cat*. Therefore, the answer is *c. cat*. A kitten is obviously not a young *claws* or a *purr*. Although the answer *animal* fits the sentence, *animal* is not specific enough.

Animal is not related to *cat* in the same way as *dog* is related to *puppy*. Analogy questions call for you to figure out relationships. You can practice doing this by making up your own analogies.

Short-Answer Questions

Short-answer questions ask you to provide a short answer for each question. Always read the directions first:

Write a complete sentence to answer the question.
Who wrote the play *Julius Caesar*?

William Shakespeare wrote Julius Caesar.

Write the answer to the question.
Who is credited with inventing the airplane?

Wilbur and Orville Wright

In the first example, the directions say to write a complete sentence. In the second example, the directions do not ask for a complete sentence; therefore, it may be correct to simply write the word or phrase that provides the answer. However, check with your teacher to be sure.

Essay Questions

Essay questions ask you to write a paragraph or more to answer a question. Because you will not have much time or space to answer the question, you must simplify the steps in your writing process. Plan your answer the way you would plan any piece of writing. First identify your purpose. To do this, read the question carefully to find out what it asks you to write about.

1. Contrast the form of government in the United States with the form of government in the Soviet Union.
2. Describe a typical settler's house on the Great Plains in the early 1800's.

The first example above asks you to contrast two things. **Contrast** means to discuss differences. Therefore, you would write about the ways in which the Soviet Union's government is different from the government of the United States. The question does not ask you to write everything about each government—only the things that can be contrasted.

The second question asks you to **describe** what something consists of or looks like. You would write everything you know about the settlers' houses. Make sure you use specific details in your answers.

Other essay questions may ask you to list or outline events, discuss ideas, or explain why things happen. Read each question carefully before planning your answer. It is also a good idea to list and organize your ideas on a piece of scratch paper.

Exercise

Write whether each question is a *True-False*, *Multiple Choice*, *Matching*, *Fill-in-the-Blanks*, *Analogy*, *Short Answer*, or *Essay*.

1. A transparent prism separates the colors in light.
2. The colors we are able to see are in the _____ .
3. Explain why rainbows appear after a rain.
4. When a rainbow appears, tiny droplets of water act as
   a. dyes. c. colors.
   b. prisms. d. bubbles.
5. Which colors are known as primary colors? _____
6. The eye sees color by using nerves called *cones*.
7. All males have red-green color blindness.
8. How fast do light waves travel?

_____

9. Light is to dark as bright is to _____.
10. Write the number of the correct definition beside each term.

Looking Up, New York. Robert Amft.

   _____ a. prism   1. a band of colors
   _____ b. opaque   2. a transparent geometric shape
   _____ c. spectrum   3. basic name of a color
   _____ d. hue   4. not able to transmit light

3
What to Do During the Test

While taking a test, follow these steps:

1. **Skim the test.** Look over the whole test to see what types of questions it has and how long it is.
2. **Judge the time.** First read all the directions. Decide which questions may take you more time. An essay question, for example, will take more time than short answer questions.
3. **Read all directions carefully.** Ask questions if you do not understand the directions. Follow the directions exactly.
4. **Read each test item carefully.** If answer choices are provided, read all the choices before choosing the best one.
5. **Answer easy questions first.** Then go back to harder ones. Allow more time for harder questions.
6. **Review your answers.** Be sure you have not accidentally left out any answers. Also, change confusing answers and unreadable handwriting.

Using Answer Sheets

Answer sheets are used mostly in standardized tests. The answer sheets are usually scored by machines, not people. Therefore, it is important to mark the sheet correctly. Study the following examples:

Correctly marked
Part 1

Incorrectly marked
Part 2

Do two important things when using any answer sheet:

1. **Keep your place.** Be sure you are marking in the correct part of the answer sheet. Make sure you are marking the correct item numbers as well.
2. **Mark neatly; erase neatly.** This is important because the scoring machine cannot figure out stray marks or incomplete erasures. When you erase an answer, erase gently but completely. Never cross out an incorrect answer.

Hints for Marking an Answer Sheet

These hints may help you mark answer sheets correctly:

1. Read the heading of each part when you start marking it.
2. Be sure each heading matches the one in the test booklet.
3. Read each item number on the answer sheet as you mark it. Be sure it matches the question you are answering. Every four or five answers, check to make sure that you are answering the question in the right place on the answer sheet.
4. Fill in only one answer per line.
5. Do not press so hard that your pencil marks go through the paper. Do make heavy, dark marks that show clearly.
6. Practice marking and erasing a few times on scratch paper. Try to erase neatly without tearing the paper.

Exercise

Write *True* or *False* for each of the following statements.

1. You should take your time on each test question.
2. Skim the whole test before you start answering questions.
3. Answer the easiest questions first.
4. When answer choices are provided, choose the first one that contains correct information.
5. Never make any changes to your answers.
6. Always check to make sure that you are marking the correct part of the answer sheet.
7. Machines are usually used to score standardized tests.
8. Incomplete erasures may be scored as wrong answers on answer sheets.
9. Press as hard as possible to mark answer sheets.
10. Do not answer questions that are hard.

Crossroads

English and Reading

Most standardized tests that you will take include a section that contains a paragraph for you to read and analyze. Following each paragraph are questions about the text. The following steps will help you with reading comprehension questions.

1. Read the questions below the paragraphs first. This will give you the best idea of what your purpose in reading will be.
2. Next, read the paragraph carefully. Keep your eyes open for references to the topics of the questions.
3. Reread the questions. Then skim the paragraph to locate the places where you are likely to find each answer.
4. Answer each question as best you can.

Activity With these steps in mind, read the following paragraph and answer the questions that follow.

> Historians have known for a long time that Christopher Columbus never actually landed on the mainland of America. They have disagreed for years about where he did land with his Spanish ships. Most historians thought that he landed on Watlings Island off the Florida coast. Now historians think he landed on the island of Samana Cay in the Bahama Islands chain. The geography and location of Samana Cay match the ship's log.

1. What is now believed to be Columbus's landing point?

   a. Florida   b. Samana Cay   c. Watlings Island   d. Spain

2. From where was Columbus sailing?

   a. America   b. Spain   c. Portugal   d. Italy

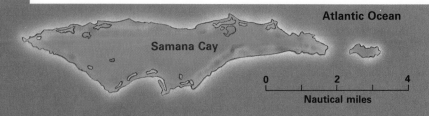

Atlantic Ocean

Samana Cay

0   2   4

Nautical miles

Application and Review

Understanding Test-Taking Skills Write the letter of the best answer to each question.

1. How should you prepare for a standardized test?
   a. Study hard the night before the test.
   b. Study a little at a time for several weeks.
   c. Reread as many textbooks as you can.
   d. Get a good night's sleep the night before the test.
2. For a course or textbook test, you should
   a. study all the materials you have used in the course or textbook.
   b. study the material that the test will cover.
   c. rest and relax instead of studying.
   d. study late the night before the test.
3. A true-false statement is always false if
   a. the word *never* is used.
   b. the word *all* is used.
   c. the words *some, most, many, usually,* or *often* are used.
   d. any part of the statement is incorrect.
4. Why should you read all multiple-choice answers provided?
   a. All the answer choices may be incorrect.
   b. Two answer choices may be equally correct.
   c. Two choices may be correct, but one may be more complete.
   d. There may be no best answer.
5. What kind of question requires you to write a paragraph or more?
   a. essay   c. matching
   b. short answer   d. multiple choice
6. What should you do when you have finished a test?
   a. Cross out any answers of which you are unsure.
   b. Hand it in immediately.
   c. Scan your answers to find out if any are missing or confusing.
   d. Use any extra time to read or study for another class.

20
Writing Letters and Filling Out Forms

ORDER NOW!
The Ultimate T-Shirt!
Indicate size, color, and quantity.
Include cash, check, or money order.

Whenever you order a product or write a letter, you are using the writing skills you have studied in this book to provide information to others.

In this chapter you will learn about writing friendly letters and business letters. You also will learn how to fill out forms correctly.

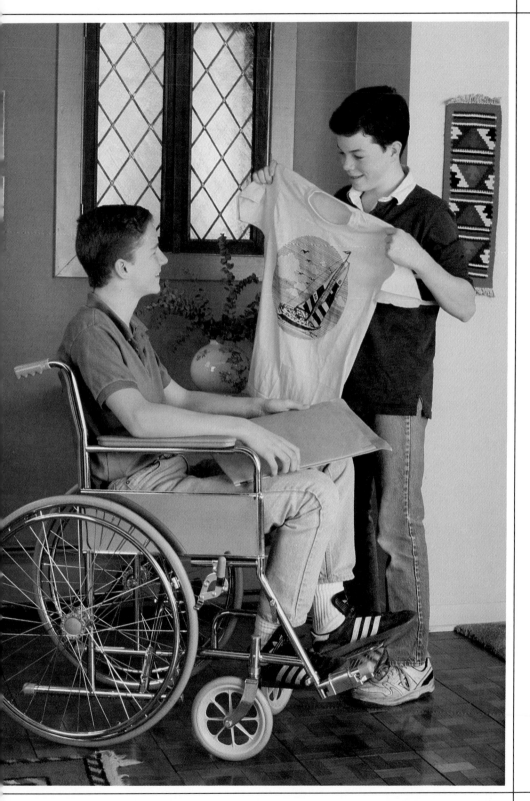

1
Writing Friendly Letters

When you write a friendly letter, keep these ideas in mind: you want to make the content of the letter interesting, and you want to write a letter that is neat and in correct form.

In a friendly letter, you are writing to someone you know well—someone with whom you have shared many experiences and who wants to know what you are doing. The most enjoyable letters to receive are those that sound as if the writer is actually speaking to you. Try to create that tone in the letters you write. Use original and colorful language to describe your experiences. Then your letter will be interesting to read.

A Friendly Letter

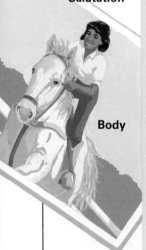

Heading

Salutation

Body

Closing
Signature

603 Pine Street
Alton, Pennsylvania 18106
August 7, 1988

Dear Beth,

I enjoyed your last letter so much that I had to hurry and answer it. How did you learn to ride a horse so quickly? In the photo you sent me, you look very impressive up there in the saddle. Do you ride in shows or just for fun?

My fun activity for the summer has been learning how to scuba dive at the local pool. Our class is even going on a diving trip to the Jersey shore next week, so I'll get to test my new skills. Wish me luck!

Write and tell me more about your wilderness rides. Say "hi" to your family for me.

Your friend,
José

In your letter, include information that interests you and that will interest the person to whom you are writing. Then the person will be eager to answer your letter. If you are replying to a letter, answer any questions the person has asked and make additional comments.

Parts of the Friendly Letter

Using the correct letter form helps you organize your letter. Each friendly letter has five main parts: heading, salutation, body, closing, and signature.

The **heading** of a letter tells where you are and when you are writing. It gives your street address on the first line; your city, state, and ZIP code on the second line; and the month, day, and year on the third line. You write it in the upper right corner of your paper. Commas go between the name of the city and the state and between the day and the year. No comma is needed to separate the state and the ZIP code.

The **salutation**, or greeting, is the way you say "hello." You write it on the line below the heading, beginning at the left margin. You capitalize the first word and any other nouns. A comma follows the salutation in a friendly letter, as in the following examples:

Dear Mike,   Hi Marcia,   Greetings Holly,

In the **body** of a friendly letter, you talk to your friend. If you're responding to a letter, begin by answering the other person's questions or reacting to her or his information. If the letter is a good one, it will make your friend feel as if you were there in person. When your friend finishes the letter, he or she will want to reply as soon as possible.

The **closing** is a simple way of saying "goodbye." Some closings, such as *Love*, *Sincerely*, and *Your friend*, are common. Other closings are original, such as the following:

Missing you,   Anxiously,   Still waiting,

Capitalize only the first word of the closing, and use a comma at the end. The closing should line up with the heading.

When you write a letter to someone who will recognize you by your first name, use your first name as your **signature**. Otherwise, sign your full name, beginning it under the closing.

Guidelines for Writing Friendly Letters

1. Write naturally, as if you were speaking to the person.
2. If you are responding to a letter, begin by answering the other person's questions or by commenting on her or his letter.
3. Write about things that are interesting to both of you.
4. Add details and use a variety of descriptive words.
5. If you are writing a thank-you letter, be sure to thank the person for thinking of you.
6. Indent each paragraph and start a new paragraph for each new idea you write about.
7. Use the five-part form for friendly letters correctly.
8. Keep your margins straight and clear so that the reader can follow what you are saying.
9. Use blue or black ink so that your writing can be read easily, and keep your handwriting as neat as possible.

Exercises

A In your best handwriting, write the heading, salutation, closing, and signature for each of the following letters. Use the correct form, margins, punctuation, and capitalization. For the body of the letter, skip two lines and print the word *BODY*.

1. From sara mason, camp tomahawk, raleigh, north carolina 27608, to her mother.
2. From terry orlanda, 114 north hermitage avenue, trenton, new jersey 08618 to his teacher, ms. barker.
3. From ricardo perez, 818 harrison street, boston, massachusetts 02118, to his sister maría.

B Write a friendly letter to one of your friends. You may use the following situation, or you may write a letter you will actually mail to a friend.

> Your friend has written to tell you that he is on the school soccer team. He plays goalie and loves it, even though practice is hard. He is also writing sports news for the school paper. Remember to tell your friend what's going on in your life.

2
Writing Business Letters

A business letter is written for a specific purpose—for example, requesting information or ordering a product. It requires a different, more formal writing style and a different form than a friendly letter.

There are two forms for writing business letters: modified block form and block form. In **modified block form**, the paragraphs are indented, and the closing and signature are in line with the heading, just as in a friendly letter. Handwritten letters always use modified block form. (*See the letter on page 382.*)

In **block form**, all parts of the letter begin at the left margin. The paragraphs are not indented. Instead, there is a space between paragraphs. Block form is used only when a letter is typewritten.

Parts of the Business Letter

The business letter contains one part that the friendly letter does not: the inside address. The **inside address** contains the name of the individual to whom you are writing, if you know that person's name. It also contains the name and address of the organization to which you are writing. Place the inside address below the heading and at the left margin.

The **salutation** of the business letter is more formal than that of a friendly letter. If you are writing to a specific person, use *Dear* and then the person's name followed by a colon. An example is *Dear Ms. Kent:* If you do not know the name of the person who will read your letter, use a general greeting such as *Dear Sir or Madam:*

The **body** of a business letter is usually short. It should be courteous and should state your business clearly.

The **closing**, like the heading, follows the same rules for a business letter as for a friendly letter. The only difference is that it is always formal. *Sincerely,* and *Yours truly,* are examples.

For the **signature** of a business letter, skip four spaces below the closing, print or type your name, and write your signature in the space.

A Business Letter (*Modified Block Form*)

Heading

> 1104 Balsana Avenue
> Boulder, Colorado 80302
> April 27, 1988

Inside
Address

> Sports Extras Company
> 2134 Peachtree Avenue
> Atlanta, Georgia 30308

Salutation

> Dear Sir or Madam:

Body

>   In the March issue of <u>Runner's World</u> I saw your advertisement for visor headbands. Please send the item indicated as soon as possible.
>
> 1 light blue headband with
>   white visor $4.50
> postage and handling .50
> $5.00
>
> I am enclosing a money order for the amount of $5.00. Thank you for your prompt response.

Closing
Signature

>   Sincerely,
>   Pat Williams
>   Pat Williams

Exercises

A Write a letter for the situation below. Make up any names and facts needed for a complete letter, but sign your own name.

> You want to order a T-shirt with a picture of your dog reproduced on the front. Give the size and color of the T-shirt you want and enclose a picture of your dog. The price is $6.95 plus $.75 handling. The company is T-Shirts, Inc., 1130 Nicollet Avenue, Minneapolis, Minnesota 55403. You want your picture returned. (Do not send the letter.)

B Bring to class an advertisement for a company. Write to that company requesting information about its product.

3
Addressing Envelopes

If you address your envelope accurately, your letter will get to the right place. A simple mistake could cause your letter to be returned to you or sent to the Dead Letter Office.

Although you should not use abbreviations in the heading or inside address of a letter, you may wish to abbreviate the state on the envelope. Be sure that you also include the ZIP code. If you do not know the ZIP code, call the post office.

If you are using a business envelope, put the name and address of the person or organization to whom you are writing halfway down and halfway across the envelope. Put your own address, the **return address**, in the upper left corner of the envelope.

If you are sending a friendly letter in a small square envelope, you may put the return address on the back flap instead of on the front of the envelope. The address of the person to whom you are writing should then be centered on the front of the envelope.

Business Envelope

Return Address

Ms. Laura Daniels
2202 Sunnyside Avenue
Salt Lake City, UT 84108

Address

Walter Drake Interiors
P.O. Box 12684
Dallas, TX 75225

Exercise

Draw three business envelopes. Put each address below in proper form where it should appear on an envelope.

1. the athlete's foot 825 chicago avenue evanston illinois 60202
2. the harper company 12 oak road columbus ohio 43216
3. campfitter inc p o box 6745 providence rhode island 02940

4
Completing Forms

Of course, letters are only one way of giving information. Forms are another. You have probably completed various kinds of forms in your everyday life. You may have used a form to order a product, to register for classes at school, or to apply for membership in an organization.

Companies, schools, governments, and other organizations use forms to collect information. By asking people to complete a form, these organizations get the same kinds of information from every person, and they get all the information they need for a specific purpose.

The sample bicycle registration form on the following page, for example, asks for the bicycle owner's name, address, and phone number. It also asks for information about the bicycle: frame style, size, color, make, and serial number. This information would help the police identify the bicycle and its owner if it were stolen, or if it were parked illegally.

Guidelines for Completing Forms

1. Look over the entire form before you write anything.
2. Read all directions carefully. Follow any special instructions, such as *Please print* or *Use black ink*.
3. Collect all the facts you need to complete the form.
4. Get the proper writing instrument (pen, pencil, or typewriter) and an eraser or correction fluid.
5. Complete the form one line at a time, rereading each part of the directions as you come to it.
6. Be sure you put something in every blank. If a question does not apply to you, write *N/A* in the blank to indicate *not applicable*.
7. Proofread your answers and correct any errors neatly.
8. Make a photocopy of the complete form for your records.
9. Take or mail the completed form to the correct person and place.

Bicycle Registration No. 45872   **City of Red Valley**

Owner			
Street Address			Phone Number
Make	Frame	Size	Color
Serial Number			
Other Identification			

I hereby certify that the bicycle described above belongs to me and that I will follow the cycling rules of the road and parking regulations of the City of Red Valley.

Signature _____ **Date** _____

Return one copy of this registration form in person to:

Police Department
Bicycle Records Officer
513 Main Street
Red Valley, Oklahoma
Keep Your Copy of This Registration in a Safe Place

Exercises

A Find a catalog of bicycling equipment including helmets, clothing, safety vests, and other items. Complete an order form from this catalog. Follow the guidelines for completing forms on page 384. (Do not mail the form.)

B Go to the public library and get an application for a library card. Follow the guidelines for completing forms to fill in the blanks on the application. To actually get a library card, you may have to show the library clerk some identification.

English and Social Studies

Letters and forms are two of the most common ways for our government to conduct its business. You'll use forms to receive a driver's license, register a new bicycle, or apply for a city job, for example.

Letters are also useful for government business. Government officials can inform you of the opening of a new city pool, or persuade you to vote in the next election. Letters can let you communicate with someone in the city, state, or national government.

In addition to receiving letters from government officials, you will sometimes want to write to them yourself. There are two main types of letters you can write to government officials. In the first type, you share an idea for a project with an official who can help you make it work. For example, you might have an idea about adding a soccer field to your neighborhood park. A letter to the mayor may help make your plan a reality. In another type of letter to government officials, you express your opinions on certain issues.

Activity You have been chosen as the leader of your school improvement group. The group has decided to work to improve something about the school but is having trouble doing it alone. First, identify a real problem at your school. Next, come up with a possible solution. Then, write a letter that could go to the principal of your school telling about the problem and your idea for a solution.

Application and Review

A Writing Letters and Addressing Envelopes Answer each of the following questions.

1. When you are responding to letters from friends, where should you answer their questions?
2. Do business and friendly letters both use headings?
3. On what letters can you sign your first name only?
4. In a friendly letter, why do you include information that will interest your friend?
5. What item can you abbreviate when addressing envelopes?
6. Where can a return address be positioned on a friendly letter's envelope?
7. What part does the business letter include that the friendly letter does not?
8. What punctuation mark follows the salutation in a friendly letter?
9. What punctuation mark follows the salutation in a business letter?
10. In block form, each part of a business letter begins where?

B Completing Forms Identify each of the following statements as *True* or *False*.

1. People seldom have to complete forms until they are adults.
2. On a form, you should fill in everything that seems obvious first, and then read the directions.
3. You can get the details you need as you fill in the blanks.
4. It is not necessary to read the directions more than once.
5. Using forms helps companies get specific information.
6. Every form should be completed with a pencil.
7. You should write *N/A* if a question doesn't apply to you.
8. It is acceptable to leave some of the blanks empty.
9. You do not need to proofread a completed form.
10. You should keep a copy of the completed form.

Grammar, Usage, and Mechanics

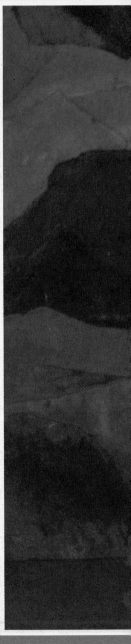

*Although paintings may look very different from
each other, most do have a few basic similarities.
That is because most painters agree to follow
certain rules, or conventions. Writers also follow
certain rules. These are the conventions of
language. Good writers master these rules so
that they can write in a way that is natural and
individual yet still conventional enough to
be understood.*

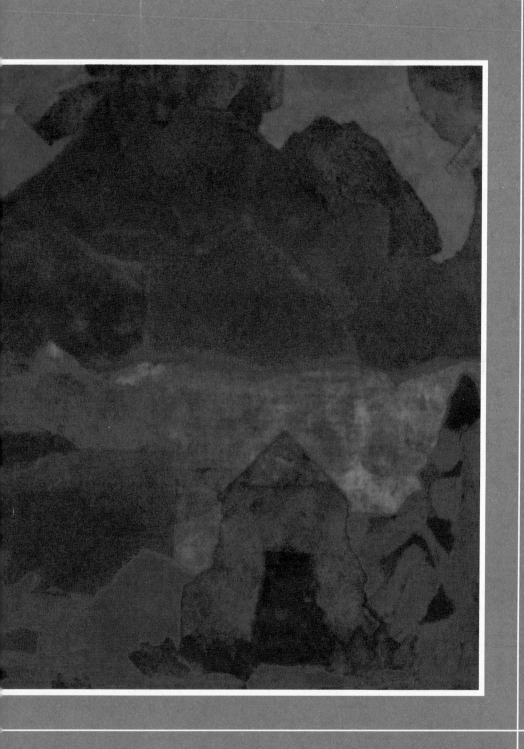

21
Understanding Sentences

Launching a rocket requires the combined efforts of a team of scientists, engineers, and technicians, all working together. Unless all systems are "Go," the rocket will not be cleared for blast-off.

All parts of a sentence must be working together if the sentence is to express the ideas intended by the writer. If even one word or phrase is misused, the meaning of the entire sentence may be affected.

The sentence is the key unit of communication. In this chapter you will learn about the parts of the sentence and how they work together to express a complete thought.

1
The Parts of a Sentence

A *sentence* is a group of words that expresses a complete thought. A sentence must have a subject and a predicate.

A sentence expresses a complete thought. It may make a statement about something. It may ask a question or tell someone to do something. It may also express strong feeling. Every sentence always has two parts. One part tells whom or what the sentence is about. That is the **subject**. The second part tells something about the subject. This is the **predicate**. Subjects and predicates can be short or long, as you can see from the following examples.

Subject *(Who or what)*	Predicate *(What is said about the subject)*
Beth	smiled.
The boys	had gone.
Each participant	received a certificate.
The two racing cars	nearly collided.

One way to understand the parts of a sentence is to think of a sentence as telling who did something or what happened. The subject tells *who* or *what*. The predicate tells *what was done* or *what happened*. You can divide sentences, then, in this way:

Who or What	What Was Done or What Happened
Juanita	arrived.
The ice	melted.
The subway	was crowded with people.
Many of my friends	entered the talent show.
The runner in the red shirt	won the race.

Exercises

A Write the following sentences. Draw a vertical line between the subject and the predicate.

> EXAMPLE   The whole crowd | cheered

1. An alligator slid into the water.
2. Both dogs circled the water hole.
3. Thunder rumbled in the distance.
4. The boy across the street raises rabbits.
5. Terry saw the music show on Channel 4.
6. A large crowd watched the basketball game.
7. A powerful earthquake damaged San Francisco in the spring of 1906.
8. The sand dunes baked in the sun.
9. Nancy's Labrador retriever jumped the fence.
10. The yardstick snapped in two.

B Decide whether each group of words below is a subject or a predicate. Then use each group of words to write a complete sentence. Your completed sentences will tell about work on a school newspaper.

> EXAMPLE   wrote the sports news (predicate)
> Karen wrote the sports news.

1. works on the school newspaper
2. our photographer
3. the editor-in-chief
4. both of my brothers
5. draws the cartoons
6. the latest issue
7. our movie reviewer
8. interviewed the principal
9. writes about music
10. enjoy our newspaper

C *Write Now* Create a new national holiday to celebrate an event or a notable person. Write a paragraph telling what or whom it honors and how it should be celebrated. Make sure that each of your sentences is complete.

2
Simple Subjects and Predicates

> The *subject* of a sentence tells *whom* or *what* the sentence is about. The *predicate* tells what the subject *does* or *is*.

In every sentence there are a few words that are more important than the rest. These key words make the basic framework of the sentence. Study these examples:

Subject	Predicate
A cold, driving **rain**	**fell** throughout the night.
Rain	**fell.**

The subject of the first sentence is *A cold, driving rain*. The key word in this subject is *rain*. You can say *Rain fell throughout the night*. You cannot say *cold fell throughout the night*. Nor can you say *driving fell throughout the night*.

The predicate in the first sentence is *fell throughout the night*. The key word is *fell*. Without this word you would not have a sentence.

The key word in the subject of a sentence is called the **simple subject**. It is the subject of the verb.

The key word in the predicate is called the **simple predicate**. The simple predicate is the **verb**. Hereafter we will use the word *verb* rather than the phrase *simple predicate*.

The verb and its subject are the basic framework of every sentence. All the rest of the sentence is built around them. To find this framework, first find the verb. Then ask *Who?* or *What?* This will give you the subject of the verb.

> Two girls in our class made puppets.
> *Verb:* made *Who made puppets?* girls
> *Subject of verb:* girls

Diagraming Verbs and Their Subjects

A diagram helps you see how a sentence is put together. To diagram a sentence, begin with a horizontal line. Write the subject on the left side of the line. Write the verb on the right side of the line. Then draw a vertical line between the subject and the verb.

EXAMPLE   Dogs bark.

Exercises

A Write each verb and its subject.

1. My cousins live in Indianapolis.
2. The swimmers waited for the whistle.
3. Nancy plays the flute in the band.
4. Almost all beekeepers wear protective masks.
5. Jack helped with the chores after school.
6. The two boys built a chicken coop.
7. Julie caught the ball easily.
8. The copilot radioed the tower.
9. Tall elms lined the avenue.
10. The three girls walked home together.

B Draw a diagram to show the verb and its simple subject in each of the following sentences. Write only one word for the verb and one word for its subject.

1. A large, colorful umbrella shaded the chairs.
2. Curtis posted the names of the winners.
3. A squirrel started a nest in the attic.
4. The clock in the hallway needs new hands.
5. Eliza sat near the brook.
6. The photographs fell out of the folder.
7. Barbara's dresser fit next to the window.
8. A majestic eagle soared overhead.
9. Watermelon tastes good in hot weather.
10. Dr. Harvey's cat wore a tin bell.

3
Finding the Verb

A *verb* expresses an action, states that something exists, or links the subject with a description.

To understand a sentence, you must find the verb. Here are some guidelines that tell you what verbs do. These guidelines can serve as clues to help you find the verb in a sentence.

Some verbs tell about action:

> Tom *paddled* the canoe.
> Ann *caught* the ball.
> Shana *wrote* a letter.

Sometimes the action shown by the verb is an action you cannot see:

> Jan *wants* a bicycle.
> Jim *remembered* the story.
> Wilson *enjoys* math.

Some verbs tell that something *is* or *exists*. We say that such verbs tell a *state of being:*

> The doctor *is* here.
> How many planets *are* in the solar system?

Some verbs link a subject to a description of it.

> The road *looked* slippery.
> The wind *felt* cold.

Exercises

A Write the verb in each sentence. It may express an action you can see, an action you cannot see, or a state of being.

> EXAMPLE   Tina ran across the field
> Verb: ran

1. Skiers dream about snow.
2. I imagined the old fishing wharf.

3. Roberto and Maria are from Argentina.
4. The three boys were cousins.
5. All the campers have flashlights.
6. My dog never trusts the mail carrier.
7. Roy and Danny raced across the playground.
8. The ice looked too thin.
9. Mark had an idea.
10. That record sounds scratchy.

B Write the verb in each sentence. Then write whether it expresses an action or a state of being.

1. Scientists know little about the faraway planets of Uranus and Neptune.
2. Clyde Tombaugh discovered the planet Pluto in 1930.
3. Our sun is an enormous ball of hot gas.
4. Earth is the fifth largest planet in the solar system.
5. One of Saturn's moons is larger than the planet Mercury.
6. Thick clouds cover the planet Venus.
7. Some people call Venus the Morning Star.
8. Earth is the third planet from the sun.
9. Perhaps as many as twenty-three moons circle Saturn.
10. "Shooting stars" are really meteors.

c *Write Now* Make a list of possible jobs in health care such as doctor, therapist, nurse, or dental hygienist. Find out more about these jobs by talking to adults you know or using the encyclopedia. Choose one of these jobs that you might like to do. Then imagine what a typical work day would be like in your new job. Write an imaginary journal entry describing what you did that day. Write ten sentences and be sure that each sentence has at least one verb.

4
Main Verbs and Helping Verbs

A *helping verb* helps the main verb make a statement or express action.

There are certain words you can count on as verbs.

Words you can count on as verbs			
am	was	has	do
is	were	have	does
are	be	had	did

Sometimes these words are used alone. Sometimes they are used as **helping verbs** with a **main verb**.

Jay *will paint* the fence.   The actor *has visited* the school.

A verb may consist of a main verb and one or more helping **verbs**.

Yolanda *did win* the race.   Tony *should have run* faster.

Sometimes the main verb ends in *-ing*:

We *had been playing* the piano.

How to find the verb in a sentence

1. Look for a word that tells the main action, expresses a state of being, or links the subject with a description.
2. Look for helping verbs. Examples are *is, am, are, was, were, be, been, have, has, had, do, does, did, shall, will, should, would,* and *could.*
3. Look for all the verbs that make up the verb phrase.

Exercises

A Make two columns on your paper. Label them *Helping Verbs* and *Main Verbs*: Write the helping verbs from the following sentences in the first column. Write the main verbs in the second column.

1. The grandfather clock had stopped.
2. Andy was bracing himself against the shelf.
3. Two ducks were huddling near the pond.
4. The Mulligans have had a good time at Six Flags.
5. Kathy had been ready for over an hour.
6. The outcome had seemed uncertain.
7. Really, I do try.
8. At four o'clock the plumber was working on the drain in the kitchen sink.
9. The sky has looked stormy all afternoon.
10. Twice recently the car has needed a new front tire.

B Write the verb and its simple subject from each of the following sentences. If a sentence has a helping verb and a main verb, write both of the verbs.

1. Victor's parents got him a new camera for his birthday.
2. He has been interested in photography for several months.
3. Now, Victor could take a photography class.
4. He went to the community center.
5. There, he joined a class.
6. A woman taught the class.
7. Victor had heard about Marge's popular class.
8. He studied light meters and time exposure.
9. Marge also demonstrated film development.
10. Victor might become a wildlife photographer for *National Geographic* someday.

C *Write Now* Suppose you are a junior counselor at a summer camp. The campers are all from the city and this is their first time camping out. One night you are asked to tell a ghost story to the younger campers around the campfire. Write five spooky sentences that would be part of your ghost story. Use helping verbs in three of your sentences.

Separated Parts of a Verb

Sometimes the parts of a verb are separated by words that are not verbs. In the sentences below, the verbs are printed in bold type. The words in between are not part of the verb phrase.

That bus **has** often **been** late.
The temperature **had** rapidly **dropped**.
We **had** not **seen** the accident.
The clerk **did**n't **understand** my question.

Notice that *not* and the ending *n't* in contractions are not parts of the verb even though they do change the meaning of the verb.

Exercises

A Write the complete verb for each sentence.

1. Ted is not writing the script for the skit.
2. Nora has never been in Florida.
3. Four students were already serving refreshments.
4. Lou will probably return your tape recorder today.
5. My brother did not arrive until after the thunderstorm.
6. The weather is now becoming cooler.
7. The next players are already waiting for the court.
8. I have not gone to the dentist's office this week.
9. Patrick had never eaten spaghetti.
10. The key to the art room is not hanging on that hook.

B Write the helping verbs and the main verb for each of the following sentences.

1. She had recently photographed the Florida Everglades.
2. Chuck did not enjoy the play.
3. Bison do still graze on wildlife preserves.
4. Minnesota has often been called the land of ten thousand lakes.
5. We have never visited the Milwaukee Zoo.
6. Jane's spirits were obviously rising.
7. Negotiations between the countries have progressed.
8. The waves were viciously splashing the deck.
9. The school had probably closed because of the weather.
10. The elevators in our building are usually running.

c *Write Now* Imagine that you have a summer job as a lifeguard at a swimming pool. Write a paragraph telling the things that you did and saw in one day on the job. As a prewriting activity, you might make a list of swimming safety rules. Such rules include "Always swim with a partner" and "Do not run along the edge of a pool." These rules will remind you of the things a lifeguard has to watch for at a pool and give you some ideas on what to put in your paragraph.

When you are finished, underline the verbs you have used. Label each helping verb *HV* and each main verb *MV*.

Grammar in Action

One way to make your writing lively and interesting is to use a variety of verbs. You can build one kind of paragraph by starting with a general statement about a subject and then use action verbs to provide specific details about the subject. The example below follows this model:

> I think Washington, D.C., is a great place to visit. Last spring I explored the city with my friends. We roamed all over the National Air and Space Museum and were thrilled by the real rockets we saw there. We also pressed our faces against the White House fence and imagined the President at work inside.

Writing Activity Write a paragraph about a trip you have taken. Use a variety of main verbs and helping verbs in your sentences.

5
Compound Subjects and Compound Verbs

> A *compound subject* or a *compound verb* has two or more parts.

Look at these two sentences. How do they differ?

Bob went to the game.   Bob and Tony went to the game.

In the first sentence, the subject is *Bob*. In the second sentence, both *Bob* and *Tony* are subjects. Two or more subjects joined together are called a **compound subject**. The word *compound* means "having more than one part." Notice how a compound subject can help make your writing precise. It also makes your writing more efficient. You can tell about Bob and Tony in the same sentence.

Verbs can be compound, too. How do these sentences differ?

We hammered.   We hammered and sawed.

In the first sentence the verb is *hammered*. In the second, the **compound verb** is *hammered* and *sawed*. Again, the second sentence is more precise and efficient than two separate sentences.

The word *and* joins the compound subject and the compound verb above. Words that join words and groups of words in this way are called **conjunctions.** The word *and* is a conjunction.

Diagraming Compound Subjects and Verbs

To diagram a compound subject, split the subject line. Put the conjunction on a connecting dotted line.

EXAMPLE   Don and Mrs. Parish have left.

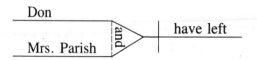

Compound verbs are similarly diagramed.

EXAMPLE   Linda read, slept, and swam.

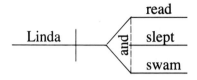

Exercises

A Make two columns on your paper. Label them *Subjects* and *Verbs*. Write the subjects from the following sentences in the first column. Write the verbs in the second column.

1. Monet and Manet were both French impressionist painters.
2. Marie and her father skate and ski together.
3. The carpenter cut, sanded, and painted the lumber.
4. The plants grew quickly and bloomed by late April.
5. Her character and determination impressed the students.
6. Thunder and lightning preceded the rain.
7. The width and depth of the stage were unusual.
8. Ruth and Phil stood and waited two hours for the bus.
9. The wind and the tide were perfect.
10. Martha Graham choreographed and performed dances.

B Combine the following sentence pairs into sentences with either compound subjects or compound verbs.

1. The workers cut the pipe. The workers threaded the pipe.
2. New cars were on display. New trucks were on display.
3. Laura cut the colored paper. Laura pasted the colored paper.
4. His shirt looked torn. His pants looked torn.
5. Ann lifted the old flute. Ann cleaned the old flute.
6. Krista ran to the bus stop. Katie ran to the bus stop.
7. Dina swept the bleachers. Ted swept the bleachers.
8. Jeff packed by noon. Jeff left by noon.
9. Pete smiled at the audience. Pete waved at the audience.
10. Alex tripped over the rock. Alex fell over the rock.

6
Kinds of Sentences

There are four kinds of sentences: *declarative, interrogative, imperative,* and *exclamatory.*

You use language for several different purposes. Sometimes you want to tell something. Other times you might want to ask a question or tell someone to do something. Sometimes you just want to show how strongly you feel about something. There is a different kind of sentence for each of these purposes. A **declarative sentence** is a sentence that makes a statement. An **interrogative sentence** asks a question. An **imperative sentence** tells or requests someone to do something. An **exclamatory sentence** is used to express strong feeling. Following is a list of the four kinds of sentences with examples of each kind.

1. A sentence that makes a statement is called a declarative sentence.

   The outfielder dropped the ball.
   Her story was short.
   The sun is shining.

2. A sentence that asks a question is called an interrogative sentence.

   Where do you go to school?
   Has anyone seen my dog?
   Do you know the final score of the game?

3. A sentence that tells or requests someone to do something is an imperative sentence.

   Finish the assignment soon.   Be here at nine o'clock.
   Turn down your radio.   Please raise the window.

4. A sentence that is used to express strong feeling is an exclamatory sentence.

   How Sherry yawned!   Dad, the garage is on fire!
   Help! I can't swim!   Oh, what fun scuba diving was!

Exercises

A For each of the following sentences, write *Declarative, Interrogative, Imperative,* or *Exclamatory* to show what kind it is.

1. In the woods we found kindling for our fire.
2. How do you do macramé?
3. Cut a green branch and sharpen the end.
4. Have you been here before, Sara?
5. Hold my books for a minute, please.
6. Yes, we took first place.
7. Is your watch running?
8. How the falls thundered!
9. Kate, look out!
10. Move to the rear of the elevator, please.

B Label each sentence *Declarative, Interrogative, Imperative,* or *Exclamatory*. Then write the punctuation mark that belongs at the end.

1. Help! My leg is broken
2. Have you ever had an emergency
3. Would you know what to do
4. Some people just shout
5. Help me
6. Instead, you should stay calm
7. Think about the problem
8. Then take action
9. You might call 911
10. Your decision is important

Grammar in Action

Using different kinds of sentences can make your writing more interesting and lively. Sometimes you might want to write dialogue. It is especially important that dialogue be realistic and able to hold the reader's attention. By varying sentence types, a writer can create realistic and interesting dialogue.

> "Oh, no!" cried Tina, "I think we're lost. We'll never find our way out of these woods."
> "Stay calm," Terry insisted. "Don't panic. If we can just find the trees with yellow markers we'll be back on the path."
> "Where was the last yellow marker we saw?" asked Terry.

Writing Activity Imagine that you want to go to a nearby fair or amusement park on Sunday with a group of your friends. Your parents, however, do not think you should go. Write a short conversation you might have in which you try to convince them to let you go. Include each of the four kinds of sentences in the conversation.

7
Subjects in Unusual Order

> The subject does not always come at the beginning of a sentence.

You won't have to look far in this book or any other to discover that the subject does not always come before the verb in a sentence. Placing the verb before the subject occasionally will make your writing more interesting and give emphasis to what you say.

Usual order   An odd creature hobbled into the store.
Unusual order   Into the store hobbled an odd creature.

Diagraming Sentences with Unusual Order

Unusual order does not change the positions of subjects and verbs on diagrams.

> EXAMPLE   Down the street came the procession.

procession	came

Exercises

A   Write the subjects and verbs in the following sentences.

1. Behind his sleepy face was a quick, intelligent mind.
2. From one end of the pipe scampered a frightened rabbit.
3. Across the Potomac River from Virginia stands the Washington Monument.
4. Over the city streets jogged the marathon runners.
5. High above our heads stretched the Bay Bridge.
6. From the committee in Boston came news of the prize.
7. Into Mr. Bevan's office strolled my scruffy dog.
8. From the sand along the shore came a curious glow.
9. In the corridor were special nautical exhibits.
10. Across the valley stretched fields of beautiful flowers.

B Rewrite each of the following sentences by placing the verb before the subject.

1. The wind roared across the campground.
2. The campers sat around the fire.
3. The crimson forest stood beyond the line of hills.
4. A chipmunk suddenly zoomed out of the shrubs.
5. A brilliant meteor streaked across the night sky.
6. A bear lurked in the forest.
7. The rapids lay far below the campsite.
8. A moth fluttered into the light of the campfire.
9. A loud growl came from the forest.
10. Three bickering geese rose from the river.

Grammar in Action

There are many ways to make your writing more interesting. You have learned, for example, to use different kinds of sentences. Varying the order of subjects and verbs is another way of holding your reader's attention.

Writing Activity Read the paragraph below. In each sentence, the subject comes before the verb. Rewrite the paragraph. Liven it up by changing the order of the subject and verb in at least two sentences.

> The canoe floated over the peaceful lake. Sandy sat, paddling effortlessly, in the bright red boat. A cool autumn breeze blew across the lake. Sandy stopped paddling and began to daydream. She imagined herself back hundreds of years. Skillful, silent Indian hunters roamed along the shore. Suddenly, a strange sound came from behind the boat. A croaking bullfrog woke Sandy from her daydream.

8
Subjects and Verbs in Questions, Exclamations, and Commands

Questions, exclamations, and commands often change the order of the subject and verb.

Some interrogative sentences are written in the usual order, with the subject first and the verb second.

> Whose kite flew the highest?
> (*Kite* is the subject, *flew* is the verb.)

Often, though, questions change the order of the subject and verb. Look at the following question:

> Did we bring enough chairs?
> (The subject *we* falls between the two parts of the verb.)

Some exclamatory sentences also change the order.

> Am I thirsty!   Was that music loud!

To find the subject and verb in a question or exclamation, try rewording the sentence as a declarative sentence.

> Have you heard the story?   Were we nervous!
> You have heard the story.   We were nervous.

Imperative sentences, or commands, usually begin with the verb. For example, in the command *Open the window,* the verb is the first word, *Open.* There doesn't seem to be any subject. The subject in the sentence is *you,* even though it is not expressed. We say that the subject *you* is understood.

> (you) Close the door.   (you) Get the newspaper.

Imperative sentences sometimes consist of only one word—the verb. *Stop. Look. Listen.* These are single-word sentences. The subject is the same: (*you*) *Stop.* (*you*) *Look.* (*you*) *Listen.*

Diagraming Questions, Exclamations, and Commands

To diagram a question or exclamatory sentence, place the subject before the verb.

Has Carolyn pitched before?

Carolyn	has pitched

When the subject of an imperative sentence is understood, show it on a diagram by writing (*you*).

Hurry.

(you)	Hurry

Open the door.

(you)	Open

Exercise

Write the subject and verb for each of the following sentences. If the subject is understood, write (*you*).

1. Which bicycle looks the newest?
2. Have the beaches opened yet?
3. Beat the egg whites carefully for a successful, light soufflé.
4. Did you watch the television special last night?
5. Were they surprised!
6. Has Pedro given his speech?
7. Put some spruce boughs and some dry leaves under your sleeping bag.
8. Has Harriet told you about her latest adventure?
9. Was that race close!
10. Did the officer question the suspects?

9
Sentences That Begin with There

> When *there* is used to begin a sentence, it usually serves just to get the sentence moving.

Study these sentences. What are the simple subjects?

> There were some pencils in my locker.
> There are two new swimmers on the team.

The word *there* is not the subject of these sentences. The subjects are *pencils* and *swimmers*.

> There *were* some *pencils* in my locker.
>
> There *are* two new *swimmers* on the team.

Study the following sentences. Notice that the subject is not first when *there* comes near the beginning of the sentence. Point out the subjects.

> **Are** there any **apples**?
> There **are** some **apples** in the bag.
> **Were** there many **families** at the picnic?
> **Is** there any **light**?
> There **was** a loud **crash**.

Diagraming Sentences with There

There is usually just an 'extra' word. It is placed on a separate line above the subject in a sentence diagram. Its line is not connected to other lines in the diagram.

EXAMPLE   There was a snowstorm.

Exercises

A Write the subjects and verbs from the following sentences.

1. There are some new notices on the bulletin board outside the cafeteria.
2. Are there any Canadian dimes here?
3. There were several interesting questions after Helen's presentation on the history of the movies.
4. There were two pet skunks in one cabin.
5. Were there telescopes in the observatory?
6. There was a line at the theater.
7. Are there any diseased trees in the parkway?
8. Were there many dinosaurs in North America?
9. There was an old green bicycle in the shed next to the abandoned garage.
10. There are new beakers in the science room down the hall.

B Write sentences using the following beginnings. Add the correct punctuation at the end of each new sentence that you create.

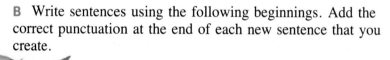

1. Were there . . .
2. There has been . . .
3. There has never been . . .
4. Has there ever been . . .
5. Will there be . . .
6. There is . . .
7. There would often be . . .
8. There will be . . .
9. Have there been . . .
10. Would there ever be . . .

c *Write Now* Suppose you went on a walk by yourself in a strange neighborhood. You walk through a large iron gate and find yourself in the most fantastic garden in the world. Write five sentences describing what you see in the garden around you. Start each sentence with the word there. When you are finished, underline each subject once and underline each verb twice.

10
Sentence Fragments and Run-on Sentences

A *sentence fragment* is a group of words that does not express a complete idea.
A *run-on sentence* occurs when two or more sentences are written as one.

Both sentence fragments and run-on sentences confuse the reader. The fragment leaves something out. The run-on sentence combines ideas that should be separate.

Sentence Fragments

A group of words that is not a sentence is called a **sentence fragment**. A fragment is only a part of something. Avoid sentence fragments in your writing.

A sentence fragment leaves out something important. Sometimes it leaves out the subject. Sometimes it leaves out the verb. As you read a fragment, you may wonder either *What is this about?* or *What happened?*

Fragment Their camping trip *(What happened?)*
Sentence Their camping trip started from Lander, Wyoming.

Fragment In the sky last night *(What is this about?)*
Sentence In the sky last night there was a strange light.

Exercises

A Write *Sentence* or *Fragment* for each of the following.

1. The dog is playing under the porch
2. Just before the end of the game
3. In our back yard
4. Down at the pharmacy in the middle of the block

5. Before the end of the day
6. We can rent a canoe
7. Came up and spoke to us during our trip to Europe last summer
8. Suddenly a fire siren screamed
9. Rain, wind, and hailstones
10. The uprooted trees landed on the garage roof

B Read the following letter. Rewrite the letter, turning the fragments into complete sentences.

Dear Rick,

    I hope your vacation is a lot of fun. It was too bad that you had to miss our last baseball game, though. A great game. Six to five over the Ashland Park Dodgers. I played first base and got two hits. A single and a triple. Donald pitched. He had eight strikeouts. His highest of the season. We really missed your bat. Almost didn't get enough hits. No errors though. The team fielded really well. It rained a little in the third inning. Almost called off. I'll see you in two weeks.

Your friend,
Delia

Run-on Sentences

    When two or more sentences are written incorrectly as one, the result is a **run-on sentence**. Sometimes no end mark is placed at the end of the first thought. At other times, a comma is incorrectly used. Here are some examples:

Incorrect   Aren't you through let me help.
Correct   Aren't you through? Let me help.

Incorrect   Pam came, we went cycling.
Correct   Pam came. We went cycling.

    The trouble with run-on sentences is that your readers don't know which words go together. Without a period and a capital letter to guide them, they believe they are following one thought. Suddenly the words stop making sense and your readers have to back up to find the start of a new idea. You can correct a run-on sentence by adding the proper end mark and capitalizing the first letter of the next sentence.

Exercises

A Rewrite the following run-on sentences correctly.

1. Balloons were stuck to the ceiling, they fell down later.
2. Dan is an artist he paints with oils.
3. We all opened our presents, then we ate dinner.
4. Kay is the sports editor she is my sister.
5. Joe caught the football he was in the end zone.
6. It rained for days, the soccer field was soaked.
7. We went to Florida, we stayed two blocks from the ocean.
8. We skated for one hour we came in to get warm.
9. I have read several biographies, I find them interesting.
10. Monica and I aren't going skiing, the snow is too slushy.

B Decide if each of the following is a complete sentence or a run-on. If it is a sentence, write *Sentence*. If it is a run-on, rewrite it correctly.

1. Lava shoots out of an erupting volcano.
2. People fear volcanoes, some eruptions have killed many.
3. The lava is very hot, it may be above 2,000° Fahrenheit.
4. Large rocks burst out of volcanoes, these are called bombs.
5. The world's largest volcano is Mauna Loa in Hawaii.
6. Mount Vesuvius erupted, three towns were destroyed.
7. Scientists who study volcanoes are called volcanologists.
8. Volcanologists predict eruptions with a tiltmeter.
9. Mount St. Helen's erupted, more than sixty people died.
10. Aconcagua in South America is an inactive volcano.

c *Proofreading* Proofread the following paragraph. Then rewrite it, correcting all errors. Pay particular attention to run-on sentences.

An interesting "careers" assembly last week. An airplain pilot explained how to fly a plane. He told us about the plane's three basic movements, *pitch, roll,* and *yaw*. Pitch describes the plane's nose moving up or down, roll describes the tipping of the wing. Yaw refers to the plane's nose turning left or right. Showed us a diagram of the plane's controls and instruments flyng a plane is quiet complicated,

Linking Grammar & Writing

A Imagine that you are on a scavenger hunt. All of the directions are written on a single sheet of paper. You and your partner have decided to separate, so you tear the paper in half in order to divide the list between you. By accident, you tear the paper the wrong way! Now each direction is only half complete. You have the right-hand half. Write what you think each direction might have originally instructed you to do. Use your imagination to make each direction a complete sentence with a subject and a verb. Be careful not to use the same subject or verb more than once.

> EXAMPLE   that you would find in a kitchen
> Bring in something that you would find in a kitchen.

1. all the colors of the rainbow
2. from another country
3. an unopened envelope
4. wrapped in tin foil
5. a blonde hair, a red hair, and a black hair
6. in three different colors
7. folded in half and marked in green eyeliner
8. postmarked this year
9. about the latest fashions
10. and bury it

B Many people have pen pals in foreign countries. Through letters, pen pals are able to learn about customs of one another's cultures. Write a letter to someone in a country where they do not celebrate Halloween. Describe how you and your friends celebrate Halloween. After you have written your description, go back and study each sentence you have written. Underline the subject of each sentence once and the predicate of each sentence twice.

Additional Practice

Parts 1 and 2 Subjects and Predicates Write the following sentences. Draw a vertical line between the subject and the predicate. Then put one line under the simple subject and two lines under the verb.

1. The two candidates agreed to a televised debate.
2. The new librarian shelved the books.
3. Picasso created many unusual and memorable works of art.
4. The President's helicopter landed in a cornfield.
5. Howard Carter discovered the tomb of King Tutankhamen.
6. My youngest sister won first prize in an essay contest.
7. Wild turkeys eat small fruits and insects.
8. Antonia Fraser writes detective stories.
9. The enthusiastic audience cheered the singer's performance.
10. Most plants manufacture their own food.

Parts 3 and 4 Identifying Verbs Write the verb in each sentence. Then write *A* if it expresses an action, *S* if it expresses a state of being, or *L* if it links the subject with a description. Underline the helping verb if there is one.

11. The sand felt hot under my bare feet.
12. The five Great Lakes are Lakes Michigan, Huron, Erie, Superior, and Ontario.
13. The runner slid across home plate.
14. President Kennedy was assassinated on November 22, 1963.
15. The Lopez family is not here.
16. Benjamin Franklin signed the Declaration of Independence.
17. My aunt has worked on many political campaigns.
18. White birches are a common sight in Minnesota.
19. Janet seems unhappy in her new school.
20. The soccer game was at Memorial Park.

Part 5 Compound Subjects and Compound Verbs Combine the following sentence pairs into sentences with either compound subjects or compound verbs.

21. The blueberries were ripe. The cherries were ripe.
22. Carol wrote her report. Carol edited her report.
23. Alan washed the kitchen floor. Alan waxed the kitchen floor.
24. Marcia danced in the play. Marcia sang in the play.
25. Orville Wright built the world's first successful airplane. Wilbur Wright built the world's first successful airplane.

Part 6 Sentence Types Label each sentence *Declarative, Interrogative, Imperative,* or *Exclamatory.* Then write the punctuation mark that belongs at the end.

26. What a magnificent sunset
27. Don't you agree that Steffi Graf is a great athlete
28. Many Americans use personal computers at home.
29. Stop tapping your pencil on the desk, please.
30. The 1988 Summer Olympics were held in South Korea.

Parts 7–9 Unusual Word Order Make two columns on your paper. Label them *Subject* and *Verb.* Write the simple subjects from the following sentences in the first column. Write the verbs in the second column. If the subject is understood to be *you,* write (*you*).

31. On the shelf sat a jar of silver coins.
32. What is the capital of Venezuela?
33. Am I glad to be home!
34. Please close the garage door.
35. From the woods came the cry of a terrified animal.
36. There are three branches of the United States government.
37. Have you seen reruns of *Leave It to Beaver*?
38. Was that dog vicious!
39. Are there any tomatoes on the vines?
40. Describe the climate of Egypt.

Part 10 Fragments and Run-ons Label each group of words *Sentence, Fragment,* or *Run-on.* Rewrite fragments and run-ons to make complete sentences.

41. On the first of the month.
42. Scott O'Dell wrote *Black Pearl,* he also wrote *The Captive.*
43. I am taking swimming lessons.
44. Tornadoes are powerful windstorms they can kill people.
45. Our terrifying ride on the new roller coaster.

Application and Review

Lesson Review

A Finding Subjects and Predicates Copy the following sentences. Draw a vertical line between each subject and predicate.

1. All the water leaked out.
2. Chris wound the thread around the bobbin.
3. His toolbox belongs in the shed.
4. Kimberly sang in the school show.
5. Meredith followed the Thanksgiving Day Parade over the Wilson Street Bridge.
6. The large brown dog rescued the child.
7. The gardener grafted the new branch onto the old tree in our front yard.
8. Peter eased his bicycle over the ditch.
9. The sleet was falling at a 40-degree angle.
10. Our entire school attended the play-off.

B Finding Simple Subjects and Verbs Write the verb and its subject for each of the following sentences.

1. The door swung soundlessly on its hinges.
2. Ann's older sister babysat for the neighbors.
3. The bluejays zigzagged past the clothesline.
4. Mr. Wilkinson's old blue van squeezed into my mother's parking place.
5. An undercoating protects a car's exterior from salt corrosion.
6. The measurements of the room surprised my father.
7. The edges of the swamp reverberated with frog sounds.
8. The computer revealed the mistake.
9. Warm weather makes me happy.
10. A beautiful flower garden surrounded the lovely old fountain in the town square.

C Finding Verbs Write the verb in each sentence. The verb may express an action or a state of being. It may link the subject to a description.

1. The Campbells had guests for Thanksgiving.
2. The sky appeared calm.
3. The porch steps are dangerous.
4. Terry had a hard time.
5. Their friendship is mutual.
6. Fran had a job at the pool for two years.
7. Mrs. Watson feels much better.
8. The farmers hoped for rain.
9. I am from Missouri.
10. The issues in the candidates' debate became more and more interesting.

D Finding Main Verbs and Helping Verbs Find the main verb and helping verb in each sentence.

1. Have you ever seen Saturn through a telescope?
2. Helen did not know the population of Maine.
3. I have never heard of an emperor called Sargon the Great.
4. We will probably stop the game at 8:30.
5. Nina may soon visit Canada with her family.
6. Peter has already left for school.
7. The explorer had never seen a cat quite like that one.
8. Vanessa will soon be here.
9. There may never be a colony on the moon.
10. The storm had suddenly stopped.

E Finding Compound Subjects and Compound Verbs Make three columns on your paper. Label them *Subjects, Verbs,* and *Conjunctions.* Fill in the appropriate columns for each sentence.

1. His shirt and tie matched.
2. Confetti and rice covered the church steps.
3. The Pep Club and the Student Council organized and presented the assembly.
4. Apples, crackers, and cheese were in big bowls on the table.

5. The plane circled once and landed.
6. After the movie, we stopped and ate dinner.
7. The cauliflower and cabbage rolled out of the bin and onto the counter.
8. Colorful stripes and spots decorated the huge poster in Elena's room.
9. Curtis and Sandra skated and skied all day.
10. Salt, pepper, and mustard are condiments.

F Identifying Kinds of Sentences For each of the following sentences, write *Declarative, Interrogative, Imperative,* or *Exclamatory* to show what kind it is. Write the correct punctuation mark.

1. What a big lawn you have
2. Follow these instructions
3. Who wants my racket
4. Terry thought and thought
5. Where is the province of Ontario
6. Go to the corner, turn right, and continue until you reach the third house
7. The dodo is a large, extinct bird
8. How empty the room seems
9. Please keep the change
10. How the mare snorted and whinnied

G Finding Subjects and Verbs in Unusual Order Write the subjects and verbs in the following sentences.

1. On the floor was a large carpet.
2. In the tower were three telescopes.
3. Under his hat were two tiny kittens.
4. In the basket sat one angry hen.
5. Into the attic flew the swarm of bees.
6. Next to the old house stood an oak tree.
7. Over the water floated the bubbles.
8. Into the yard ran the children.
9. Out of the tree flew a huge bird.
10. Inside the box was a new stereo.

H Finding the Subjects and Verbs in Questions, Exclamations, and Commands Write the subject and verb for each of the following sentences.

1. Are you going to the gymnastics meet?
2. Play that record over again, please.
3. Are Steve and Kim going to the carnival?
4. Did the referee see it?
5. Act fast.
6. Was I confused!
7. Please give me the sports page.
8. Is our team running in the district track meet?
9. Did you audition for the school play?
10. Was it hot!

I Finding the Subjects and Verbs in Sentences with *There* Write the subjects and verbs in the following sentences.

1. There were several people in line for tickets to the air show.
2. Is there any more room between the trees for my brother's tree house?
3. Has there ever been a World's Fair in this state?
4. There is an extra racket in the closet.
5. There have been many more locusts this year than last year.
6. Towards evening there is a drop in temperature.
7. Was there more paperwork than usual?
8. Have there been problems with this drill before?
9. There has been enough rain for the evergreens and the azaleas this year.
10. There was too much humidity.

J Writing Complete Sentences Add words to the following fragments to make them complete sentences. Write the sentences on a sheet of paper.

1. from the other room
2. hardly rained
3. called the library
4. across the street
5. were reflected in the glass
6. near the school
7. weeded the garden
8. Bill and Peggy
9. at the bottom
10. ate a late dinner

Chapter Review

A Finding Sentence Parts Write the verbs and their subjects in each of the following sentences.

1. A large bolt fell out of the door of the locker.
2. Onto the field raced the excited players.
3. One boy and one girl from each class should go.
4. You must wear a protective helmet at the construction site.
5. There are several Civil War battlefields in Virginia.
6. Has anyone reported the theft?
7. Fossils provide much information about the past.
8. Are the North Pole and the South Pole exactly alike?
9. Do not touch the electrical outlet!
10. Ramon and his family are traveling in Spain this summer.

B Identifying Run-ons and Fragments Write *Sentence,* *Fragment,* or *Run-on* for each of the following sentences.

1. There are huge clouds of gas and dust in deep space, they hide some of the distant stars from us.
2. Of the world's four largest cities, only Mexico City is not on a river or an ocean.
3. Shoes with cleats for basketball.
4. Very few modern Eskimos live in igloos, but many know how to build igloos from snow blocks.
5. David and Vera, the best dancers in our class.
6. A glider is an airplane without an engine, it is usually towed up into the air by an engine-powered airplane.
7. Can send out radio signals and also pick them up.
8. Viking warships were long, narrow, and fast, they were usually open on top and had flat oak bottoms.
9. Ferdinand Magellan, a Portuguese sailor.
10. Feeling great pride in my accomplishment.
11. I've visited Puerto Rico, I don't speak Spanish.
12. All along the edge of the railroad track.
13. I've got spurs, I've got chaps and boots.
14. A floodlight casts a broad beam of light.
15. The Common Market encourages trade within Europe.

22
Using Nouns

Look at the amusement park to the right and then try to imagine one in your own mind. Think of all the sights, sounds, and smells that might be there. Feel the *fun* and *thrills.* Imagine the *Ferris wheel,* the *crowds,* the *fairground,* the *lights,* the *music* and the *excitement.* The words you use to talk about these things are nouns. Nouns are words that stand for persons, places, things, or ideas.

Nouns are the basic words that create a "picture" in the reader's mind. Chapter 22 will tell you more about common and proper nouns and how to use them in your writing.

1
What Is a Noun?

A *noun* names a person, place, thing, or idea.

All words may be classified into groups. These groups are called **parts of speech**. Nouns are one of the most important of these parts of speech. The following list may be similar to ones you have written. This list will help to illustrate how important nouns are. The nouns are italicized.

To do today: Fix the *tire* on my *bike*.
Go to the *dentist* for a *checkup*.
Go to the *library* with *Pat*.
Find *books* for my *report*.
Buy dog *food* for *Champ*.
Take *Champ* to the *park*.
Call *Jan* about the *game* on *Saturday*.

You use nouns every day when you speak and write. A noun is used to name a person, place, thing, or idea.

Persons	Places	Things	Ideas
coach	New Orleans	shoe	friendship
Miguel	field	cloud	courage
friend	Disneyland	bread	honesty
skydiver	beach	tree	freedom
harpist	mountains	eraser	integrity

Nouns may name things you can see:

bike   pen   guitar   door   desk

Nouns may name emotions you can feel:

pain   love   excitement   fear   jealousy

Nouns may name ideas:

interest   education   democracy   honor   thought

In this chapter you will learn to recognize the different kinds of nouns, and you will see how they are used in writing.

Common Nouns and Proper Nouns

There are two kinds of nouns: common nouns and proper nouns. A **common noun** is the name of a whole class of persons, places, things, or ideas.

> audience   city   helicopter   intelligence

A **proper noun** is the name of a particular person, place, thing, or idea. Proper nouns always begin with capital letters.

> Carol   St. Louis   Lake Merritt   Christianity

A noun may consist of more than one word. The names of particular people or things are sometimes made up of more than one word.

Common Nouns	Proper Nouns
street	Pennsylvania Avenue
artist	Georgia O'Keeffe

Proper nouns make your writing more specific and interesting.

Exercises

A Write the proper nouns from the following sentences on your paper. Capitalize them correctly.

1. They live near the choctawhatchee river in florida.
2. The ferry to staten island passes near a famous statue.
3. One postcard was from sequoia national park.
4. The writer flannery o'connor was born in georgia.
5. In Williamsburg, we can see how americans once lived.
6. Toronto and montreal are major canadian cities.
7. A famous address in london is number ten downing street.
8. The jefferson library is equipped with computers now.
9. The cajuns of louisiana were originally from nova scotia.
10. The coast of new england has many fishing ports.

B Rewrite the following sentences. Substitute a proper noun for each italicized common noun. You may need to remove words like *a, the,* and *an* from the sentence.

1. A *boy* was reading a *newspaper* aloud.
2. The *teacher* asked a *girl* to answer the question.

3. A *doctor* visited the *school* to discuss nutrition.
4. Is the *principal* new to the *city*?
5. Please ask the *janitor* for the *book*.
6. A *man* crossed the *street* to the *shop*.
7. I lent the *magazine* to a *friend*.
8. My *uncle* wrote a *book* about an *animal*.
9. The *singer* arrived at the *hall* to give a concert.
10. In the backpack were a *snack*, a *drink*, and a *magazine*.

c *Write Now* In books or movies you meet characters you like and some you dislike. When you need a character for a story you are writing, you might use as a model a character you remember. Make a list of such characters. Write a sentence about each. Tell where you encountered the character and why you either liked or disliked him or her. Capitalize all proper nouns.

Grammar in Action

Proper names let us identify with the characters in a story.

> The detective realized too late that he had fallen into his enemy's trap. Would his good friend arrive in time to save him from the world's most evil person?

Did you recognize those characters as Sherlock Holmes, Professor Moriarty, and Dr. Watson? If these names had been used, the paragraph would be more specific and interesting.

Writing Activity Write a cast of characters for your own detective series. Give the criminals interesting nicknames. Be sure to capitalize the names correctly.

| Detective | Victim | Villain |

2
Nouns Used as Subjects

A *noun* may be used as the *subject* of a sentence.

The **subject** of a sentence tells whom or what the sentence is about. Nouns are often used as subjects.

> The goalie stopped the ball.
> (The noun *goalie* is the subject of the verb *stopped*.)
> Onto the field came Sarah and Martha.
> (The nouns *Sarah* and *Martha* are subjects of the verb *came*.)

In some sentences, the subject may not be next to the verb. Other words may come between the subject and the verb.

> The edge of the rink melted.
> (What melted? Not the whole rink, just the edge. *Edge* is the subject of *melted*.)

Exercise

Write the nouns used as subjects in the following sentences. Some sentences have more than one subject.

1. In 1957, Ray Bradbury wrote *Dandelion Wine*.
2. Children and adults have read the book.
3. Readers still remember the setting and the main character, Douglas Spaulding.
4. Douglas is twelve years old, lives in Green Town, Illinois, and loves summer.
5. A pair of sneakers in a shop window catches Douglas's eye.
6. The boy asks his father for the shoes.
7. His father tells Douglas to save up for them.
8. Slowly, the money adds up.
9. The shoes seem to have magic qualities.
10. On his feet the sneakers will even be able to outrun a deer, he thinks.

3
Nouns Used as Direct Objects

A *noun* used as a *direct object* receives the action of the verb.

The arrow hit the *target*.
Peggy threw the *baseball*.

The nouns *target* and *baseball* are direct objects. They answer the questions, *Hit what?* and *Threw what?* In other words, they receive the action of the verbs *hit* and *threw*.

Remember, direct objects always answer the questions *whom* or *what*, and they are always nouns or pronouns.

Diagraming Direct Objects

When you diagram a sentence, place the direct object after the verb on a horizontal line. Draw a vertical line between the verb and the direct object.

EXAMPLE Shari enjoys music.

<u>   Shari | enjoys | music   </u>

For compound direct objects, make the horizontal line longer after the verb. Then split the line as shown below. Each direct object should be put on a separate parallel line. Draw the vertical line before the split to show that all the words that follow it are direct objects.

EXAMPLE We met Jean, Jesse, and Eric.

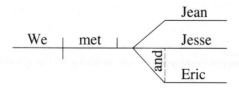

Exercises

A Write the direct objects from the following sentences.

1. Did you wash the dog?
2. I've heard that song before.
3. The vaporizer cleared my head.
4. The mechanic installed a new muffler and tailpipe.
5. Wilhelm Roentgen discovered X-rays in 1895.
6. Adam took a big piece of watermelon.
7. Inez helped her brother with his boots and jacket.
8. The lighthouse keeper swiftly and grimly climbed the stairs.
9. Roberto dropped the book into the return slot.
10. Leif Ericsson may have reached Virginia in the year 1000.

B Write the following sentences, underlining the direct objects. If a sentence does not have a direct object, provide one and underline it.

1. The children picked peaches from the tree.
2. Each school held a pageant for the holiday.
3. In the last race, Mario won.
4. Katrina adopted a chimpanzee at the zoo.
5. Please pass the salad.
6. The junior high school students read each afternoon for an hour.
7. Is Debra calling?
8. A windstorm blew the roof off the courthouse.
9. The committee chose Mr. Ling.
10. Take your jacket to the cleaners.

C *Write Now* Sportswriters are among the most colorful writers in America. When they report a day's games, they choose words that excite the imagination. Chris Evert doesn't "serve" the ball; she "smashes" it into the opposite court. Jim Rice "sails" the ball into the bleachers. Michael Jordan "dribbles" the ball and then "taps" it into the basket. A good sportwriter makes the game come alive for readers. Imagine that you are a sportswriter. Write a column about your favorite sport or game. Use direct objects in your writing.

4
Nouns Used as Indirect Objects

> The *indirect object* of the verb generally tells to whom or for whom an action is done.

A sentence may contain an indirect object only if it also has a direct object. The **indirect object** comes before the direct object and says to whom (or to what) or for whom (or for what) something is done. The word *to* or *for* never appears before the indirect object.

Subject	Verb	Indirect Object	Direct Object
Sarah	gave	Renee	a kite.
Alex	threw	Doreen	the football.
Marc	brought	Ms. Dole	flowers.

Diagraming Indirect Objects

Write the indirect object on a horizontal line lower to the right of the verb. Then draw a diagonal line from the verb to that line.

EXAMPLE Anne showed Tad the camera.

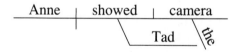

For compound indirect objects, make as many parallel indirect object lines as you need.

EXAMPLE Beth wrote Dave and Pat a letter.

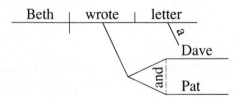

Exercises

A Write the direct objects from the following sentences.

1. Angelo served the guests fruit.
2. Mrs. Meyers gave the boys some sweaters.
3. Constantin bought his brother and sister a game.
4. Mike sent Joe and Ilene invitations.
5. Our class gave the patients a show in mime.
6. Give that chair a second coat of paint.
7. Marla taught the children Spanish.
8. We offered Greg help with his math.
9. Gina sent the class postcards from the lake resort.
10. Tracy told Sara a fascinating story about the deserted house down the block.

B Write the direct and indirect objects from the following sentences. Label them direct or indirect. Some sentences do not have indirect objects.

1. Scientists have taught chimpanzees sign language.
2. The scouts showed our class slides of their camp.
3. Tibor showed Lara a shortcut to the bus stop.
4. Give the committee a report of your activities.
5. The patient showed signs of progress.
6. I gave Pete my hat to wear in the sun.
7. Dr. Barnes gave Dr. Ortega the results of the X-rays of my swollen ankle.
8. Mail the letter in the morning.
9. We showed Pat the bread we made.
10. Rhoda sent her sister to the dime store.

C *Write Now* Think of the people you like best. Next, imagine that you are very old and very rich. You are making out your will. You are leaving something special to each one. Make a list of their names along with your bequests as shown below.

"I give (name) (gift) because (same name) gave me (love, understanding, etc.)."

5
Predicate Nouns

Predicate nouns are nouns in the predicate that explain or identify the subject.

When a linking verb connects the subject of a sentence with a noun in the predicate, that word is a **predicate noun**.

Jade is a very hard *stone*.   Sylvia is my best *friend*.

Stone and *friend* are predicate nouns. They mean the same thing as the subject or explain the subject in some way. Often the subject and the predicate noun are roughly equal.

Diagraming Predicate Nouns

The diagram for a sentence containing a predicate noun is different from the diagram for a sentence containing a direct object.

EXAMPLE   Mrs. Williams is the president.

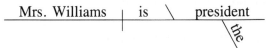

Notice that the predicate noun is on the horizontal line in the same position as the direct object. The line that separates the predicate noun from the verb is a diagonal one that slants toward the subject to show its close relationship to the subject. For sentences with a compound predicate noun, use parallel lines. The diagonal line comes before the split in the main line.

EXAMPLE   Tiger was a poor pet but a good watchdog.

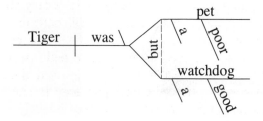

Exercises

A Write the subjects and predicate nouns from the following sentences.

1. Malta is an island south of Sicily.
2. The Texas Building is a seventy-five-story skyscraper in Houston.
3. Greenland is the largest island in the world.
4. *Lord of the Flies* is an interesting book.
5. Hernando de Soto was a Spanish explorer.
6. Pablo Picasso was one of the greatest painters of our century.
7. Franklin D. Roosevelt became President in 1933.
8. Oak Park is a suburb of Chicago.
9. London is the most populous city in England.
10. My uncle has been a policeman for a year.

B Write the predicate nouns from the following sentences. Some sentences do not have predicate nouns.

1. The ancestors of the Eskimo-Americans were Asians.
2. They had probably crossed the Bering Sea in umiaks.
3. Umiaks are large boats made of skin.
4. Eskimos are skilled and efficient hunters.
5. Eskimos are also talented storytellers.
6. Their stories are traditional tales.
7. These tales describe the Eskimos' life in a harsh climate.
8. They also tell about courage and love of family.
9. Eskimo stories are a record of the past for the young people.
10. Many of these stories are passed from one generation to the next.

C *Write Now* Imagine that you are about to write a play about an exciting adventure. Your play has a cast of ten characters. For example, the setting of the play might be a seemingly deserted planet just discovered by a crew of astronauts. It might be the deck of a pirate ship, where the crew is preparing for a night attack on a Spanish galleon. Describe each character in one sentence. Use a predicate noun in each sentence.

Grammar in Action

With a little imagination, you can brighten your writing with metaphors. A metaphor compares two different things without using *like* or *as*.

> The moon is in the dark sky.
> The moon is a shiny button sewn to the velvet sky.

The second sentence is a metaphor. It compares the moon to a button. A metaphor contains a subject (moon) and a predicate noun (button).

> The river is a glistening snake sliding through the marshes.
> The old woman's face was an apple browned by the sun.

In the first metaphor, the river (subject) is compared to a snake (predicate noun). In the second, the old woman's face (subject) is compared to an apple (predicate noun).

Writing Activity Think of five comparisons you can make with metaphors. Choose as subjects things you see every day at home or in the classroom. Be as creative as possible.

Thinking up metaphors takes concentration. Look at an object. What is its shape, its color? Is it heavy or light? Is it rough or smooth? What is it used for? Sometimes it is interesting to compare a thing to something that is extremely different. For example, compare a bridge to a cobweb. Practice using metaphors whenever you can.

6
The Plurals of Nouns

A *singular noun* names one person, place, thing, or idea.
A *plural noun* names more than one person, place, thing,
or idea.

Many writers have trouble spelling the plural forms of words.
For example, they know how to spell the singular form of the
word *avocado*. They are not sure whether the plural form is
spelled *avocados* or *avocadoes*. (The former is preferred.) Here
are seven rules for forming the plurals of nouns:

1. To form the plural of most nouns, add -*s*:

     pencils   cows   buildings   friends   games

2. When the singular ends in *s, sh, ch, x,* or *z*, add -*es*:

     losses   brushes   porches   boxes   buzzes

3. When the singular ends in *o*, add -*s*:

     studios   radios   sopranos   altos   Eskimos

   Exceptions: For a few words ending in *o* preceded by a
   consonant, add -*es*:

     potatoes   tomatoes   heroes   echoes   vetoes

4. When the singular noun ends in *y* preceded by a consonant,
   change the *y* to *i* and add -*es*:

     baby—babies   country—countries   hobby—hobbies

   If the *y* is preceded by a vowel, do not change the *y* to *i*. Just
   add -*s* to the singular.

     boy—boys   play—plays   day—days
     valley—valleys   monkey—monkeys   tray—trays

5. For most nouns ending in *f*, add -*s*. For some nouns ending in
   f or *fe*, however, change the *f* to *v* and add -*es* or -*s*:

     chief—chiefs   leaf—leaves   half—halves   self—selves
     dwarf—dwarfs   elf—elves   calf--calves   wolf—wolves

6. Some nouns are spelled the same in the singular and the plural:

deer	tuna
trout	moose
sheep	elk

7. Some nouns form their plurals in ways that are unusual or unique to them:

child—children	foot—feet
mouse—mice	tooth—teeth
woman—women	man—men

Exercises

A Write the plural of each of these nouns.

1. table	7. loaf
2. dress	8. lady
3. key	9. photo
4. daisy	10. piano
5. desk	11. tomato
6. echo	12. thief

B Write the correct plurals. Some may already be correct.

1. patch	7. foxes
2. potatos	8. taskes
3. buses	9. joys
4. baby	10. wolves
5. twos	11. churches
6. thiefs	12. partys

C *Write Now* Unusual rhymes can add humor and interest to your poetry. For example, you could rhyme *buses* and *hippo-potamuses.* You might write: "When I am riding trains or buses, I always chat with hippopotamuses." Unusual or silly rhymes were made popular by Ogden Nash, an American poet. Once, he wrote about a chipmunk, "He moves with flickering indecision/ Like stripes across the television." Write five pairs of sentences, using animals' names in rhymes. Rhyme the animals' names with anything you like—the sillier, the better. Be sure to use plural nouns in at least three rhymes. Underline all plural nouns.

7
Possessive Nouns

A *possessive noun* shows who or what owns something.

The **possessive noun** may show different kinds of ownership. It may refer to something we possess. It may refer to something that is a part of us—our bodies, our emotions, the baby's mouth, the person's anger.

Forming the Possessive of Singular Nouns

Carolyn's cassette   the boy's tape

Look at the two phrases shown above. An apostrophe and an *s* have been added to *Carolyn* and *boy* to show possession.

To form the possessive of any singular noun, add an apostrophe and *s*:

the boss's idea   Kay's poetry   the man's tie

Forming the Possessive of Plural Nouns

Remember these rules when you write the possessive of a plural noun:

1. If the plural noun ends in *s,* simply add an apostrophe: *teams' uniforms, runners'* shoes, *teachers'* notes.
2. If the plural noun does not end in *s,* add an apostrophe and *s*: *men's* voices.

Diagraming Possessive Nouns

In a diagram, possessive nouns are written on diagonal lines under the nouns they modify.

EXAMPLE   This is Dore's coat.

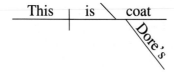

Exercises

A Rewrite each of the following phrases, using a possessive.

> EXAMPLE   the path of the locusts
> the *locusts'* path

1. the violin of the musician
2. the chair of my grandfather
3. the two cases of the travelers
4. the howling of the dogs
5. the weight of the baby
6. the voices of the sopranos
7. the five geese of the poultry farmer
8. the pearls of the duchess
9. the names of the students
10. the fins of the fish

B Write the plural possessive for each noun in the list.

1. teacher	11. child	21. coach
2. Smith	12. captain	22. hand
3. woman	13. man	23. clerk
4. player	14. researcher	24. artist
5. editor	15. mother	25. leader
6. designer	16. sailor	26. girl
7. plumber	17. boy	27. typist
8. mouse	18. astronaut	28. sheep
9. group	19. secretary	29. pilot
10. scientist	20. father	30. student

C *Proofreading* Copy the following paragraph and correct the errors you find. Pay particular attention to possessives.

Folk tales and farey tales are sometimes about a Persons three wishes. An elfin creatures' ring is lost, the princess sharp eyes find it, and the elfs wishes are given to the princess in exchainge for the ring. The humans wishes are always used carelessley. A writers' imagination could create such a story in a modern setting. A neighbors ring is found, and the man who found it is rewarded with three weeks of the neighbors landscaping services.

Linking Grammar & Writing

After seeing a bad movie, you have probably said to yourself, "I could write a better movie than that!" Well, this is your chance! Choose the setting for a movie—outer space or a haunted house, for example. Decide what characters you will put in the movie. Make a list of them. Then write at least three sentences describing the part each character will play. Use this style:

Menace Manor

List of characters:

Sam Spatter — Sam's sister, Pam, has inherited an old house called Menace Manor. Mysterious things are happening there. Sam is a detective, and he wants to solve the mystery.

Pam Spatter — Pam is Sam's sister. She came into possession of Mallory Millstone's house after his strange disappearance seven years ago. Millstone's relatives, the Carruthers, want Pam to sell the house to them.

Continue with the list of characters, describing at least four more. In your descriptions, use common and proper nouns, including predicate nouns and possessives.

439

Additional Practice

Part 1 Identifying Nouns List the nouns in each sentence. After each noun, tell whether it refers to a person, place, thing, or idea. Underline all proper nouns.

1. The Empire State Building is in New York City.
2. Ian will need a pencil, a ruler, and a compass.
3. Alice Walker is a novelist as well as a poet.
4. Carolyn invited my sister and brother to her party.
5. Brazil is the largest country in South America.
6. The pioneers faced many dangers and hardships.
7. The lawyer defended the innocence of the man.
8. The librarian suggested that Inez look for information in an encyclopedia.
9. Last night, the members of our club elected a new president.
10. Dr. Jonas Salk developed a vaccine for polio.

Parts 2–5 Functions of Nouns Make four columns on your paper. Label them *Subjects, Direct Objects, Indirect Objects,* and *Predicate Nouns*. List each noun in the following sentences in the appropriate column.

11. My little sister delivers newspapers.
12. Jane passed Judy the potatoes.
13. The Minnesota Twins have won the World Series once.
14. A salamander is an amphibian.
15. Our new neighbor is an athlete.
16. Tammy showed Sean her coin collection.
17. Abraham Lincoln wrote and delivered the Gettysburg Address.
18. Ms. Gale bought her son a new skateboard.
19. Contemporary Japan is an industrial giant.
20. Robert showed Dennis the secret handshake.

Part 6 Singular and Plural Nouns Change each noun in italics to the plural form. Write the nouns on your paper.

21. The *baby* crawled across the carpet.

22. What could possibly be in the *box*?
23. The earth shook as the *giant* approached the frightened villagers.
24. Hot gases and lava erupted from the *volcano*.
25. The glass *shelf* fell to the floor and broke.
26. The *child* refused to eat the vegetables.
27. The passengers on the train were annoyed by the *delay*.
28. The logger had forgotten to sharpen his *ax*.
29. It was a good thing that the *hero* came along to save the day.
30. We could see the wild *sheep* climbing up the side of the mountain.
31. Mr. Bucek's dentist told him that she would have to pull the *tooth*.
32. The *salmon* swam upstream for many miles.
33. The home-grown *tomato* tasted delicious.
34. Marianne and Fred both screamed when they saw the *mouse*.
35. Did you see the *donkey* pulling the cart down the gravel road?

Part 7 Possessive Nouns Rewrite each italicized phrase in the following sentences using a possessive.

> EXAMPLE   the coats of the women
>   the women's coats

36. The *paws of the dog* were caked with mud.
37. The *names of the guests* were easy to remember.
38. The *lines of the actors* were quite funny.
39. Dr. Martin Luther King, Jr., was influenced by the *ideas of Mohandas Gandhi*.
40. The *wings of the bird* were covered with oil.
41. The *teeth of a lion* are designed for killing and eating other animals.
42. A police officer found the *tools of the thieves*.
43. Each morning, Mr. Chen makes the *lunches of the children*.
44. An insect was trapped in the *web of the spider*.
45. The *knives of the juggler* were quite dull.

Application and Review

Lesson Review

A Identifying Nouns Write the nouns in each of the following sentences. Then underline each proper noun.

1. The state has passed laws against pollution.
2. Throughout the game last week, the fans cheered the team vigorously.
3. While in Washington, D.C., we visited the Pentagon and the White House.
4. A penguin waddled down the ramp.
5. South of the border is Mexico.
6. Happiness is a warm blanket.
7. The new address is Riverboat Drive, Cary.
8. Energy has been the topic of many programs on television lately.
9. Our school is the largest in North Carolina.
10. That robin just flew away with your bread.

B Identifying Nouns as Subjects Write the nouns used as subjects in each of the following sentences.

1. Clouds hid the top of the mountain from sight of the tourists.
2. Plastic bags are lighter than paper ones.
3. Every fact had been checked.
4. A cool breeze aired the room.
5. The greenhouse was hot and humid.
6. Did Marilee and Frank come with you?
7. The third hole on the golf course is on the longest fairway.
8. The second chapter of the book is easier.
9. Dishes littered the picnic table.
10. The horn on Jonathan's new bicycle sounded like a trumpet.

C Identifying Nouns as Direct Objects Write the nouns used as direct objects in each of the following sentences.

1. The cat yawned and closed its eyes.
2. The police directed traffic around the accident.
3. A mockingbird built its nest in the tulip tree.
4. Dick simply couldn't believe his eyes.
5. The contractor calculated the cost of labor.
6. Grate the rind of one lemon.
7. Kimberly rode her bicycle from Milwaukee to Kenosha.
8. We had just transplanted the evergreens.
9. Gina owns the Sunshine Plant Shop.
10. Please bring your money for the tickets tomorrow.

D Identifying Nouns Used as Indirect Objects Write the indirect objects from the following sentences. Use diagrams or whatever method your teacher suggests.

1. Uncle Ted and Aunt Marie gave my brother a new baseball and mitt.
2. Joyce showed her friends the music box.
3. Carlos baked Donna a cake for her birthday.
4. Mary Ellen might have offered the elephants her bag of peanuts.
5. Mayor Otaki showed the visitors Riverside High School on Friday.
6. Phil cooked the family a hot supper.
7. The footprints gave the police their first clue to the suspect.
8. Barb offered Lou her umbrella.
9. Did you buy your cousin that book?
10. The club members gave the meeting room a thorough cleaning last night.

E Finding Predicate Nouns Write the predicate nouns from the following sentences.

1. That van is also a camper.
2. Laura was the messenger.
3. Benji is a movie dog.
4. Susan became an architect.
5. The cherry blossom is the Chinese symbol for happiness.

6. Botswana is a country in Africa.
7. To his father, Billy was a genius.
8. Phil is the owner of the torn, dirty sneakers on the floor of the locker room.
9. Peaches and apricots were the dessert at Jerome's birthday party.
10. The thistle is the national flower of Scotland.

F Forming Plurals of Nouns Write the correct plural form of each of the following words. Some forms may already be correct.

1. feet	11. crashs	21. roachs
2. valleys	12. lifes	22. securities
3. ashes	13. tusks	23. paper
4. keys	14. cuckoos	24. patchs
5. sheeps	15. rodeos	25. tomatoes
6. wolfs	16. buzzs	26. cry
7. watchs	17. mans	27. pianoes
8. selfs	18. elkes	28. countrys
9. duos	19. bunches	29. citys
10. lobbys	20. ladies	30. leaves

G Forming the Possessives of Nouns Write the possessive forms asked for in parentheses.

> EXAMPLE   (singular possessive of Joan) towel
>   Joan's towel
>   the (plural possessive of dog) food
>   dogs' food

1. the (plural possessive of *bird*) claws
2. (singular possessive of *Melinda*) calendar
3. Bobbie (singular possessive of *Jones*) house
4. the (singular possessive of *parrot*) colors
5. the (plural possessive of *horse*) manes
6. the (singular possessive of *student*) book
7. (singular possessive of *James*) clock
8. the (plural possessive of *woman*) club
9. the (singular possessive of *mouse*) whiskers
10. the (plural possessive of *baby*) habits

Chapter Review

A Identifying Nouns and Their Uses Write the italicized word or phrase in each sentence. Identify the item as a subject, direct object, indirect object, or predicate noun.

1. Marc is studying underwater *photography*.
2. Bad *weather* ruined the fireworks display.
3. Today is the *anniversary* of the expedition.
4. Chad and Melita served *Tanya* lunch.
5. Charlie Chaplin was a *comedian* in silent films.
6. The *umpire* called the game because of rain.
7. We showed the *children* several exercises.
8. Take the *bus* to the corner of Market Street.
9. Tell *Lorna* the route to your cabin.
10. *Charles* took the shore road yesterday.
11. Karen has become the best *cyclist* on the team.
12. The *ice* on the river formed unusual shapes after the boat broke through it.
13. Laura writes numerous poems and *short stories* every week for her evening class.
14. William makes his *parents* a delicious dinner every Friday evening.
15. Allyson hopes to be the best *flutist* in the all-city music competition.

B Correct the Errors These sentences contain fifteen errors in the plural and possessive forms of nouns. Write the sentences on your paper, correcting the errors.

1. David's key's fell out of his jean's.
2. Dr. Weiss' offices are next to Leslie's shop.
3. The Womens' Council voted for the candidate's program.
4. The fishermen's catch included two trouts.
5. The farmers's auction was held in one farmers' shed.
6. The chefs' recipe calls for new potatos.
7. Childrens' feets need shoes that fit well.
8. Each racers' car was given a thorough checkup.
9. Both partys expect to win in next week's election.
10. In many countrys, highways join major citys.

23
Using Pronouns

Journal   June 8

<u>My</u> *mind wasn't on how many fish*
<u>we</u> *would catch. Instead* <u>I</u> *was*
thinking about <u>my</u> *Dad.* <u>He</u> *said* <u>we</u>
would someday buy a boat and just
the two of <u>us</u> *would fish from* <u>it</u>.

The underlined words above are called *pronouns*.
Pronouns may seem unimpressive, but they are
actually powerful words that allow you to speak and
write with greater ease. They help you avoid
repetition of the same nouns. They can also link
ideas between sentences and paragraphs.

In this chapter you will study the many different
forms of pronouns and learn how and why they are
so helpful.

1
What Is a Pronoun?

> A *pronoun* is a word that is used to take the place of a noun or another pronoun.

Like nouns, pronouns are used to refer to people, places, things, and ideas. Unlike nouns, pronouns change form according to their use. Study these pairs of sentences.

Nouns	Pronouns
Jerry pruned the tree.	*He* pruned the tree.
Mr. Barnes helped *Jerry*.	Mr. Barnes helped *him*.
Mr. Barnes is *Jerry's* father.	Mr. Barnes is *his* father.
The *books* came yesterday.	*They* came yesterday.
Ms. Franks ordered the *books*.	Ms. Franks ordered *them*.

The Forms of Pronouns

Pronouns have three forms: *subject, object,* and *possessive.*

She came. (*She* is the subject.)
I saw *her*. (*Her* is the direct object.)
It is *hers*. (*Hers* is possessive.)
It is *her* book. (*Her* is also possessive.)

The pronouns listed below are called **personal pronouns**. Each has a subject, object, and possessive form.

	Forms of the Personal Pronouns		
	Subject	**Object**	**Possessive**
Singular	I	me	my, mine
	you	you	your, yours
	she, he, it	her, him, it	her, hers, his, its
Plural	we	us	our, ours
	you	you	your, yours
	they	them	their, theirs

Substituting Pronouns for Nouns

The form that a pronoun takes depends on its use. Subject pronouns are used as subjects; object pronouns, as direct and indirect objects; and possessive pronouns, to show possession.

> The girls are here. *They* arrived early. (subject)
> The workers left later. Ann saw *them*. (direct object)
> Carlos came. Terry showed *him* the map. (indirect object)
> The Satos have moved. Carl has *their* address. (possessive)

Exercise

Change the italicized proper nouns in the following sentences to pronouns as directed in parentheses.

> EXAMPLE   Ms. Vickers gave Kate and Todd the ball
> and net.   (You are Kate. Use one word
> for Kate and Todd.)
> Ms. Vickers gave us the ball and net.

1. *Joel* is captain of the soccer team. (You are Joel. Change the verb.)
2. *Joyce* and *Craig* want to try out for the team. (You are Craig. Use two words for the people.)
3. Toss the ball to *Paula*, please. (You are Paula.)
4. *Sherry* and *Shelly* both want to play goalie. (You are Shelly. Use one word to refer to both people.)
5. *Sara* and *Sam* are experienced players. (Use one word.)
6. *Tatu* and *Karl-Heinz Granitza* are famous soccer players. (Use one word.)
7. The team presented *Jim* with a trophy. (You are not Jim.)
8. Kevin got *Winning Soccer* and *Championship Soccer* from the library. (Use one word for the two books.)
9. Please direct *Ms. Slater* and *Claire* to the soccer field. (You are Claire. Use one name and one pronoun.)
10. *Mr. Gray* and *Ms. Criticos* taught Jennie to play soccer. (Use one word for Mr. Gray and Ms. Criticos.)

2
Subject Pronouns

The pronouns *I, you, he, she, it, we,* and *they* are *subject pronouns.* Use them as subjects of the sentence or after linking verbs.

The subject form of a pronoun is used as the subject of a sentence or as a predicate pronoun following a linking verb in a sentence. A **predicate pronoun** is a pronoun that renames, or refers to, the subject. Consider the following examples of pronouns in subject form:

Subject	Predicate Pronoun
She and *I* went.	The students were *she* and *I.*
You and *he* came.	The visitors were *you* and *he.*
They and *we* walked.	The experts are *they* and *we.*

Predicate pronouns are used in speaking and writing to identify people and things: The winner was *he.*

To identify predicate pronouns, remember the following points:

1. Predicate pronouns follow linking verbs such as *am, is, are, was, were, shall be,* and *will be.*
2. The predicate pronoun renames, or refers to, the subject of the sentence.
3. A sentence with a predicate pronoun will usually make sense if the subject and the predicate pronoun are reversed.

Study the following examples:

Subject	Verb	Predicate Word
The visitor	was	he.
He	was	the visitor.
The captains	were	Rita and I.
Rita and I	were	the captains.
The winners	are	they.
They	are	the winners.

Exercises

A Write the correct form of the pronouns given in parentheses in the following sentences.

1. Kathy and (me, I) work together.
2. Mary Leakey and (him, he) searched for fossils in Tanzania.
3. The base runners were Mark and (I, me).
4. Al and (them, they) live next door.
5. (We, Us) and the Bradleys play touch football.
6. It was Todd and (me, I) in the photograph.
7. Lee and (them, they) saw an interesting Picasso exhibit at the museum.
8. There are Ginny and (I, me) on TV!
9. (Us, We) and the rest of the class visited the planetarium in the city.
10. The owners are (they, them) and their brothers.

B Substitute a pronoun for the word or words printed in italics in the following sentences. After the pronoun, write *S* if it is used as a subject pronoun or *P* if it is used as a predicate pronoun.

1. It's *Chris*. (You are Chris.)
2. The Hawk Pack and the *Eagles* were friends at camp. (Your group is the Eagles.)
3. Angie and *Darlene* helped make the salad.
4. The most frequent winners of hurdles races were Chris and *Bobby Jeanne*.
5. Robin and *Jessica* both played tennis.
6. The authors of the script were *Marion and John*.
7. *Cassandra* and I will see you tonight.
8. The boy on the right is *Dennis*.
9. Michele and *three friends* kept movie scrapbooks.
10. *Peter and Carmella* were almost late to homeroom. (You are Carmella. Use one pronoun.)

C *White Now* Suppose you are going to write a short story about two characters. Write ten sentences describing your characters. Use the characters' names as subjects in five of your sentences. Use pronouns as subjects in the other five sentences.

3
Object Pronouns

The pronouns *me, you, him, her, it, us,* and *them* are *object pronouns.* Use them as objects of the verb or as objects of a preposition.

Look at the examples below. They illustrate the uses of object pronouns.

Direct Object	Ted saw *him* and *her.*
Indirect Object	Lynn asked *me* a question.
Object of Preposition	We talked about *them* all evening.

You will learn all about prepositions on pages 544–553.

Pronouns in Compound Objects

A compound object may consist of two pronouns joined by *and, or,* or *nor.* It may also consist of a noun and a pronoun. The object form of pronouns is used in all compound objects.

Direct Object	They saw *Terry* and *me.*
	He directed *him* and *her.*
Indirect Object	Please give *Alice* and *me* your address.
	She gave *us* and *them* the records.
Object of Preposition	I'll play my guitar for *you* and *Tim.*

Exercises

A Write the correct pronouns given in parentheses in the following sentences.

1. Eric was teaching (he, him) and his sister how to play racquetball.
2. The snow gave (they, them) and the other hikers trouble.
3. Sharlene gave (her, she) an interesting puzzle.
4. Jan bought (them, they) and their friends subway tokens.
5. Have you seen John and (he, him) this morning?
6. The veterinarian told Anita and (we, us) about chimpanzees.

7. Rosellen made (he, him) a hooked rug.
8. Mother gave (them, they) and (us, we) a ride to school.
9. Jack told (me, I) about the Louistown flood.
10. Give the tickets to (he, him) and his friends.

B Write the correct pronouns given in parentheses. After each object pronoun, write *DO* for direct object, *IO* for indirect object, or *OP* for object of the preposition.

1. Our geography teacher told (we, us) about Thailand.
2. She gave a report topic to each of (us, we).
3. Su Linn gave (I, me) some help with my report.
4. Su Linn told (I, me) that Thailand was once called Siam.
5. She brought in some information for Saundra and (I, me) about the King of Siam.
6. The people of Siam greatly respected (he, him).
7. The musical *The King and I* features (he, him).
8. The king did a lot for (they, them).
9. The king gave (they, them) freedom.
10. The teacher asked Su Linn to talk more about (he, him).

Grammar in Action

Proper use of pronouns is important for effective writing and speaking. When you are using two pronouns together, you may find it hard to decide on the correct form. To write compound pronoun objects in the correct form, first look at each pronoun separately in the sentence.

> Mr. Jackson showed *him* and *me* the computer.
> Mr. Jackson showed *him* the computer.
> Mr. Jackson showed *me* the computer.

Writing Activity Imagine that your town or city has just given you an award for saving the lives of four children. Their names are Jason, Tim, Melissa, and April. Write a brief description of how you saved their lives. Use at least four sets of compound objects made up of pronouns or nouns and pronouns.

4
Possessive Pronouns

Possessive pronouns are personal pronouns used to show ownership or belonging.

Like nouns, pronouns have special possessive forms. The possessive form of a noun is made with an apostrophe. Possessive forms of pronouns are not made with an apostrophe:

The Possessive Pronouns	
my, mine	our, ours
your, yours	
his, her, hers, its	their, theirs

Possessive Pronouns and Contractions

Many people confuse the possessive forms of some pronouns with the contractions they resemble.

its—it's   your—you're   their—they're

The first word in each pair is a **possessive pronoun**. It shows possession, or ownership. The second word is a contraction made from a pronoun and a verb.

The bird preened *its* feathers. (possessive pronoun)
It's time to leave. (contraction meaning *it is*)

May I read *your* poem? (possessive pronoun)
You're late. (contraction meaning *you are*)

My brother raked *their* yard. (possessive pronoun)
I know where *they're* going. (contraction meaning they *are*)

Remember that if the word you are using takes the place of two words, it is a contraction. Also remember that a possessive pronoun does not contain an apostrophe. If you understand the difference between possessive pronouns and contractions, you will be able to write more precisely.

Exercises

A Write the correct pronoun or contraction given in parentheses in the following sentences.

1. The turtle pulled into (its, it's) shell.
2. Max said that (your, you're) moving away.
3. (Their, They're) basement flooded last spring.
4. If (its, it's) possible, (their, they're) going to win.
5. (Its, It's) the first day of winter today.
6. (Their, They're) going to Mexico on (their, they're) trip.
7. (Your, You're) next in line, Su Ling.
8. (Its, It's) only a short walk to (their, they're) house.
9. What do you have in (your, you're) gym bag?
10. The football team lost (its, it's) best players to injuries.

B Write the correct pronoun or contraction given in parentheses in the following sentences.

1. As a citizen, (your, you're) responsibility is to vote.
2. The cat licked (its, it's) paws.
3. (Their, They're) leaving (their, they're) house now.
4. When (your, you're) late, (its, it's) hard to be calm.
5. The sisters sang (their, they're) songs for us.
6. The club held (its, it's) meetings at my house.
7. Did (your, you're) painting fall off (its, it's) easel?
8. (Their, They're) waiting for the coach.
9. If (your, you're) interested in biking, come with us.
10. (Its, It's) a great day for (their, they're) camping trip.

c *Write Now* Imagine that you are reporting on the first two people to communicate with beings from another world. Write a one-paragraph news story describing this event. Be sure to tell what you, your friends, and the aliens said to each other. Use pronouns to clarify who is speaking and who is being discussed.

5
Pronoun Problems

Phrases in which *we* or *us* is used with a noun sometimes cause problems. For example, when do you say *we students?* When do you say *us students?* To decide which is correct, try saying the pronoun alone with the verb.

> (We, Us) campers hiked five miles.
> (Subject form: *We* hiked.)
> The conductor asked (we, us) musicians for silence.
> (Object form: Asked *us*.)

Who and *whom* are often used to ask questions. When they are used in this way, they are called **interrogative pronouns**. *Who* is the subject form and *whom* is the object form.

> *Who* is on the committee? (*Who* is the subject of *is*.)
> *Whom* did you ask? (*Whom* is the direct object of *did ask*.)
> From *whom* will we get the equipment? (*Whom* is the object of the preposition *from*.)

Exercise

Write the correct pronouns given in parentheses.

1. (We, Us) runners prefer the outdoor track.
2. The librarian helped (we, us) students find the book.
3. (We, Us) dancers will perform the opening number.
4. Mrs. Sullivan took (we, us) boys on a camping trip.
5. (We, Us) band members need new uniforms.
6. (Who, Whom) is the Secretary of State?
7. (Who, Whom) did Great Britain elect as Prime Minister?
8. (Who, Whom) was the star of that movie?
9. (Who, Whom) painted that mural?
10. (Who, Whom) did Grant Wood paint in *American Gothic*?

6
Pronouns and Their Antecedents

> The *antecedent* of a pronoun is the noun or another pronoun for which the pronoun stands.

Notice the pronouns in the following sentences. The pronouns all have **antecedents**, or words for which the pronoun stands.

> *Larry* came today and brought *his* tools.
> (*Larry* is the antecedent of *his*.)

> *Debbie* and *Tom* came in. *They* were laughing.
> (*Debbie* and *Tom* are the antecedents of *They*.)

The antecedent usually appears before the pronoun. Sometimes, as in the second example, the antecedent is in the sentence before it.

Exercises

A Make two columns on your paper. Label them *Pronouns* and *Antecedents*. Write the pronouns from the following sentences in the first column. Write their antecedents in the second column.

> EXAMPLE   Aunt Carol and Uncle Jim like Fran. They told her stories about the old mining town.

Pronouns	Antecedents
they	Aunt Carol, Uncle Jim
her	Fran

1. Randy had the radio with him.
2. Luis wrote a report on Einstein and Fermi. They were physicists.
3. Jane Addams is known for her social work.
4. Marsha is at home now. She is mowing the lawn.
5. Before Mary got there, Frank cooked their meal.
6. Jim and Liz brought their dog.

7. Wayne sanded and painted his table.
8. Peter put his camera on Nancy's chair.
9. Mrs. Foster bought six bananas. They were quite ripe.
10. Katie went out to walk her dog.

B Make two columns on your paper. Label them *Pronouns* and *Antecedents*. Write the pronouns from the following sentences in the first column. Write their antecedents in the second column.

1. Saturn is the second largest planet in the solar system. It is much larger than the earth.
2. Saturn is surrounded by rings. They are made of rock and ice.
3. Recent observations of the rings show that they are about ten miles thick.
4. Galileo first saw Saturn in 1610, but his telescope was not strong enough to show the rings.
5. Galileo was mistaken when he thought that Saturn was really three planets.
6. Saturn has at least seventeen satellites. They revolve around the huge planet.
7. One satellite is called Titan. It is the largest of Saturn's moons.
8. Christian Huygens discovered Titan. He discovered the satellite in 1655.
9. Huygens also discovered Saturn's rings. He thought that there was only one large ring, however.
10. W. T. Hay was an amateur astronomer known for his discovery of a huge spot on Saturn's surface.

Agreement of Pronouns and Antecedents

Use a singular pronoun for a singular antecedent. Use a plural pronoun for a plural antecedent. This is called **agreement** in number. When you write and speak, be sure that each pronoun agrees in number with its antecedent.

> *Snow* (singular) covered the hills. *It* (singular) was a foot deep.
> The *members* (plural) of the class gave *their* (plural) ideas.

Exercise

Complete the following sentences with the correct pronouns.

1. Juan put a van Gogh print on _____ wall because _____ liked _____ bright colors.
2. Mr. O'Shea moved _____ lawn sprinkler. _____ was getting water on _____ car. _____ dragged _____ over near the bushes.
3. Elliot had rice, beans, and spices in _____ kitchen. _____ mixed _____ to make a New Orleans style dish.
4. Kim and Tina put _____ return bottles on the counter. _____ got almost a dollar. _____ took the money home.

Grammar in Action

You can avoid repetition in your writing by using pronouns effectively:

Original   Last night there was a thunderstorm. The thunderstorm caused a rain gutter to fall off the house.

Revised   Last night there was a thunderstorm. It caused a rain gutter to fall off the house.

Read the following paragraph. Notice how difficult it is to read when there are no pronouns.

> Ivan wanted to make the gymnastics team. The parallel bars were Ivan's strong point. The parallel bars were also Ivan's favorite activity. Best of all, only one other person was better than Ivan on the parallel bars. Unfortunately, Mr. Cook, the gymnastics coach, favored the rings. The rings were very difficult for Ivan. Ivan seemed to have a fear of height when Ivan was up on the rings. If the rings were only a few feet closer to the ground, Ivan could relax and concentrate.

Writing Activity Rewrite the paragraph above, using pronouns in place of repeated nouns.

7
Indefinite Pronouns

An *indefinite pronoun* is a pronoun that does not refer to a particular person or thing.

Some pronouns, such as *anybody* or *each*, do not refer to a definite person or thing. These are called **indefinite pronouns**.

		Singular Indefinite Pronouns	
another	each	everything	one
anybody	either	neither	somebody
anyone	everybody	nobody	someone
anything	everyone	no one	

The singular possessive pronouns *his, her,* and *its* are used with singular indefinite pronouns.

> Someone forgot *her* scarf.
> Nobody was unhappy with *his* assignment.
> Everyone brought *his or her* ticket.

His or her may be used when the person referred to could be either male or female. A few indefinite pronouns are plural.

Plural Indefinite Pronouns			
both	few	many	several

Use the plural possessive *their* with plural indefinite pronouns:

> Both offered *their* seats.
> Many of the travelers lost *their* luggage.

To avoid awkward agreement problems, you may sometimes use a plural noun instead of an indefinite pronoun:

> *Each* of the students brought his or her book.
>   (indefinite pronoun)
> The *students* brought their books. (plural noun)

Exercises

A Write the correct possessive pronouns given in parentheses in the following sentences.

1. Not many have cast (his or her, their) votes yet.
2. Each of the drivers started (her, their) car.
3. Everybody in the aerobics class checks (his, their) heart rate.
4. Someone left (her, their) bicycle unlocked.
5. Several missed (his, their) planes.
6. Both agreed that (they, he) should leave.
7. Somebody just turned on (his, their) stereo.
8. Does everyone have (his, their) sheet music?
9. Few regretted (his, their) choice.
10. Everything on the rack had (its, their) sale price marked.

B Make two columns on your paper. Label them *Possessive Pronouns* and *Antecedents*. Write the correct possessive pronouns in the first column. Write their antecedents in the second column.

1. Either of the plans would have (its, their) advantages.
2. Has anybody completed (his, their) experiment yet?
3. Nobody wants to give up (her, their) place in line.
4. Many lost (his, their) money in the 1929 stock market crash.
5. One must protect (his or her, their) rights.
6. Nobody wants (his, their) name used in the article.
7. Both researched Margaret Mead for (her, their) reports.
8. Everybody wants (his, their) chance for success.
9. No one may open (his or her, their) test booklet yet.
10. Few weave (his, their) own cloth anymore.

C *Proofreading* Proofread the following paragraph. Then rewrite it correctly. Pay particular attention to errors in the use of pronouns.

> The junior high school finaly got computers this year. Their all in one special room called the computer lab Each student may spend one of their free periods in the lab each day. a representative from the computer company will teach both students and teachers how to use the new mashines.

Linking Grammar & Writing

A Imagine that you and your friends are starting a magazine. Decide on the purpose and activities of your magazine. Make a set of ten or more guiding principles by which your magazine will operate. In each of your statements use *we writers* or *us writers*.

B Imagine that you have been chosen to act as principal of your school for a day. What will you do? Write a paragraph in which you tell how you would change school rules during your day as principal. Use at least six of these indefinite pronouns as antecedents in your narrative: *another, anybody, anyone, anything, each, either, everybody, everyone, everything, neither, nobody, no one, one, somebody, someone, both, few, many,* and *several.*

C Think of a person who would be the ideal guest for a party you are planning. The person may be a sports figure, a movie star, or some other kind of celebrity. Write a paragraph telling why the person would be a good guest.

   In your paragraph use subject, object, possessive, and interrogative pronouns. Underline each pronoun you use in your paragraph.

Additional Practice

Parts 1–3 Subject and Object Pronouns Write the correct pronoun from the parentheses in each sentence.

1. (Us, We) asked the astronauts to describe the inside of the space shuttle.
2. The police officer gave (them, they) directions to the ballpark.
3. Julie and (me, I) sell the jewelry that we make.
4. The winners of the race were (her, she) and Dan.
5. Ann Landers gave (he, him) some good advice.
6. Mr. Woodruff and (they, them) are good mechanics.
7. It was (her, she) who ran for Vice-President of the United States.
8. You and (they, them) need to discuss this matter.
9. My favorite poets are Emily Dickinson and (he, him).
10. Although I liked (her, she), I voted for the other candidate.
11. There at the table are my sister and (she, her).
12. The judge told (they, them) to sit down and be quiet.
13. Alice asked (me, I) not to tell anyone about her illness.
14. They and (him, he) agree that Kirk Gibson is a great baseball player.
15. (Her, She) and Joan always walk to school together.

Part 4 Possessive Pronouns Write the correct pronoun or contraction from the parentheses in each sentence.

16. (Its, It's) supposed to rain later this afternoon.
17. (You're, Your) going to be late if you don't leave soon.
18. Olympic athletes who win (they're, their) events receive gold medals.
19. Did you remember to do (you're, your) homework?
20. In ancient Rome, many children received (their, they're) schooling in (their, they're) homes.
21. Have you ever seen a newt shed (it's, its) skin?
22. (Their, They're) hoping to make a million dollars from (their, they're) invention.

23. The doctor says that (its, it's) necessary to perform an operation.
24. Chicagoans had to rebuild (they're, their) city after the 1871 fire.
25. Frank said that (you're, your) getting a new bike.

Part 5 Special Pronoun Problems Write the correct pronoun from the parentheses in each sentence.

26. (Who, Whom) is the main character in *The Witch of Blackbird Pond*?
27. (We, Us) students have to present our views to our teachers.
28. (Who, Whom) will win this year's Oscar for best director?
29. Our parents showed (we, us) how to program the videocassette recorder.
30. With (who, whom) do you share your locker?

Parts 6 and 7 Antecedents and Indefinite Pronouns Some of the following sentences contain an error in pronoun agreement. Rewrite the sentences that need correction. If a sentence has no error, write *correct*.

31. Each of the students in the class gave their report.
32. Everyone should remember to cast their vote.
33. Both wanted to give their opinions on the issue of nuclear energy.
34. Has anyone finished their science project?
35. She was afraid that one of the students might lose their place.
36. Each of the speakers was eager to give his or her speech.
37. Neither of the girls wanted to eat their dinner.
38. In 1980, Ronald Reagan chose George Bush as his running mate.
39. Several of my friends asked his or her parents for a larger allowance.
40. Both of my brothers are planning to open his own business.
41. In a well planned workshop, everything is in its place.
42. Many of the monks elaborately decorated his manuscripts.
43. Either of my sisters is eager to tell their side of the story.
44. Only a few of the chefs would reveal his recipes.
45. Anyone who forgets their permission slip cannot go.

Application and Review

Lesson Review

A Using Pronouns to Replace Proper Nouns Rewrite the following sentences on your paper, changing all the italicized proper nouns to pronouns.

1. Please give *Joy Tim's* coat to take on the bus to the championship game.
2. *Ryan* has wanted to climb *Mount Washington* ever since he visited there two years ago.
3. Throw *Fred* the ball.
4. Will you lend *Ron* and *Peg* your baseball, glove, and bat this afternoon?
5. *Mr. Leham* took *Dee's* picture.
6. *Tony* and *Anton* help their parents harvest corn on their farm in Iowa.
7. The social studies teacher will certainly ask *Benji* the first question.
8. Has anyone in the Spanish Club called *Denis* to discuss plans for the fund-raising carnival?
9. *Carolyn* reads the classified advertisements in our local newspaper every day.
10. Tell *Billy Karen's* address at her grandparent's house in the country.

B Using Subject Pronouns Write the correct pronouns given in parentheses in the following sentences.

1. Larry and (him, he) mowed the grass of every house in their neighborhood.
2. Ryan and (I, me) are the best players on the East Junior High School soccer team.
3. (They, Them) and the two file clerks share an office down the hall.

4. (Us, We) and Ted like to sit in the back row at the movie theater.
5. The best ice skating pair might have been Frank and (I, me) after all.
6. (Him, He) and Paula raked the lawn on the hill behind our house yesterday.
7. The best cooks in our home economics class are (him, he) and (she, her).
8. (We, Us) and Ms. Mooney won a toaster and a color television set.
9. The first ones to leave the football stadium were (they, them).
10. Dorinda and (I, me) finished the work on our science project three days ago.

C **Using Object Pronouns** Write the correct pronouns given in parentheses in the following sentences.

1. Mr. Fox awarded the other players and (we, us) the silver trophy.
2. Ms. Phillips took (they, them) and (us, we) to the play at the theater downtown.
3. My sisters took (they, them) to the North Dakota State Fair last July.
4. The manager told Len and (he, him) the same thing about the job requirements.
5. The school basketball team chose (she, her) and (I, me) as co-captains.
6. Gail invited Joan, Jim, and (I, me) to the party at her house in the city.
7. The colorful new band uniforms will fit both (they, them) and (we, us).
8. The time change every spring and every fall confuses (me, I) and other people.
9. Mr. Litt dropped Kristie and (she, her) off at the art fair in Oak Park.
10. A strong wind blew Elaine and (I, me) off balance in the little sailboat.

D Using Pronouns and Contractions Write the correct pronoun or contraction given in parentheses in each of the following sentences.

1. (Its, It's) time for a break from learning this new computer program.
2. The elephant sprayed (its, it's) back with water.
3. (Their, They're) opening a new fitness center in the shopping mall.
4. Snakes shed (their, they're) outer layer of skin as they grow larger.
5. If (your, you're) number is called, you will win the special prize.
6. (Your, You're) the sixth person I've spoken to about this matter.
7. If (your, you're) finished with dinner, we'll all wash the dishes.
8. The silver cup has lost (its, it's) shine because it was not wrapped before it was put away.
9. When (its, it's) cold outside, even the best maintained car won't start.
10. (Their, They're) going to the Wisconsin Dells for (their, they're) vacation.

E Using Problem Pronouns Write the correct pronouns given in parentheses in the following sentences.

1. (We, Us) students must stick together.
2. Ms. McKlintock coached (we, us) girls.
3. (We, Us) girls will organize the art fair.
4. It would take (we, us) boys too long to walk all the way to the station.
5. (We, Us) two did it.
6. (Who, Whom) is your doctor?
7. (Who, Whom) did you invite?
8. (Who, Whom) will the judges choose?
9. (Who, Whom) won the 1983 World Series, Baltimore or Philadelphia?
10. (Who, Whom) is that man in the gray suit?

F Finding Antecedents Make two columns on your paper. Label them *Pronouns* and *Antecedents*. Write the pronouns from the following sentences in the first column. Write their antecedents in the second column.

1. The chair has lost three of its rungs.
2. The girls played their new records several times this morning.
3. Mother called Pete and asked him to help move the furniture.
4. The hikers were studying their maps of the many mountain trails.
5. That book has its cover on upside down.
6. Ms. Evans bought a car. It cost $5,500.
7. Grandfather is a welder. He wears goggles every day at work.
8. Donna bought Kent a card and mailed it from the post office on Friday.
9. Glenn spoke to Mr. Sakata this morning and found him quite interesting.
10. Rosita rearranged the room. It looked great.

G Using Indefinite Pronouns Write the correct possessive pronouns given in parentheses in the following sentences.

1. Nobody hits (his, their) stride in the first mile of a long marathon race.
2. Someone has (their, her) eyes shut.
3. Has anybody got (her, their) tools handy?
4. Both accepted (his, their) awards personally.
5. No one has bought (his, their) ticket to the music festival yet.
6. Has everybody made (their, his) bed?
7. Many of the students typed (his or her, their) papers.
8. Each of the girls was in (her, their) place near the door to the auditorium.
9. Several of the actors in the school play forgot (his, their) lines.
10. Everyone has (her, their) ups and downs.

Chapter Review

A Using Pronouns Write the correct pronouns given in parentheses in the following sentences.

1. My brother and (I, me) are very close.
2. The art exhibition gave Patty and (her, she) many good ideas.
3. The tenth caller was (he, him).
4. The coach instructed the halfbacks and (they, them).
5. (You're, Your) stepping on my toe!
6. Please tell me when (its, it's) lunchtime.
7. (We, Us) baseball fans can't wait until the season opens in April.
8. (Who, Whom) shall we invite to the New Year's Eve party?
9. Someone has left (their, his or her) sweater in my locker at school.
10. Both students eagerly researched (his, their) reports on ancient Egypt.

B Using Contractions and Possessive Pronouns The following paragraphs contain ten errors in the use of contractions or pronouns. Rewrite the paragraphs on your paper, correcting the errors.

Not many people can express they're feelings musically. Your very lucky if you can, and you should use your musical ability whenever its possible.

If you're parents offer to pay for music lessons, take them up on their offer. If you're not able to take lessons, your going to have to learn by yourself. Its not impossible. Practice is the key, whether or not you take lessons.

Ask your friends who play musical instruments to suggest they're favorite pieces. Perhaps they can recall their early lessons. If they're willing, its possible that they can even teach you. If their teaching is successful, be sure to show you're appreciation. Let them know your happy to be able to express your feelings musically.

Cumulative Review

A Identifying Subjects and Verbs Write the verbs and their subjects in each of the following sentences.

1. The enormous balloon lifted the basket very slowly.
2. Anybody can memorize phone numbers, addresses, and multiplication tables.
3. Do not take the dog to school.
4. Out of the cave flew thousands of bats.
5. Several cities in the United States are named Cairo.
6. An elephant and two camels led the circus parade through the city streets.
7. Were Stuart and Alan both late for class?
8. Did Thomas Jefferson write most of the Declaration of Independence?
9. Chicago and its suburbs grow larger every year.
10. The earth revolves around the sun and at the same time rotates on its own axis.

B Identifying Nouns Write the italicized word in each sentence. Then label each one as a *Subject, Direct Object, Indirect Object,* or *Predicate Noun.*

1. The *echo* sounded clear enough to be another person.
2. Marissa and Latasha gave *Rebecca* their tickets.
3. Edgar Allen Poe was a *writer* of extraordinary tales.
4. Volcanoes have formed many *islands* in the Pacific Ocean.
5. The Sears Tower is the tallest *building* in the world.
6. *John Hancock* signed the Declaration of Independence in large, clear letters.
7. "Avoid the *iceberg* at all costs!" roared the captain.
8. The *Incas* made beautiful objects from precious metals.
9. France sold the *United States* the huge Louisiana Territory.
10. Give *me* an apple, please.

C Using Pronouns Correctly Write the correct pronoun given in parentheses.

1. The youngest person in the family was (she, her).
2. Both girls left (her, their) muddy boots outside the door.
3. Try to keep (your, you're) footing on the slippery ice.
4. The huge lizard flicked (its, it's) tongue at us.
5. (Who, Whom) was the president of your class?
6. (Us, We) winners are going to have a group picture taken.
7. The old dog and (me, I) play every day.
8. Did you pick up Tammy and (she, her) at the library?
9. Can anyone lend me (his or her, their) ruler for a minute?
10. My parents invited the teachers and (they, them) to the Masquerade Ball next week.
11. Some people asked my sister and (me, I) for directions.
12. Did one of the girls lose (her, their) notebook?
13. The last person in the door was (her, she).
14. The day after tomorrow, (your, you're) going to the dentist.
15. (Whom, Who) did the noise wake?
16. Some turned in (his or her, their) homework early.
17. (It's, Its) my birthday tomorrow.
18. The other runners and (I, me) are ready to start.
19. The air show thrilled (we, us) spectators.
20. The graduates and (them, they) wore robes.

D Combined Review Make two columns. Label them *Complete Subject* and *Complete Predicate*. Put the parts of each sentence in the appropriate column. Then underline each noun once and each verb twice.

1. Many lakes in North America were formed by glaciers.
2. Glaciers were huge sheets of ice.
3. They were hundreds of miles long.
4. The glaciers moved slowly over the land.
5. The glaciers dragged enormous stones with them.
6. The glaciers scooped great holes into the earth.
7. All this activity happened millions of years ago.
8. The glaciers melted gradually.
9. The new water from the glaciers filled huge holes.
10. New lakes were created by this method.

24
Using Verbs

**". . . Only five seconds *are* left in the game.
Michael Jordan *drives* toward the basket.
He *stops*. He *shoots*. He *scores*!"**

Without a verb, a sentence would be as lifeless as
an empty basketball court. The verb is the most
important part of every sentence. No sentence is
complete without one.

In this chapter you will learn about the types of
verbs. You will learn how to use them to add
movement, activity, and life to your sentences.

1
What Is a Verb?

> A *verb* expresses an action, states that something exists, or links the subject with a word that describes or renames it.

The verb is the most important part of every sentence. Without a verb, a sentence cannot be complete or make sense.

Action Verbs

An **action verb** says what the subject of the sentence does. For example, "The baseball *flew* into the stands." The action may be one that you cannot see, as in "Shana *knew* the answer." Look at the difference colorful action verbs make in this sports column.

SHOE by Jeff MacNelly   Reprinted by permission: Tribune Media Services.

Linking Verbs

A **linking verb** states that something exists, or *is*. It does not refer to an action. Often, a linking verb links the subject of the sentence with a word in the predicate that modifies the subject.

> Yes, they *are*. (states that some group exists)
> Yes, they *are* fresh. (links *they* with *fresh*)

The most common linking verbs are *am, are, were, being, is, was, be,* and *been.* Other familiar linking verbs include *look, appear, seem, become, remain, feel, sound, taste, grow,* and *smell.* Many linking verbs can also be used as action verbs.

> The sky *looked* cloudy. (linking verb)
> Jackie *looked* at the sky. (action verb)

Exercises

A Write on your paper the verbs from the following sentences.

1. Al Rosen's dog followed us to the movies.
2. Jenny's sister repairs cars.
3. Ricardo painted this picture.
4. Our class decorated the hall for the bazaar.
5. Actors and actresses often become directors of films.
6. That guitar music sounds difficult.
7. The newspaper printed a special section on photography.
8. Dolphins and porpoises are very intelligent and friendly mammals.
9. I remember this old house.
10. Many hotels in Europe were once castles.

B Make two columns on your paper. Label them *Action Verbs* and *Linking Verbs.* Write the verbs from the following sentences in the correct column.

1. The Republic of Minerva is very small.
2. It includes two coral reefs.
3. The Pacific Ocean covers these coral reefs at high tide.
4. Sealand is even tinier.
5. It is the size of a baseball diamond.
6. It lies in the English Channel.
7. Beethoven's Fifth Symphony became the national anthem of the island nation of Morac-Songhrati-Meads.
8. Two figs in a white star adorn the flag of that island nation.
9. The national motto begins, "Conscience, Intelligence, Courage."
10. Meads Island, the capital of this country, is absent from most atlases.

2
Verbs and Direct Objects

> The *direct object* is the noun or pronoun that receives the action of the verb.

In many sentences, the subject and verb alone can express a complete thought.

Subject	Verb
Snow	fell.

In some sentences, the thought is not complete until one or more words have been added after the verb.

Linda lifted   Mel prepared

You wonder what Linda lifted and what Mel prepared. Suppose you complete the sentences.

Linda lifted *the child*.   Mel prepared *the dinner*.

In the sentences above, the word *child* receives the action of the verb *lifted*, and the word *dinner* receives the action of the verb *prepared*. *Child* and *dinner* are direct objects of the verbs.

Recognizing Direct Objects

To find the direct object in a sentence, ask *what* or *whom* after the verb. The word that answers *what* or *whom* is the **direct object**. If you cannot answer the questions *what* or *whom* after the verb, there is no direct object in the sentence.

Vera watched the parade. (Watched what? *parade*)

Exercises

A Write each sentence on your paper. Underline each verb once and each direct object twice.

1. A breeze suddenly puffed the sail.
2. This jug contains fresh water.

3. Dandelions covered our lawn.
4. The players rushed the goalie.
5. My brother collects stamps.
6. Mud splattered the windshield.
7. Roberta called her sister.
8. Barry mailed the letter.
9. Melissa sews her own clothes.
10. The Chinese invented fireworks.

B Write direct objects to complete the following sentences.

1. Emil and Alicia painted the _____ bright blue and green.
2. Lia and Bob saw a _____ on their trip to the aquarium.
3. Our school principal introduced the new _____ .
4. Nathan opened the _____ .
5. The snowstorm delayed the _____ for several hours.
6. The hot tea warmed my _____ .
7. The carpenter created a beautiful oak _____ .
8. Performers enjoy the _____ of their audiences.
9. Donald practices the _____ for an hour every night.
10. Martina made the _____ for her friend Rosa.

Grammar in Action

Colorful action verbs help make your writing interesting. Don't imagine, however, that you must write about rapid or dramatic action before you can use action verbs. You can create a vivid image for many different situations.

> As the fire blazed and crackled, we huddled close to it and told scary stories.

Writing Activity Write a paragraph in which you describe being in a peaceful place. What do you see and hear around you? Use colorful action verbs to describe those actions and sounds.

3
Transitive and Intransitive Verbs

A verb that has a direct object is called a *transitive verb*. A verb that does not have a direct object is called an *intransitive verb*.

The following are examples of **transitive** and **intransitive verbs**.

> Cheryl *wrapped* the package beautifully. (*Wrapped* is transitive; *package* is the direct object.)
> This game *requires* two batteries. (*Requires* is transitive; *batteries* is the direct object.)
> The disappointed fans *groaned*. (*Groaned* is intransitive; it has no direct object.)
> The boat nearly *rammed* into the pier. (*Rammed* is intransitive; it has no direct object.)

Recognizing Transitive and Intransitive Verbs

To determine whether the verb is transitive or intransitive, first determine whether the sentence contains a direct object. If the sentence has a direct object, the verb is transitive. If there is no direct object, the verb is intransitive. Remember that a direct object does not tell *when*, *where*, or *how*.

Some verbs are always transitive. They must always take a direct object. An example is *bring*. Other verbs are always intransitive. They can never take a direct object. An example is *arrive*. Most verbs can be used with or without direct objects. They can be transitive in one sentence and intransitive in another. An example is *sing*. Here are some examples of verbs that can be either transitive or intransitive.

Transitive	**Intransitive**
Alicia studies Spanish.	Alicia studies at home.
The monkeys ate bananas.	The monkeys ate quickly.

Exercises

A Make three columns on your paper. Label them *Transitive Verbs, Intransitive Verbs*, and *Direct Objects*. Write the verbs from the following sentences in the correct column. Write the direct objects of the transitive verbs in the third column.

1. Isabel fired her clay pot in the kiln.
2. The farmer helped the calf to its feet.
3. My friend from camp writes very well.
4. Celia and Victoria quickly raked the front lawn.
5. The school bus arrived late.
6. Big elm trees shade our street.
7. The crowd cheered for the team.
8. Louisa draws in charcoal.
9. Jorge played his favorite album for us.
10. The tide comes in quickly.

B For each of the following verbs, write two sentences. In the first sentence, make the verb transitive. In the second sentence, make the verb intransitive. Write *Transitive* after the first sentence and *Intransitive* after the second.

> EXAMPLE   see
>
> I see an eagle. *Transitive*
> I see well. *Intransitive*

1. read	5. wrinkle	8. sail
2. use	6. burn	9. unpack
3. turn	7. wash	10. act
4. ring		

C *Write Now* Imagine that you were at the zoo when one of the chimpanzees escaped and was recaptured. You even witnessed its capture. Now, the editor of your school newspaper wants you to write an article about this event. In one paragraph, describe the capture. Use strong action words. Then label each action verb transitive (*T*) if it has a direct object or intransitive (*INT*) if it does not.

4
Linking Verbs and Predicate Words

A *linking verb* connects, or links, the subject with a word in the predicate that modifies or renames the subject.

A **linking verb** connects the subject with a word in the predicate. The word that follows the linking verb says something about the subject.

> The movie *was* long.   The room *seemed* empty.
> The forest *looked* dark.   The wind *sounds* fierce.

Long says something about the *movie*; *dark*, about the *forest*; *empty*, about the *room*; and *fierce*, about the *wind*. *Long, dark, empty,* and *fierce* are all adjectives.

The words that follow linking verbs and modify or rename the subject may be adjectives, nouns, or pronouns. Because they appear in the predicate, these words are called **predicate words**.

Do not confuse a linking verb with a transitive verb. A transitive verb has a direct object. A linking verb connects the subject with a word in the predicate that says something about the subject. Predicate words identify, rename, or explain the subject.

> The yogurt tasted delicious. (*Delicious* is a predicate word that says something about the subject, *yogurt*; *tasted* is a linking verb.)
> Ned tasted the yogurt. (*Yogurt* is the direct object of *tasted*; *tasted* is a transitive verb.)
> Yogurt is a dairy product. (*Product* is a predicate word that says something about the subject, *yogurt*; *is* is a linking verb.)

Remember, the words *am, is, are, was, were,* and *be* are often used as linking verbs. Other words often used as linking verbs are *seem, look, appear, smell, taste, feel, sound, remain, grow,* and *become.*

Exercise

Make two columns on your paper. Label them *Linking Verbs* and *Transitive Verbs*. Write the verbs from the following sentences in the correct column.

1. At seventeen, Henry VIII became King of England.
2. He employed many great thinkers and artists.
3. Sir Thomas More, a philosopher and scholar, was an advisor to Henry.
4. Henry is famous for his six marriages and for the fate of his wives.
5. Henry had three children.
6. All three children eventually ruled England.
7. Henry enjoyed sports and games.
8. He looked handsome and dashing in his youth.
9. But Henry grew fat in his later years.
10. The Tower of London still displays Henry's enormous jousting armor.

Henry VIII of England.
Hans Holbein.

Grammar in Action

In persuasive writing—the kind of writing used by advertisers—linking verbs and predicate words are used to create favorable descriptions of products.

> This orange juice tastes like a glass of sunshine.
> Your wash will smell like springtime.

In the sentences above, the linking verb connects the subject with a descriptive predicate word that conveys a positive impression of the product.

Writing Activity Write five advertising slogans to "sell" products of your choice. Your "products" may include such things as homeless kittens or your own leaf-raking services. Be sure your sentences have linking verbs and predicate words.

5
Verb Phrases

> A *verb phrase* consists of a main verb and one or more helping verbs.

Often the **main verb** of the sentence appears with one or more helping verbs. A main verb with one or more helping verbs is called a **verb phrase**. The most common helping verbs are forms of *be, have,* and *do*. These and other helping verbs are shown below in italics.

will go	*may* go	*could* go
shall go	*would* go	*might* go
can go	*should* go	*must* go

A verb phrase may consist of a main verb and two helping verbs. *Have* is often the middle word of a three-word verb phrase.

will have gone	*may have* gone	*could have* gone
shall have gone	*would have* gone	*might have* gone

The words that make up a verb phrase are not always together. Sometimes the helping verbs and the main verb are separated by words that are not verbs. Notice that *not* and its contraction, *n't*, are not verbs.

can hardly *wait*	*could* not *have come*	*did*n't *see*

Exercises

A Write the complete verb phrases from the sentences below.

1. Therese would like concert tickets.
2. The class must meet here.
3. The Great Lakes have never frozen completely even during the month of January.
4. Our neighbors are always planning something.
5. The driver could have told him about the traffic jam.
6. Twelve states are named after Indian tribes.

7. Shall I bring the plates and cups?
8. I really don't have time for a movie.
9. The message may have fallen off the desk.
10. Plants cannot live without sunlight.

B Make two columns on your paper. Label them *Helping Verbs* and *Main Verbs*. Write the helping verbs in the following sentences in the first column. Write the main verbs in the second column.

1. We could not have run the sale without you.
2. Carrie has won the tennis tournament.
3. The fragrance of marigolds will keep mosquitoes away.
4. Mr. Steed must have traveled to dozens of countries.
5. My bicycle will definitely need new brakes soon.
6. Will you take the bus with me?
7. Renaldo can repair just about anything.
8. Have you ever seen a cranberry bog?
9. Why don't you run for student council president?
10. I really should not have stayed so late.

Daniel Greysolon, Sieur Dulhut at the Head of the Lakes—1679. F. L. Jaques.

c *Write Now* Imagine that you were one of the first explorers to travel west of the Mississippi River. Write a paragraph about your adventures. Begin it with the phrase "If I had gone West in the 1800's. . . ." Underline all the main verbs once and all the helping verbs twice.

6
The Tenses of Verbs

> Different forms of the verb are used to show the time of an action or of a state of being. These forms are called the *tenses* of the verb.

A verb has different forms called **tenses** to indicate whether an action takes place or a condition exists in the present, past, or future. The tenses of the verbs you use tell your readers clearly when something happened or when a condition existed.

The **present tense** places the action or condition in the present.

> I *jog* after school. I *am* a jogger.

The **past tense** places the action or condition in the past.

> I *skated* a lot last winter. I *was* a hockey player.

The **future tense** places the action or condition in the future.

> I *will play* football this fall. I *will be* a quarterback.

Tense changes are made in three ways:

1. By a change in the ending: *walk, walked*
2. By a change in the spelling: *sing, sang, sung*
3. By a change in the helping verbs: *has walked, will walk*

Tenses of Verbs		
Present Tense	She walks	We choose
Future Tense	She will walk	We shall choose
Past Tense	She walked	We chose
Present Perfect Tense	She has walked	We have chosen
Past Perfect Tense	She had walked	We had chosen

Looking at the chart, you can see that three different tenses may be used to show the time of a past action or condition: the *past*, the *present perfect*, or the *past perfect*. You will learn two things about them.

1. The past tense form of the verb is used alone. It is never used with a helping verb.

> we cleaned   you ran

2. The present perfect tense is formed by using the helping verbs *has* or *have* with the main verb. The past perfect tense is formed by using the helping verb *had* with the main verb.

> he has cleaned   you had run

Exercises

A Make two columns on your paper. Label them *Verbs* and *Verb Tenses*. Write the verbs from the following sentences in the first column, and write their tenses in the second column.

1. The goalie wore a face mask.
2. Gayle carries her camera everywhere.
3. Mitch has weeded the garden.
4. I will sing with you.
5. You bought flowers for me?
6. Eugene will find the note on the table.
7. I had opened the kitchen window just after the storm.
8. I will be a lifeguard this summer.
9. Polly had taken French horn lessons.
10. Makiko studies Japanese on Saturdays.

B Complete the following sentences with the verb forms given in parentheses. Write the complete sentences.

1. Cleopatra (past perfect of *become*) ruler of Egypt by the time she was seventeen.
2. Our class (future of *see*) a movie about her next week.
3. We (past of *learn*) that Cleopatra and Julius Caesar traveled together down the Nile.
4. I wonder if the moviemakers (present perfect of *include*) her 300-foot barge.
5. After Caesar (past perfect of *help*) Cleopatra to defeat her brother, she decided to return to Rome with him.
6. Cleopatra (past of *leave*) Rome after Caesar was murdered.
7. After Caesar's death, Cleopatra (past of *travel*) to Asia to ask for Mark Antony's help.

8. She and Antony eventually (past of *marry*).
9. But the Roman senate (past of *take*) away Mark Antony's power because of the marriage.
10. Our class (present perfect of *enjoy*) studying about this fascinating woman.

c *Proofreading* Proofread the following paragraph. Rewrite the message, correcting all errors. Pay particular attention to verb tenses.

> We spends all are time at the Ocean. Yesterday, we sail aboard a big saleboat. It is really more like an old sailing ship. It even had a figurehead. We notice that the name of the ship was the *siren*. Legend says that sirens used to call sailors out to see. today we will goes out on another boat, which will took us out to see humpback whales. Then tommorow we goes to the beach.

7
The Principal Parts of Verbs

Verb tenses are made using the three *principal parts* of verbs: the *present*, the *past*, and the *past participle*.

The different tenses of a verb are all made from three basic forms of that verb. Those forms are called the **principle parts** of the verb. They include the **present**, **past**, and **past participle**.

Another form, the **present participle**, is sometimes called the fourth principal part. This part is formed by adding *–ing* to the present: *call—calling*. The present participle is often used with a helping verb to make a verb phrase such as *is calling*.

Regular Verbs

Most English verbs are regular. For a regular verb, the past is formed by adding *-ed* or *-d* to the present. The past participle is the same as the past and is always used with a helping verb.

Present	Past	Past Participle
talk	talked	(have) talked
sip	sipped	(have) sipped

Irregular Verbs

For some verbs, the forms of the past and the past participle do not follow the same rules. Those verbs are called **irregular verbs**. In some cases, the past and the past participle forms of an irregular verb are spelled the same:

Present	Past	Past Participle
bring	brought	(have) brought
say	said	(have) said

Often, the past and past participle are not the same:

Present	Past	Past Participle
do	did	(have) done
go	went	(have) gone

Mistakes in verb forms are commonly made in writing and speaking. Remember the following rules:

1. The past form of the verb is used alone, without a helping verb: the pond *froze* during the night.
2. The past participle is used with a helping verb: the pond *has frozen* since yesterday.

The list below gives the principal parts of the most common irregular verbs. Refer to this list whenever you are unsure about which form to use. The principal parts of irregular verbs are also given in most dictionaries. Remember that the past participle is always used with a helping verb. As you study the list of irregular verbs, practice saying the word *have* in front of each past participle.

Irregular Verbs

Present	Past	Past Participle	Present	Past	Past Participle
begin	began	(have) begun	ride	rode	(have) ridden
break	broke	(have) broken	ring	rang	(have) rung
bring	brought	(have) brought	rise	rose	(have) risen
choose	chose	(have) chosen	run	ran	(have) run
come	came	(have) come	say	said	(have) said
do	did	(have) done	see	saw	(have) seen
drink	drank	(have) drunk	sing	sang	(have) sung
eat	ate	(have) eaten	speak	spoke	(have) spoken
fall	fell	(have) fallen	steal	stole	(have) stolen
freeze	froze	(have) frozen	swim	swam	(have) swum
give	gave	(have) given	take	took	(have) taken
go	went	(have) gone	teach	taught	(have) taught
grow	grew	(have) grown	throw	threw	(have) thrown
have	had	(have) had	wear	wore	(have) worn
know	knew	(have) known	write	wrote	(have) written

Practice Pages on Irregular Verbs

Irregular verbs can cause problems in writing and in speaking. The following pages provide practice in the correct use of irregular verbs.

How well do you use these verbs? The exercise on the next page will tell you. If you need more practice with certain verbs, your teacher may ask you to do the exercises on the following pages. For each verb there are many sentences that will help you to "say it right," "hear it right," and "write it right."

Exercise

Write on your paper the correct form of the verb in parentheses.

1. The jury (bring, brought) in the verdict.
2. Michael had (broke, broken) his leg while water-skiing.
3. Ruth had (came, come) to the meeting with us.
4. Rosa has (chose, chosen) a biography for her report.
5. After we had (did, done) all the work, we went tobogganing.
6. Have you and Michael (drank, drunk) all the lemonade?
7. When I came home, everyone else had (ate, eaten) dinner.
8. The tomatoes in our yard have (froze, frozen).
9. Mr. Lorenzo has (gave, given) us our assignment.
10. All of us have (gone, went) to the science fair.
11. Have you (grew, grown) strawberries or raspberries?
12. How long have you (knew, known) the MacArthurs?
13. Sara and Rick (ran, run) in the relay race yesterday.
14. At camp, the dinner bell (rang, rung) every night.
15. I have never (rode, ridden) in a helicopter.
16. Lisa and Perry have (sang, sung) that duet many times before.
17. I have (saw, seen) every one of the regular season games.
18. Ms. Bell has (spoke, spoken) to me about a job at her shop.
19. Last summer I (swam, swum) across the lake.
20. The pitcher had (threw, thrown) the ball to first base.
21. He must have (wore, worn) his lucky cap.
22. Always proofread what you have (wrote, written).

Say It Right   Hear It Right

Break
Broke
Broken

A Say these sentences over until the correct use of *broke* and *broken* sounds natural to you.

1. I broke the dish.
2. The dish is broken.
3. The window had been broken.
4. She broke the record.
5. The tool was broken.
6. They broke the news.
7. Jason had broken his arm.
8. Christie broke the lamp.

Bring
Brought
Brought

B Say these sentences over until the correct use of *bring* and *brought* sounds natural to you.

1. What have you brought?
2. Did you bring your bicycle?
3. I brought mine.
4. Keith brought his lunch.
5. Laura will bring the fruit.
6. We brought you a gift.
7. I wish I'd brought my jacket.
8. Did you bring the tickets?

Write It Right

Write on your paper the correct form of the verb given in parentheses.

1. Jill (broke, broken) her wristwatch.
2. Pat has (broke, broken) another window.
3. We have (broke, broken) the tape player.
4. My dad's car (broke, broken) down on the expressway yesterday.
5. The runner has (broke, broken) the previous high school record.
6. Ted's fishing pole (broke, broken) in half.
7. That clock in the gymnasium has been (broke, broken) for over a year.
8. Did you (bring, brought) your camera?
9. I (bring, brought) two rolls of film.
10. Have you (bring, brought) the report to class?
11. Yes, I have (bring, brought) mine.
12. I will (bring, brought) you a surprise.
13. Haven't you (bring, brought) anything?
14. Peg (bring, brought) her new racket to class.
15. The paramedics did (bring, brought) him to the hospital as quickly as possible.

Say It Right   Hear It Right

A Say these sentences over until the correct use of *chose* and **Choose**
chosen sounds natural to you. **Chose**
Chosen

1. The actors have been chosen.
2. Our band was chosen to play.
3. The class chose these books.
4. Everybody has been chosen.
5. Student Council chose Lou.
6. Was Liz chosen?
7. Have you been chosen?
8. Dick chose a yellow shirt.

B Say these sentences over until the correct use of *came* and **Come**
come sounds natural to you. **Came**
Come

1. Jennifer came yesterday.
2. Has Jay come yet?
3. Amy and Tad came home.
4. He should have come.
5. Has the plumber come yet?
6. They came on Sunday.
7. We came on the early bus.
8. Eric has come for me.

Write It Right

Write on your paper the correct form of the verb given in parentheses.

1. We (chose, chosen) to go camping this summer.
2. I (chose, chosen) watermelon instead of fresh peaches for dessert.
3. Have you (chose, chosen) the color you want on your walls?
4. The team has (chose, chosen) Chris as captain.
5. We have (chose, chosen) new books for our library.
6. At camp we (chose, chosen) Rico as our group leader.
7. Ruth has been (chose, chosen) as class president for three years in a row.
8. I (chose, chosen) to work on the mural.
9. I saw the accident just as I (came, come) along.
10. The exhibit will (came, come) this way in July.
11. I wondered why the mail carrier (came, come) to our house so early.
12. They had arrived long before we (came, come) home.
13. A loud cheer (came, come) from the fans.
14. My sister has (came, come) home from college this weekend.
15. She (came, come) last weekend, too.

Say It Right   Hear It Right

Do
Did
Done

A Say these sentences over until the correct use of *did* and *done* sounds natural to you.

1. Art did his homework.
2. Ellen has done hers.
3. Tim did his quickly.
4. Jo has done ten problems.
5. Darla did only three.
6. Mark has done only one.
7. I did the dishes.
8. Jim has done the laundry.

Drink
Drank
Drunk

B Say these sentences over until the correct use of *drank* and *drunk* sounds natural to you.

1. I have drunk the lemonade.
2. Ann has drunk three glasses.
3. Ray had drunk only one.
4. Carol drank iced tea.
5. Linda drank cider.
6. Carla drank water.
7. Tim had drunk juice.
8. Kim and Lisa drank milk.

Write It Right

Write on your paper the correct form of the verb given in parentheses.

1. The school band has never (did, done) so well in the state competition before.
2. No one could have (did, done) those problems.
3. Have you (did, done) your homework?
4. The team (did, done) the best it could.
5. Have you (did, done) the math exercises yet?
6. Juan (did, done) a good job on that model airplane.
7. Jane (did, done) that scale model of a pyramid.
8. The seventh graders (did, done) well in the school spelling contest.
9. I have (drank, drunk) eight glasses of water today.
10. Jamie and Steve (drank, drunk) the juice.
11. Have you ever (drank, drunk) goat's milk?
12. The baby has (drank, drunk) from a bottle for at least three months now.
13. We (drank, drunk) lemonade at the picnic.
14. Josh has never (drank, drunk) iced tea.
15. At the end of the trail, the hikers (drank, drunk) water from the well on the farm.

Say It Right   Hear It Right

A Say these sentences over until the correct use of *ate* and *eaten* sounds natural to you.

Eat
Ate
Eaten

1. I ate breakfast.
2. Dana has eaten breakfast at the diner.
3. Sam ate later.
4. Beth ate slowly.
5. We ate macaroni and cheese.
6. We had eaten dinner.
7. I ate very little.
8. Shelly had eaten more than usual.

B Say these sentences over until the correct use of *froze* and *frozen* sounds natural to you.

Freeze
Froze
Frozen

1. Mother froze the meat.
2. The yogurt was frozen.
3. The milk had frozen.
4. Rain froze into hail.
5. We nearly froze.
6. Bus windows were frozen.
7. My fingers froze.
8. The chicken was frozen.

Write It Right

Write on your paper the correct form of the verb given in parentheses.

1. We had (ate, eaten) before going to the game.
2. Sue (ate, eaten) her supper too quickly.
3. I (ate, eaten) very fast.
4. Scott has (ate, eaten) all the peanut butter sandwiches we made.
5. Lucy had (ate, eaten) lunch at a friend's house.
6. She has (ate, eaten) there lots of times.
7. Dave had (ate, eaten) slowly.
8. We (ate, eaten) at my cousin's last night.
9. This is the first winter the river has (froze, frozen) so quickly.
10. The water pipe has (froze, frozen).
11. We (froze, frozen) the leftovers.
12. Waiting for the school bus, we nearly (froze, frozen).
13. Linda's toes were almost (froze, frozen).
14. The lake was (froze, frozen) halfway out from shore.
15. The azaleas in our garden (froze, frozen) in late autumn.

Say It Right Hear It Right

**Give
Gave
Given**

A Say these sentences over until the correct use of *gave* and *given* sounds natural to you.

1. I gave my speech yesterday.
2. Jo gave her speech today.
3. Jim had given his speech last week.
4. My aunt gave me a watch.
5. She has given a party.
6. I gave the baby a toy.
7. I was given the day off.
8. Sue gave Bob a rare stamp.

**Go
Went
Gone**

B Say these sentences over until the correct use of *went* and *gone* sounds natural to you.

1. Allison went skiing.
2. John had gone last winter.
3. I went to the museum.
4. We went swimming yesterday.
5. Have you gone to Disneyland?
6. I went there last summer.
7. Dee went this spring.
8. Mom went to her office.

Write It Right

Write on your paper the correct form of the verb given in parentheses.

1. Their team seemed to have (gave, given) up.
2. You should have (gave, given) better directions.
3. Sally (gave, given) me a jigsaw puzzle.
4. We (give, gave) our teacher a present yesterday.
5. Our coach has always (gave, given) us praise when we win.
6. Sometimes he has (gave, given) us a lecture.
7. Mrs. Anzalone (gave, given) us a spelling test.
8. Jeremy and Beth (went, gone) to the meeting.
9. Jonathan and Liz have (went, gone) hiking.
10. I have (went, gone) fishing only once.
11. Rob has (went, gone) swimming at the public pool every day this summer.
12. Mary has always (went, gone) to the library on Saturday.
13. The children (went, gone) down to the farmers' market.
14. My sister has always (went, gone) to summer camp in the mountains.
15. Ann has (went, gone) away for the summer.

Say It Right   Hear It Right

A Say these sentences over until the correct use of *grew* and *grown* sounds natural to you.

Grow
Grew
Grown

1. We grew a garden.
2. We grew our own lettuce.
3. Have you ever grown beets?
4. The tree has grown tall.
5. The grass grew quickly.
6. I had grown tired of weeding.
7. The house has grown old.
8. We have all grown a lot.

B Say these sentences over until the correct use of *knew* and *known* sounds natural to you.

Know
Knew
Known

1. I knew the owner.
2. I have known her for years.
3. Ed had known the results.
4. I had known Jim in camp.
5. They knew it would rain.
6. Have you known Kim long?
7. Lola knew her well.
8. Rhea knew Celie from band.

Write It Right

Write on your paper the correct form of the verb given in parentheses.

1. George has (grew, grown) two inches since last fall.
2. The Jeffersons (grew, grown) their own vegetables.
3. Ana (grew, grown) ten different kinds of plants for her experiment.
4. Our class (grew, grown) flowers for the army hospital.
5. We have (grew, grown) radishes every summer.
6. Mother (grew, grown) catnip for our cat.
7. The sunflowers have (grew, grown) six feet tall.
8. They have (knew, known) each other since fifth grade.
9. I have never (knew, known) a busier person.
10. We never (knew, known) the game was postponed.
11. Mike had never (knew, known) anyone from Japan before.
12. We (knew, known) the Jacksons.
13. Clara has (knew, known) how to swim since she was three years old.
14. The hikers (knew, known) they were lost.
15. Before she started school, Kathy (knew, known) how to read.

Say It Right   Hear It Right

Ride
Rode
Ridden

A Say these sentences over until the correct use of *rode* and *ridden* sounds natural to you.

1. Pat has ridden a horse.
2. I rode one last summer.
3. We rode our minibikes.
4. We have ridden them before.
5. We rode to the lake.
6. Have you ridden a camel?
7. Josh rode the Ferris wheel.
8. I have ridden it often.

Ring
Rang
Rung

B Say these sentences over until the correct use of *rang* and *rung* sounds natural to you.

1. Has the bell rung yet?
2. I thought it rang.
3. Who rang the doorbell?
4. The mail carrier rang it.
5. The church bells rang.
6. The victory bell rang.
7. The fire alarm rang again.
8. It had rung earlier.

Write It Right

Write on your paper the correct form of the verb given in parentheses.

1. Have you (rode, ridden) in a 747 jet?
2. My brother (rode, ridden) in a dirt bike race at the park last Saturday.
3. Our club (rode, ridden) in the bike-a-thon to raise money.
4. My uncle (rode, ridden) his bicycle to work.
5. Garry has (rode, ridden) in many horse shows, but this is his first blue ribbon.
6. Helen has (rode, ridden) in a hot-air balloon.
7. Have you ever (rode, ridden) in a rodeo?
8. The telephone (rang, rung) earlier.
9. The cathedral bells (rang, rung) this morning.
10. The camp dinner bell had (rang, rung) twice.
11. The doorbell (rang, rung) three times.
12. All the church bells had (rang, rung).
13. The fire alarm had (rang, rung), but it was a false alarm.
14. The student who (rang, rung) the fire alarm was expelled from school.
15. When the ceremony ended, all the bells (rang, rung).

Say It Right   Hear It Right

A Say these sentences over until the correct use of *ran* and *run* sounds natural to you.

Run
Ran
Run

1. We ran along the shore.
2. Al had just run all the way.
3. We ran the battery down.
4. Has our time run out?
5. Barb ran the school store.
6. The joggers ran for miles.
7. Steve has run three miles.
8. Has the relay race been run yet?

B Say these sentences over until the correct use of *saw* and *seen* sounds natural to you.

See
Saw
Seen

1. I saw you yesterday.
2. We haven't seen him before.
3. Jay saw the All-Star game on television.
4. Antonio saw it, too.
5. Eve saw us at the pool.
6. We have seen that movie.
7. Michelle has seen the play.
8. Have you seen our new station wagon?

Write It Right

Write on your paper the correct form of the verb given in parentheses.

1. The car has (ran, run) out of gas.
2. Rhonda and Janet (ran, run) four miles today.
3. The race was (ran, run) at the high school.
4. Who (ran, run) in the relays?
5. Viola had (ran, run) until she was exhausted.
6. When my little brother saw Dad coming, he (ran, run) to meet him.
7. Have you ever (ran, run) in a three-legged race?
8. We (saw, seen) the World Series.
9. I (saw, seen) Mr. and Mrs. Barton at the Auto Show.
10. My family (saw, seen) the Olympic Games.
11. Darcy has (saw, seen) the film before.
12. We (saw, seen) the King Tut exhibit in Chicago.
13. I have never (saw, seen) a professional football game, except on television.
14. Have you (saw, seen) the movie *It's a Wonderful Life*?
15. Ian (saw, seen) a deer in the woods last weekend.

Say It Right   Hear It Right

Sing
Sang
Sung

A Say these sentences over until the correct use of *sang* and *sung* sounds natural to you.

1. We sang in chorus yesterday.
2. She had sung that before.
3. They sang with the band.
4. Who sang at the concert?
5. The choir had sung.
6. Kirsten sang two songs.
7. George has sung one song.
8. Have you ever sung a solo before?

Speak
Spoke
Spoken

B Say these sentences over until the correct use of *spoke* and *spoken* sounds natural to you.

1. Has Don spoken to you?
2. He spoke to Julie.
3. The principal spoke to us.
4. We had spoken to her.
5. The baby spoke one word.
6. Mother spoke to my teacher.
7. Lou has not spoken to me.
8. Who spoke at the meeting?

Write It Right

Write on your paper the correct form of the verb given in parentheses.

1. The quartet (sang, sung) in the mall last weekend.
2. Have you ever (sang, sung) in a chorus?
3. Paul (sang, sung) a solo.
4. Roger and Donna had (sang, sung) a duet.
5. Sara, Lois, Sam, and Chuck (sang, sung) a medley of jazz tunes.
6. Ginny (sang, sung) her solo beautifully.
7. Her cousin had (sang, sung) just before she did.
8. We (sang, sung) around the campfire every night on our hike.
9. Tim (spoke, spoken) to the new students.
10. The first speaker (spoke, spoken) on solar energy.
11. The second speaker (spoke, spoken) on nuclear energy.
12. They had both (spoke, spoken) to us before.
13. I have (spoke, spoken) to three movie stars.
14. The coach (spoke, spoken) to us enthusiastically about our performance.
15. He has often (spoke, spoken) to us that way.

Say It Right Hear It Right

A Say these sentences over until the correct use of *swam* and *swum* sounds natural to you.

Swim
Swam
Swum

1. Wayne and I swam in the pool.
2. Sherry has swum there, too.
3. We swam after school.
4. Mandy swam for an hour.
5. I have swum three laps.
6. The salmon swam upstream.
7. Roy swam in the river.
8. Dozens of fish had swum by the dock.

B Say these sentences over until the correct use of *threw* and *thrown* sounds natural to you.

Throw
Threw
Thrown

1. We threw open the doors.
2. The ball was thrown wildly.
3. The mayor threw out the ball.
4. He threw his cap in the air.
5. Who threw that pass?
6. Have you thrown it away?
7. Yes, I have thrown it away.
8. The pitcher threw a curve ball.

Write It Right

Write on your paper the correct form of the verb given in parentheses.

1. Our team (swam, swum) laps for an hour.
2. Dolphins (swam, swum) around our boat.
3. We have (swam, swum) in that race every year.
4. Sally (swam, swum) faster than I did.
5. Only one goldfish (swam, swum) in the bowl.
6. Sharks (swam, swum) in those waters.
7. Curt has (swam, swum) in races for years.
8. The trout (swam, swum) toward the bait.
9. Our newspaper had been (threw, thrown) into the bushes again on Sunday.
10. Kent (threw, thrown) the winning pass.
11. They had (threw, thrown) out bread for the birds.
12. Lynn (threw, thrown) the ball to Tanya.
13. The wrestler has (threw, thrown) his opponent.
14. The cargo was (threw, thrown) out of the train by the blast and caught fire.
15. We (threw, thrown) out the spoiled leftovers.

Say It Right   Hear It Right

Wear
Wore
Worn

A Say these sentences over until the correct use of *wore* and *worn* sounds natural to you.

1. I wore out my shoes.
2. Ryan had worn his jacket.
3. José wore glasses.
4. Gail had worn out the record.

5. Libby wore her jeans.
6. We all wore sandals.
7. They had worn masks.
8. I have worn out my pen.

Write
Wrote
Written

B Say these sentences over until the correct use of *wrote* and *written* sounds natural to you.

1. Who wrote that play?
2. Shakespeare wrote it.
3. Rebecca has written a letter.
4. Who wrote this song?

5. Carmela has written a song.
6. We wrote the assignment.
7. I had written two thank-you letters.
8. Doug had written a poem.

Write It Right

Write on your paper the correct form of the verb given in parentheses.

1. We all (wore, worn) costumes to the party.
2. I have never (wore, worn) roller skates before.
3. Holly and Juanita were (wore, worn) out from the hike up the mountain.
4. My sandals (wore, worn) out.
5. I have already (wore, worn) out her jeans.
6. My sister (wore, worn) her new blazer.
7. We had (wore, worn) our heavy gloves to shovel snow out of the driveway.
8. To whom have you (wrote, written)?
9. Who (wrote, written) "The Raven"?
10. Edgar Allan Poe (wrote, written) it.
11. We had (wrote, written) our friends in Indiana.
12. Emily Dickinson (wrote, written) many poems.
13. Have you ever (wrote, written) to the President of the United States?
14. How many letters have you (wrote, written) now?
15. Adam (wrote, written) a science fiction story.

8
Choosing the Right Verb

Several pairs of verbs cause confusion. These include *let* and *leave*, *lie* and *lay*, and *sit* and *set*.

Sometimes people confuse one verb with another one. For example, they do not know whether to say, "Let me help" or "Leave me help."

In this lesson, you will study several pairs of verbs that often cause difficulty. Notice the correct way to use these verbs.

Using Let *and* Leave

1. *Let* means "to allow" or "to permit."

> EXAMPLE   *Let* me go.

2. *Leave* means "to depart" or "to let stay or be."

> EXAMPLE   They always *leave* rehearsals early.

The principal parts of the verbs *let* and *leave* are:

let, let, let

Present	I let you read my book.
Past	I let you read it yesterday.
Past participle	I have let you read it often.

leave, left, left

Present	Leave your book here.
Past	I left my book on the table.
Past participle	I have left my book at home.

Exercise

Write the correct verb given in parentheses.

1. (Let, Leave) me take those packages.
2. Shouldn't we (let, leave) Carlie join us?
3. Please (let, leave) these paintings dry.
4. We will (let, leave) a note for him.
5. Will you (let, leave) Mark and Trisha go with you?

6. (Let, Leave) us help you wash the dishes.
7. (Let, Leave) me hold one of the new puppies.
8. Randy will (let, leave) on her vacation tomorrow.
9. Did you (let, leave) your hat and scarf at home?
10. The Jansens have (let, left) us use their tree swing.

Using Lie and Lay

1. *Lie* means "to rest" or "to recline." It does not take an object.

> EXAMPLE   I often *lie* on the couch.

2. *Lay* means "to put or place something." It takes an object.

> EXAMPLE   Wanda *laid* the dress pattern out on the
> kitchen table.

The principal parts of the verbs *lie* and *lay* are:

lie, lay, lain
Present   My dog lies on the porch when it's hot.
Past   The cyclist lay under the tree for a rest.
Past participle How long has that shovel lain there?

lay, laid, laid
Present   Megan always lays her coat on that chair.
Past   He laid his books on the table.
Past participle She has laid the picnic blanket on the lawn.

Exercise

Write the correct verb given in parentheses.

1. Ricardo (lay, laid) his head on the pillow.
2. Please (lie, lay) those photographs on the table.
3. I'm going to (lie, lay) on the beach for an hour or so.
4. Where did you (lie, lay) the scissors?
5. Freida (lies, lays) her pen down while she thinks.
6. The nurse advised me to (lie, lay) down for a while.
7. David and Brian had (lain, laid) their skateboards in a
   dangerous place.
8. Annie (lay, laid) in the sun during lunch.
9. Several runners did (lie, lay) down after the race.
10. If you will (lie, lay) all the drawings on this counter, we
    will choose the best one.

Using Sit and Set

1. *Sit* means "to be in a seat" or "to rest." It does not take an object.

> EXAMPLE   We often *sit* on the front porch after dinner.

Sat is the past tense of *sit*. It means "was seated," or "was rested." Because it is a form of *sit*, *sat* does not take an object.

> EXAMPLE   We *sat* on the front porch after dinner.

2. *Set* means "to put or place something." It takes an object.

> EXAMPLE   Please *set* the dishes on the table.

The principal parts of the verbs *sit* and *set* are:

sit, sat, sat

Present	Our cat sits in the sunlight.
Past	Jay sat in the first row.
Past participle	I have sat there many times.

set, set, set

Present	Set the bowl on the counter.
Past	I set the packages there last night.
Past participle	Carol has set the plants on the porch.

Exercise

Write on your paper the correct verb given in parentheses.

1. Do you want to (sit, set) on the balcony?
2. I would prefer to (sit, set) on the main floor.
3. Please (sit, set) the groceries on the table.
4. We (sat, set) in the front row at the outdoor concert in the park.
5. Marlene and Rhoda will (sit, set) near the fifty-yard line.
6. Will you (sit, set) the luggage on the curb, please?
7. I thought I had (sat, set) my lunch tray on this table by the window.
8. Sandy (sat, set) the mail on the counter.
9. Won't you (sit, set) down and join us for dinner?
10. The drivers (sat, set) waiting for the race to begin.

Linking Grammar & Writing

A Verbs can be vivid and descriptive. If you say that a person walks, you have not given a precise picture. However, if you say that a person shuffles, you have created a vivid image; the verb *shuffle* is more descriptive than the verb *walked*. If, instead, you say that a person scurried, you have created a vivid but different picture; a scurrying movement varies greatly from a shuffling one.

Think of ten animals. Write a sentence about each one. In each sentence, use a verb that vividly describes the way the animal moves. For example, an elephant *lumbers*; a butterfly *flits*.

B Imagine that you are a sports announcer. You are watching a World Series game. It is the bottom of the ninth inning. The score is tied 1–1. There are two outs and nobody is on base, but then Homer Casey comes up to bat. If he can score a run, the game will be over. How does the team in the field react? What does the pitcher do? What do the outfielders do? Does Homer Casey score the winning run? Write a present-tense account of what happens when Casey comes to bat. Use lively verbs.

C Imagine that you were the young pitcher in the World Series game that you described in exercise B. Thirty years have passed, and you are describing the game to your grandchildren. Write an account of what happened. Use a combination of past, past perfect, and present perfect tenses.

500

Additional Practice

Parts 1–3 Identifying Verbs Make three columns. Label them *Transitive Verbs, Intransitive Verbs,* and *Direct Objects*. Write the verbs from the following sentences in the correct column. Write the direct objects of the transitive verbs in the third column.

1. The *Titanic* sank after a collision with an iceberg.
2. Fran trimmed her neighbor's shrubbery.
3. Emily Dickinson was born in Amherst, Massachusetts.
4. The stock clerk stacked the cans on the shelf.
5. On our fishing trip we caught twenty bluegills.
6. Billie Holiday sang the blues with strength and tenderness.
7. More than sixty million Americans bowl each year.
8. I eat cereal for breakfast every morning.
9. Many young people watch music videos.
10. The sun will set at exactly seven o'clock on both Tuesday and Wednesday this week.

Part 4 Linking Verbs and Predicate Words Make three columns. Label them *Linking Verbs, Transitive Verbs,* and *Predicate Words*. Write the verbs from the following sentences in the correct column. Write the predicate word or words of the linking verbs in the third column.

11. The music from the jukebox sounded old-fashioned.
12. Hernando de Soto explored the American Southeast in an unsuccessful search for gold.
13. Bill Cosby is a popular entertainer.
14. Last summer my sisters painted the barn.
15. That steaming bowl of chili smells delicious.
16. Harriet Tubman, once a slave herself, led many slaves to freedom.
17. The morning sunlight brightened the room.
18. The child seemed happy and carefree.
19. My cousin is an actress and singer.
20. Alabama became a state in 1819.

Part 5   Verb Phrases   Copy each sentence. Then underline each helping verb once and each main verb twice.

21. The princess will someday become queen of her country.
22. I could not find the square root of the number.
23. The squirrels and other animals are busily preparing for winter.
24. Wayne Gretzky could have remained with the Edmonton Oilers.
25. We might not have finished it without your help.

Parts 6 and 7   Verb Tenses and Principal Parts   Write the complete verb in each sentence and identify its tense (*Present, Future, Past, Present Perfect,* or *Past Perfect*).

26. Abigail Adams was a strong supporter of women's rights.
27. Mark will write to his grandparents about his summer vacation plans.
28. A large number of Americans eat many of their meals away from home.
29. Walt Disney created Donald Duck and Mickey Mouse.
30. Carolyn has never seen snow before.
31. I will join our school's soccer team.
32. Craig had washed the dinner dishes.
33. The chorus performed again this evening.
34. Have you ever gone tobogganing?
35. Air pollution poses a serious problem in many parts of the world.

Part 8   Choosing the Right Verb   Write the correct form of the verb in parentheses.

36. Our cat likes to (lay, lie) on the windowsill.
37. (Set, Sit) down and relax until they return.
38. Please (set, sit) the house keys on the kitchen table.
39. My little brother would not (leave, let) me help him.
40. Phyllis (laid, lay) the notebook on her desk.
41. The hoe is (lying, laying) in the garden where you left it.
42. (Leave, Let) your brother alone and don't argue.
43. The fork (sits, sets) to the left of the plate.
44. The teller (lay, laid) the coins on the counter.
45. Don't (sit, set) the ladder on unlevel ground.

Application and Review

Lesson Review

A Identifying Verbs Make two columns on your paper. Label them *Action Verbs* and *Linking Verbs*. Write the verbs from the following sentences in the correct column.

1. The deer appeared frightened.
2. Martina Navratilova won the tennis tournament.
3. The recital lasted for over three hours.
4. Jack went to Florida with his parents.
5. Is Penny on the volleyball team?
6. The fog horn sounded all night.
7. That new sofa looks great in here.
8. The car suddenly skidded out of control.
9. Mindy and Denise walked out on the pier by the ocean together.
10. I really did all my homework in just two hours.

B Recognizing Direct Objects Make two columns on your paper. Label them *Action Verbs* and *Direct Objects*. Write the verbs and direct objects from the following sentences in the correct column.

1. Judy and I weeded the garden.
2. Please close the locker.
3. Cora and Emanuel mistakenly hung the painting upside down.
4. Marilee read the biographies of every one of her favorite songwriters.
5. I heard that song on the radio early this morning.
6. After our fancy Italian dinner, Gabriel washed the dishes.
7. Alexis opened the trunk quietly and carefully.
8. The state police officer ticketed the speeder.
9. Sip the hot chicken soup slowly.
10. Scott met his uncle at the airport.

C Recognizing Transitive and Intransitive Verbs Make three columns on your paper. Label them *Transitive Verbs, Intransitive Verbs,* and *Direct Objects*. Write the verbs from the following sentences in the correct column. Write the direct objects of the transitive verbs in the third column.

1. Dave leaned his bicycle against the building.
2. The construction workers hammered all day long.
3. Weeds grew in the garden.
4. Turn the thermostat to seventy degrees.
5. The sun set at 6:20.
6. Jackie swept the front porch in a hurry.
7. I understand the arrangement.
8. That gymnast's performance amazed us.
9. The paramedics ran as fast as possible.
10. The librarian whispered the answer to José's question.

D Identifying Linking Verbs Make three columns on your paper. Label them *Subjects, Linking Verbs,* and *Predicate Words*. Write the subjects, linking verbs, and predicate words from the following sentences in the correct column.

1. Spaghetti is my favorite food.
2. The sauerkraut smells strong.
3. At sunset, the pink clouds became brighter.
4. Nelson seemed annoyed.
5. The grass became awfully tall last summer.
6. Those blue stripes look violet to me in this light.
7. My older brother was a busboy last summer.
8. The goalie looked ready for anything.
9. The old tomcat remained absolutely motionless all afternoon.
10. The freshly painted room smelled awful for several weeks.

E Identifying Main Verbs Make two columns on your paper. Label them *Helping Verbs,* and *Main Verbs*. Write all the parts of the verb phrases in the following sentences in the correct column.

1. May I take your coat?
2. The Rosenfelds might have an extra outdoor thermometer.

3. Shall I put the fish in the freezer?
4. It might have happened anyway.
5. Bridget must have practiced her speech a hundred times.
6. Our class is going to the art museum.
7. I would never have forgotten your birthday.
8. Jim would ordinarily have put the mitt in the hall closet.
9. Franny couldn't have taken Dad's camera with her.
10. The book has obviously been out in the rain.

F Recognizing Tenses Make two columns on your paper. Label them *Verbs* and *Verb Tenses*. Write the verbs from the following sentences in the first column. Write their tenses in the second column.

1. Brenda brought her backpack.
2. Rick steals bases all the time.
3. My mother will write a letter to the newspaper.
4. Fernando has walked the dog.
5. The Domingo family had known us for years.
6. Shall I heat the stew?
7. The pitcher's arm gave out.
8. Have you two already met?
9. Will you sign the card too?
10. Nancy runs a mile every morning.

G Recognizing Principal Parts Make three columns on your paper. Label them *Present, Past,* and *Past Participle*. Write the verbs from the following sentences in the correct column. Then label each helping verb *HV*.

1. Grandma has shoveled the snow off the sidewalk.
2. Sea monkeys need food every four days.
3. The Great Lakes were formed by a glacier.
4. My mother has sewn a dress for me.
5. Cherry trees grow all over Washington, D.C.
6. You sure have taken your time.
7. We watched the sky for meteors.
8. The actress has used many different accents.
9. We make our own peanut butter.
10. The wasps buzzed around the patio umbrella.

H Using Irregular Verbs Complete the following sentences with the verb forms given in parentheses. Write the complete sentences.

1. Huge hailstones (past of *fall*) from the sky.
2. Ramona (past of *catch*) a lot of trout on our trip.
3. Mark (past of *speak*) to the manager about a job.
4. We (future of *eat*) only the ripe bananas.
5. What time does the sun (present of *rise*) tomorrow?
6. Peter and Michael have (past participle of *swim*) in Walden Pond.
7. Have you ever (past participle of *ride*) in a horse-drawn carriage?
8. My father (future of *come*) to school tomorrow.
9. I have (past participle of *see*) cardinals in those trees many times.
10. Does Sheri (present of *know*) the actor's name?

I Choosing the Right Verb Write the correct verb given in parentheses.

1. (Let, Leave) some lettuce in the hamster's cage.
2. Rob's mother (lay, laid) his new suit out on the bed.
3. Bert (sat, set) the milk on the table.
4. My parents (let, left) me stay up late last night.
5. The rake has (lain, laid) in the snow rusting all winter.
6. Those dishes have (sat, set) in the sink for days.
7. We had (let, left) the basketball game before our team even scored.
8. We (lay, lie) our clothes out on the railing to dry.
9. My brother once (sat, set) in a park in Vienna where peacocks roamed around in the open.
10. The crew will (lie, lay) the railroad tracks right behind the factory.
11. The jeweler (sat, set) the diamond in the center of a wide gold band.
12. We (let, left) the carrots cook too long.
13. (Lie, Lay) that treasure map out on the table.
14. Regis (sat, set) the hands of the clock ahead an hour.
15. The sick horse has (lain, laid) in the stable for days.

Chapter Review

A Recognizing Verbs Make five columns. Label them
*Transitive Verbs, Intransitive Verbs, Linking Verbs, Direct
Objects,* and *Predicate Words.* Write the verbs from the
following sentences in the correct column. Write the direct
objects of the transitive verbs in the fourth column. Write the
predicate words in the last column.

1. Nancy enjoys classical music.
2. The cafeteria is open now.
3. Snow has covered the fields.
4. Are the chemicals dangerous?
5. Those two dogs always fight.
6. Millions of football fans watched the Super Bowl on TV.
7. The preschool children at the day care center nap every day
   after lunch.
8. Calvin read the biography of Aaron Burr on the long bus
   ride.
9. Could the weather forecaster have predicted the tornado any
   sooner?
10. The milk doesn't smell fresh.

B Using Verbs Correctly Write the correct verb form given in
parentheses.

1. With our band in the lead, the Columbus Day parade
   (began, begun) at noon.
2. Have you (chose, chosen) a captain for the soccer team yet?
3. Antonia (ran, run) for class president last semester.
4. Gregory could have (swam, swum) faster than I.
5. For parents' night, our class has (wrote, written) a skit about
   Abraham Lincoln.
6. The tired harvesters (lay, laid) in the shade of the barn.
7. My father accidentally (let, left) his keys in the car.
8. Joel has (wore, worn) that same black sweatshirt in every
   game this season.
9. Clara (sit, set) the box of slides on the closet shelf beside
   the microscopes.
10. The librarian has (spoke, spoken) in whispers for years.

25
Using Adjectives

What would it be like to live in a black-and-white world? There would be no canary yellow vintage coupes, just old black cars. We would have no rainbow-hued chalksticks, just white ones. Colors make the world more interesting.

Language needs color, too. Adjectives add color by modifying nouns and pronouns and making their meanings more precise or vivid. In this chapter you will learn how to recognize adjectives and how to use them to add color and precision to your speaking and writing.

1
What Is an Adjective?

> An *adjective* is a word that modifies a noun or pronoun.

In talking with a friend, you might say, "We have bats in our garage." Your friend might not know that you are talking about baseball bats instead of animals. What you meant to say was, "We have *three baseball* bats in our garage."

The words you left out—*three* and *baseball*—would have made your statement clearer. They answer the questions *How many* and *What kind*. They are adjectives.

Adjectives are words that modify or clearly define the nouns and pronouns you use in your speaking and writing. You can usually tell whether a word is an adjective by asking if it answers the questions *what kind, how many,* or *which one*. Look at how well the Peanuts gang uses adjectives.

Proper Adjectives

Adjectives can be made from nouns. *Salty, mountainous,* and *colorful* are adjectives made from nouns. When an adjective is made from a proper noun, it is called a **proper adjective**. Like proper nouns, proper adjectives are always capitalized.

A proper noun does not always change its form to become an adjective. It may become an adjective simply by being used to describe another noun as in *June wedding* and *Friday night*. However, sometimes an ending such as *-an, -ian, -n, -ese,* or *-ish* is added to the noun to make it an adjective. In this way, the proper nouns *China* and *Mexico* become the proper adjectives *Chinese* and *Mexican*.

Articles

The words *a*, *an*, and *the* are special adjectives called **articles**. *The* is the **definite article**. It points out one specific person, place, thing, or idea. *A* and *an* are **indefinite articles**. They are less specific.

When you speak or write, you refer to specific persons, places, things, and ideas with the word *the*. When you want to be less specific, use *a* or *an*.

> Hand me *the* pen, please. (one specific pen)
> Hand me *a* pen, please. (any pen).

Diagraming Sentences Containing Adjectives

On a diagram an adjective is shown on a line that slants down from the noun or pronoun the adjective modifies.

EXAMPLE   A tall tree shades the old cabin.

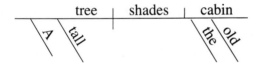

Exercises

A Write the adjectives from the following sentences on your paper. Do not write articles.

1. The old car needs constant attention.
2. Princeton is an Eastern college.
3. Sheep and wriggly lambs crowded into the empty shed.
4. Round objects roll.
5. Rob whipped up a hot, peppery, Mexican sauce.
6. The silly, bespectacled clown led the parade.
7. Egyptian kings were buried in gigantic tombs with priceless treasures.
8. The weathered windmill made a weird, screechy sound.
9. A ferocious otter ruled the small pond.
10. A playful, young Alaskan husky pranced happily ahead of the sled.

B Make two columns on your paper. Label them *Adjectives* and *Words Modified*. Write the adjectives from the following sentences in the first column. Write the words they modify in the second column. Be aware that nouns can also be used as adjectives in some situations. Do not write articles.

1. Sculptures have been made from many different materials.
2. The first sculptors used bone and ivory.
3. Greek sculptors carved huge marble blocks into human forms.
4. Ancient Greeks also made colossal bronze statues.
5. African masks have been sculpted from wood.
6. At Mt. Rushmore, a magnificent sculpture of four presidential faces has been cut into a craggy mountain.
7. One artist piled rocks in a lake and called the arrangement a modern masterpiece.
8. A French chef in New York chisels ice sculptures.
9. Machine parts are used to form mechanical sculptures.
10. Even neon lights have been used to create art works.

Grammar in Action

Adjectives are like colors. Both help to create more vivid and interesting pictures. For example, which of these two sentences helps you see the person and the place best?

> The detective entered the room.
> The rumpled detective entered the elegant drawing room.

Writing Activity Rewrite the paragraph below. Replace the underlined adjectives with one or more vivid and specific adjectives.

> Dave bought a <u>new</u> bicycle for the <u>long</u> bike trip he planned to take. He also got a <u>nice</u> helmet and a <u>good</u> pair of biking shorts. He thought the bike trip would be <u>fun</u>. It would be five hundred <u>long</u> miles over <u>difficult</u> roads, but he felt ready.

2
Predicate Adjectives

A *predicate adjective* is an adjective that follows a linking verb. It describes the subject of the sentence.

Adjectives usually come before the words they modify:

The *tired, thirsty* scouts crawled up the hill.

Sometimes they appear after the words they modify:

The scouts, *tired* and *thirsty,* crawled up the hill.

Varying adjective position adds variety to sentences.
In some sentences, the verb separates an adjective from the word it modifies:

The clouds are *billowy.* (*billowy* modifies *clouds*)
Does the water look *murky?* (*murky* modifies *water*)
The banners were *large* and *colorful.* (*large* and
    colorful modify *banners*)

The adjectives *billowy, murky, large,* and *colorful* are in the predicate of their sentences, but each of these adjectives modifies the subject of its sentence. Each one is linked to the subject it modifies by a *linking verb.* For this reason these adjectives are given a special name: **predicate adjectives**.

Diagraming Predicate Adjectives

You show predicate adjectives on diagrams just as you show predicate nouns. Place them on the horizontal line following the verb, and separate them from the verb by a line slanting back toward the subject.

EXAMPLE   The stairs seem steep.

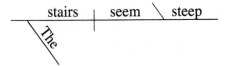

Exercises

A Make three columns on your paper. Label them *Subjects, Linking Verbs,* and *Predicate Adjectives.* Write the subjects, linking verbs, and predicate adjectives from the following sentences in the correct column. There might be more than one predicate adjective in a sentence.

1. The old house looked drab and dingy.
2. Spinach often tastes gritty.
3. In the spring, the woods smelled fresh and earthy.
4. Sometimes, bears look ferocious.
5. Before dinner, the kitchen was bright and noisy.
6. That story sounds suspicious to me.
7. In Bob's opinion, the peaches were sweet and juicy.
8. The old rug is smelly and dusty.
9. In the morning light, the river seems dirty.
10. During the race, the runner looked sweaty but joyful.

B Make two columns on your paper. Label them *Adjectives* and *Words Modified.* Write the adjectives from the following sentences in the first column. Write the words they modify in the second column. Then, rewrite the sentences, replacing the predicate adjectives with different predicate adjectives.

1. As we approach, the volcano seems gigantic.
2. The fish tastes salty.
3. The trophy was heavy and cold.
4. After Dad repaired it, the raft looked safe.
5. Though they were on different teams, the players appeared friendly.
6. Outside my window, the leaves are orange and red.
7. On a foggy day, marshes often look eerie.
8. The water feels greasy and cold.
9. The petals look soft and velvety.
10. After we did push-ups, our muscles were tense.

C *Write Now* Write ten sentences to describe the experiences in taste, touch, smell, sight, or sound you might encounter on a picnic at the beach in July. Use a predicate adjective in each of your sentences.

3
Adjectives in Comparisons

Use the *comparative form* of an adjective to compare two things.
Use the *superlative form* of an adjective to compare more than two things.

We often use adjectives to compare two or more people or things.

> Rachel is *taller* than Susan.
> Rachel is the *tallest* girl in our class.

When adjectives are used in comparisons, they have special forms or spellings.

The Forms of Adjectives in Comparisons

When we compare one thing or person with another, we use the **comparative form** of the adjective. When we compare a thing or person with more than one other, we use the **superlative form**.

Short adjectives, like *tall* and *new*, change their forms by adding *-er* for the comparative or *-est* for the superlative. Notice that adjectives ending in *y* change the *y* to *i* before adding these endings.

Adjective	Comparative Form	Superlative Form
light	lighter	lightest
sweet	sweeter	sweetest
happy	happier	happiest
shiny	shinier	shiniest

Longer adjectives, like *accurate* and *peculiar*, use *more* for the comparative and *most* for the superlative.

Adjective	Comparative Form	Superlative Form
wonderful	more wonderful	most wonderful
capable	more capable	most capable
important	more important	most important

Use only one form of comparison at a time. Do not use *more* and *-er* together, or *most* and *-est* together.

Incorrect Goalie is the most hardest position to play.
Correct   Goalie is the *hardest* position to play.

Incorrect This comedian is much more funnier than that one.
Correct   This comedian is much *funnier* than that one.

The Forms of Good and Bad

A few adjectives change their forms by using totally different words for the comparative and superlative forms. Here are two important ones to remember.

Adjective	Comparative Form	Superlative Form
good	better	best
bad	worse	worst

Exercises

A Write the correct form of the adjectives given in parentheses.

1. Which high school is (bigger, biggest), Wilson or Nichols?
2. These woolen gloves are the (warmest, most warmer) of all my gloves.
3. Golf courses are always (busiest, most busy) on weekends.
4. Of the two city parks, this one is (gooder, better).
5. This is the (baddest, worst) tennis match of the season.
6. Is a ton of iron (heavier, more heavy) than a ton of feathers?
7. It was (warmer, warmest) in Texas than in Florida that day.
8. This is the (awfullest, most awful) movie I've ever seen.
9. Ian's books looked even (raggeder, more ragged) than yours.
10. Tony was the (most careful, carefullest) camper on our overnight trip.

B Write the correct form of the adjective given in parentheses.

1. These ice skates have (comparative of *sharp*) blades than those.
2. This is the (superlative of *good*) fish I've ever tasted.
3. The rinse water for the dishes was (comparative of *soapy*) than usual.

4. This is the (superlative of *bad*) weather for kite flying.
5. The pond is the (superlative of *clear*) I've ever seen it this year.
6. Greg politely took the (comparative of *small*) piece.
7. That's the (superlative of *bright*) star in the whole sky.
8. This problem is (comparative of *hard*) than that one.
9. He was (comparative of *underweight*) than his brother.
10. The bus driver was (comparative of *careful*) than most I have seen.

Grammar in Action

Your science and social studies assignments will often involve comparing two things. You may be asked to compare the growth rate of two different plants, or you may want to compare the nutritional value of two different foods.

Tuna offers more protein than cereal.

When you edit your writing, make sure you have used the correct forms of comparison.

Writing Activity Find the five errors in the following paragraph. Write each comparison correctly.

Ducks and geese are both web-footed birds. Ducks have more shorter necks than geese, and they have the smallest wings. Geese live in all parts of the world. In fact, about thirteen kinds of geese live in the United States and Canada. Of the two kinds of birds, geese are largest. Geese are the best swimmers, also, and they are more better at flying long distances.

4

Possessive Pronouns Used as Adjectives

A *possessive pronoun* usually modifies a noun. Then the pronoun functions as an adjective that tells *which one* or *which ones* about the noun.

When used with a noun, a possessive pronoun can help make the meaning of a noun more definite: not any pencil, *your* pencil.

> *your* pencil *her* shirt *our* class *their* decision

When possessive pronouns are used to limit the meaning of nouns, they can be classed as adjectives. In the examples above, *your, my, her, his, our, its,* and *their* are all possessive pronouns being used as adjectives.

Exercise

Make two columns on your paper. Write the possessive pronouns and the words they modify in the two columns.

1. My class visited the Egyptian art exhibit.
2. Our teacher Ms. Chambers accompanied us.
3. She answered my questions about the ancient paintings.
4. She told our group about the rules Egyptian artists followed.
5. Their rules were extremely strict.
6. Artists had to paint the heads, shoulders, and feet of their figures from the angle that each part looked its best.
7. If you were a model in Egypt, you would stand with your head and feet pointed to the sides.
8. Then you might get a stiff neck because your head and shoulders would have to face forward.
9. An artist also had to paint the most important people larger than the other people in his picture.
10. Each colorful wall was supposed to tell its own story.

5
Demonstrative Adjective or Demonstrative Pronoun?

A *demonstrative pronoun* such as *this, that, these,* or *those* points out a specific person or thing. When such a word is used as a modifier, it becomes a *demonstrative adjective.*

The words *this, that, these,* and *those* can be used to modify nouns or pronouns.

> Did you buy tickets for *this* concert or *that* one?
> *Those* oranges are ripe, but *these* peaches aren't.

When used as modifiers, *this, that, these,* and *those* are called **demonstrative adjectives**. They tell *which one* or *which ones* about words they modify.

Keep in mind that these words can also be used by themselves. Then they are called **demonstrative pronouns**.

Demonstrative Adjective	Demonstrative Pronoun
Did you taste *this* chili?	Did you taste *this*?
I heard *that* bulletin.	I heard *that*.
These flowers are lovely.	*These* are lovely.

Using Demonstrative Adjectives Correctly

This, That, These, and Those *This* and *that* modify singular nouns. *These* and *those* modify plural nouns.

> *this* skateboard   *these* skateboards
> *that* club   *those* clubs

Kind and Sort The nouns *kind* and *sort* are singular. They are used with the demonstrative adjectives *this* and *that*. The nouns *kinds* and *sorts* are plural. They are used with the demonstrative adjectives *these* and *those*.

> *this* kind   *these* kinds   *that* sort   *those* sorts

Never use *here* or *there* with demonstrative adjectives.

Incorrect I made this here table.
Correct I made *this* table.

Incorrect Hand me that there saw.
Correct Hand me *that* saw.

Exercises

A Make two columns on your paper. Label them *Demonstrative Adjectives* and *Demonstrative Pronouns*. Write the demonstrative adjectives from the following sentences in the first column. Write the demonstrative pronouns in the second column.

1. This moped carried my brother through the storm.
2. Nobody thought that mighty oak would ever die.
3. This is the field where we lost to the Mayfield Pirates.
4. That woman looked into my eyes and told my fortune.
5. These are my good and loyal friends, Terry and JoAnn.
6. That was my final trip to the orthodontist.
7. Don't these pictures make you think of a shipwreck in the Arctic?
8. This is the second time I've lost my bike.
9. Do you see those airplanes flying together like a flock of geese?
10. I challenge you to knock over these bowling pins in one turn.

B Each sentence contains an error in the use of demonstrative pronouns, demonstrative adjectives, or the words that accompany them. Rewrite the sentences on your paper, correcting the error.

1. This here wire should be replaced.
2. Mario doesn't like these sort of games.
3. The committee never purchases those kind of supplies.
4. Did you read that there poster about the carnival?
5. Those kind of tricks take years of practice.
6. The museum has several of these sort of exhibits.
7. These here instructions are difficult to understand.
8. The farmer harvested that there field last week.
9. I hate being outside in this kinds of weather.
10. This sorts of glass comes from Italy.

c *Proofreading* Rewrite the following paragraph, correcting the errors you find. Pay particular attention to the use of comparative and demonstrative adjectives.

> Have you ever been to a diveing meet. Skillful divers are graceful and dareing. They try to spin and twist more better than other divers. These here atheletes sometimes dive from platforms higher than three-story buildings.

Grammar in Action

Sales clerks, teachers, tour guides—those who point things out and answer questions—often use demonstrative pronouns and demonstrative adjectives for specific persons or things. Demonstrative adjectives are used to clarify which person or which thing.

> That is a beautiful scarf in the shop window.
>   (demonstrative pronoun)
> That scarf costs twenty dollars. (demonstrative adjective)

Writing Activity Imagine you are going to conduct a tour of your town. Write out what you will say during the tour. Use demonstrative pronouns to point things out. Use demonstrative adjectives for clarity. Then, underline the demonstrative pronouns once and the demonstrative adjectives twice. Your speech should be no longer than one page.

Linking Grammar & Writing

A Think of the scariest thing you have ever seen or done. Describe the experience in as much detail as you can. Be sure to involve all of your senses in describing it. What happened? Were there any sounds? Were there any smells? Did you touch anything? Did you eat anything?

After you have written your description, underline all the adjectives you used.

B Compare a typical meal in the lunchroom at your school with a special meal you have eaten in a restaurant or at someone's home. Include details in your comparison (a flimsy plastic fork compared with a heavier, shining stainless steel fork; a sticky bench compared with a comfortable old, cushioned chair). Use the comparative form of adjectives when appropriate.

C Imagine that you have just come home from a trip to Mexico, where you visited friends of your family. Your family's friends live in a rural mountain village on a sheep farm. You met a lot of interesting people, tasted unusual foods, and learned new customs while you were there. Now, write a story about your trip. Try to make this story so detailed and descriptive that when your friends read it, they'll feel as though they have visited your Mexican village. Your story should include many adjectives as well as demonstrative adjectives. You may need to do some research in an encyclopedia.

Additional Practice

Part 1 Identifying Adjectives Make three columns on your paper. Label them *What Kind, How Many,* and *Which One.* Then list all the adjectives in the following sentences in the correct columns. Do not include articles.

1. That movie had an exciting ending.
2. Those Asiatic elephants will be moving to a new zoo in the spring.
3. The football coach at Lake Bluff Junior High owns two antique cars.
4. I just finished reading a mystery novel with a clever plot.
5. The rundown old house stood at the top of a steep hill.
6. Florida has many miles of beautiful sandy beaches.
7. Crows have shiny black feathers.
8. That chicken pie has a tender, flaky crust.
9. After the Boston Marathon, sweat poured from the many exhausted runners.
10. Jim Thorpe was an outstanding athlete.

Part 2 Predicate Adjectives Copy the following sentences. In each sentence, draw one line under any predicate adjective. Then draw two lines under the word or words it modifies.

11. The woman on the park bench looked lonely.
12. The flowers, china, and crystal looked beautiful on the table.
13. Even from a distance, the shark seemed enormous.
14. That trick seems difficult and dangerous.
15. The mashed potatoes were fluffy and warm.
16. A Labrador retriever's coat is thick.
17. My brothers seemed upset after their argument.
18. Are the math problems difficult?
19. Charles Lindbergh became famous after his flight across the Atlantic Ocean.
20. *The Wind in the Willows*, a well-known children's book by Kenneth Grahame, is very amusing.

Part 3 Adjectives in Comparisons All of the following sentences contain errors in comparisons. Write each comparison correctly.

21. Which do you like best, hot dogs or hamburgers?
22. Carl Lewis is one of the most fastest runners in the world.
23. In a division problem, does the divisor have to be more small than the dividend?
24. It was the beautifulest sunset we had ever seen.
25. The weather forecaster said that tomorrow will be more warmer than today.
26. Frieda received the worse grade among the three of them.
27. Houston has a more larger population than Dallas.
28. That skyscraper is one of the more tall buildings in the world.
29. We all agreed that it was the most ugliest animal we had ever seen.
30. I feel more happy today than I did yesterday.

Parts 4 and 5 Possessive Pronouns and Demonstrative Adjectives All of the following sentences contain errors in the demonstrative adjectives or in the words that accompany them. Rewrite the sentences on your paper, correcting the errors. Then underline all possessive pronouns.

31. Those there paintings are the work of the Spanish artist Francisco Goya.
32. I don't like those kind of apples.
33. Our class voted to take a field trip to that there natural history museum.
34. This sorts of chain letters are illegal because they ask people to send money to other people.
35. May I eat my dinner on those snack tray?
36. Meryl Streep won an Oscar for her performance in this here movie.
37. Those building is the Sears Tower, the world's tallest skyscraper.
38. Our parents told us not to let those sort of thing happen again.
39. Frank Lloyd Wright designed that there house.
40. Does your uncle still own this here farm?

Application and Review

Lesson Review

A Identifying Adjectives Make two columns on your paper. Label them *Adjectives* and *Words Modified*. Write the adjectives from the following sentences in the first column. Write the words they modify in the second. Do not write articles.

1. Robin is a good writer.
2. The gold coin had strange words on it.
3. The old boat slid over the calm, smooth waters.
4. The tiny red wagon had been left out in the rain.
5. The Peruvian bell had a tiny, tinny sound.
6. The immediate echo startled him.
7. There was a long line at the new Greek restaurant.
8. I learned it from a reliable source.
9. The enormous jet cannot land on the short runway.
10. High winds and a heavy surf damaged many of the vacant homes.

B Identifying Linking Verbs and Predicate Adjectives
Make three columns on your paper. Label them *Subjects, Linking Verbs,* and *Predicate Adjectives*. Write the subjects, linking verbs, and predicate adjectives from the following sentences in the correct column.

1. The apples taste sour.
2. This bread is stale.
3. We were tired after the rehearsal.
4. The room appeared ready for the banquet.
5. Our Dalmatian is always playful.
6. The music sounded louder in the gymnasium.
7. Their apartment looks great.
8. A change appears certain.
9. My sore throat feels better today.
10. The new magazine looks slick.

C Using Comparative and Superlative Forms of Adjectives Write the correct form of the adjectives given in parentheses in the following sentences.

1. Kent is the (shortest, most short) person on the team.
2. That trail was (rougher, roughest) than the other.
3. The Sears Tower is the world's (tallest, most tall) building.
4. Of the three restaurants, Manda's is (closer, closest).
5. He gave the (completest, most complete) answers of all.
6. Have you ever heard a (gooder, better) band than this?
7. That question seems a lot (harder, more harder).
8. These math problems are (easier, easiest) than the others.
9. This room looks (brighter, brightest) than that one.
10. Her costume looks (more creative, creativer) than his.

D Identifying Possessive Pronouns and the Words They Modify Make two columns on your paper. Write the possessive pronouns and the words they modify in the two columns.

1. Gretchen returned my books to the library.
2. The Canadian bluejay fed its young.
3. Paul's mother borrowed his hat.
4. Our automatic timer started its cycle.
5. Jeremy's sister is washing her car.
6. The fox hid some of its food in the woods.
7. Nan gave me her eyeglasses to hold.
8. The air has lost its chill.
9. Randi and Marlene were showing the others their prizes.
10. The hailstorm certainly took its toll.

E Identifying Demonstrative Adjectives and Pronouns Write correctly on your paper each of the following sentences, deleting any unnecessary words. Underline the demonstrative adjectives once and the demonstrative pronouns twice.

1. This here is the first daffodil I've seen.
2. Ms. Cook always reads that kind of mystery story about private investigators.
3. Those books about South America are mine.
4. That there clock has stopped.
5. Take these shoes with you.

Chapter Review

A Identifying the Adjectives Write on your paper the adjectives from the following sentences. Identify predicate adjectives, demonstrative adjectives, proper adjectives, and possessive pronouns. Do not write articles.

1. The brown puppy is the friskiest of the litter.
2. Some Indian leaders met the weary settlers.
3. Those Hawaiian print shirts are colorful.
4. Several stamps in my collection are old and rare.
5. Melissa is a better sprinter than she is a long-distance runner.
6. The Italian sausage is spicy and rich and is also inexpensive.
7. The juice in the red cup seems colder than my icy lemonade.
8. Keith put a new battery in his digital clock.
9. That rickety staircase is not a safe place for small children.
10. That kind of skateboard is sturdier than a wooden one.

B Using Adjectives Correctly All of the following sentences contain errors in the use of adjectives. Rewrite the sentences on your paper, correcting the errors.

1. The knit gloves are the warmer of all the pairs I could find in the closet.
2. At this time of year, this kinds of days are dreary and long.
3. Which band is best, Dynamite or the Elements?
4. This here watch ticks loudest of the three.
5. Of those three bowling contest prizes, the minibike is the expensivest.
6. Jeanette's cough was worst today than yesterday.
7. The earliest of the two buses makes more stops and is usually most crowded.
8. These fraction problems are more easier than those decimal problems we did yesterday.
9. Of all the teachers I've ever had, Ms. Butler explains things better.
10. There are more accidents on this kinds of days than on warmer days.

26
Using Adverbs

At the winter carnival, the contestants are completing their creations. You are impressed by the artists and their sculptures. You notice that the woman works <u>carefully</u> and <u>methodically</u> on her ice sculpture. You comment that the snow dragon looks <u>almost</u> alive.

The three underlined modifiers in the paragraph above are adverbs. In Chapter 25 you learned to make your writing more precise by using adjectives to modify nouns and pronouns. Now you will learn to recognize and use adverbs to modify verbs, adjectives, and other adverbs.

1
What Is an Adverb?

An *adverb* modifies a verb, an adjective, or another adverb.

Suppose you were writing a letter to a friend about an exciting ballet performance. You might write that the dancers leaped *high* and twirled *gracefully*. You could say that you saw the ballet *yesterday, onstage,* and that it was *quite* enjoyable. You would be using adverbs to help your friend understand exactly what attending the ballet was like.

Adverbs tell *how, when, where,* or *to what extent* about the words they modify. In this chapter you will learn to use adverbs correctly to modify verbs, adjectives, or other adverbs. As you can see from the examples given below, adverbs add specific details to make statements clear and interesting. The adverbs turn flat statements into expressive ones.

Adverbs Modify Verbs
We walked.
How?   We walked *slowly*.
Where?   We walked *out*.
When?   We walked *yesterday*.

Adverbs Modify Adjectives
It was a *clear* day.
How clear?   It was a *fairly* clear day.

I was *late*.
To what extent?   I was *very* late.

Adverbs Modify Other Adverbs
Joe talked *fast*.
How fast?   Joe talked *extremely* fast.

Irene danced *happily*.
How happily?   Irene danced *very* happily.

The team practices *often*.
To what extent?   The team practices *quite* often.

Exercises

A Write the adverbs on your paper.

1. Tod's presentation was very interesting.
2. We will explore Mars tomorrow.
3. The gymnast gracefully performed her floor exercise.
4. Scott danced extremely well.
5. The Warners had parked nearby.
6. Ken cleared the hurdle easily.
7. The water in the lake is too cold.
8. The most beautiful roses are yellow.
9. The bicycle racers pedaled quite swiftly.
10. The base runner easily stole second.

B Make two columns on your paper. Label them *Adverbs* and *Words Modified*. Write the adverbs from the following sentences in the first column. Write the words they modify in the second.

1. Our sense of smell is very important.
2. In fact, scientists believe it is even more important than taste.
3. Taste buds only detect salty, sweet, bitter, and sour.
4. People recognize different smells very quickly.
5. Certain smells very often trigger memories.
6. The smell of smoke quickly alerts people to fire.
7. Even faintly sweet smells of baking can make us hungry.
8. Very frightened animals leave scents to warn others of danger.
9. Perfumes sometimes give people a feeling of confidence.
10. Napoleon often wore perfume into battle.

c *Write Now* Write a paragraph about an adventure you've had. It might be about a vacation, a competition, or a new sport you've tried. Use adverbs to make your writing more precise. Remember that adverbs can modify adjectives, verbs, and other adverbs.

The Position of Adverbs

When an adverb modifies an adjective or another adverb, it usually comes before the word it modifies: *very* hot, *quite* still, *not* often. When an adverb modifies a verb, its position is not usually fixed. It can come after the verb, at the beginning of the sentence, or just before the verb.

Diagraming Sentences Containing Adverbs

Adverbs, like adjectives, are diagramed on slanting lines attached to the words they modify. The following diagram shows an adverb modifying a verb.

EXAMPLE   Finally the lazy boy raised his hand.

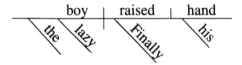

Notice that *Finally,* the first word in the sentence, keeps its capital *F* in the diagram.

The next diagram shows one adverb modifying an adjective and another modifying an adverb.

EXAMPLE   Some fairly young children play musical instruments quite well.

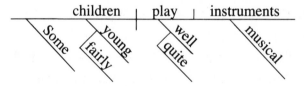

Notice how the adverbs are attached to the words they modify.

Exercises

A Write on your paper an adverb that answers the question after each sentence. Try to be creative in your choice of adverbs. Avoid using words such as *very*.

1. Bring your books. *When?*
2. The monkey disappeared. *When?*

3. The elevator climbed. *How?*
4. The sunset was beautiful. *How beautiful?*
5. The damaged plane landed. *When?*
6. The runners rounded the turn. *How?*
7. Jack slept soundly. *How soundly?*
8. Emily's speech was long. *How long?*
9. My friend arrived late. *To what extent?*
10. The bird flew. *Where?*

B Write five sentences on your paper. Use a different adverb from the following list in each sentence. Then rewrite the sentences, replacing the adverbs with different ones from the list.

often	over	then	sometimes
in	finally	out	together
already	there	away	quietly

Grammar in Action

In descriptive writing, you will often need to use adverbs. One adverb that is often overused, however, is the adverb *very*. Notice how the following lines are improved when *very* is replaced by a variety of adverbs.

It was ~~very~~ *terribly* cold and ~~very~~ *miserably* gloomy that day. My friends and I couldn't raise very much enthusiasm for exploring the cave Tania found last week. ~~Very~~ soon, though, Kate convinced us to start and we became ~~very~~ *awfully* excited. We ran ~~very~~ quickly into a narrow ravine.

Writing Activity Write a paragraph about what you think might happen if you went camping in a desert. Use a variety of adverbs.

2
Adverbs in Comparisons

Use the *comparative form* of an adverb when you compare two actions. Use the *superlative form* of an adverb when you compare more than two actions.

Suppose you were talking about locomotion in animals. You might use sentences like the following:

A turtle moves *slowly*, but a snail moves *more slowly*.
A sloth moves the *most slowly* of all creatures.

In the sentences above, *slowly*, *more slowly*, and *most slowly* are all adverbs. They are all forms of *slowly*. They compare the movement of the animals.

The adverb *slowly* describes the action of one animal, the turtle. The comparative adverb *more slowly* compares the actions of two animals, the turtle and the snail. The superlative adverb *most slowly* compares the actions of all animals, including the sloth.

Most adverbs that end in *-ly* form the comparative with the word *more*. They form the superlative with the word *most*.

Adverb	Comparative	Superlative
quickly	more quickly	most quickly
deeply	more deeply	most deeply

Some adverbs add *-er* for the comparative and *-est* for the superlative.

Adverb	Comparative	Superlative
close	closer	closest
late	later	latest

Some adverbs change completely to form the comparative and superlative.

Adverb	Comparative	Superlative
well	better	best
much	more	most
little	less	least

Exercises

A Write the correct modifiers given in parentheses in the following sentences.

1. We must bury the treasure (more deeply, more deeper).
2. Jon will spell his teacher's name (carefuller, more carefully).
3. I wish you would eat (more slow, more slowly).
4. Now the sting hurts (littler, less) than before.
5. Amy fields the ball (more better, better) than anyone else.
6. He types (faster, fastest) early in the morning.
7. Follow this (more closely, closer).
8. My dog drinks (noisiest, more noisily) than most dogs.
9. Pat threw the ball (harder, more hard) that time.
10. In that event, Doug jumped (highest, most high).

B Complete the following sentences with the correct adverb form of the word given in parentheses.

1. Of all the bikers, Steve rides (fast).
2. Janie walks (graceful) of all the dancers.
3. We dove (deep) than usual last summer.
4. Dr. Parr got home (soon) than her postcards.
5. No one draws (good) than Suzanne.
6. Ted usually wakes up (early) than I do.
7. Doris sings the (loud) of everyone in the school choir.
8. David handles the animals (gentle) than other zookeepers.
9. I read books (often) in the summer.
10. Our friends stayed (long) than usual.

C *Proofreading* Rewrite the following paragraph, correcting the errors you find. Pay particular attention to the form of adjectives and adverbs.

Skateboarding is the most best sport I know, but many people think its dangerous. If you were protective clothing, it can be more safer than many other sports. What you need for the most protection is a special helmet and hard-coated knee and elbow pads. Carefuler skateboarders never go into the street. They go to places designed special for skateboarding.

3
Adjective or Adverb?

An *adjective* describes a noun or pronoun. An *adverb* modifies a verb, an adjective, or another adverb.

Sometimes an adjective or adverb is misused because the speaker or writer did not recognize which part of speech was needed. You must learn to analyze carefully how the word you are considering is being used. Try the method described in the examples below:

1. Cynthia reads (good, well).

   Problem   Is the needed word an adjective or an adverb?
   Question Would the word answer the question *how*, *when*, *where*, or *to what extent?*
   Answer   Yes—it tells *how* Cynthia reads.
   Solution The word *well*, an adverb, should be used to modify the verb *reads*.

2. The situation is (real, really) funny.

   Problem   Is the needed word an adjective or an adverb?
   Question What would the word do?
   Answer   It would modify *funny*. It would tell *how funny*.
   Question What is *funny*?
   Answer   The word *funny* is a predicate adjective.
   Solution The word *really*, an adverb, should be used to modify the adjective *funny*.

Using Adjectives and Adverbs

Since adjectives and adverbs are used in similar situations, writers sometimes confuse them. Words that follow linking verbs are the most commonly misused modifiers.

To avoid making mistakes when you use an adjective or an adverb, check to see what kind of word you want to modify. Choose an adjective to modify a noun or a pronoun. Choose an adverb to modify a verb, an adjective, or another adverb.

Notice the reasons for the type of modifier chosen in each of the following sentences.

> He writes (beautiful, <u>beautifully</u>).
> (The word *beautifully* is an adverb modifying the verb *writes*.)
> Roses smell (<u>sweet</u>, sweetly).
> (*Sweet* is a predicate adjective.)
> We were (terrible, <u>terribly</u>) late.
> (*Terribly*, an adverb, modifies *late*, a predicate adjective.)
> It tastes (<u>bad</u>, badly).
> (*Bad* is a predicate adjective.)

Exercises

A Write the correct modifiers given in parentheses.

1. The auctioneer nodded (brief, briefly).
2. That bread smells (wonderfully, wonderful).
3. The telephone operator's voice sounded (pleasant, pleasantly).
4. Your centerpiece looks (beautiful, beautifully).
5. Bob answered again (more gently, more gentle).
6. The team looked (anxious, anxiously) at the wet field.
7. The explorers traveled (safe, safely) through the dense jungle.
8. Jon felt (terrible, terribly) after the accident.
9. Doug ran (real, really) well in the qualifying race.
10. The students moved (quiet, quietly) through the halls during the fire drill.

B Write the correct modifiers given in parentheses in the following sentences.

1. Babe Didrikson Zaharias was one of the (best, better) athletes of all time.
2. She was a (fine, most fine) basketball player.
3. She (actual, actually) won two gold medals in the 1932 Olympics.
4. In the 1940's, she began to play golf (enthusiastic, enthusiastically).

Babe Didrikson Zaharias, Women's Amateur Golf Champion, 1947.

5. Babe could (easily, easy) hit a golf ball the length of two football fields.
6. She played (more competitively, most competitively) than others and won seventeen tournaments in a row.
7. She attracted (largest, large) crowds with trick shots.
8. Babe believed that women should wear clothes that felt (comfortably, comfortable).
9. She was (brave, bravely) enough to wear pants when participating in athletic events.
10. In 1947, Babe Didrikson Zaharias became (real, really) competitive as a pro golfer.

Grammar in Action

Adverbs add depth and color to your writing. One way to make them even more effective is to vary their position in sentences.

The swarm of bees chased us angrily.
Angrily the swarm of bees chased us.

The Prime Minister's helicopter landed suddenly.
Suddenly the Prime Minister's helicopter landed.

In each pair of sentences above, the second sentence sounds more dramatic. However, you don't always want to put an adverb at the beginning of a sentence. The dramatic effect would be lost if every sentence used this same device.

Writing Activity Write a paragraph about a visit to your community by a world leader. Use adverbs in various positions.

4
Using Negatives

Never use a *double negative* when you write or speak.

A negative is a word that says "no." The most common negative words are *no, none, not, nothing,* and *never.*

If two of these words are used in a sentence when only one is needed, the result is a **double negative**.

Mistakes made in using double negatives occur most often when one of the negatives is in the form of a contraction. *Can't, don't, doesn't, won't, wouldn't, isn't,* and *aren't* are negatives. Each of these words contains the shortened form of *not: n't.* When this kind of contraction is used in a sentence, there is no need for another "no."

Incorrect   He isn't never going back to that store.
Correct   He isn't ever going back to that store.

Incorrect   She doesn't have nowhere to go.
Correct   She doesn't have anywhere to go.

Exercise

Write the words given in parentheses that correctly complete the following sentences.

1. Sheila could talk to (nobody, anybody) else.
2. I haven't had (no, any) lunch.
3. Those hornets (won't, will) never come back.
4. He doesn't (never, ever) want to sing in public.
5. Is there (any, no) water in this canteen?
6. Nobody (can, can't) walk through such deep snow.
7. They haven't done (none, any) of the yard work.
8. We haven't heard (nothing, anything) about the test scheduled for tomorrow.
9. I can't tell you (nothing, anything) about the plans for the assembly.
10. We can't go (nowhere, anywhere) until we have eaten.

Linking Grammar & Writing

A Imagine that you are a playwright. Write stage directions for the entrance of three actors—a teenager, a military officer, and a person wearing a cast for a broken leg. Use many adverbs to describe exactly the way you want each actor to move.

B Critics sometimes compare two performances. Think of two performances you have seen—live, on television, or at the movies. Write a one-page comparison of the two performances. You may choose to compare two rock singers, two comedians, two actors, or an old movie and the remake of it.

C If your desk could talk, how would it describe a typical day? Write a narrative from the point of view of your desk. Use adverbs to tell how, when, where, and to what extent things happen to your desk.

D Imagine you are an undersea explorer. You are equipped with a microphone and have been asked to describe what you see to tourists on a nearby ship. Tell what you see happening on the ocean floor. Use precise verbs and adverbs to describe clearly the movement you see around you.

Additional Practice

Part 1 Identifying Adverbs Number your paper from 1 to 10. Write each adverb and the word that it modifies.

1. Diamonds are quite expensive.
2. The high jumper easily and gracefully cleared the bar.
3. Cheetahs can run swiftly.
4. My older sister always beats me at chess.
5. Mr. Goldstein has an exceptionally attractive yard.
6. When the boat suddenly sank, we were very glad to be wearing our life jackets.
7. Although the test was unusually difficult, Bonnie finished quickly.
8. Jazz musician John Coltrane played the tenor saxophone beautifully.
9. I cook dinner for our family quite frequently.
10. I laugh hysterically when I watch reruns of *I Love Lucy*.

Part 2 Adverbs in Comparisons Complete the following sentences with the correct adverb form of the word given in parentheses.

11. Grandmother stayed up (late) than Grandfather.
12. Our gymnastics teacher says that we will have to learn to move even (gracefully).
13. Ted swims the (well) of everyone on the swim team.
14. African crocodiles can move (quickly) than American alligators.
15. Tammy spoke (excitedly) than usual.
16. My father drives (slowly) than my mother.
17. Some Americans are watching television (little) than they used to.
18. Of all the software programs I've used, that was the (easy) one to learn.
19. Rose bushes have to be planted (deeply) in cold-weather areas than in warm-weather ones.
20. Walter is (bitterly) opposed to the idea than George.

Part 3 Using Modifiers Correctly Choose the right modifier,
and write it on your paper. Next write the word it modifies.
Finally, write *Adjective* or *Adverb* to show how the modifier is
used.

>EXAMPLE The new cotton blanket felt (soft, softly).
>soft, blanket, Adjective

21. Patricia felt (badly, bad) when her dog died.
22. Those canaries sing (sweetly, sweet).
23. Don't you think the doctor looks (worriedly, worried)?
24. The gorillas adjusted (beautiful, beautifully) to their new
    surroundings.
25. Willa Cather wrote a number of (real, really) fine novels.
26. Christopher Columbus and his crew felt (happy, happily)
    when they finally sighted land.
27. When Columbus returned to Spain, King Ferdinand and
    Queen Isabella received him (grand, grandly).
28. This food tastes (dreadful, dreadfully).
29. Silver maple trees grow (rapidly, rapid).
30. My brother seemed (grateful, gratefully) for the help I had
    given him.

Part 4 Using Negatives Correctly Rewrite the following
sentences on your paper, correcting the errors in the use of
negatives. Some of the sentences may be corrected in more than
one way.

31. Haven't you ever seen no films starring Dean Martin and
    Jerry Lewis?
32. The suspect would not say nothing until her lawyer arrived.
33. We don't have no intention of doing all this work ourselves.
34. Elizabeth got into trouble because she didn't do none of the
    things her mother had asked her to do.
35. Most Americans hope that their country won't never fight
    another war.
36. I haven't no idea about how to make spaghetti.
37. Oil won't never mix with water.
38. Don't go nowhere near the construction area.
39. Isn't there no law about jaywalking?
40. They aren't never going to know my secret.

Application and Review

Lesson Review

A Identifying Adverbs Make two columns on your paper. Label them *Adverbs* and *Words Modified*. Write the adverbs from the following sentences in the first column. Write the words they modify in the second column.

1. The fresh bread was very warm.
2. Her letter came amazingly soon.
3. The police helicopter was terribly noisy landing on the hospital roof.
4. Gretchen arrived too late.
5. He goes to Knoxville regularly.
6. The tomato plants probably have overripe tomatoes on them.
7. I'm awfully glad you've finally arrived.
8. They smiled at each other very mischievously.
9. She was quite passionate about saving every endangered species.
10. Emily moved to Phoenix from Philadelphia fairly recently.

B Using Adverbs Write the correct modifiers given in parentheses in the following sentences.

1. The tennis team practiced (longer, more long) than ever before this last tournament.
2. The party guests ate (less, littler) food than Nicolas had expected them to eat.
3. Beth got home from the library (latest, later) than her brother.
4. Our kitten jumped (higher, highest) of the six kittens.
5. I cook (carefully, more carefully) than my sister.
6. Press the (hardest, harder) you can against the door, and turn the handle.

7. Lynn has been playing the piano (longer, more longer) than Robin.
8. This glue dries (fastest, most fast) of all.
9. This movie ends the (horriblest, most horribly) of any movie I've ever seen.
10. Turn the volume (higher, more high).

C Using Modifiers Write the correct modifiers given in parentheses in the following sentences.

1. The goat gave an (occasionally, occasional) bleat.
2. Just then Sandra looked up (brightly, bright).
3. Tape is sometimes (usefuller, more useful) than glue.
4. He went (most recent, most recently) to Pakistan.
5. The backpackers grew (uneasy, uneasily) as they approached the summit.
6. Willie retraced his steps (more carefully, most carefully) the second time.
7. This calculator is (more better, better) than that one for the kind of work you are doing.
8. Kris came (more later, later).
9. Ms. Larson gave us unannounced quizzes (oftener, more often) than the other teachers.
10. My math grades have improved (considerable, considerably) since last term.

D Using Negatives Rewrite the following sentences on your paper, correcting the errors in the use of negatives. Some of the sentences may be corrected in more than one way.

1. I haven't had no cold this year.
2. Mike couldn't find no stamp for the letter.
3. Tina didn't eat none of the peaches.
4. My Uncle Frank isn't really no relative of mine.
5. Don't make no salad for my dinner.
6. We haven't done nothing wrong.
7. The computer didn't fix no mistakes.
8. I couldn't find my other sock nowhere.
9. Nobody never read the whole book at once.
10. I don't get no fun from shoveling snow.

Chapter Review

Using Adverbs and Adjectives Write the correct modifiers given in parentheses in the following sentences.

1. The reading assignment for social studies sounds (interesting, interestingly).
2. Gayle (quick, quickly) wrote a note to Jenny.
3. (Eager, Eagerly) we chose our grab bag gifts from the pile on the table.
4. Tennis shoes are (comfortable, comfortably).
5. The problems become (increasing, increasingly) difficult toward the end of the chapter.
6. In June, our lilacs smell (wonderful, wonderfully).
7. I (desperate, desperately) want to go camping in Yellowstone National Park next summer.
8. The runners are trying (real, really) hard to break the record.
9. Apples taste (delicious, deliciously) in October, when they have just been picked.
10. Donna was not feeling (cheerful, cheerfully) enough to come to the party.

B **Using Adverbs** Rewrite the following sentences on your paper, correcting the errors. Some of the sentences may be corrected in more than one way.

1. You must sing more louder in the auditorium than in the classroom.
2. Sam had his hair cut recent.
3. Courtney draws cartoon characters careful.
4. Everybody was real happy after the awards assembly at school.
5. Nobody couldn't solve the mystery.
6. It is terrible important that you lock the door when you leave.
7. Ms. Simpson won't allow no street shoes on the wood floor of the gym.
8. Of the two movies, I liked *Gone with the Wind* best.
9. Brian is the less motivated person in the whole class.
10. We could not imagine a more longer report.

Cumulative Review

A Recognizing Verbs Make five columns on your paper and label them *Transitive Verb, Intransitive Verb, Linking Verb, Direct Object,* and *Predicate Word*. Then write the verbs from the following sentences in the correct columns. If a verb is transitive, write its direct object in the fourth column. If a verb is a linking verb, write its predicate word in the last column.

1. The pitcher quickly threw the ball.
2. Most people sleep eight hours every night.
3. All the windows in that house are plastic.
4. Is the water too cold?
5. Trees don't grow above the mountain timberline.
6. Twelve exchange students visited the Soviet Union.
7. Should the driver have stopped the bus closer to the corner?
8. Marve likes sports of all kinds.
9. The chorus has sung four new songs.
10. The whole top of the mountain exploded.

B Identifying Adjectives Write all the adjectives from each sentence. Then label those that are *Predicate Adjectives, Demonstrative Adjectives, Proper Adjectives,* and *Possessive Pronouns*. Some adjectives will not have labels. Do not write articles.

1. The happy tourists rode on an open sleigh.
2. The German food at this restaurant is delicious.
3. Latin is the ancient Roman language.
4. Your old alarm clock is louder than my new one.
5. That article is a good description of the French countryside.
6. The brown shoes are smaller than the black ones.
7. The full pitcher of orange juice made a sticky mess on our clean floor.
8. The American flag waves outside many buildings.
9. Was that automatic pencil very expensive?
10. The English queen is known as Her Royal Highness.

11. The valuable ring was saved from the huge fire.
12. Black squirrels are unusual in this area.
13. Twelve angry ducks quacked loudly at his dog.
14. The Hawaiian islands have few active volcanoes.
15. Her tortilla chips fell into the hot sauce.

C Identifying Adverbs Write all the adverbs from each of the following sentences.

1. North Dakota is very cold in the winter.
2. Peter quickly wrote his name and address on the application.
3. The late bell will ring soon.
4. Those lima beans look too pale.
5. Please stop the car now so that I can get out.
6. Jan easily jumped over the last hurdle.
7. The history test was pretty hard.
8. Each dancer leaped lightly into the air and landed on only one foot.
9. Is the stove very hot?
10. He played so well that he won the most important award.
11. The artist tried hard to copy the dark green color.
12. Mark arrived very late at the party.
13. The molasses dripped extremely slowly out of the bottle.
14. Paulo stood nearby while Angie knocked hard on the door.
15. Hercules is often used as a symbol of strength.

D Combined Review Write the correct word or phrase from each pair in parentheses in the following sentences.

1. Some teams have (chose, chosen) their players already.
2. Which lake is (deeper, deepest), Erie or Superior?
3. Emily accepted the award (proudly, proud).
4. Tai could have (wrote, written) the story in two languages.
5. The rain became (steadily, steady) heavier.
6. This is the (more intelligent, most intelligent) of all three puppies in the litter.
7. These coins are (newer, more newer) than any of mine.
8. Yesterday the boss (give, gave) Ellie her first paycheck.
9. They walked (careful, carefully) across the rocky field.
10. Which answer choice is (good, better), A or B?

27

Using Prepositions, Conjunctions, and Interjections

The Golden Gate Bridge is an elegant steel structure that links the city of San Francisco with its northern suburbs. The simple stone bridge pictured above is a link between parts of a town. Language has its bridges, too. In your speaking and writing, prepositions and conjunctions link words, ideas, and sentences.

In this chapter you will discover how to use prepositions and conjunctions to make connections in your writing. You also will learn how to use interjections to add emotion and emphasis to your statements.

1
Prepositions

A *preposition* is a word that relates its object to some other word in the sentence. The noun or pronoun following the preposition is called the *object of the preposition.*

When you write or speak, you use certain kinds of words to show relationships between ideas. These words are called **prepositions** and **conjunctions**.

> The roller coaster sped *along* the track. It dipped *and* turned. It rolled slowly *up* the incline *and* then plummeted *down* the hill.

In the paragraph above, the prepositions *along, up,* and *down* show the relationships between *track* and *sped,* between *incline* and *rolled,* and between *hill* and *plummeted.* The conjunction *and* also shows relationships. You will study conjunctions in Part 5 of this chapter.

The word *preposition* has two parts: *pre,* meaning "before," and *position.* A **preposition** is a word that is positioned before its object and shows the relationship between that object and another word in the sentence. The noun or pronoun following a preposition is the **object of the preposition**.

> *to* the store (*to* is the preposition; *store* is its object)
> *along* the street (*along* is the preposition; *street* is its object)

Remember that the real job of a preposition is to tie its object to another word in the sentence. Usually this other word appears just before the preposition.

> We walked *to* the store.
> We strolled *along* the street.

In the first example above, *store* is connected with *walked* by the preposition *to.* In the second example, *street* is connected with *strolled* by the preposition *along.* Choose prepositions that express relationships between words as precisely as possible.

You have seen that you often cannot tell what part of speech a word is until you see how the word is used in a sentence. However, listed below are some words that are often used as prepositions.

Words Often Used as Prepositions

about	below	from	past
above	beneath	in	through
across	beside	inside	to
after	between	into	toward
against	beyond	near	under
along	but (except)	of	underneath
among	by	off	until
around	down	on	up
as	during	out	with
before	except	outside	within
behind	for	over	without

Preposition or Adverb?

You may notice that a number of words in the list above can be used not only as prepositions but also as adverbs. When they are used as adverbs, however, they do not have objects.

> Tony walked *on*. (adverb)
> Tony walked *on* the sidewalk. (preposition)

When you have a question about whether a word is an adverb or a preposition, think about how the word is used. If it has an object and shows the relationship of one word to another in the sentence, it is probably a preposition. If it is used alone, it is probably an adverb.

Exercises

A Write on your paper the prepositions from the following sentences.

1. Lee stumbled up the steps.
2. Thursday comes before Friday.
3. What do you know about fleas?

4. In the box on the desk was a small tape recorder with headphones.
5. Chris always drives under the speed limit.
6. The fresh apricots are on the small table near the refrigerator.
7. The pitchfork was leaning against the door and fell into the haystack.
8. Nobody is here but me.
9. The new indoor ice skating rink will be built between these two houses.
10. The extra tennis balls rolled across the court and out the gate.

B Make two columns on your paper. Label them Prepositions and Adverbs. Write the italicized words from the following sentences in the first column if they are prepositions. Write them in the second column if they are adverbs.

1. Firefighters work *on* unusual schedules.
2. They often work three days at a time and have the rest of the week *off*.
3. Every fire station has a kitchen *for* the firefighters, so they can cook for themselves.
4. They sleep in a big room *above* the garage at the fire station.
5. Some days many fires keep the firefighters busy *outdoors*.
6. Other days they have little work to do, and they may exercise to keep busy *during* slow periods.
7. Many firefighters play basketball on courts *outside* the fire station.
8. Some fire stations even have racquetball courts *downstairs*.
9. Firefighters do most of their work *outside* in the sun, rain, or snow.
10. During big fires, Red Cross volunteers may bring refreshments *to* the firefighters.

2
Prepositional Phrases

> A *prepositional phrase* is a group of words that begins with a preposition and ends with its object.

The group of words that includes a preposition and its object is called a **prepositional phrase**. Words that modify the object are also part of the phrase. Prepositions along with their objects can add precision and clarity to an idea.

> Jim found my book *in his locker*.
> Jody wrapped the present *with bright green paper*.

The prepositional phrases in the sentences above are *in his locker* and *with bright green paper*. In the first sentence, the preposition is *in*, the object is *locker*, and the modifier is the pronoun *his* used as an adjective. The preposition in the second sentence is *with*, the object is *paper*, and the modifiers are *bright* and *green*.

Compound Objects

When a preposition has two objects, the construction is called a **compound object**. Both objects are part of the prepositional phrase. These sentences contain compound objects.

> My gift *from Mom and Dad* was a watch.
> We walked *past the school and the store*.

Exercises

A Make two columns on your paper. Label them *Prepositional Phrases* and *Objects of Prepositions*. Write the prepositional phrases and the objects of the prepositions in the correct columns.

1. BASIC is a computer language that is commonly taught by schools and camps.
2. Experts speak of BASIC as a simple language.

3. Many computer programs are written in BASIC.
4. Instructions to the computer are given in special languages.
5. Information is translated by a computer into a series of digits.
6. The only digits used by the machine are zero and one.
7. Inside a computer you find many circuit boards.
8. Circuit boards hold semiconductors in place.
9. Tiny wires wind in a maze.
10. Electrical pulses go through the wires, sending messages to the computer.

B *Write Now* Suppose you have invented a new kitchen appliance. Write a paragraph explaining what it does and how it works. Use prepositional phrases to make your explanation clear.

Grammar in Action

Sometimes you can combine two sentences by using a prepositional phrase. Combining sentences can improve your writing by adding variety and by producing smoother sentences.

Two Sentences   Hal went sailing today. He went sailing with Pedro.

Combined   Hal went sailing today *with Pedro*.

Writing Activity Rewrite the paragraph below, using prepositional phrases to combine at least three pairs of sentences.

> Candice enjoys writing computer programs. She writes them in a language called BASIC. One of her programs calculates checkbook balances. Candice developed that program for her mother. Another program calculates batting averages. Candice's brother asked for that disk. Candice also uses prepackaged software. She uses that for word processing. She likes to write letters. She does that with a word processing program.

3
Pronouns as Objects of Prepositions

When a pronoun is used as the object of a preposition, its *object form* must be used.

The object of a preposition is often a noun, but sometimes it is a pronoun taking the place of a noun. When a pronoun is the object of a preposition, we use the object form. The **object forms** are *me, us, you, her, him, it, them,* and *whom.*

> I think often of *her.*   The dog sat between *us.*

When a preposition has only a single pronoun as its object, there is seldom a problem. When a preposition has a compound object, however, some people do not know which form of the pronoun to use.

Simple Object   Come with *me.*
Compound Object   Come with the *usher* and *me.*

To make sure you use the correct pronoun in a compound object, say the pronoun alone with its preposition first.

> These tickets are for Pam and (he, him).
> These tickets are for *him.*
> These tickets are for Pam and *him.*

Who and Whom Remember that the word *whom* is the object form of the interrogative pronoun. *Who* is the subject form.

> *Who* has the camera?   To *whom* did you speak?

Between and Among *Between* and *among* are often confused. Remember that you use *between* when speaking of two people or things. Use *among* when speaking of three or more.

> Ginny sat *between* Nick and me. (two people)
> Divide the profits *among* them all. (more than two)

Exercises

A Write the correct form of the pronouns given in parentheses in the following sentences.

1. Give the tickets to Craig and (me, I).
2. The article was written by Cora and (she, her)
3. Between Lisa and (he, him), sauntered the cat.
4. The folk song was sung by Paula and (her, she).
5. The reporter arrived after Larry and (they, them).
6. Ms. Cowles was looking for Sally and (she, her).
7. The electric socks are from Elise and (us, we).
8. The quarterback waved to Terry and (I, me).
9. Before Katie and (me, I), marched the majorettes.
10. To (whom, who) did Sherlock Holmes send the message?

B Complete the following sentences with *between* or *among* or with a pronoun in the correct form.

1. Hal sat _____ the pine trees, the ferns, and the deer.
2. We gave the score sheets to the coach and _____ .
3. The nurse looked skeptically at Bill and _____ .
4. Bounding _____ the five Smith children were their prize-winning Doberman Pinschers.
5. We gave many books about astronomy to Judy and _____ .
6. Mr. Sims bought circus tickets for Jonathan and _____ .
7. _____ the two of us, we had not heard from Sarah.
8. The Grand Canyon lay far below Thomas and _____ .
9. To our dismay, the ball landed _____ Susan and me.
10. Near Jack and _____ stands a huge redwood tree.

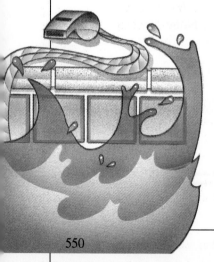

C *Proofreading* Proofread the following paragraph. Then rewrite it correctly. Pay particular attention to the form of pronouns used as objects of prepositions.

Doug invited me to go swiming with Helen and he. I asked if Matt could come with us. Sitting between Matt and I on the edge of the pool, Doug began splashing both of we. Then Doug and i slid into the water. Matt climbed in at the shallow end and waded toward Helen and us. Soon the lifeguard bagan shouting at he.

4
Using Prepositional Phrases

> A prepositional phrase, like an adjective or an adverb, modifies a word in the sentence.

Prepositional phrases do the same kind of work in sentences that adjectives and adverbs do. A prepositional phrase that modifies a noun or pronoun is an **adjective phrase**.

> The bottom *of the jar* was dirty.
> I was washing the window *over the sink*.

A prepositional phrase that modifies a verb is an **adverb phrase**.

> They swam *under the bridge*.
> The geyser erupted *at noon*.

Beginning Sentences with Prepositional Phrases

Sometimes, for the sake of emphasis or variety, we begin a sentence with a prepositional phrase.

> We saw a brilliant flash at that very moment.
> At that very moment, we saw a brilliant flash.

It is not necessarily better to start a sentence with a prepositional phrase. However, if many of the sentences in your composition start with the subject, you may want to change the beginning of a few of them to add interest.

Placing Prepositional Phrases Correctly

Some prepositional phrases can be moved from one position to another without changing the meaning of the sentence. Sometimes, however, the position of a prepositional phrase makes a great deal of difference to the meaning of the sentence.

Unclear   Patrick met the mail carrier in his robe.
Clear   In his robe, Patrick met the mail carrier.

The first example sentence at the bottom of page 551 is unclear because the adjective phrase *in his robe* seems to modify *mail carrier*. The second sentence brings the phrase where it should be: closer to *Patrick*, the word it modifies.

Diagraming Prepositional Phrases

Since a prepositional phrase does the work of an adjective or an adverb, you diagram it the same way. Write the preposition on a line slanting down from the word modified. On a horizontal line attached to the preposition line, write the object. Anything modifying the object slants down from it. In the diagram below, the object of a preposition is modified by another phrase.

EXAMPLE   In the morning we walked to the rim of the volcano.

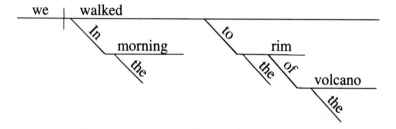

Exercises

A Make three columns on your paper. Label them *Adjective Phrases, Adverb Phrases,* and *Words Modified.* Write the prepositional phrases from the following sentences in the correct column. Write the word each phrase modifies in the third column.

1. Jenna heard a noise in the back yard.
2. Many of my friends like baseball and soccer.
3. At the corner they built a new sign.
4. The buttons on my sleeve caught in the door.
5. Four well-known scientists from the space center waited in the office.
6. Put the magician's props behind the big box.
7. Dad had already put the pizzas in the oven.
8. I saw a strange Siamese cat in the alley.

9. The hikers had blisters on their feet.
10. Our cousins from Indiana visited this summer.

B Write on your paper the following sentences, moving prepositional phrases so they are close to the words they modify.

1. The clock stopped by the water fountain at 3:30.
2. A rabbit ran across the street with long ears.
3. That girl caught the ball with a striped T-shirt.
4. With the big straw stomach, Al laughed at the scarecrow.
5. John reached for the string beans with long arms.
6. Underneath the earth in Ohio we passed many mines.
7. At Bunker Hill we read about an important Revolutionary War battle.
8. We saw a horse beside a brook with a long, flowing tail.
9. In the cages we saw many exotic animals.
10. The coins are for the tollway on the dashboard.

Grammar in Action

Prepositional phrases can be moved from one position to another in a sentence, as long as the sentence is clear. Sometimes using a prepositional phrase at the beginning of a sentence can provide a welcome change of rhythm.

> First put the eggs into the bowl. Beat them with a fork. Then add milk to the mixture. Shake in the spices next. Into the hot pan it all goes!

As you read the directions above, you see that the writer catches your attention with the last sentence by starting with a prepositional phrase.

Writing Activity Write a paragraph to a friend, giving directions for making something—a recipe, a model car, anything you know how to make. Use prepositional phrases and vary their sentence positions. Make sure you are saying exactly what you want to say.

5
Conjunctions and Interjections

A *conjunction* is a word that connects words or groups of words.

An *interjection* is a word or short group of words used to express feeling.

Conjunctions and interjections are the only two parts of speech we have not discussed so far. **Conjunctions** move a sentence along and can be used to combine sentences or sentence parts. **Interjections** add excitement, realism, emphasis, and a sharp, quick rhythm to your writing.

Coordinating Conjunctions

What is missing in these sentences?

The chimp _____ his brother swung from the rope.
John went, _____ Lee didn't go with him.
Will he go to the police station _____ just go home?

The missing words—*and, but,* and *or*—are coordinating conjunctions. **Coordinating conjunctions** join words or groups of words that are of equal importance. Most words or groups of words joined by coordinating conjunctions are called **compound constructions**. The sentences below use coordinating conjunctions to connect words of equal importance.

Mark or Joan will fix it. (*Or* connects *Mark* and *Joan*, making them a **compound subject** of the verb *fix.*)
We need string and tape. (*And* connects *string* and *tape*, making them a **compound direct object** of the verb *need.*)

Conjunctions also connect other parts of the sentence, including phrases. Conjunctions can even connect sentences.

Interjections

Read the two sentences below. Each uses an interjection.

Hooray! We won.   Oh no! I forgot my homework.

The expressions *hooray* and *oh no* are interjections. An **interjection** is a word or group of words that expresses feeling. Interjections usually come at the beginning of a sentence. If an interjection expresses strong emotion, it is punctuated with an exclamation mark. However, when an interjection expresses only mild emotion, it is punctuated with a comma.

Hey, how are you?

Exercises

A Write each conjunction in the following sentences.

1. Will we lose this game and the next one, too?
2. The enormous crowd cheered and applauded.
3. The train whistle sounded loud but mournful.
4. Would you prefer eggs or pancakes for breakfast?
5. My soccer coach always wears a jacket or a sweater.
6. The bedraggled hikers seemed tired but happy.
7. Music and animals are Jill's main interests.
8. Parts of the dress and jacket are made of cotton.
9. The drum major tripped and stumbled.
10. I like spaghetti with tomato sauce or clam sauce.

B Write the conjunctions and interjections in the following sentences.

1. Ballet dancers and football players are both athletes.
2. Willie Gault is a football player, but he also studies ballet.
3. Dancers move gracefully but powerfully.
4. Are football players or ballet dancers better athletes?
5. Both kinds of athletes need healthy food and enough rest.
6. Amazing! Did you see how high that dancer leaped?
7. Does dance require more physical strength, or does football?
8. They each require a different kind of strength and control.
9. In football, contact is brief but often painful. Ouch!
10. In dance, the contact is planned and graceful.

Linking Grammar & Writing

A Think of an inanimate (nonliving) object such as an old gym shoe, a favorite T-shirt, or a chewed pencil. Bring the object to life by writing a story from the object's point of view. Pretend you are the object. What would you feel, think, say, and do? Try to use at least eight prepositional phrases in your story.

B A new student has just arrived in your town and wants to meet other students. Give the student directions from school to a popular meeting place. Be specific because this person is not familiar with your town. Be sure to include in your directions the exact name of the place and its distance from school. Try to use prepositional phrases in the beginning and middle of your sentences rather than just at the end. Also try to make three of these adverb phrases and three adjective phrases.

C Choose one of the ideas below or one of your own. Write instructions telling how to accomplish this task properly. Make your instructions very detailed. Include proper equipment and materials needed, where and when the activity takes place, and how it is done. Use at least three compound constructions and five prepositional phrases.

Story Ideas

How to Prepare a Meal in Ten Minutes
How to Earn Extra Money
How to Create a Computer Program
How to Groom Your Dog (or Cat)
How to Juggle
How to Change a Tire on a 10-speed Bicycle
How to Take a Good Photograph

Additional Practice

Part 1 Prepositions Make two columns on your paper. Label them *Prepositions* and *Adverbs*. Write the italicized words from the following sentences in the first column if they are prepositions. Write them in the second column if they are adverbs.

1. A mosquito landed *near* my arm and suffered the consequences.
2. It was raining, so the children had to play *inside*.
3. Courage can only be found *within* yourself.
4. Lloyd works as a lifeguard *during* the summer.
5. Alice stood at the corner and looked *around* for her friend.
6. Wildflowers had grown *around* the abandoned house.
7. The animal sensed that a human being was *near* and ran *away*.
8. The doctor told the patient to look *away* from the needle.
9. We worked *outside* until it was dark.
10. The speed limit changes *beyond* the city limits.

Part 2 Prepositional Phrases Write the prepositional phrases from the following sentences. Draw a line under the object or objects of each preposition.

11. Most frogs lay their eggs in water.
12. The campers hiked through the muddy forest.
13. Do you see the green snake beneath that mossy log?
14. Clara Barton traveled to Civil War battlefields and nursed the wounded.
15. My father built a tall fence around our property.
16. The students were studying the myths of ancient Greece and Rome.
17. The firefighters arrived within three minutes.
18. I go jogging every day except Sunday.
19. What do you know about country music and its origins?
20. Sierra Leone is a small country in western Africa.

Part 3 Pronouns and Prepositional Phrases Write the correct form of the pronouns or prepositions given in parentheses.

21. Let's keep this secret (between, among) you and me.
22. This gift is for Frank and (him, he).
23. The catcher fired the ball to (I, me).
24. The woman in the movie froze in panic as the elephant charged toward (she, her).
25. They had less than ten dollars (between, among) the three of them.
26. The reporter wrote an article about Michael Jackson and (him, he).
27. To (who, whom) should I direct my complaint?
28. The lead roles in the film were performed by Dustin Hoffman and (her, she).
29. The voters had to decide (among, between) the two candidates.
30. Joan is reading about Winston Churchill and (him, he).

Part 4 Adverb and Adjective Phrases Write the prepositional phrases from the following sentences on your paper. Label them as *Adjective Phrases* or *Adverb Phrases*.

31. My mother repaired the light in the attic.
32. With our telescope, we could see the rings around Saturn.
33. Hitler's troops marched into Paris.
34. The painting above the sofa is quite old.
35. The soup can be reheated in a microwave oven.

Part 5 Conjunctions and Interjections Make two columns on your paper. Label them conjunctions and interjections. Write the conjunctions and interjections in the following sentences.

36. Oxygen and hydrogen are chemical elements.
37. Whew! That was a close call!
38. Pam wants to become a carpenter or an electrician.
39. I wanted to make lasagna, but I didn't have enough tomato sauce.
40. Hooray! Our team scored a touchdown with only ten seconds left on the clock.

Application and Review

Lesson Review

A Identifying Prepositions Make two columns on your paper. Label them Prepositions and Adverbs. Write the prepositions in the first column and the adverbs in the second column.

1. That poem was written by Julie.
2. The storm is very near.
3. Ryan ran down the street to the store.
4. Beside the river were several picnic tables with benches.
5. Near the shore the two wet puppies lay down.
6. The cropduster flew low over the field.
7. During supper we received six phone calls.
8. Tom strolled past the bank.
9. The crate of watermelons fell from the truck.
10. Emily grows flowers in small pots.

B Identifying Prepositional Phrases Write the prepositional phrases from the following sentences.

1. The helicopter rumbled across the sky.
2. We went to the restaurant near the theater.
3. She rode to the parade with her brother.
4. They stood by the table eating chips with salsa.
5. She covered the rising bread dough with a cloth .
6. We played tennis at the public courts.
7. Two letters arrived for my grandfather.
8. The plane landed near Atlanta.
9. The people on the snowmobiles raced over the hill.
10. For a minute the eagle stared at Sandy.

C Using Pronouns as Objects of Prepositions Write the correct form of the pronouns given in parentheses.

1. To (whom, who) does this yellow bicycle belong?
2. The cashier pointed toward Eliza and (we, us).

3. The work was divided among Rosa, Jeremy, and (he, him).
4. Lyn went on the roller coaster with Sue and (them, they).
5. The calf circled around my brother and (I, me).
6. Near (who, whom) did Ms. Ramirez seat you?
7. The party can't start without Janie and (her, she).
8. Tell that joke to my friends and (I, me).
9. Everybody except Nicole and (he, him) rides the bus.
10. To Eileen and (us, we), it seemed a long time.

D Using Prepositional Phrases Make two columns on your paper. Label them *Adjective Phrases* and *Adverb Phrases*. Write the adjective phrases from the following sentences in the first column. Write the adverb phrases in the second column.

1. The oven heats in a few minutes.
2. The music box in Murphy's store looks expensive.
3. An ant highway ran between the bucket and the pump.
4. The bear cubs went into their den.
5. Several students in Peter's class work with Dr. Parker.
6. From the trunks of the maple trees hang tin pails.
7. We built a greenhouse near the toolshed.
8. They should arrive around noon.
9. The umpire behind home plate is Mr. Edens.
10. The pilot of that plane is my sister.

E Recognizing Conjunctions and Interjections Make two columns on your paper. Label them *Conjunctions* and *Interjections*. Write the conjunctions in the first column. Write the interjections in the second column.

1. Ladybugs and spiders help gardeners.
2. Give me butter but no jam, please.
3. Watch out! There's a hole in the road.
4. Ouch! The sand is hot.
5. We used paint and wallpaper to fix the old kitchen.
6. I like to run slowly but smoothly.
7. Did red or blue stripes decorate the new awning?
8. Oh, I must have the wrong number.
9. The coach will give Ben or me special instructions.
10. Near the school and the park we planted the seedlings.

Chapter Review

A Using Prepositional Phrases Rewrite each sentence, adding the prepositional phrase shown in parentheses. Be careful to place the phrase correctly. Then tell whether you used the phrase as an adjective or as an adverb.

1. The child looked at the wrapped package. (with a sly grin)
2. Rick held his breath as the stunt plane soared. (through the ring of fire)
3. The conductor ran when the woman screamed. (after the purse snatcher)
4. The girl asked for the movie star's autograph. (in the pink sweatshirt)
5. The young man showed us where to sit. (in the dark suit)
6. The confused monkey appeared on my window ledge. (from the zoo)
7. The elephant grabbed the peanuts from the small child. (with its trunk)
8. The distance is called the circumference. (around a circle)
9. The boy told how he learned to swim. (in his speech)
10. She hung her coat on the hook. (with a long sigh)

B Using Conjunctions and Interjections Make two columns on your paper. Label them *Conjunctions* and *Interjections*. Write the conjunctions from the following sentences in the first column. Write the interjections in the second column.

1. Sue lives near John and Simon.
2. Ugh! This milk is spoiled.
3. Look! There goes your favorite movie star.
4. The party was given by Antonio and her.
5. I sat near the front door but left by the back.
6. Goodness! I haven't seen a car like that in years.
7. Well, I haven't seen you for a while.
8. All students have given their social studies reports except Michael and me.
9. No one could throw the ball far enough or high enough to win a prize.
10. The women did not give the book to Harold or me.

28
Using Compound Sentences

If railroads could move freight only one boxcar at a time, transportation would be quite inefficient. Similarly, if writers could only use simple sentences with simple ideas, communication would be inefficient.

Boxcars, however, can be linked together behind powerful locomotives. Simple sentences can be linked too, forming compound sentences that make communication more powerful and efficient.

This chapter explains how compound sentences are formed and how they can be used to add variety and richness to your writing.

1
What Are Compound Sentences?

A *compound sentence* consists of two or more simple sentences joined together.

You have learned that the word *compound* means "having two or more parts." You have worked with compound subjects, verbs, and objects.

So far, however, you have been dealing with simple sentences. A **simple sentence** is a sentence with only one subject and one predicate. It is called simple even though both the subject and the predicate may be compound. Note the following examples of simple sentences that contain compound constructions:

> The *co-captains* and the *coach* accepted the trophy.
> (compound subject)
> We *sat* and *listened* to the demonstration of laser
> technology. (compound verb)
> The movie scene required *robots* and *motorcycles*.
> (compound object)

Now we come to a different kind of sentence, a sentence that can have more than one subject and more than one predicate— the **compound sentence**. The parts of a compound sentence are joined by either a comma and a coordinating conjunction or by a semicolon (;).

> My uncle gave me a book**, and** I read it from cover
> to cover.
> We need scientists**, but** we need laboratory workers
> even more.
> You can take the course now**, or** you can take it
> next year.
> Mom threw my sneakers away**;** they were worn out.

The main parts of each compound sentence could be written as separate sentences, as in the examples on page 563.

My uncle gave me a book. I read it from cover to cover.
We need scientists. We need laboratory workers even more.
You can take the course now. You can take it next year.
Mom threw my sneakers away. They were worn out.

Compound Sentence or Compound Verb?

The first sentence below is a simple sentence with a compound verb. The second sentence is a compound sentence. Notice the difference in punctuation.

> The storm raged and howled for hours. (This is a simple sentence. It has only one subject. The conjunction *and* joins two parts of a compound verb.)

> The storm raged, and the wind howled for hours. (This is a compound sentence. It contains two simple sentences, each with a subject, *storm*, *wind*, and verb, *raged*, *howled*. The two simple sentences are joined by *and* to form the compound sentence.)

Diagraming Compound Sentences

It is not difficult to diagram compound sentences if you already know how to diagram simple sentences. Review page 395 for diagraming simple sentences. A compound sentence is really two or more simple sentences joined together. Therefore, you diagram the first half of the sentence, draw a dotted-line "step" between the verbs for the conjunction, and then draw the diagram for the second half.

EXAMPLE   John slept soundly, but the other boys did not close their eyes.

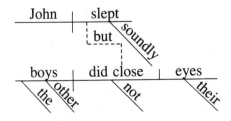

Exercises

A Write *S* for simple sentences and *C* for compound sentences.

1. The blue jay called, and three other jays answered.
2. Marge Piercy is a poet; Saul Bellow is a novelist.
3. You must practice often, or you will not improve.
4. Cheryl plays backgammon, but she prefers chess.
5. One dancer tripped and lost his balance.
6. Mark Twain and Emily Dickinson are American writers.
7. The river overflowed and damaged much property.
8. The clouds are low, but it still isn't raining.
9. He's buying radish seeds, and I'm getting green beans.
10. Quarter horses and Arabians are kinds of saddle horses.

B Write *S* for each simple sentence and *C* for each compound sentence. Write every subject and verb for each sentence.

Gold Incan artifact, Peru.

1. The Incas were a South American Indian people; they ruled vast stretches of South America.
2. Their empire stretched up the Pacific coast of South America and was called the *Four Quarters of the Earth*.
3. Much Incan history has been lost, but archeologists have found many Incan artifacts.
4. Incan artisans made beautiful gold works of art, and Incan workers built enormous stone buildings.
5. Many of these works of art were melted for their gold, but some pieces have been discovered in tombs.
6. The Incas' stone buildings have survived earthquakes.
7. The Spaniards conquered the *Four Quarters of the Earth* and captured the Incas' gold.
8. In 1553, the Spaniards captured the last Incan emperor and demanded a huge ransom.
9. The emperor filled a seventeen-foot by twenty-two-foot room with gold, and the Spaniards seized it.
10. The Spaniards killed the emperor and melted the gold.

2
Punctuating Compound Sentences

When the parts of a compound sentence are joined by a coordinating conjunction, a *comma* precedes the conjunction. Otherwise, the parts are separated by a *semicolon*.

Since compound sentences are made up of two or more simple sentences, they are sometimes long. To help readers keep the information in order, you must separate the parts of compound sentences. Do this by putting either a comma and a coordinating conjunction or a semicolon between the parts of the compound sentence. Remember that the coordinating conjunctions are *and*, *but*, and *or*. (See page 554 for a review of conjunctions.)

> Patti did a routine on the parallel bars**, and** Liz and
>   Amy performed on the trampoline.
> Nelson swam a mile**;** then he jogged home.

If the comma hadn't been used in the first example above, a reader might have been confused. The comma clarifies what Patti did, so the reader can see that Liz and Amy did something else. If the semicolon hadn't been used in the second example, the reader would think two sentences had been carelessly run together.

You have already learned that a compound sentence requires a comma to separate its parts. However, you do not need a comma to separate the two parts of a compound subject, a compound verb, or a compound direct object.

Incorrect	The students from the seventh grade, and those from the eighth formed a soccer team.
Correct	The students from the seventh grade and those from the eighth formed a soccer team. (compound subject)
Incorrect	We walked into the office, and talked with the manager.
Correct	We walked into the office and talked with the manager. (compound predicate)

Finally, the comma is not necessary in very short compound sentences.

We skated and we skied.
Fred walked here but I rode.

Exercises

A Rewrite each compound sentence, adding a comma or a semicolon where needed.

1. The walls were brick and the roof was slate.
2. The old bathtub had legs its feet looked like lion's paws.
3. We could hear the rumbling of thunder and Tim could see flashes of lightning across the lake.
4. Ms. Hart and the members of the camera club will be putting on an exhibit of indoor photography I would like to see it.
5. The concert was almost sold out but Carmen managed to get tickets.
6. Juan went mountain climbing his sister went white-water rafting.
7. The hiking club has already taken several training walks it is planning a walkathon for next month.
8. The old wooden chest is an antique and Carrie was fascinated by its design.
9. I like all sports but I enjoy soccer the most.
10. Dennis wears hip boots and fishes right in the stream but Lisa prefers to fish from the shore.

B Rewrite each compound sentence, adding a comma or a semicolon where needed. For each simple sentence, write *Correct*.

1. They folded the raft and Mr. Russell stowed it in the trunk of his car.
2. The sky grew dark and soon large hailstones were hitting our house.
3. A chain saw can be very dangerous it can cause accidents.
4. Peter drove for twenty minutes and finally reached Concord.

5. An electric typewriter is very sensitive and types at the lightest touch.
6. Amelia Earhart successfully flew across the Atlantic Ocean alone in 1932 but her plane disappeared over the Pacific Ocean in 1937.
7. We will eventually use the metric system but we are adjusting to it with difficulty.
8. I sent the book third-class mail I sent everything else by first-class mail.
9. We repaired our bikes and cycled to the lake.
10. Our tomcat chewed through the screen door flies and mosquitos soon got in.

c *Proofreading* Copy the following paragraph and correct the errors. Pay particular attention to the punctuation of compound sentences.

When I heard that our police oficers were going to use radar guns, I was quite surprized. The words sounded menacing, I thought they referred to some space-age weapon. I soon learned, however, that a radar gun is harmless, in fact, it is extremely helpful. By shooting week microwaves at a car, the police can tell if the car is speeding. The radar gun compares the speed of the outging waves with the speed of those that bounce back. Then a number apears on the gun, the number tells how many miles per hour the car is traveling:

Grammar in Action

Because you could write all sentences as simple sentences, you may wonder why compound sentences are important. Read the following passage. As you can see, a series of short sentences can be monotonous and dull:

Chicago is the birthplace of the skyscraper. The first one was built there in 1885. This first skyscraper was ten stories high. It was not the height that made the building a skyscraper. It was the frame. A steel "skeleton" or frame supported the building. This frame made it strong. The building could support many stories. Thanks to this early technology, today's skyscrapers reach heights of more than one hundred stories.

Writing Activity Rewrite the paragraph, combining some of the simple sentences into compound sentences. Use the conjunction *and* only once. Keep in mind that an interesting paragraph has a variety of simple and compound sentences.

3
Using Compound Sentences

The parts of a compound sentence must be related in thought.

You have learned that the parts of a compound sentence are of equal importance because each part is a simple sentence. This means that the parts balance one another grammatically. They must also balance in thought. That is, the parts of a compound sentence must express thoughts that are related to each other. Review the Grammar in Action exercise on page 568. Did each of your compound sentences express related thoughts?

Making Compound Sentences

Some pairs of sentences make good compound sentences, and some do not:

1. It looked like rain. We went to the fair anyhow. (Will these simple sentences make a good compound sentence? Yes. Use *but*.)
2. I like horseback riding. Arabian horses are beautiful. (The ideas are not closely related enough to make a compound sentence.)
3. Pete flew his kite. I have never built a kite. (The ideas are not closely related enough to make a compound sentence.)
4. Give me your boat. I'll give you my ski poles. (These two may be made into a compound sentence. Use *and*.)

Exercises

A Rewrite each pair of sentences as a compound sentence.

1. Ann goes horseback riding every weekend. She rides in the annual horse show every summer.
2. You must wake up early today. You will miss the bus.
3. The fan belt on the station wagon was worn out. There was nothing wrong with the engine.
4. Disneyland is in California. Disney World is in Florida.

5. That rough-barked wood is hickory. This smoother wood is maple.
6. Builders use those concrete blocks for walls. My brother uses them with boards for furniture.
7. We should practice every day this week. We will not be ready for Saturday's game.
8. Jim wanted to see the movie. It was not playing in Memphis.
9. Marilyn and Phillip were going to the carnival. The thunderstorm changed their plans.
10. Don't go too far into the woods. You might become lost.

B Tell whether each of the following pairs of sentences might be made into a compound sentence. For pairs that can be made into compound sentences, indicate the conjunction that should be used. For pairs that cannot be joined write *no compound*.

1. Elizabeth has the mumps. She has never felt this sick before.
2. The game opened with the raising of the flag. Our team gained twenty yards on the first play.
3. Cross-country skiing is a popular winter sport in many areas. Many Midwestern states have excellent indoor ice skating rinks.
4. Have a good time in New York City. See as much as possible.
5. You can make a puppet from pâpier-mâché. You can try another kind of material.
6. The sweet potatoes were raw. The barbecued chicken was burned.
7. Arizona is a beautiful state. Nevada and California lie west of it.
8. Tennis players can use a two-handed backhand. They can use a one-handed grip.
9. Most trees lose their leaves in winter. Evergreens live up to their name.
10. Todd and Doug won easily. It started to snow after the match.

Grammar in Action

The following paragraph could be improved by the use of some compound constructions.

My friend Tony was going to the baseball game. I wanted to go, too. Mother objected. I hadn't mowed the lawn. I hadn't watered the garden. I could go to the game. I had to work first. Tony was getting impatient. Then I had an idea. There was a patch of delicious strawberries in our garden. Tony loves strawberries. I talked my idea over with Mom. Then, I talked it over with Tony. Soon Tony was watering the garden. I was mowing the lawn. Before long we left for the game. Tony was carrying a box of strawberries.

Writing Activity Using what you have learned about compound constructions, rewrite the paragraph. Be sure that the parts of each compound sentence express related thoughts. Remember that a good paragraph has a variety of sentence constructions.

Linking Grammar & Writing

A Imagine you have been given complete control of Earth. What is the first thing you would do to improve conditions on the planet? Write a paragraph explaining what you would do and tell why you think it is important. Use *and, but,* or *or* in at least three compound sentences.

B Read the paragraph below, and use it as the beginning of a story of your own. In your story, include at least three simple sentences with compound verbs and at least three compound sentences.

> Paul and his friend Bob were camping outside one night when they were awakened by the rustling of leaves and the cracking of twigs. As they emerged from their tent, they saw three pairs of red eyes glaring at them from the dark forest.

C Write a paragraph describing an accomplishment of which you are proud. Tell how you managed to achieve this feat and why it means a lot to you. Be sure to combine related thoughts into compound sentences in your paragraph.

Additional Practice

Part 1 Identifying Compound Sentences Write *S* for each simple sentence and *C* for each compound sentence. Write every subject and verb for each sentence.

1. Ted likes classical music; Gina prefers rock.
2. Alexander Hamilton signed the United States Constitution.
3. Anne weeded and watered the vegetable garden.
4. Ruth thinks Robin Williams is the funniest person alive, but I think Jay Leno is even funnier.
5. The Mississippi River is 2,348 miles long.
6. My sister bought Dad a birthday gift, and I wrapped it.
7. First multiply the numerators and denominators; then write the product in its simplest form.
8. Billie Jean King has played an important role in women's professional tennis.
9. I enjoy golf, but my father does not.
10. We can do our homework now, or we can wait until later.
11. Great Britain entered World War II in 1939; the United States entered the war in 1941.
12. Katharine Hepburn had a brilliant acting career.
13. My cat and my parakeet do not like each other.
14. Jamie woke up early, but then she fell asleep again.
15. Tom mowed the lawn, and Christine cleaned the garage.

Part 2 Punctuating Compound Sentences Rewrite each compound sentence, adding a comma or semicolon where needed. For each simple sentence, write *S*.

16. Orson Welles produced a radio broadcast based on *The War of the Worlds*.
17. The runner pulled a muscle during the race she was unable to continue.
18. Many people tried to flee in their cars others went into shock.
19. Karen wants to go to the concert but she has not saved enough money for the ticket.

20. Clark Gable played Rhett Butler in *Gone with the Wind* and Vivien Leigh played Scarlett O'Hara.
21. Deciduous trees drop their leaves each year but evergreen trees do not.
22. A dictionary and a thesaurus are useful tools for a writer.
23. Mary Ann walks to school Joanne takes the bus.
24. At the nature center we hiked and then had a picnic.
25. I walk my dog every morning and then I eat breakfast.

Part 3 Using Compound Sentences Ten of the following pairs of sentences may be written as compound sentences. Rewrite these sentences, using the correct punctuation and/or conjunctions.

26. An octagon has eight sides. A hexagon has six.
27. Sandra Day O'Connor is an associate justice of the United States Supreme Court. She was born in Texas.
28. You can have a baked potato with your steak. You can have another kind of potato.
29. Please close the window. Draw the curtains.
30. Australia is a country. It is also a continent.
31. Oklahoma was the forty-sixth state to be admitted to the United States. Oklahoma City is the capital of Oklahoma.
32. Mrs. Allen likes to sing. She does not have a good voice.
33. My cousin graduated from law school in June. He did not find a job until September.
34. Thomas Jefferson wrote the Declaration of Independence. He played the violin every day.
35. You can mop the floor. You can vacuum the rugs instead.
36. I wanted to buy a new jacket. I didn't have any money.
37. Three inches of rain fell last night. Oregon often has rainy weather.
38. Come to my house after school. I'll listen to you rehearse your speech.
39. Bicycle racing is extremely popular in Europe. Henry is in training for an important bicycle race in France.
40. Tanya wanted to go home for lunch. She had forgotten her house key.

Application and Review

Lesson Review

A Analyzing Compound Sentences Write *S* for each simple sentence and *C* for each compound sentence.

1. I collect silver coins, and Liz collects two-dollar bills.
2. William made the announcements for the day, but the intercom didn't work.
3. Beatrice discovered and replaced the worn-out needle on her record player.
4. We sometimes play miniature golf on Saturday, but last week we went to the museum.
5. Snow whirled around the buildings and settled into deep drifts.
6. Last summer we went to the Grand Canyon, but this summer we will be backpacking in Maine.
7. Sara and Max designed and built a booth for the school carnival.
8. The cable car ride up the mountain was fun, but I was frightened at first.
9. Our home room won the intramural trophy for soccer, and we were victorious in field hockey, too.
10. The moon rose, and the whippoorwill started its endless call.

B Punctuating Compound Constructions Rewrite each compound sentence, adding a comma or a semicolon in the appropriate place. For each simple sentence, write *Correct*.

1. The links in the chain were as big as saucers they clanked against each other.
2. Our neighbors from Germany boil and dye their Easter eggs with red onion skins.
3. Trays of chicken salad sandwiches and fresh vegetables were next to the juice.

4. We looked in the shed behind the school but the shovels were not there.
5. Jack brought and set up the movie projector for the public meeting.
6. An electric knife vibrates a lot it works well on both bread and meat.
7. The grapefruit tree next door was in bloom it smelled pungent and fresh.
8. Dina stumbled and fell but a moment later she was jogging again.
9. We all went to the baseball game and we later came home for a barbecue.
10. The photographs of Mars didn't show much and Roberto was very disappointed.

C Making Compound Sentences Rewrite each of the following pairs of sentences as a compound sentence. Be sure to use the correct punctuation.

1. Do you want a turkey sandwich? Would you prefer a tossed salad?
2. Many early attempts were made with a flying machine. The Wright Brothers are credited with the invention.
3. Jonathan, Linda, and I visited Universal Studios. We also went to Knotts Berry Farm.
4. Tierra del Fuego is at one end of the Pan American highway. Fairbanks, Alaska, is at the other end.
5. Green Lake, Wisconsin, is a great place for cross-country skiing. Door County is even better.
6. Our intramural softball game was postponed. We were able to play it on Friday.
7. In science we studied a unit on insects. I didn't find it very interesting.
8. Jim, you should take home economics. You will never learn to cook.
9. Rick hit the ball deep into left field. The umpire called it a foul.
10. You can go to the movie. You can spend all evening preparing for the exam.

Chapter Review

A Analyzing Compound Sentences Write *S* for each simple sentence and *C* for each compound sentence. Rewrite each compound sentence, adding a comma or a semicolon in the appropriate place.

1. The teacher walked around the room he stopped at John's desk.
2. Calvin opened the letter it was from Greg.
3. Albert laughed and cried during the movie.
4. Elsa entered the computer contest.
5. I started this science fiction book Monday and I haven't been able to put it down.
6. It is summer but the weather is cool.
7. The Mets loaded the bases but the next batter struck out.
8. People cheered and laughed at the antics of the clowns.
9. Gus is an excellent artist but he works too quickly.
10. The driver of the oncoming car hit the brakes and swerved to the side.

B Using Compound Sentences Six of the following pairs of sentences can be written as compound sentences. Rewrite those sentences, using the correct punctuation and/or conjunctions.

1. We can watch television. We can go out and jog instead.
2. They may hike all day. The backpacks were new.
3. A cat ran into the room. The science room keeps white mice.
4. Morgan wanted the videocassette. He had no money.
5. My brother drove carefully. We still couldn't avoid skidding on the ice.
6. A great storm arose. John was always afraid of sailing.
7. Being a teenager isn't easy. Being an adult is probably hard, too.
8. Jeff tried to improve his grades. Science is his favorite subject.
9. Ruth built the scenery. Barbara controlled the stage lights.
10. You can buy that shirt. You can save the money for something else.

29
Understanding Subject and Verb Agreement

What would happen if you walked out of your house wearing a striped shirt, checkered pants, mismatched socks, and two different shoes? It's possible you would be complimented on your unique fashion sense, but more likely your friends would laugh and say that your clothes weren't getting along too well. The parts of a sentence must "get along" with each other, too. The subject and verb of a sentence must match, or agree. If they do not, the sentence as a whole will not work well. In this chapter you will learn how to make subjects and verbs agree in many different types of sentences.

1
Singular and Plural Forms

Certain groups of words have different forms depending on whether they are *singular* or *plural*.

A noun that stands for one person, place, thing, or idea is **singular**. A noun that stands for more than one is **plural**.

Verbs, too, have singular and plural forms. Most singular, third person verbs are formed by adding *s*. Most plural verbs are formed by dropping the *s*.

Singular	runs	finds	carries	wishes
Plural	run	find	carry	wish

In a sentence, the verb must agree in number with its subject. A subject and verb agree in number when they are both singular or both plural.

Singular	The student *cooks*.	The class *votes*.
Plural	The students *cook*.	The classes *vote*.

Exceptions to the agreement rule are the singular pronouns *I* and *you*, which take plural verbs. *I cook. You vote.*

Special Forms of Certain Verbs

Am, Is, Was, Are, and Were   The verb forms *is*, *am*, and *was* are singular. The forms *are* and *were* are plural.

Singular	Pat *is* helpful.	Pat *was* helpful.
Plural	The books *are* helpful.	The books *were* helpful.

Has and Have   The verb form *has* is singular. *Have* is plural.

Singular	Colleen *has* new shoes.
Plural	They *have* new shoes.

Does and Do   The verb form *does* is singular. *Do* is plural.

Singular	He *does* the dishes.
Plural	Sam and Frank *do* the dishes.

Exercises

A Make two columns. Label them *Singular* and *Plural*. Write the following words in the correct column.

1. table	6. activity	11. they	16. holidays
2. walks	7. cook	12. writes	17. live
3. horse	8. arena	13. I	18. sports
4. have	9. was	14. draws	19. travel
5. papers	10. laughs	15. mouse	20. do

B Write on your paper the *Subjects* and *Verbs* from these sentences. Indicate whether the subjects and verbs are *Singular* or *Plural*.

1. On our visits, my grandfather tells us stories about Ireland.
2. Jane helps me with my preparation for the talent show.
3. The team members practice hard.
4. Lyn's plans were too complicated.
5. These dogs need new flea collars.
6. Mrs. Morey is helpful to all the new students.
7. The Feather River waterfalls look spectacular this spring.
8. Shadow puppets perform behind a screen.
9. Pewter is a metal alloy, and it consists mainly of tin.
10. These apples are MacIntosh, and their juice is light and tart.

C *Write Now* Study the following photograph. What could be happening? Write a paragraph in which you describe what the people might be watching. Include in your paragraph sentences that have plural subjects (the people in the crowd) and singular subjects (a person in the crowd).

2
Agreement of Subject and Verb

> A verb must agree with its subject in *number.*

The **number** of a word refers to whether it is singular (one thing or action) or plural (more than one thing or action). When we say that one word **agrees** with another, we mean that it is the same in number.

> The *boys* (plural) *were* (plural) fixing a toboggan.
> *She* (singular) *does* (singular) not have her coat.

Often a phrase appears between the subject and the verb. The simple subject is never part of such a phrase. Don't mistake the phrase or any word in it for the subject.

> *One* (of the glasses) *was* broken.
> The *horses* (in the barn) *were* restless.

The Pronoun You

The pronoun *you* is unusual for two reasons. It has one form for both singular and plural. In addition, it takes a plural verb, even if it refers to a singular noun.

> Donna, you *have* my best wishes. (not *has*)
> Christine and Gary, you *are* next on the list. (not *is*)

The Pronoun I

Although the pronoun *I* stands for a single person, it does not usually take a singular verb. The only singular verb forms used with it are *am* and *was*.

> I *am* the captain.   I *was* here yesterday.

Except with *am* and *was*, the pronoun *I* takes a plural verb.

> I *play* guitar and drums. (not *plays*)
> I *live* on the next block. (not *lives*)

Exercise

Write the simple subjects from the following sentences.
Beside each one write the correct form of the verb given in
parentheses.

1. Some inventions dramatically (changes, change) our lives.
2. Many inventions that we take for granted (is, are) recent.
3. The jet plane (was, were) first flown in 1939.
4. Now many people (travels, travel) on jets.
5. Television (is, are) also a fairly new invention.
6. Dad (remembers, remember) when few homes had TV's.
7. He (says, say) that familes listened to radio instead.
8. Today many people (relies, rely) on computers.
9. The first computer (was, were) completed in 1946.
10. I (wonders, wonder) what inventions people will take for
    granted in the next century.

Grammar in Action

The following examples will help you understand the
importance of subject–verb agreement in your writing.

Incorrect   The doors on our house *is* blue.
Correct   The doors on our house *are* blue.

The first example could confuse your readers. Since the
singular verb (is) agrees with the wrong noun (house), your
readers might think that the house is blue. In the second
example, the plural verb (are) sends them to the correct noun
(doors).

Writing Activity Edit the following paragraph so that each verb
agrees with its subject.

> Cyclists on the river path loves sunny fall days
> like today. A sailboat on the river appear to glisten
> in the sun. The trees along the way treats cyclists to
> a variety of fall colors. The cars on the bridge
> overhead seems to be in another world.

3
Verbs with Compound Subjects

A *compound subject* has two or more subjects that share the same verb.

Compound Subjects Joined by and

If two or more subjects share a verb, they are a **compound subject**. When a compound subject contains the conjunction *and*, it is plural; a plural verb must be used with it.

> Meg and Lee *are* here. (*Meg* and *Lee* is the compound subject. The verb *are* is plural.)

> My friends and I *are* downstairs. (*Friends* and *I* is the compound subject. The verb *are* is plural.)

Compound Subjects Joined by or or nor

When the parts of a compound subject are joined by *or* or *nor*, the verb agrees with the nearer subject.

> Lisa or Ted *is* the one to call. (*Ted* is the subject nearer the verb, so the verb is singular.)

> Neither Beth nor her sisters *have* curly hair. (*Sisters* is the subject nearer the verb, so the verb is plural.)

Exercises

A Write the correct form of the verbs given in parentheses.

1. Shqiperia and Albania (is, are) names for the same country.
2. The president or the vice-president (take, takes) charge.
3. Neither Steve nor Dave (is, are) trying out for hockey.
4. Neither the Grammy nor the Emmy (is, are) a movie award.
5. Carol and you (have, has) overdue books.
6. Neither the milk nor that chicken (smell, smells) fresh.

7. The elm and those birch trees (was, were) just planted.
8. Jane and I (does, do) imitations of popular singers.
9. Either the band or the chorus (performs, perform) Friday.
10. Mom or my brothers (meet, meets) Dad at the airport.

B Make two columns on your paper. Label them *Simple Subjects* and *Verbs*. Write the simple subjects from the following sentences in the first column. In the second column, write the correct form of the verb. Some subjects will be compound.

1. Ellen and I (am, are) going hot-air ballooning.
2. Neither Ellen nor I (has, have) been in a balloon before.
3. The calm air and cooler temperature (makes, make) morning the best time to fly.
4. Our pilot and co-pilot (tells, tell) us that ballooning began in France.
5. Balloons (rises, rise) because they are filled with warm air.
6. Our brightly colored balloon (lifts, lift) off smoothly.
7. The air inside floating balloons (is, are) over 200 degrees.
8. The fields and streams (seems, seem) very far away.
9. Pilots and passengers (has, have) to bend their knees as the balloon lands.
10. Our first flight (ends, end) much too soon.

c *Write Now* You have been asked to write a travel brochure for a ten-day wilderness adventure. Your goal is to make the trip sound so exciting that many people will want to take it. Describe what the participants will see and do during their ten days in the wilderness. Use at least four of the following compound subjects in your paragraph. Make sure that subjects and verbs agree.

A clear pool and a waterfall . . .
Neither the soil nor the water . . .
Either rain or dark clouds . . .
Neither animals nor vegetation . . .
Food or water . . .
Fuel and supplies . . .
Animal tracks and other signs of life . . .
Either this hill or the hills on the horizon . . .
Neither this volcano nor any of the others . . .

4
Agreement in Inverted Sentences

Word order does not affect subject–verb agreement.

Usually, the subject comes before the verb. A person is likely to say, for example, "Our house lies just beyond those woods." For emphasis, however, a writer or speaker may say, "Just beyond those woods lies our house." The second sentence is called an **inverted sentence**. In each sentence, however, the subject is *house* and the verb is *lies*. The subjects and verbs of both sentences must agree.

> Above the plaza flutter a thousand flags. (flags, flutter)
> On the field is a huge parade. (parade, is)
> To the games go tourists by the thousands. (tourists, go)
> Does Mom or Dad have the keys? (Mom or Dad, does have)

Notice the last example above. For questions, inverted order is the ordinary order.

Exercises

A Write on your paper the correct form of the verbs given in parentheses in the following sentences.

1. (Does, Do) the story end well?
2. Down the road (thunders, thunder) a lumber truck.
3. Beside the bench (is, are) a tool box.
4. Far underground (rumbles, rumble) subway trains.
5. After "Oceans" (come, comes) the chapter called "Space."
6. In moist places (lives, live) many insects.
7. Into the bird bath (jump, jumps) two happy sparrows.
8. Near the fire (snuggle, snuggles) a dog and a cat.
9. At the end of the big load (flaps, flap) the red flag for danger.
10. (Is, Are) the geese flying south already?

B Make two columns on your paper. Label them *Simple Subjects* and *Verbs*. Write the simple subjects from the following sentences in the first column. In the second column, write the correct form of the verbs given in parentheses.

1. After the parade floats (come, comes) the Marshfield band.
2. Round and round (whirls, whirl) his thoughts.
3. On the wall (hang, hangs) a movie screen and maps.
4. In the protected park (graze, grazes) giraffes and zebras.
5. On the bookcase (is, are) Dad's keys and wallet.
6. Around that dinner table (sit, sits) our entire family.
7. In the midst of the crowd (stand, stands) a juggler.
8. (Has, Have) Marilyn and Jackie finished their tree house?
9. Near that barn often (prowl, prowls) two foxes or a coyote.
10. (Do, Does) one or two maples shade that house?

c *Write Now* Write a paragraph that describes exactly where you are right now. Begin by describing the things or people nearest to you. Then move outward until you have created the scene. Begin half of your sentences in inverted order. You may use the following words and phrases or words and phrases of your own.

To my immediate right . . .	Above . . . / Below . . .
Beside . . .	Slightly beyond . . .
Upon . . .	Along the . . .

Verbs with There, Where, *and* Here

The words *there*, *where*, and *here* often begin sentences. Their job is to get the sentence moving. When *there*, *where*, or *here* begins a sentence, look for the subject later in the sentence.

Here is a book on magic tricks.
(*Book* is the subject.)

Where are my keys?
(*Keys* is the subject.)

There are no questions.
(*Questions* is the subject.)

As in any other sentence, the subject and verb must agree. The singular subject *book* takes the singular verb form *is*. The plural subjects *questions* and *keys* take the plural verb form *are*. When *there*, *here*, or *where* begins a sentence, be careful to make the verb agree in number with the subject of the sentence.

When *there* is used near the beginning of an inverted sentence, the sentence is usually a question. Look for the subjects later in these sentences as well.

Were there any empty seats?   Was there a party?
(*Seats* is the subject.)   (*Party* is the subject.)

Exercises

A Write on your paper the correct form of the verbs given in parentheses.

1. (Is, Are) there any milk in the house?
2. Here (is, are) my art assignment.
3. There (was, were) a symphony on the radio late last night.
4. Where (has, have) the ten eggs that were in this carton gone?
5. Where (were, was) the ring when you found it?
6. Where (is, are) the active volcanoes in Alaska?
7. (Was, Were) there a very large crowd at the Friday night baseball game?
8. Here (sit, sits) the Speaker of the House of Representatives.
9. There (was, were) three chores I had to do before I left for the party.
10. (Have, Has) there been any visitors yet?

B *Proofreading* Imagine that you have written a children's story to entertain your younger cousin. Now you need to proofread it. Begin by proofreading the following paragraph. Pay particular attention to subject-verb agreement. Then, rewrite the paragraph correctly.

In a land far, far away, there are a kingdom. in this kingdome, on a hi hill, there stand a palace. In one of the very top rooms of this palace, there sit a prince, and beside this prince lie the worlds smartest dog. How smart is he. Well, he only know twelve languages, including dolphin, zebra, and chinese. We talking about one smart dog

Grammar in Action

You can gain or lose a reader's attention with your very first sentence. That's why your topic sentence should introduce the rest of the paragraph in an interesting way.

Topic sentences that begin with *There is* or *There are* are usually general enough, but they are often boring. Try to avoid beginning your topic sentences with either of these phrases. Notice the difference between the two sentences below.

Boring   There are many Spanish words now used in English.

Better   *Banana, patio,* and *mosquito* are just a few of the words we have taken from the Spanish language.

Sometimes a topic sentence can be improved by changing it into a question.

Boring   There is a garden of glass flowers at Harvard University in Cambridge, Massachusetts.

Better   Can you imagine walking into a garden of glass flowers?

Writing Activity Revise the following topic sentences so that they are more interesting. Your revisions should not begin with *There is* or *There are.* Do not make more than two of your revisions questions. Write the revised topic sentences on your paper.

1. There are many strange creatures in caves.
2. There are many ways to protect your home from fire.
3. There is a time capsule buried on the Oglethorpe University campus.
4. There is one of the world's most crowded cities in Japan.

Now use one of these topic sentences to write a paragraph. Vary the beginnings of your sentences, but make sure that the subject and verb of each sentence agree. You may need to do some research to write the paragraph.

Linking Grammar & Writing

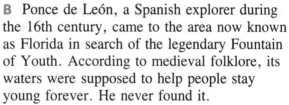

A Write a one-page fantasy about what the products in a grocery store would say to each other if they could talk. Imagine what they might say about the customers, employees, and each other. Would they complain about the way they are squeezed and jostled? Would they argue over who is fresher or more wholesome? Write in the present tense, using as many vivid action verbs as possible. Begin one sentence with *There*, make at least two sentences questions, and use compound subjects occasionally. Make sure that the subject and verb agree in each sentence. (Refer to page 644 for information on punctuating dialogue.)

B Ponce de León, a Spanish explorer during the 16th century, came to the area now known as Florida in search of the legendary Fountain of Youth. According to medieval folklore, its waters were supposed to help people stay young forever. He never found it.

Imagine that you have just found this fountain. What are your thoughts and feelings at this moment? Do you want to drink from it? Are you thinking of the Spaniards who searched in vain for the fountain? Are you worried about how people will react when news of your discovery leaks out? Are you excited by the idea of being young forever?

Write two or three paragraphs describing the fountain, its special powers, and your thoughts and feelings about this discovery. Write your paragraph primarily in the present tense. Use inverted order to write at least one of the sentences. Use at least two compound subjects. Form one of these compound subjects with *or* or *nor*, and use *there* before a verb once. Then, make sure that within each sentence the subject and verb agree.

Additional Practice

Parts 1 and 2 **Agreement in Number** Make each of the following sentences singular or plural as directed. Write the correct choices of the words in parentheses on your paper.

1. Our television (set, sets) (are, is) broken. *Plural*
2. The (wrestlers, wrestler) (spend, spends) four hours a day in training. *Singular*
3. (They, He) (was, were) the first to arrive at the party. *Plural*
4. The (trains, train) always (passes, pass) through the village at night. *Plural*
5. The (candidates, candidate) often (speaks, speak) without notes. *Singular*
6. (One, Two) of the horses (were, was) quite old. *Plural*
7. (Both, Neither) of the watermelons (were, was) ripe. *Singular*
8. The (entrance, entrances) to the woodchuck's hole (were, was) blocked. *Singular*
9. (She, They) never (eat, eats) dinner before six o'clock. *Singular*
10. (We, I) (were, was) late for soccer practice yesterday. *Plural*
11. The (scientist, scientists) (work, works) in the field of cancer research. *Singular*
12. (They, You) (think, thinks) of everything. *Singular*
13. (One, Most) of the dishes (is, are) dirty. *Plural*
14. The (states, state) (provides, provide) scholarships for deserving students. *Plural*
15. The computer (program, programs) (gives, give) on-screen instructions to the user. *Singular*

Part 3 Agreement with Compound Subjects Write the correct form of the verbs given in parentheses.

16. Caroline and Megan (lives, live) next door to each other.
17. Either Mrs. Morgan or her secretary (answer, answers) the telephone.

18. New Hampshire, Massachusetts, and Connecticut (is, are) in New England.
19. Neither an earthworm nor a snail (have, has) backbones.
20. Mr. Feinstein or Ms. Cunningham (are, is) the person to see for tickets.
21. My mother and father (wants, want) to take a trip around the world.
22. Ray Bradbury and Isaac Asimov (write, writes) science fiction.
23. Neither Jim nor Bud (are, is) going to the track meet.
24. Egypt, Libya, and Turkey (border, borders) on the Mediterranean Sea.
25. Neither she nor they (want, wants) to go to the beach today.
26. Toni Morrison or Tom Wolfe (are, is) going to win the award.
27. My coaches and I (is, are) worried about this week's game.
28. Jewels and pottery (was, were) found in the pharaoh's tomb.
29. Minnows or worms (are, is) suitable bait for these fish.
30. Jim or the other boys (have, has) left the ball at the park.

Part 4 Agreement in Inverted Sentences Make two columns on your paper. Label them *Simple Subjects* and *Verbs*. Write the simple subjects from the following sentences in the first column. In the second column, write the correct form of the verbs given in parentheses.

31. On the highest branch of an oak tree (sit, sits) a blue jay.
32. (Does, Do) Aunt Edna and Uncle John have a new car?
33. On Longboat Key, Florida, (are, is) many hotels and condominiums.
34. Across the top of the fence (walk, walks) a fat gray squirrel.
35. On the top shelf of the cabinet (are, is) Mother's cut-glass vases.
36. Down the street (runs, run) four members of our school's track team.
37. (Does, Do) the Democratic or Republican candidate have the better chance of winning the election?
38. Up and down (bounces, bounce) the children on the trampoline.
39. Into second base (slides, slide) José Canseco.
40. From my sister's room (come, comes) the sound of Ella Fitzgerald's voice.

Application and Review

Lesson Review

A Identifying Singular and Plural Forms Copy these sentences. Underline each subject once and each verb twice. Then identify the forms as *Singular* or *Plural*.

1. The computer in the library works well.
2. Two cabbages are enough for this recipe.
3. Miniature lions live in the Mau forest of Kenya.
4. Judy has a new dog.
5. My parents do their errands on Saturdays.
6. Lindsay does her homework before dinner.
7. The tomatoes were delicious.
8. This plywood is damp.
9. Everyone's locker was full of books.
10. For breakfast this morning we had eggs and potatoes.

B Making the Subject and Verb Agree in Number Write the correct form of the verbs given in parentheses.

1. One of my friends (walk, walks) home with me.
2. Lionel, you (takes, take) this bus, right?
3. I (remember, remembers) everyone's name.
4. Those two seventh-graders (does, do) well in the orchestra.
5. Each of the players (has, have) a number.
6. Several starlings (were, was) eating the cherries.
7. You (has, have) just won a skateboard!
8. The lights of the city (are, is) visible below.
9. I often (do, does) the cooking at home.
10. The number of boys and girls (was, were) about equal.

C Using Verbs with Compound Subjects Write the correct form of the verbs given in parentheses.

1. Chris and her sister (ride, rides) their bikes to school.
2. Neither the actors nor the dancers (was, were) on time.

3. Neither Wendy nor Marcia (has, have) finished the project.
4. Dr. Keifer and her assistants (works, work) at the clinic.
5. The book on the desk and the one on the shelf (is, are) Joe's.
6. Either peas or corn (come, comes) with your meal.
7. Either Jim or his friends (deliver, delivers) papers.
8. Mike and the Simpsons (is, are) old friends.
9. Neither the tap shoes nor the ballet slippers (was, were) big enough.
10. Shells, seaweed, and sand (covers, cover) the seashore.

D Using Verbs in Inverted Sentences Write the correct form of the verbs given in parentheses.

1. Here and there (rises, rise) the smoke of a campfire.
2. When (does, do) the snow fall?
3. Overhead (hover, hovers) a long-tailed kite.
4. Between the passengers (squeeze, squeezes) Ramón with his guitar case.
5. In the front of the house (are, is) four columns.
6. Near the farm turn-off (is, are) a stone bridge.
7. (Do, Does) two chairs fit in here?
8. After graduation (comes, come) the party.
9. Suddenly, as if from the waves, (appear, appears) the sun.
10. In the park (stand, stands) two Civil War cannons.

E Using Verbs with *There, Here,* and *Where* Write on your paper the correct form of the verbs given in parentheses.

1. There (was, were) many tough exam questions.
2. (Is, Are) there any stamps for these letters?
3. There (was, were) not another boat in sight.
4. (Is, Are) there any good movies on TV tonight?
5. Here (is, are) the felt-tipped pens you misplaced.
6. Where (are, is) the other screwdriver?
7. Here, in the aquarium, (was, were) all the tadpoles for biology class.
8. Where (is, are) the scarf I gave you?
9. (Weren't, Wasn't) there a picture on this wall?
10. There (is, are) a half an hour before curtain time.

Chapter Review

A Using Verbs Write the correct form of the verbs given in parentheses.

1. On the stage of this theater (has, have) stood many great actors and actresses.
2. There (go, goes) the commuter train.
3. Motorboats, water skiers, and sailboats (crowd, crowds) the once peaceful lake.
4. (Are, Is) there any more questions about the history test tomorrow?
5. Regina, (does, do) you know if Doctor Harrison makes house calls?
6. One of the dogs (keep, keeps) barking in the yard all night every night.
7. Either my older brother or my dad (cook, cooks) dinner on Wednesday night.
8. Both John and Sue (were, was) great in the spring musical production.
9. Neither my classmates nor I (wants, want) the school year to end yet.
10. An acrobat or a juggler (perform, performs) at noon in the gymnasium.

B Making Subjects and Verbs Agree Some of the following sentences contain errors in subject–verb agreement. Write the incorrect sentences, using the correct verb form. If a sentence is already correct, write *Correct*.

1. The homecoming king and queen wears crowns.
2. Tom, Leo, or you bats first.
3. There was another one of those plates in the sink.
4. Neither thunder nor lightning scare me.
5. Brothers and sisters often has disagreements.
6. Those roses and that geranium is red.
7. Either Wendy or Lisa plays the guitar.
8. People all over the world celebrates birthdays.
9. Do you has an extra pen?
10. Neither my sisters nor I wants separate rooms.

Cumulative Review

A Identifying Prepositional Phrases Write all the prepositional phrases from each of the following sentences. Then write whether each phrase is used as an adjective or an adverb.

1. The name of this game is Boggle.
2. In a shaky voice, the leader said, "Who's there?"
3. The fossils in that stone tell of life in ancient times.
4. Jon peered cautiously around the corner at the stranger.
5. Both rabbits in the cage were watching the cat walk around the room.
6. Many tourists travel in boats to the island.
7. Trey spoke with assurance about the reasons for his actions.
8. Christopher Columbus looked beyond the horizon.
9. The red-haired girl under all the sweaters was Patty, our next door neighbor.
10. Down the stairs came the bag of dirty laundry.

B Identifying Compound Sentences Write *C* for each compound sentence and *S* for each simple sentence below.

1. Colin entered the yard; his eyes took in the scene.
2. Queen Elizabeth and Prince Philip are the highest ranking royalty in Great Britian.
3. Pioneers in America had to grow their own food and build their own houses.
4. The moon revolves around the earth, and the earth revolves around the sun.
5. The weather is warm but too windy today.
6. Did Kim borrow my eraser, or have I lost it again?
7. Washington, D.C., is the capital of the United States, but New York is our largest city.
8. The president banged the gavel and called the meeting to order.
9. The lights went out; the show had started.
10. Reptiles are coldblooded, and mammals are warmblooded.

C Showing Subject–Verb Agreement Write the correct form of the verbs given in parentheses in the following sentences.

1. On the dining-room table (was, were) dozens of yellow marbles.
2. (Was, Were) there enough paper plates and cups for everyone?
3. Either soccer or volleyball (is, are) fine with me.
4. Neither the clowns nor the trapeze artist (are, is) here.
5. Both the radio and the television set (is, are) blaring.
6. Those fleas on the dog (is, are) biting him.
7. The bushel of apples (is, are) mine.
8. On the mountain top (stands, stand) the three climbers.
9. (Has, Have) Chad and Evelyn memorized the poem?
10. Above the cabinets (sit, sits) a heavy kettle.
11. There (were, was) enough jobs for everyone.
12. (Is, Are) there some water on the roof?
13. There (was, were) neither swimmers nor boats on the lake.
14. The pumpkins in the field (are, is) ripe.
15. Dina, (has, have) you built your project yet?
16. The amount of water and milk (are, is) equal.
17. Either two tablets or one notebook (is, are) enough.
18. From the window ledge (hang, hangs) two pennants.
19. Where (is, are) the box of tools?
20. Both Lee and his brother (sings, sing) well.

D Combined Review Rewrite the following paragraph on your paper, and correct any errors you find. Pay particular attention to run-on sentences and possible subject–verb agreement problems.

Ken and Roberta wants to take the train into the city they will ask their parents for permission. Roberta's parents do not mind, but Ken's father do not agree. Since they do not have permission to go into the city, Ken and Roberta decides to ride their bikes to the local zoo. Ken like the chimpanzees there Roberta is fond of the puffins and other birds. Ken and Roberta take along a picnic lunch and have a good day after all.

30
Capitalization

Imagine that you have just returned from a trip, and you want to share your adventures with a friend. You write a letter describing the spectacular, grand canyon you saw. If you capitalize *Grand Canyon,* however, your friend will know immediately that you are describing a specific place, not just any impressive valley.

Capitalizing names of specific places is just one rule of capitalization. There are many other rules of capitalization that help you make your writing and ideas clear. This chapter will help you become familiar with most of them.

1
Proper Nouns and Proper Adjectives

Capitalize proper nouns and proper adjectives.

The use of capital letters is called **capitalization**. When you use a capital letter at the beginning of a word, you say that you have capitalized the word.

A **common noun** is the name of a whole class of persons, places, things, or ideas. It is not capitalized.

boy   girl   town   street   honesty

A **proper noun** is the name of a particular person, place, thing, or idea. It is capitalized.

Joe   Elizabeth   Sweden   Oak Street   Congress

A **proper adjective** is an adjective formed from a proper noun:

English   Elizabethan   Swedish   Congressional

There are many different types of proper nouns. The following rules along with their examples will help you solve problems in capitalizing proper nouns and proper adjectives.

Names and Titles of Persons

Capitalize the names of persons and also the initials or abbreviations that stand for those names:

Melinda R. Eaton   Lauren A. Banfield   William J. Franklin, Jr.

Capitalize titles used with names of persons and abbreviations standing for those titles.

Doctor Maria A. Sandquist   Dr. Maria A. Sandquist

Do not capitalize titles that are used as common nouns.

One of our police captains is Captain Daniel Jeffries.
The presiding officer was President Mary Gomez.
She will be president again next year.

Capitalize titles of people and groups whose rank is very important.

Titles of important people in unique positions, such as those of the President and Vice-President of the United States, are capitalized even when these titles are used without proper names.

> The **V**ice-**P**resident presides over the **S**enate.
> The **Q**ueen attended the opening of **P**arliament.
> The **P**resident addressed his remarks to **C**ongress.

Family Relationships

Capitalize such words as *mother, father, aunt,* and *uncle* when these words are used as names.

> Hello, **M**other. Has **D**ad left yet?
> **A**unt **H**elen took movies of the parade.
> We're meeting **U**ncle **E**d at the train.

These words are not used as names when they are preceded by a possessive or by such words as *a* or *the*.

> We met the **f**ather of the boy.
> My **a**unt will pick me up later.

The Pronoun I

Capitalize the pronoun *I*.

> Did you get the postcard **I** sent?

The Deity

Capitalize all words referring to the Deity, to the Holy Family, and to religious scriptures.

> **G**od   the **B**ible   the **T**orah
> **J**esus   the **G**ospel   **A**llah

Exercises

A Write the following sentences using correct capitalization.

1. My favorite aunt is aunt rose.
2. Ladies and gentlemen, the president of the United States.

3. Four players in the Baseball Hall of Fame are ernie banks, jackie robinson, sandy koufax, and mickey mantle.
4. Do you know the last name of the prince of monaco?
5. For his sermon, dr. chester took a story from the bible.
6. My sister and i ate swedish pancakes for breakfast.
7. Muslims study the koran and jews study the torah.
8. "Did dad bring the camera?" mother asked.
9. We met the japanese manager of melinda's new company.
10. The actor p. j. geddes said i had a good voice.

B Write the following sentences using correct capitalization. Some words are incorrectly capitalized.

1. Did the president of the United States speak at the admiral's funeral?
2. The names on the door were dr. natalie j. sanders and martin able, jr.
3. Barbara took mom to the open house at school and darnell took his Father.
4. Traditionally, Sundays have been days when my Brother and i spend time together.
5. Christmas is the celebration of the birthday of jesus.
6. In 1953, Edmund hillary and Tenzing Norkay climbed the Highest Mountain in the world.
7. The queen of england made hillary a knight.
8. Christopher columbus sailed under the spanish flag.
9. William h. bonney was better known by his nickname, billy the kid.
10. The coast of south america was explored by portuguese sailors.

c *Write Now* Think of five characters from movies or books. Now think of a prize that could be named for each of them—for example, The Donald Duck Award for Plain Speaking. Plan a publicity campaign for each award. Give names of newspapers that will be sent press releases. List the television programs and cities to be included on a speaking tour. Be sure to capitalize the titles correctly.

The DONALD DUCK AWARD for Plain Speaking

2
Geographical Names

Capitalize major words in geographical names. Also capitalize names of sections of the country but not compass directions.

Following are examples of geographical names:

Continents	North America, Europe, Asia
Bodies of Water	the Red Sea, Lake Erie, Baffin Bay
Land Forms	the Rocky Mountains, the Syrian Desert
Political Units	Ohio, the British Isles, San Diego
Public Areas	Gettysburg National Park, Fort Niagara, Mount Rushmore, Statue of Liberty
Roads and Highways	Central Avenue, Route 447, Garden Parkway, the Ohio Turnpike, State Street

Directions and Sections

Capitalize names of sections of the country but not directions of the compass.

Cotton was king in the **S**outh.
Cities in the **S**outhwest are flourishing.
They flew **e**ast and then **n**orth of the storm.

Capitalize proper adjectives derived from names of sections of the country or the world. Do not capitalize adjectives derived from words indicating directions.

an **E**astern school   a **s**outherly course   an **e**astern route

Exercises

A Write the following phrases, using correct capitalization.

1. a street in paris, france
2. in huron bay, ontario
3. near pikes peak
4. ships on the red sea

5. north of first avenue
6. near the rocky mountains
7. along the gulf of mexico
8. soldiers of the south
9. on state street, chicago
10. the five great lakes

B Write the following sentences, using correct capitalization.

1. There are many streets named elm and oak in the united states.
2. The song "Give My Regards to broadway," however, refers to only one street, the one in new york city.
3. A song is also named after state street in chicago.
4. The song "highway 61" is about a road in minnesota.
5. Some famous roads, like alligator alley in florida's everglades, have distinctive nicknames.
6. Another nicknamed street is sunset strip in california.
7. Some roads are sightseeing routes like the paseo del rio along texas's san antonio river.
8. Other well-known routes for sightseeing are highway 1 in california, and the blue ridge parkway in virginia.
9. There are roads like london's whitehall that are world famous as centers of government.
10. One of the oldest roads is the appian way in italy.

Grammar in Action

Too much capitalization in your writing, especially if it's incorrect capitalization, distracts your reader. You make a word seem more important when you capitalize it.

> We all watched the Pilot land the Helicopter in the field North of our School.

The sentence above overemphasizes words by using incorrect capitalization. Only *We* needs to be capitalized.

Writing Activity   Write a paragraph about a trip that you might take. Use geographical names, directions, and sections of the country. Remember not to use unnecessary capitalization.

3
Organizations, History, and Time

Capitalize the names of:
- organizations
- institutions
- historical events
- documents
- periods of time
- months
- days
- holidays

Organizations and Institutions

Capitalize all the important words in the names of organizations and institutions.

Rogers and Mark Corporation   Stacy Memorial Hospital
Nichols Junior High School   Bank of England

Do not capitalize such words as *school*, *college*, *church*, and *hospital* when they are not used as names.

the emergency entrance at the hospital
the football team of our school

Events, Documents, Periods of Time

Capitalize the names of historical events, documents, and periods of time.

Industrial Revolution   World War II
Declaration of Independence Middle Ages
Magna Charta   Renaissance

King Arthur and knights.

Months, Days, Holidays

Capitalize the names of months, days, and holidays, but not the names of seasons.

February   Wednesday   Labor Day
April   winter   New Year's Day

Exercises

A Write each of the following groups of words. Use correct capitalization.

1. the month of march
2. veterans day, november 11
3. the band at eisenhower high school
4. the battle of bunker hill
5. the house of representatives
6. a weekend in june
7. louisiana state university
8. the civil war
9. Industries and colleges in the state
10. fire prevention Week

B Write the following sentences using correct capitalization.

1. The green bay packers played the new york jets.
2. Emerson High school dramatized the signing of the constitution.
3. In april, we took a tour of the guggenheim museum.
4. Mardi gras is celebrated with parades in New orleans.
5. Melanie is a student at West technical school.
6. The emancipation proclamation was written during the civil war.
7. The bill of rights guarantees specific personal freedoms.
8. The fourth thursday in november is thanksgiving day.
9. The Barnes and Smith corporation offered a scholarship.
10. The Great depression was a troubling time for Americans.

c *Write Now* During the late 1700's in the United States, several major historic events took place. Write a paragraph naming some of those that you can think of or that you can find in your history books. Use correct capitalization.

4
Languages, Peoples, Transportation, and Abbreviations

Languages, Races, Nationalities, Religions

Capitalize the names of languages, races, nationalities, and religions, and also the adjectives derived from them.

Irish linen	Oriental features	French
Italians	Lutheran hymn	African art
Scottish tweeds	Spanish king	Native American

Ships, Trains, Aircraft, Automobiles

Capitalize the names of ships, trains, and aircraft. Capitalize brand names of automobiles.

U.S.S. *Constitution*	Concorde
Wabash *Cannonball*	Bolt Sport Coupe
Apollo *II*	*Spirit of St. Louis*

Abbreviations

Capitalize the abbreviations *B.C.* and *A.D.*

Julius Caesar was born in the year 100 **B.C.**
Christopher Columbus landed in the New World
    in **A.D.** 1492.

Capitalize the abbreviations *A.M.* and *P.M.*

The bus leaves at 8:05 **A.M.** every weekday morning.
It returns promptly at 5:30 **P.M.**

Exercises

A Write each of the following phrases, capitalizing correctly.

1. the new african nations
2. a scottish writer
3. a methodist minister
4. a car called the tornado
5. the spanish language
6. 2:30 p.m.
7. 10:00 a.m.
8. the year 40 b.c.
9. a.d. 300
10. the s.s. *france*

B Copy each of the following sentences. Wherever necessary, change small letters to capitals.

1. We will sail on the s.s. *queen elizabeth* in may.
2. In Haiti, many people speak french.
3. The buddhist religion originated in India.
4. Banking hours are from 8:30 a.m. to 5:00 p.m.
5. We boarded the *metroliner* in Newark, New Jersey.
6. irish and italians immigrated to the United States.
7. I speak spanish, french, and english.
8. The first modern Olympics were held in a.d. 1896.
9. Many people of european ancestry are of the caucasian race.
10. Many Rhode Islanders are italian and most are catholic.

Grammar in Action

Capitalization is very important for clarity. A capital letter or a lower-case letter in the wrong place can interfere with accuracy.

The general from the north met with the general
from the south at the end of the civil war.

Do the generals represent opposite ends of a field or of a nation? Are they meeting after a polite war (*civil* can mean "polite") or after the American Civil War?

Writing Activity Write a paragraph about a historic event. Use correct capitalization.

5
First Words

Capitalize the first words in:
- sentences
- most lines of poetry
- quotations
- outline entries
- greetings and closings of letters
- important words in titles

Sentences

Capitalize the first word of every sentence.

The images in modern art can be unusual.

Poetry

Capitalize the first word in most lines of poetry.

A word is dead
When it is said,
    Some say.
I say it just
Begins to live
    That day.
        —*Emily Dickinson*

Sometimes in modern poetry, a poem's lines do not begin with a capital letter.

Man in the Bowler Hat, 1964. René Magritte.

Quotations

Capitalize the first word of a direct quotation.

"Close the window, please," Ms. Cortez said to Jerry.
Sarah said, "The next bus is due in an hour."

When a quotation is interrupted, it is called a **divided quotation**. Do not capitalize the first word of the second part of a divided quotation unless it starts a new sentence.

"Close the window," Ms. Cortez said. "It's getting chilly."
"I have some time," Sarah said, "before my bus comes."

Outlines

When you write an outline, capitalize only the first word in each line.

    II. Things to be considered
        A. Small breeds
           1. Kinds of dogs
           2. Uses of dogs
        B. Large breeds

Letters

In the greeting of a letter, capitalize all the important words.

Dear Sir: **Dear Ms. A**shley: **Dear S**ir or **M**adam:

In the closing of a letter, capitalize only the first word.

Sincerely yours,   **Y**ours very truly,

Titles

Capitalize the first word, the last word, and all important words in titles.

Book	*The Fellowship of the Ring*
Poem	"The Road Not Taken"
Newspaper	*The Wall Street Journal*
Play	*The Diary of Anne Frank*
Painting	*Sunflowers*
Musical composition	*Peter and the Wolf*
Short story	"The Ransom of Red Chief"
Movie	*Star Wars*
Article	"Space Age Grand Tour"

Exercises

A Write the words that should be capitalized.

1. the doors open early. no one can enter after 2 P.M.
2. II. poetry
    A. american
        1. country poems
        2. city poems
    B. british

3. "three may keep a secret," said Benjamin Franklin, "if two of them are dead."
4. a harvest mouse goes scampering by
   with silver claws and a silver eye.
5. sailing is a favorite sport of visitors to Cape Cod.
6. sincerely yours,
7. Shakespeare wrote *othello* and *romeo and juliet*.
8. it was many and many a year ago,
   in a kingdom by the sea,
9. "there's no school," said heather. "it's memorial day."
10. dear ms. martin:

B Write the words in the following sentences that should be capitalized. Use correct capitalization.

1. Carl Sandburg's *chicago poems* was published in 1916.
2. One of his children's books included a story, "The two skyscrapers who decided to have a child."
3. Sandburg's *the american songbag* included folk songs.
4. *harvest poems* is a fifty-year collection of his works.
5. Sandburg called Chicago, "City of the Big shoulders."
6. The first part of Sandburg's biography of Abraham Lincoln was titled *abraham lincoln: the prairie years*.
7. The second part, *abe lincoln grows up*, won a Pulitzer Prize.
8. Sandburg loved language and described that feeling vividly in his *notes for a preface*.
9. In the poem "fog," he describes the fog as a cat.
10. The poem "grass" shows his opposition to war.

c *Proofreading* Copy the following paragraph, correcting each error you find. Be sure to capitalize correctly.

yesterday, aunt cheryl went to a travel agent and got some travel folders. I asked her, "are you taking a trip?"

"I don't have any money," she replied, "so i'm going to travel in my imagination instead."

we spent the day "traveling" to hawaii, tahiti, and sydney, australia. We might be their yet if the phone hadnt rung.

Linking Mechanics & Writing

A Many states are advertising on television, hoping to attract tourists and thereby build up the state's economy.

Imagine that you have been assigned the task of writing ads to attract tourists to your community. Begin by telling where your community is and how it can be reached from major highways. Describe your city or surrounding cities, lakes, rivers, mountains, famous sites, and landmarks. You may decide to devote one ad to scenery and peace and quiet and another to entertainment. When you have finished, check your ads to be sure that you have used correct capitalization.

B Write a letter to the editor of your local newspaper. Choose an article from the newspaper to write about. Choose one about which you have a strong opinion. In your letter list the title of the article, the section of the newspaper in which you found it, and the author of the article. When you have completed the letter, address an envelope as though you were going to mail it. (You may send it if you wish.) Check for correct capitalization.

C Imagine you are planning a trip to a historic town (like San Antonio, Texas). As you plan your trip, include all the things you would love to do there. Mention a historic event that took place there. Don't forget to make hotel and travel reservations. You'll also need to reserve tickets for shows or games you want to see. How are you going to travel, by air or train? Another reservation! Draw up an itinerary showing what you will be doing on every day. Check the capitalization.

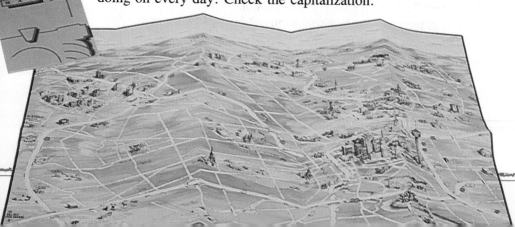

Additional Practice

Parts 1–5 Using Capital Letters Write the words that should be capitalized in the following sentences. Change small letters to capital letters.

1. Cole porter wrote many beautiful songs, including "Night and day."
2. My father is a teacher at Central Junior high school.
3. The italian renaissance began in the fourteenth century.
4. The mayo Clinic is located in rochester, Minnesota.
5. dr. liange hopes that either his daughter or his son will also become a physician.
6. Mother asked aunt Pearl if she would like to go camping with our family.
7. The first five books of the bible make up the torah.
8. Mr. Evans has a 1950 packard that is in nearly perfect condition.
9. William Randolph Hearst owned many newspapers, including the *san francisco examiner*.
10. Have you ever read *treasure island* by Robert louis Stevenson?
11. The cold front was heading towards the southern states.
12. Three countries in south America are Peru, ecuador, and Venezuela.
13. Prince Charles will one day become the ruler of great Britain.
14. My favorite cousin is coming home from college the day before thanksgiving.
15. Maria Martinez was a pueblo indian.
16. The ancient Olympic Games ended in a.d. 394.
17. We plan to visit the wisconsin dells this summer.
18. "If you want to go fishing with me tomorrow morning," said mom, "you had better set your alarm for 4:30 a.m."
19. *The grapes of wrath* by John steinbeck was made into a movie starring Henry Fonda.
20. Henry Fonda's children, jane and peter, are also actors.

21. "Let's go to the mall after school," said Penelope. "my mother will drive us there."
22. Pastor Anderson quietly asked us to open our bibles to the gospel of Matthew.
23. Franklin Delano Roosevelt was elected president of the united states four times.
24. Jane austen wrote six novels, including *Pride and prejudice* and *persuasion.*
25. Grenada is an island in the caribbean sea.
26. The five major romance languages are french, italian, spanish, portuguese, and romanian.
27. The astronaut Sally Ride completed her first space-shuttle mission in june 1983.
28. Every day after school, i walk ms. singh's dogs.
29. Demeter is the greek goddess of agriculture.
30. Ernest lawrence thayer wrote a famous poem about baseball called "casey at the bat."
31. My great-grandfather served in France during world war I.
32. on Memorial day, we always are invited to our neighbor's house for a barbecue.
33. part of Niagara falls is in the United States, and part is in canada.
34. *Meet the austins,* a novel by madeleine L'Engle, was first published in 1960.
35. "Let's have swedish pancakes for breakfast," said dad. "I'll make the batter, and you set the table."
36. To get to my house from school, walk three blocks east on maple street.
37. *The miracle worker* is a famous play about Annie Sullivan and helen keller.
38. The composer Stephen Foster wrote Kentucky's state song, "my old Kentucky home."
39. The American red cross provides food, clothing, and other services to disaster victims.
40. At our school, classes always begin at 8:30 a.m. and finish at 3:00 p.m.
41. Tom paine said, "these are the times that try men's souls."
42. The p.j. smith company published the book *cyclist's guide.*
43. We elect u.s presidents on the second tuesday in november.
44. The spacecraft *discovery* orbits over the equator.
45. My uncle traveled throughout the midwest on his job.

Application and Review

Lesson Review

A Capitalizing Proper Nouns and Proper Adjectives Write the sentences below, using correct capitalization.

1. My favorite poet is gwendolyn brooks.
2. ted williams was baseball's greatest hitter, mom says.
3. The vice-president of the united states is in africa.
4. Is dr. lewis in the swiss alps this year or in finland?
5. Janelle and i showed origami to ms. wilson's class.
6. Did i tell you i saw loretta lynn in concert?
7. The nobel peace prize was awarded to elie wiesel.
8. In some faiths, god and jehovah are names for the deity.
9. "Well, i can't wait," ms. garvey said. "i need it monday."
10. One of america's most famous athletes was jim thorpe.

B Capitalizing Geographical Names Write the words in the following sentences that should be capitalized.

1. The bermuda triangle is an odd area of the atlantic ocean.
2. Go through the swamp from naples to fort lauderdale.
3. The mississippi river borders illinois and iowa.
4. gettysburg national park is near the pennsylvania turnpike.
5. Lake ontario flows into the saint lawrence river in canada.
6. Is greenleaf avenue four blocks north of maple street?
7. Part of the soviet union is in europe, and part is in asia.
8. I think of cowboys when you mention the west.
9. The atacama desert in chile is one of the world's driest spots.
10. Harvard is a well-known eastern university.

C Capitalizing Names Relating to Organizations, History, and Time Write the following sentences using correct capitalization.

1. Our game is on friday not saturday.
2. Those students are from benjamin harrison high school.

3. I was at the april fool's day carlton city council's parade.
4. I always send valentine's day cards on february 14.
5. After graduation, Jan will attend antioch college.
6. My plane leaves Tucson on monday and arrives on tuesday.
7. In 1917, the russian revolution drove the Czar from power.
8. The space age began on october 4, 1957.
9. The river dell high school soccer team plays on memorial day.
10. On january 30, 1649, King Charles of england was beheaded.

D Capitalizing Languages, Peoples, Transportation, and Abbreviations Correctly write the words that should be capitalized.

1. Was there really a ship called h.m.s. *bounty*?
2. Everyone in Elena's family speaks both spanish and english.
3. I hope some day to be able to speak italian fluently.
4. The original inhabitants of Tahiti were polynesians.
5. The *enola gay* dropped the atomic bomb on Japan.
6. In a.d. 1492, columbus discovered america.
7. The language spoken on the island of ponape is ponapean.
8. The *carpathia* rescued survivors of the sinking *titanic*.
9. The emperor romulus augustulus ruled until a.d. 476.
10. g. b. shaw wanted to simplify the english alphabet.

E Capitalizing First Words and Titles Correctly write the words that should be capitalized.

1. "are you going to answer," dr. fields asked, "or shall I?"
2. Charlene and I saw *the monster from the deep lagoon*.
3. the world is weary of the past,
   oh, might it die or rest at last!
4. many think that *guernica* is Picasso's greatest work.
5. Jerry asked, "do you know how to juggle?"
6. He intends to read my short story "the snowgirl."
7. I found a copy of *the black stallion* and began to read it.
8. dear Neighbor:
   yours truly,
9. Did you read "making perfect pancakes" in last Sunday's *gazette*?
10. Mother's favorite song is "twilight time."

Chapter Review

A Using Capital Letters Write the following sentences using correct capitalization.

1. the fourth of july is the most patriotic of our american holidays.
2. dr. burger, a surgeon, practices at community general hospital.
3. in the declaration of independence, thomas jefferson presented the demands of the american colonies.
4. president theodore roosevelt established yellowstone national park.
5. the union-pacific railroad was the first transcontinental railroad in america.
6. "dad, may i see the movie *computer creatures* on tuesday evening?"
7. the methodist minister discussed the bible and the koran.
8. my brother usually vacations in the east during july.
9. the fbi found counterfeit american and canadian currency.
10. my sister's favorite subjects at northwood junior high school are english and french.

B Using Capital Letters Write the words that should be capitalized in the following sentences. Use correct capitalization.

1. My family always takes a trip around labor day.
2. this year we decided to take the durango train west.
3. Before we left, i went to the river grove public library.
4. i found *signs of the west* and *western tourist attractions*, both written by c. a. lott.
5. After reading the books, i couldn't wait to visit the west.
6. at 5:00 a.m. dad woke us by playing *the star-spangled banner* over the stereo.
7. I dressed in my T-shirt and bermuda shorts.
8. at main street station we boarded our train, *the pride of america*.
9. i chose a seat on the east side to see the sunrise.
10. The conductor called, "all aboard," and our western trip began.

31
Punctuation

What a traffic jam Paul it was a mess

Without punctuation, your writing is like a downtown street at rush hour when the traffic signals fail. Confusion reigns!

Commas, periods, question marks, and other punctuation marks are like traffic signals. They tell your reader when to pause or stop. They indicate your intentions. For these reasons, it is important to use punctuation correctly. This chapter will show you how.

"What a traffic jam, Paul. It was a mess!"

1
End Marks

Use a *period,* a *question mark,* or an *exclamation point* to
end a sentence.

In speaking, your tone of voice helps you to communicate
your message. For example, it tells your listener when you are
excited, when you are asking a question, or when you have
completed a thought. In writing, you must use punctuation marks
to give your reader such messages. Each punctuation mark will
tell your reader something different. Three punctuation marks
show where a complete expression ends. These **end marks** are
the **period**, the **question mark**, and the **exclamation point** (or
exclamation mark).

The Period

Use a period at the end of a declarative sentence.

A **declarative sentence** makes a statement. Use a declarative
sentence when you want to tell somebody something.

> My brother is a good skater.
> Roland left for a vacation.

Use a period at the end of an imperative sentence.

An **imperative sentence** makes a request or tells someone to
do something. Use a period at the end of an imperative sentence
unless you wish to express excitement or emotion at the same
time. In that case, use an exclamation point.

> Please open the window.   Look out!

Use a period at the end of an indirect question.

An **indirect question** reports what someone asked, without
using the speaker's exact words. Use a period, not a question
mark, at the end of a sentence with an indirect question. A **direct
question**, or a quoted question, is written exactly as it was originally asked. Use a question mark at the end of a direct question.

Indirect Question Judy asked whether the movie was worth
seeing.

Direct Question Judy asked, "Is the movie worth seeing?"

The Question Mark

Use a question mark at the end of an interrogative sentence.

An **interrogative sentence** is a sentence that asks a question.

> Has anyone seen my dog?
> Do you know about the new drama club?

The Exclamation Point

Use an exclamation point at the end of an exclamatory sentence.

An **exclamatory sentence** expresses strong feeling.

> What a terrific game that was!
> Please give me some help!

Use an exclamation point at the end of an imperative sentence expressing emotional excitement. Other imperative sentences should be followed by a period.

> Hurry up!   Please shut the door.

Use an exclamation point after an interjection or any other exclamatory expression.

An **interjection** is a word or group of words used to express strong feeling.

> Oh! How beautiful!
> Wow! What an exciting movie!

Use an exclamation point after a declarative sentence that you want to emphasize.

Declarative sentences generally end in periods. However, you may want to add extra feeling to the sentence by using an exclamation point instead of a period.

> You almost hit that car. (declarative sentence)
> Be careful! You almost hit that car! (exclamation)

Exercises

A Add proper end marks to the following sentences.

1. Look out That shelf is falling
2. How did the cat get into the birdcage
3. How peaceful it is here Is it always this way
4. Did you get the directions to the restaurant
5. Myron is in charge of the decorations
6. Help This carton is too heavy for me
7. How dare you say that
8. Wow That was an exciting race
9. Move The can of paint is falling off the ladder
10. Please let me see that book Is it yours

B Write on your paper the following paragraph, adding the proper end marks.

> Have you ever seen a Venus' flytrap These strange-looking plants actually eat insects Did you ever wonder how the plant catches its prey Each leaf of the flytrap has three sensitive hairs Whenever anything touches these hairs, the two leaves of the plant snap shut like a jaw Can you believe that the leaves close in only half a second The leaf then secretes a sap that digests the insect It takes ten days for the flytrap to finish digesting How amazing The flytrap is a fascinating plant

C *Write Now* Imagine that you and a friend are discussing one of the biggest news stories of the year. Make two columns on your paper. In the first column, write what you might say. In the second column, write what your friend might say. Altogether, include at least two declarative sentences, two interrogative sentences, and one exclamatory sentence or expression.

Other Uses of the Period

Use a period after most abbreviations and after initials.

A period is used in other places besides the end of a sentence. Periods are also used after most abbreviations and initials.

An **abbreviation** is a shortened, or abbreviated, form of a word or phrase. Notice how the periods are used in the following:

in. (*inch* or *inches*)   Dr. (*Doctor*)
Sept. (*September*)   Tues. (*Tuesday*)
A.D. (*Anno Domini*)   M.A. (*Master of Arts*)

Some abbreviations do not need a period. When you are not sure about whether to use a period after an abbreviation, look up the abbreviation in the dictionary.

FM (*frequency modulation*)
mph (*miles per hour*)
mm (*millimeter*)
NASA (*National Aeronautics and Space Administration*)

Many abbreviations are not acceptable in formal writing. These include abbreviations for personal titles; names of cities, states, or countries; and names of days of the week and months.

Put a period after the initials in a name. An **initial** is the first letter of a person's name. It is used alone to stand for the name. Put a period after an abbreviation of a person's title.

O. J. Simpson (*Orenthal James Simpson*)
Susan B. Anthony (*Susan Brownell Anthony*)
Mr. J. P. Cortez
Ms. Ellen Jacobsen

Put a period after the letters or numbers in an outline or list.

Outline	List
I. Trees	1. corn
A. Shade trees	2. potatoes
1. Elms	3. hamburger
2. Maples	4. milk
B. Evergreen trees	5. orange juice
II. Flowers	6. bread

Exercises

A Write the following sentences on your paper, adding periods where necessary. If a sentence is correct, write *Correct*.

1. John F Kennedy was inaugurated as President of the United States on Jan 20, 1961.

2. We listen to the news broadcast every day at 6:00 PM
3. Ms Sue M Horton teaches swimming at the YWCA.
4. Did you know that Bill Cosby has a Ph D ?
5. Her card says, "Dr Stephanie James, D D S "
6. My plane left Boston, Mass at 11:45 A M and arrived in St Louis, Mo at 2:15 P M.
7. Tia asked P J if he is collecting money for UNICEF this year.
8. Pete asked me whether I had seen Dr M J Thomas.
9. I like FM radio stations better than I do AM stations.
10. Please add to the outline under your heading: A Bicycles.

B Write the following sentences and phrases, adding periods where necessary. If a sentence or phrase is already correct, write *Correct*.

1. Julius Caesar was killed in 44 B C
2. My brother enjoys listening to AM radio stations.
3. Ms McGill will meet with Rev Henry R Cole at 7:30 P M tomorrow.
4. I   Popular literature
    A   Best sellers
       1   Fiction
       2   Nonfiction
    B   Magazines
   II   Classical literature
5. Baseball Equipment
    1   bats
    2   baseballs
    3   gloves
6. R G Grogan Bros hires students who possess M S degrees in chemistry.
7. Gen Dwight D Eisenhower became President in Jan 1953.
8. Eslinger & Co recently completed a study of the Environmental Protection Agency and titled it "The EPA and You."
9. The old car rarely traveled faster than 45 mph.
10. Mr John Yee will arrive on Wed ,Sept 22 at 8:00 A M

Grammar in Action

Abbreviations are not always acceptable in formal writing—for example, some abbreviations for the titles of persons and for the names of days of the week, months, and countries. Look at the following example of informal writing that has been revised to be more formal.

              Tuesday

That ~~Tues.~~ was a crucial turning point in the life

of Thomas J. Croeker. At 10:00 A.M. he received
       Lieutenant Colonel   *United States*

his appointment as ~~Lt. Col.~~ in the ~~U. S.~~ Army and
        West

was assigned a post in ~~W.~~ Germany.

Writing Activity Imagine that you have written the following paragraph to a friend. Now you wish to have it published in your community newspaper. Rewrite the passage, making the necessary corrections to make it formal.

    The race was held on a Sat. A.M. It was the longest race Dr. James T. McConnell had ever attempted. Sponsored by the Amer. Red Cross, it was to benefit people in the flooded areas of Ken., Tenn., and W. Va. Dr. McConnell finished the race in three hrs. and twenty min., and he donated five hundred dol.

2
Commas That Separate Ideas

<hr/>

> Use a *comma* before the conjunction in a compound
> sentence and to separate items in a series.

In speaking, you do not say everything at the same speed. You
pause when there is a break in your thought. You put words into
groups and pause between the groups to help your listeners
understand which words go together. In writing, commas are like
pauses. Use them to make your meaning clearer or to help the
reader understand which words go together.

Commas in Compound Sentences

A **compound sentence** is a sentence in which independent
sentences are joined together with a conjunction.

**Use a comma before the conjunction that joins two
sentences in a compound sentence.**

> Chris got back from his trip, and now he's sleeping.
> Isabel loves the flute, but she plays trombone.

In a very short compound sentence, it is not necessary to put a
comma before *and*, but it is necessary to put a comma before *but*
or *or*.

No Comma	We were thirsty and we were hungry.
Comma	We were thirsty, but we weren't hungry.
Comma	We may be thirsty, or we may be hungry.

In a sentence with a compound predicate made up of two parts,
do not use a comma between the parts. In a compound predicate
made up of three parts, use a comma after the first two parts.

Two-Part Compound Predicate	We can stop here or go on to Toronto.
Three-Part Compound Predicate	We came early, worked hard, and left late.

Exercises

A Write the following sentences, adding commas where necessary. After the two sentences that need no commas, write *Correct*.

1. I'd like to go to the show but I have work to do.
2. The movie was excellent but I didn't enjoy waiting in line.
3. We stopped on the side of the road and ate our lunch.
4. On the moon, the temperature rises to over 200° F in the daytime but it drops far below zero at night.
5. There was a noise in the car but we could not find it.
6. Jorge hiked in the forest and swam in the Pacific Ocean.
7. Can you stay for dinner or are you leaving early?
8. The coach drew a diagram and the players studied it.
9. We raked the leaves but the wind blew them away.
10. These jeans are too long and they don't fit at the waist.

B Write the following paragraph. Add commas where they are necessary and delete commas where they are not necessary.

Elizabeth Cady Stanton was one of the most important writers, and speakers of the nineteenth century women's suffrage, or right to vote, movement. She gained her early political experience in the antislavery movement. In 1840 Elizabeth Cady Stanton traveled to London, and took part in the World Antislavery Convention. Women at the convention could not vote speak or even sit with the men. Elizabeth Cady Stanton and the other women delegates protested but the male delegates would not change their minds. Stanton decided women should hold their own convention. The delegates at the Women's Rights Convention stated that "all men and women are created equal." The Women's Rights Convention marked the beginning of Stanton's women's rights work and she continued this work until she was eighty-seven. Women finally earned the right to vote in 1920.

Commas in a Series

Use a comma after each item in a series except the last.

A **series** consists of three or more items of the same kind written one after the other in the sentence.

> We packed, ate, and left for home. (verbs in a series)
> Tom, Mary, Eve, and Ray won prizes. (nouns in a series)
> The arms of the machine moved up and down, in and out, and back and forth. (groups of adverbs in a series)
> Will your ride to the old mill, to the beach, or over Sunset Hill? (prepositional phrases in a series)
> It was getting dark, a wind blew down from the mountain, and Henry began to wonder where he was. (independent sentences in a series)

When two or more adjectives precede and modify the same noun but do not express a closely related thought, use a comma after each adjective except the last one.

In a series of adjectives, the conjunction is sometimes omitted. Often two or more adjectives precede and modify the same noun. If you can use *and* between these adjectives without changing the meaning, use a comma to indicate a pause after each adjective except the last one.

> It was a bright, brisk, invigorating day.
> The new, blue uniforms look excellent.

Sometimes two adjectives preceding the noun are used together to express a single idea. In such a case, do not use a comma between the adjectives.

> A *red pickup* truck pulled into the driveway.
> Ina bought a *gray wool* scarf.

Exercises

A Write on your paper the following sentences, adding commas where necessary. If the sentence is correct, write *Correct*.

1. I will get a book make an outline and then write my report.
2. He ran swiftly easily and gracefully to win the race.

3. We brought a picnic lunch three straw hats and our swimsuits on the canoe trip.
4. My new puppy has big floppy ears.
5. Ted fed chickens brought in cows and hoed weeds.
6. Rafting canoeing and hiking are María's favorite activities.
7. Just go through the woods up the hill and over the bridge.
8. The sun is hot the waves are high and there's a cool breeze.
9. Karen likes peanut butter and jelly tomato and bacon ham and cheese and egg salad sandwiches.
10. I want a new vest with stripes pockets and a collar.

B Write on your paper the following sentences, adding commas where necessary.

1. I saw them slide scramble and tumble down the slope.
2. We unloaded the car set up the tent climbed into our sleeping bags and went to sleep.
3. The large striped fish jumped in front of our eyes.
4. Do you want to go to the pool to the park or into town?
5. I stir-fried some vegetables boiled rice and baked muffins.
6. Karen Jack and Juanita went swimming.
7. The curious black-masked raccoons sat on the picnic table.
8. Marvin studied his notes slowly quietly and thoroughly.
9. It's a sunny day the courts are dry and I want to play tennis.
10. Did you see a wolf a skunk or a bear?

C *Proofreading* Proofread the following paragraph. Then rewrite it correctly on your paper. Add commas where necessary and remove unnecessary commas.

In the United States many different types of energy are used to heat homes, including oil kerosene electricity and natural gas. Each type has its advantages and disadvantages. Kerosene heaters, for example, are inexpensive but if they are not well maintained, they give off thick, black smoke. Electric heatees seem cosy in drafty rooms but they can cause fires if their wiring is bad. Also, they should not be used around small children pets and furniture.

3
Commas That Set Off Special Elements

Use a *comma* to set off introductory elements, interrupters, nouns of direct address, and appositives.

In speaking, you pause to set off special elements in a sentence. In writing, you use commas for the same purpose. Special elements include introductory words or phrases, interrupters, nouns used in addressing a person or persons directly, and appositives. These elements add extra information but could be left out without changing the meaning of the sentence.

Commas After Introductory Elements

Use a comma after an introductory word or phrase to separate it from the rest of the sentence.

An **introductory word or phrase** introduces the sentence. Put the comma after an introductory word or phrase where you would pause if you were saying the sentence aloud.

> Yes, Paula is my sister.
> Climbing down the tree, I ripped my pocket.

If the pause after the introductory element would be only a short one, you may omit the comma.

> At last the plane landed.

Commas with Interrupters

Use commas before and after interrupters.

Interrupters are words or phrases that interrupt, or break, the flow of thought in a sentence. The commas used with interrupters mark pauses before and after the interruption.

> This bike, however, is in better physical condition.
> The answer, I suppose, will never be known.

Exercises

A Write the following sentences, adding commas where needed.

1. The committee as I said earlier will meet on Tuesday.
2. No I haven't seen that movie.
3. The test results I suppose will be posted tomorrow.
4. Abraham Lincoln it is said walked twenty miles a day to study law.
5. After all Fernando is a senior.
6. This paper for example has no watermark.
7. In spite of its strange style I wore the shirt.
8. Running to third I tripped and sprained my ankle.
9. Did you hear by the way who made the team?
10. Chess on the other hand is a game of skill.

B Write on your paper the following sentences, adding commas where necessary. If a sentence is correct already, write *Correct*.

1. In the past few years many geologists have tried to find the cause of earthquakes.
2. From their research the geologists know that most earthquakes are caused by the underground movement of large, flat sections of earth.
3. By using instruments scientists can measure these movements.
4. Twelve miles below the surface of the earth the flat sections called plates slide smoothly against each other.
5. Closer to the surface however the plates grind together.
6. As they grind together the plates produce friction.
7. Eventually the friction reaches very high levels.
8. Finally the plates break apart and cause the earth to shake.
9. This shaking referred to as seismic waves by geologists is what we commonly call an earthquake.
10. Despite all their work, however, geologists still cannot accurately predict when an earthquake will occur.

C *Write Now* Review examples of introductory elements and interrupters. Now imagine that you are interviewing a historical person whom you admire. Write the interview, using introductory elements or interrupters in at least half of the sentences.

Commas with Nouns of Direct Address

Use commas to set off all nouns used in direct address.

A **noun used in direct address** is the name or title of the person to whom you are speaking. Look at the following examples:

Incorrect   Help me bake John and you may have some lasagna too.

Correct   Help me bake, John, and you may have some lasagna too.

Incorrect   Call me Jane if you can go swimming.

Correct   Call me, Jane, if you can go swimming.

The incorrect sentences are confusing because the names John and Jane have not been set off with commas.

Commas with Appositives

Use commas to set off most appositives.

An **appositive** is a noun or phrase that identifies the person or thing preceding it. When an appositive is used with modifiers, the entire group of words should be set off with commas.

Ms. Bell, our science teacher, will not be back.
Joe, the boy in the blue shirt, is Al's cousin.

In these examples, the appositives are *our science teacher* and *the boy in the blue shirt*.

When the appositive is a short name, it is not usually set off by commas:

The rock star Sting is my favorite singer.

Exercises

A On your paper, combine each pair of sentences into one sentence, using an appositive.

1. There was only one hit against Tate. It was a single.
2. We have a favorite horse. Her name is Daisy Belle.
3. The author is Mark Twain. He knew a lot about people and had a keen sense of humor.

4. The largest state is Alaska. It has the smallest population.
5. The fastest runner in our class is Penny. She is on the track team.
6. Karin is on the swimming team. She is my classmate.
7. The third largest city in the United States is Chicago. It was incorporated in 1837.
8. The pitcher is Tom Seaver. He has won more than 300 games.
9. Ms. Ling is our band director. She plays the trombone.
10. One of my favorite books is *The Member of the Wedding*. It is about a girl named Frankie.

B Write on your paper the following sentences, adding commas where necessary. If a sentence is already correct, write *Correct*. After each corrected sentence, write *Noun of Direct Address* or *Appositive* to identify any special elements in the sentence.

1. Mother have you heard of this rock group?
2. Ms. Mantoya this is my father.
3. Mr. Ingram our English teacher is standing there.
4. Yes Crystal I'll join you at the skating rink.
5. Carl Sandburg a poet wrote a biography of Abraham Lincoln.
6. The winner of the school dance contest was my brother Andre.
7. Well folks dinner will be ready any minute now.
8. Mary this is my classmate Tanya.
9. My sister Teresa speaks highly of you.
10. Gustav Mahler a famous Austrian composer wrote that majestic symphony.

c *Write Now* Imagine that you are making the introductions at your school club. Write sentences about various club officers and members in which you use the following phrases.

1. the biggest fundraiser
2. champion of the debating team
3. secretary of the club
4. president of the French club
5. one of the halfbacks
6. a whiz in math
7. a science major
8. vice-president of the club
9. captain of the team
10. a new student

Grammar in Action

You can often make choppy writing smooth by combining sentences and using appositives.

My sister's name is Ruth. She lifts weights every day.
My sister Ruth lifts weights every day.

Tokyo is a city in Japan. It is a center for world trade.
Tokyo, a city in Japan, is a center for world trade.

Writing Activity The following paragraph is written in a very choppy, abrupt style. Rewrite the paragraph, making the writing style smoother by combining sentences and using appositives. Remember to punctuate all appositives correctly.

Portrait of Marco Polo.

Brothers Nicolo and Maffeo Polo with their caravan, painted circa 1270.

Marco Polo was a famous Venetian explorer. He traveled to China when he was seventeen. Marco's father and uncle were Venetian merchants. They had journeyed to China two years before their trip with Marco. Marco, his father, and his uncle traveled over land from Hormuz to Peking. Hormuz is a city on the Persian Gulf. This journey lasted for three years. In China the Polos worked for Kublai Khan. Kublai Khan was the ruler of China. The Polos remained in China for seventeen years. When Marco returned to Venice he wrote a book about his journey. This book is called *The Travels of Marco Polo*.

4
Other Uses of the Comma

> Use a *comma* to set off quotations, dates, addresses, and parts of a letter. Also use a comma to help prevent misreading.

There are specific elements in your writing that will always require commas. In this section you will learn about these elements.

Commas in Quotations

Use commas to set off the explanatory words of a direct quotation.

A **direct quotation** is a restatement of someone's exact words. These exact words are enclosed in quotation marks.

A direct quotation may be introduced by or followed by an explanatory phrase. Use a comma after explanatory phrases that precede a direct quotation and after direct quotations that are followed by an explanatory phrase.

> Jeff said, "A group of circus clowns just passed our house."
>
> "Let's see the bodybuilding contest on Channel 3," said Lucita.

A direct quotation may be separated into two parts with an explanatory phrase between them. Such a form is called a **divided quotation**. In a divided quotation, a comma is used after the last word of the first part of the quotation. Another comma is used after the last word in the explanatory phrase.

> "If it rains this afternoon," Pat said, "it will probably not rain long."

An **indirect quotation** is a restatement in different words of something that was said. An indirect quotation is usually introduced by the word *that* and does not require a comma.

> Ms. Malone said that she enjoyed visiting our class.

Exercise

Write on your paper the following sentences, adding commas where necessary. If a sentence is already correct, write *Correct*.

1. Benjamin Franklin said "Lost time is never found again."
2. "London Bridge is no longer in London" Art commented.
3. Polly said "Everyone has gone to the beach today."
4. Dr. Gonzales said that Sandy had broken his arm.
5. "Did you know" asked Angie "that Alpha Centauri is the nearest star?"
6. "I like the climate of Seattle best of all" answered Tom.
7. Jo said that most tornadoes occur in spring and fall.
8. Denise asked "Have you ever flown a helicopter?"
9. "I believe" shouted Max "that we have a winner!"
10. "I can fix that faucet in ten minutes" Mary boasted.

Commas in Dates, Addresses, and Parts of Letters

Use commas to separate the parts of dates, addresses, and letters.

In writing dates, use a comma between the day of the month and the year. If no day of the month is given, it is not necessary to use a comma between the month and the year.

> On May 20, 1980, Laura arrived in Thailand.
> The party was on Thursday, November 9, 1988.
> The celebration took place in November 1982.

In writing addresses, use a comma after the name of the street and after the name of the city. Do not use a comma before the ZIP code. Study the following examples:

> The address is 25 Elm Street, Chicago, Illinois 60604.
> She lived in Cairo, Egypt, for several years after leaving Omaha, Nebraska.
> We arrived at 525 East Fiftieth Street, New York City.

In friendly letters, use a comma after the greeting. In both friendly and business letters, use a comma after the closing.

> Dear Dana,   Sincerely yours,

Exercise

Write on your paper the following sentences, adding commas where necessary. If the sentence is already correct, write *Correct*.

1. The first Boston Marathon was held on April 19, 1897.
2. Do you live in Michigan City Indiana?
3. Sherlock Holmes lived at 221B Baker Street London.
4. The only historical date I can remember is July 4 1776.
5. She was born on April 3 1963.
6. I live at 432 Center Road Aurora Colorado 80014.
7. We were in New York in November 1986.
8. Does this envelope say Gary Indiana or Cary Illinois?
9. On Monday December 1 1988, the Polar Bear Club will swim in Lake Michigan.
10. Dear Ricardo

c *Write Now* Imagine that you have just spent a month visiting many faraway cities. Write a short letter to a friend, describing your travels. Include the locations of the different sites that you visited, the addresses of the places in which you stayed, and the dates on which you traveled. Be sure to use commas correctly.

Commas to Prevent Misreading

Use a comma to separate any sentence parts that might be improperly joined or misunderstood without the comma.

In speaking, you pause to prevent this kind of confusion.

Confusing   After eating my dog takes a nap.
Clear   After eating, my dog takes a nap.

Exercise

Write the following sentences, adding commas where needed.

1. I have the potato salad and the hamburgers are there.
2. Before coloring her little sister put all her toys away.
3. Climbing Lucy and George became tired.
4. No matter what I do not want another apple today.
5. By the time she woke up the neighborhood was quiet.
6. While circling the airplane approached the field.

7. After they finished the dishes were cleared.
8. When we entered the room was empty.
9. The night before I saw her at the library.
10. While racing my brother sprained an ankle.

Grammar in Action

Too many commas can be as confusing to a reader as too many road signs are to a driver. In the sentence below, too many commas make the sentence difficult to read.

> Write, in your notebook, ten important points, from the presidential debates, that you saw last night.

Writing Activity Suppose that you are the editor of the school newspaper. A sportswriter has given you the following paragraph, but he has not punctuated it correctly. Rewrite the paragraph, deleting unnecessary commas.

> After a recent string of narrow defeats, the girls' softball team finally won one, on Tuesday, of last week. Although their best batter was injured, the girls still scored fifteen runs, with twenty hits. Their pitching, often a trouble spot, was unusually good. Smiling happily, the coach said, she was pleased with the victory.

5
The Semicolon and the Colon

Use a *semicolon* to separate the parts of a compound sentence.
    Use a *colon* to introduce lists of items, after the greeting of a business letter, and to separate hours from minutes in time expressions.

The Semicolon

An end mark indicates the end of an expression. A comma indicates a pause in a sentence. A **semicolon** (;) indicates a longer pause and a more definite break in the parts of the sentence than a comma does.

Use a semicolon to separate the parts of a compound sentence when you do not connect them with a coordinating conjunction.

Tad threw the oranges away; they were rotten.
Sarah saw that movie twelve times; it is her favorite.

Use a semicolon between the parts of a compound sentence when these clauses are long, complicated, or punctuated.

For the bowling party, James invited Lila, Nick, Thomas, and Gloria; and I asked Martina and Jules.
Marguerite grows tomatoes, cucumbers, and squash; steams them slightly; and serves them with rice, peppers, and spices.

In the first sentence, where commas are used to separate the parts of the direct object *Lila, Nick, Thomas, and Gloria,* a semicolon is used to separate the parts of the compound sentence even though the sentence has a coordinating conjunction. The semicolon breaks the sentence into clearly visible separate parts.

The second sentence has a compound predicate (*grows, steams, and serves*). The three parts of the compound predicate are separated by semicolons because two of them already contain elements that are separated by commas.

The Colon

Use a colon (:) to mark an introduction.

Use a colon to introduce a list of things, or use it after the greeting in a business letter to introduce the body of the letter.

List We need the following supplies for class: canvas, brushes, tubes of paint, and a palette.

Greetings Dear Sir or Madam:
Dear Customer Service Representative:
Dear Mr. Hernandez:

In introducing a list, a colon always follows a complete sentence; it never comes directly after the verb.

Incorrect I will bring: tea, biscuits, and jam.

Correct I will bring the following things: tea, biscuits, and jam.

Use a colon between numbers that represent hours and minutes in expressions of time.

at 9:30 A.M.   the 6:20 train   before 8:00 P.M.

Exercise

Add semicolons and colons where necessary to these sentences.

1. Fishing is a sport it can also be a job.
2. Many people start fishing before 500 A.M.
3. They nearly always bring these things fishing rods, hats, food for themselves, and bait for the fish.
4. Commercial fishing vessels often stay at sea for weeks private boats seldom stay out more than a few days.
5. Deep-sea fishing boats carry the following supplies nets, knives, and poles.
6. People who fish are called anglers they enjoy hooking fish.
7. The activity of a fish depends on many factors water temperature, water depth, and time of day.
8. Some fish must be tired out before they can be caught this process requires that the angler be very skilled.
9. Some people use worms for bait others use artificial lures.
10. Anglers must study the habits of fish and practice catching fish otherwise the angler will not be successful.

6
The Hyphen

Use a *hyphen* to mark the division of a word at the end of a line. Use a *hyphen* in compound adjectives, compound numbers, fractions, and some compound nouns.

Hyphens have many uses in writing. Using them correctly will help make your meaning clear and will show your readers you are a careful writer.

Use a hyphen to separate the parts of a word at the end of a line.

> When my grandmother makes a sweater she uses a pat-
> tern that her mother taught her.

Use a hyphen in compound adjectives when they precede the word they modify.

> I ride my ten-speed bike to school.
> Dr. Smith is a well-known scientist.
> *But:* Dr. Smith is well known.

Use a hyphen in compound numbers from twenty-one through ninety-nine and in fractions.

> thirty-two seconds   three-fourths majority

Spell certain compound nouns with hyphens. Use a dictionary if you are not sure how to punctuate a compound.

> mother-in-law   great-aunt   vice-president

Exercise

Write the following sentences, adding hyphens where needed.

1. Marilyn's sister in law works as a police officer.
2. I paid fifty nine cents for this felt tip pen.
3. Sonja's great grandparents came from Norway in 1892.
4. We need a two thirds majority to override the veto.
5. Mona's scooter has a two cylinder engine.

7
The Apostrophe

> Use an *apostrophe* to show possession, to show where letters are omitted in a contraction, and to form the plurals of letters, figures, and words used as words.

The apostrophe is most commonly used to form possessive nouns and contractions. It is also used to write special plural forms.

Apostrophes with Possessives

The **possessive form** of a noun indicates that the person named owns or possesses something.

To form the possessive of a singular noun, add 's.

girl + **'s** = girl's   man + **'s** = man's
barber + **'s** = barber's   Charles + **'s** = Charles's

To form the possessive of a plural noun that ends in *s*, add only an apostrophe.

friends + **'** = friends'   students + **'** = students'
parents + **'** = parents'

To form the possessive of a plural noun that does not end in *s*, add 's.

women + **'s** = women's   mice + **'s** = mice's

Exercises

A Write on your paper the possessive form of the following nouns.

1. doctor
2. witness
3. producer
4. elephant
5. James

6. employee
7. hostess
8. actress
9. electrician
10. artist

B Write the plural forms of the following nouns. Then write the possessive form of the plurals.

1. family
2. pilot
3. nurse
4. woman
5. child
6. wife
7. waitress
8. actor
9. goose
10. grandpa

Apostrophes with Contractions

Use an apostrophe to show where letters are omitted in a contraction.

A **contraction** is a shortened form of a word. An apostrophe is used in a contraction to show where one or more letters have been omitted. Some commonly used contractions are shown in the following chart.

Commonly Used Contractions	
we are → we're	where is → where's
she is → she's	they are → they're
here is → here's	cannot → can't
there is → there's	could not → couldn't
I would → I'd	will not → won't
we will → we'll	was not → wasn't
they will → they'll	would not → wouldn't
it is → it's	who is → who's

A common mistake is to confuse a contraction with a possessive pronoun. Remember that apostrophes are not used in possessive pronouns: *your, yours, its, his, hers, ours, their, theirs, whose.*

Contraction	Possessive
it's (*it is* or *it has*)	its
who's (*who is* or *who has*)	whose
you're (*you are* or *you were*)	your
they're (*they are* or *they were*)	their

To form the plurals of letters, figures, and words used as words, add 's.

> Children used to be told to mind their *p*'s and *q*'s.
> You should form your *3*'s and *7*'s more carefully.
> Pam's story was full of *but*'s.
> The movie took place in the 1950's.

Exercises

A Write the following sentences, adding apostrophes where needed.

1. Jim cant go because hes helping his parents.
2. Its time for class.
3. The members dues have all been paid.
4. Ill turn on Carls lamp. Wont that help you find your book?
5. Well work much better now that shes given us directions.
6. Wheres the paint for the puppets faces?
7. I really like jazz from the 1950s.
8. Whos going with you to the movies?
9. Whose soccer ball is that? Its mine.
10. Every ushers coat was red.

B Write the correct word given in parentheses.

1. (Isn't, Isnt) Mr. Lopez (they're their) social studies teacher?
2. (Who's, Whose) going with you to the concert? I hope (your, you're) seats are next to (our's, ours).
3. (Charles', Charles's) new suit is much too big for him.
4. (Here's, Heres) the pump for (you're, your) bicycle tire.
5. (We'll, Well) be disappointed if the (performers', performer's) voice is hoarse.
6. (You're, Your) the one (who's, whose) going to Mexico.
7. Are the relief (pitcher's, pitchers') uniforms here?
8. The (coach's, coaches) exercises for the team were more difficult than (yours, your's).
9. (They're, Their) wondering (who's, whose) bike is in (they're, their) driveway.
10. (It's, Its) hard to believe that the car has lost (it's, its) muffler already.

8
Quotation Marks

> Use *quotation marks* at the beginning and end of direct quotations and to set off titles of short works.

Direct Quotations

Use quotation marks to enclose direct quotations.

A **direct quotation** is the restatement of someone's exact words. Use quotation marks to show where the exact words of another speaker or writer begin and end. Quotation marks are not used with indirect quotations.

> Matt said, "I'm going to wash the family car."
> Matt said that he was going to wash the family car.

When a direct quotation is interrupted by explanatory words, enclose each part of the quotation in quotation marks.

> "Now," Matt said, "I'm going to wash the family car."

Begin the second part of a divided quotation with a small letter unless it is the beginning of a sentence, a proper noun, or the pronoun *I*.

> "If you're ready," said Paula, "we can leave now."
> "I saw Mr. Pritchard," said Amos. "He was in the store."
> "The winner was," he insisted, "George."

Quotation Marks with Other Punctuation

Sentences that contain direct quotations will contain not only quotation marks but also other types of punctuation.

Place quotation marks outside commas and end marks following direct quotations.

> My uncle promised, "I'll send you a postcard."
> "I'll send you a postcard," my uncle promised.
> "Help me find the nail," said Scott, "and then find the hammer."

"I've finished reading this," said Nikki. "It was a good story."

Use quotation marks outside exclamation points and question marks if those marks are part of the quotation itself. Place quotation marks inside exclamation points and question marks if they are not part of the quotation.

Ms. Inez asked, "Have you finished your homework?"
"Look out!" Michael shouted.

Did Rachel say, "Meet me at the library"?
What a relief it was to hear Bob say, "I'm safe"!

Exercises

A Write the following sentences, adding all needed punctuation marks.

1. Zachary announced All entries for the most beautiful baby contest must be handed in by noon today
2. The water in the pool was very cold today said Betsy
3. Did Inspector Blaine say There wasn't anything peculiar about the thief
4. No exclaimed Tiffany This is not my pet frog
5. Does anyone roller-skate to school Milton asked

B Write the following sentences as direct quotations, adding the explanatory words given in italics to the part of the sentence indicated in parentheses.

EXAMPLE *Claire agreed* It's much too cold to cycle. (end)
"It's much too cold to cycle," Claire agreed.

1. *Janice said* Let's go to the planetarium to hear the lecture on black holes. (beginning)
2. *Ellen said* Dr. García, the speaker, is a famous astrophysicist. I would really like to hear her! (middle)
3. *Dr. García asked the audience* Does anyone know what a black hole is? (end)
4. *Janice answered* I know it's a type of star, but I don't know how it's formed. (beginning)
5. *agreed Dr. García* Yes, it's a very old, very large star that has collapsed. (middle)

6. *Dr. García continued* As it collapses, the gravity inside the star increases greatly. (beginning)
7. *She explained* The gravity becomes so great that nothing can escape, not even light. (middle)
8. *Dr. García related* Since light cannot escape, we cannot actually see a black hole. (end)
9. *she explained* We can locate them because matter that is pulled into the black hole releases radiation before the matter disappears forever. (middle)
10. *Janice exclaimed* That's fascinating! (end)

Quotation Marks in Dialogue

A **dialogue** is a conversation between two or more people. When you are writing a dialogue, begin a new paragraph every time the speaker changes, and use quotation marks as you do for all direct quotations.

"Mr. Scott invited our family to his farm for the afternoon," said Jean. "He gave Dad the directions to get to the farm."

"Well," said Barbara, "did you go? Did you have fun?"

"We got to the farm. Unfortunately, our car stalled and we had to push it up the hill. That was not the best way to spend a sunny afternoon."

Exercise

Write the following conversation, making correct paragraph revisions and using the correct punctuation.

What are you reading, Deirdre asked Colette
I'm reading an autobiography of Beryl Markham

answered Deirdre Who asked Colette I've never
heard of her Oh, you should read this book Beryl
Markham was a fascinating woman Deirdre
exclaimed. She was the first person to fly alone over
the Atlantic from Europe to the Americas, and the
first professional female bush pilot in Africa

Grammar in Action

In stories, the characters seem more alive when they are
allowed to speak directly through reported speech. Use dialogue
in your writing whenever you want your audience to see your
characters more vividly.

Indirect   Ellen and Kate told us about Ellen's victory in the
bicycle race.

Direct   "I won, but it was a hard race! I crashed in one of
the turns and almost had to quit," Ellen said.
"The crowd really cheered when she got back
up," Kate added.

Admiral Robert Peary,
North Pole expedition.

Writing Activity Suppose you had written the
following paragraph for a news article:

Admiral Robert Peary and Matthew
Henson, his assistant, had just returned
from their successful expedition to the
North Pole. Peary said he was happy to
have finally reached the Pole after two
unsuccessful attempts. Peary and Henson
described the grueling conditions of the
trip, including food shortages, exhaus-
tion, and bitter cold.

Imagine, now, a conversation between the
explorers and yourself about their expedition.
Using dialogue, write your paragraph to make
it vivid and informative. If necessary use the
encyclopedia to gather information.

Titles of Short Works

Use quotation marks to set off the titles of short works: book chapters, stories, reports, articles, songs, and poems.

"The Greeks"   "Ode on a Grecian Urn"
"To Build a Fire"   "The Raven"

Titles of Longer Works

Underline the titles of longer works: books, magazines, motion pictures, television series, plays, musical compositions, and paintings. Also underline the names of ships, airplanes (but not the type of plane), spacecraft, and trains.

Terms that are underlined in writing will appear in italics in print.

The Red Badge of Courage   U.S.S. San Francisco
The Glass Menagerie   Aliens

Exercise

Write on your paper the following sentences, punctuating the titles as required.

1. James Thurber's cartoons were often published in The New Yorker magazine.
2. We saw the play Peter Pan on stage.
3. Langston Hughes's poem Mother to Son appears in my book.
4. The New York Times reported large crowds when da Vinci's Mona Lisa was exhibited at the Metropolitan Museum.
5. Cynthia wrote a story called The Purple Turtle about one of her pets.
6. My parents sailed to Europe on the Queen Elizabeth II, a famous ocean-going liner.
7. The orchestra will play Respighi's Pines of Rome next.
8. Have you read The Jungle, a powerful novel by Upton Sinclair?
9. Mr. Thomas assigned the chapter entitled Reconstruction for our next history class.
10. Everyone I know likes The Bill Cosby Show.

Linking Mechanics & Writing

A Imagine that inanimate objects could talk to each other. They would probably have a lot to say. They could discuss what kind of lives they lead, what they like and dislike, how they feel, and how they would prefer to be treated. Choose one of the pairs listed below and write a conversation that might take place between them.

- a shoe and a sock
- a gym shoe and a soccer ball
- a pile of books and a book bag
- a paintbrush and a house

B Suppose you were present at some famous moment in history. Imagine, for example, that you had witnessed the signing of the Declaration of Independence or the first moon landing. Write a few short paragraphs in which you describe the setting of the event and the people involved. Use appositives to introduce the participants; semicolons, colons, and commas to list the setting; and quotation marks to quote any speech.

C Imagine that you could interview absolutely anyone. You might choose Mozart, a movie star of today, or one of your descendants from the future. After you have chosen your subject write a one-page interview in the form of a conversation.

Additional Practice

Part 1 End Marks Write the following sentences and phrases, adding proper punctuation where necessary.

1. Be careful Those steps are very slippery
2. Why do some people absolutely refuse to leave a message on an answering machine
3. The parent-teacher meeting will be held at 7:30 PM
4. I Flowers
   - A Annuals
     - 1 Petunias
     - 2 Marigolds
     - 3 Zinnias
   - B Perennials
   - II Vegetables
5. My sister has a PhD degree in marine biology
6. What an impressive performance Mr Dugan gave
7. Could Lewis and Clark have survived their journey without Sacajawea's help
8. Denmark, the Netherlands, Norway, and the United States are all members of NATO
9. What a relief I didn't lose my keys after all
10. Marquez Products, Inc , is owned by Hector E Marquez

Parts 2–4 Commas Write the following sentences, adding commas where necessary.

11. Groucho Marx appeared in many movies and he also had his own television show.
12. No I don't want to go ice skating this afternoon.
13. "If we freeze these green beans" said Mother "we can eat them throughout the winter."
14. The Japanese Air Force bombed Pearl Harbor on December 7 1941.
15. Marie Antoinette the Queen of France was put to death in 1793.
16. Come here Joe and help me move these bookcases.

17. The workers want to pour the concrete today but it's raining.
18. Tony Kay Scott and Kristin are all running for student council offices.
19. We could not figure out what the cold sticky substance was.
20. After dusting Tim swept the floor and took out the trash.

Part 5 Semicolons and Colons Write the following sentences, adding semicolons and colons where necessary.

21. Michelle fried the eggs Marty poured the orange juice.
22. The shop sells greeting cards, wrapping paper, and stationery and this one sells books, games and toys.
23. Lloyd Alexander wrote the following books *Westmark, The Kestrel,* and *The Beggar Queen.*
24. The meeting was called to order at 800 P.M.
25. The first battle of the Revolutionary War was fought at Lexington the second was fought at Concord.

Parts 6 and 7 Hyphens and Apostrophes Write the following sentences, adding hyphens and apostrophes where needed.

26. Monica did a first rate job on her term paper.
27. The Beatles were quite popular during the 1960s.
28. Whos going to be the first to audition for the lead role in the play?
29. Jean calls her father in law by his first name.
30. Pauls instruction manual is poorly written.

Part 8 Quotation Marks and Other Punctuation Write the following sentences, adding punctuation where needed.

31. Francis Scott Key wrote the words of our national anthem The Star-Spangled Banner.
32. If you wish said Kim you can eat dinner at my house
33. The space shuttle Challenger exploded in 1986
34. Did Mr Spivak really say No one passed the test
35. Laura said Let's play touch football on Saturday
36. Ella what a beautiful hat you have said Kip.
37. At that point said Alice I called the police
38. I once read a short story called The Necklace
39. Did Coach say Run ten more laps
40. My dad wrote the article How to Fix Your Furnace

Application and Review

Lesson Review

A Using End Marks Write the following sentences, adding periods, question marks, and exclamation points where necessary.

1. Dr Peggy S Nilsen, MD, introduced Gov Brown to me
2. Are you sure that Sam has a driver's license
3. Get off that roof before you fall and get hurt
4. Send the coupon to Ms Lauren May, 619 N Lewis Rd, St Cloud, Minn, by the first of June
5. Do you think John can get seven people into that tiny car
6. Did PJ ask if she could borrow my bicycle
7. Wow What an easy test that turned out to be
8. Don't open your eyes Wait until I count to three
9. I Stringed instruments
      A Guitar
       1 Bass guitar
       2 Acoustic guitar
      B Violin
    II Percussion instruments
10. King Tutankhamen's tomb was sealed in 1352 B C

B Using Commas to Separate Ideas Write the following sentences, adding commas where necessary.

1. Laura Sally and Tad walked to the soccer match and took the bus home.
2. We cut the lawn trimmed the bushes and weeded the garden.
3. I saw the movie *A Tale of Two Cities* but I enjoyed the book even more.
4. On Saturday we went sailing but on Sunday the bad weather kept us at home.
5. Penny plays tennis racquetball and Ping-Pong very well.

6. Fran gave me a ride and also drove Glenda Peter and Ina.
7. Would you like to go with Raul Mark and me?
8. The Smithsonian Institution in Washington, D.C., is a fabulous place but it takes several days to see it all.
9. Our science class built a small greenhouse and during the year we grew plants flowers and tree seedlings.
10. Jim cleaned the kitchen Nikki vacuumed the living room and I went to the grocery store.

C Using Commas to Set Off Special Elements Write the following sentences, adding commas where necessary.

1. About midnight however I woke up.
2. Please sit quietly children while the storyteller is speaking.
3. Ms. Eaton my science teacher is from Australia.
4. We'll get back in time we hope for the performance.
5. The announcements I think have already been read.
6. Diane do you know where I left my sweatshirt?
7. One of the speakers at the career day assembly was Dr. Fisk our optometrist.
8. Barking furiously the dog ran to the window.
9. According to this map we are nowhere near the stadium.
10. Dizzy Gillespie a famous jazz trumpet player was born in South Carolina.

D Using Commas in Dates, Direct Quotations, and Addresses, and to Prevent Misreading Write the following sentences, adding commas where necessary.

1. "I liked the dancing elephants in the circus" said Peter.
2. Beth was born on November 26 1976 in a hospital in Buena Park California.
3. In the field mice had burrowed under the grass.
4. Mail your reservation to Camp Twilight 1515 North Powderhorn Road Bessemer Michigan 49911.
5. Walking past the students saw a bulletin-board notice dated Monday November 20.
6. On October 28 1886 the Statue of Liberty was dedicated as a national monument.

7. Any time you are eating your hands should be clean.
8. Johanna shouted "Let's play football!"
9. "I've been running for five miles" Chris panted "and I have three more to go."
10. Luanne and Carrie visited their grandparents in Phoenix Arizona and then flew to Atlanta Georgia to see their sister.

E Using Semicolons and Colons Write on your paper the following sentences, adding semicolons and colons where necessary.

1. The following students will please report to the office Meg Francis, Steve Jonas, and Pam Mead.
2. Patti goes to the dentist's tonight Peter will go on Saturday.
3. Call me before 230 P.M. tomorrow.
4. We need these items poster board, magic markers, and spray paint.
5. Dear Ms. Sánchez
   Enclosed please find the employment forms you requested.
6. We went to the movies they went roller-skating.
7. The mail should arrive between 1230 and 115 P.M.
8. Dear Mr. Mahony
   I am sorry I missed your call I have been away.
9. Be sure to bring these materials to sewing class tomorrow your pattern, material, thread, scissors, and a zipper.
10. The bus leaves promptly at 330 P.M. do not be late.

F Using Hyphens Write on your paper the following sentences, adding hyphens where necessary.

1. Hopkins needs a three fifths majority to win this election.
2. Jason found that he had only thirty two cents left.
3. My sister's four cylinder car gets great gas mileage.
4. We got four fifths of all the votes cast in the stu dent council election.
5. Leia's brother in law is a medical technologist at the local hospital.
6. Stephano's great grandparents are from Italy.
7. Julia's parents have their own ten speed bicycles.

8. She's a little known artist, but her paintings are excel
   lent.
9. Jenny was ninety nine percent sure the plan would work.
10. Is your birthday on the twenty third of December?

G Using Apostrophes Write on your paper the following
sentences, adding apostrophes where necessary.

1. Theres a new rock group in town tonight. Lets go with
   Kellys brother to the concert.
2. Leslies bike was stolen, so shell have to walk to school for
   the rest of the year.
3. My mothers not home yet. Ill bet she had to work late.
4. The 1970s were interesting.
5. Whose dog is this? Its the firefighters mascot.
6. Hed better be careful. Thats Ms. Jamess favorite plant.
7. The typists chair must be adjusted; its too low now.
8. I cant tell your *e*s and *i*s apart.
9. Wont you tell me whats wrong? Youre so quiet.
10. Did the kitten eat its supper? No, its still in the dish.

H Using Quotation Marks with Other Punctuation Write on
your paper the following sentences, adding punctuation where
necessary.

1. Where can we get some kite string asked Paula.
2. We have a garden in the back yard said Jane where we grow
   vegetables
3. Ann asked Does it always rain so much here
4. Wow exclaimed JoséThat helicopter ride was exciting
5. It's three o'clock said Ms. O'Neil Let's start the walk
6. Lola said John and Ina, this is Mr. Davis, my ballet
   instructor
7. The airport is closed repeated the radio announcer All flights
   have been canceled
8. If we don't panic said Marcia calmly we'll find our way
   back to the campground
9. Did Alan say That is not the best route to take
10. Bret said that she was an excellent teacher Sue added

Chapter Review

A Using Commas Write on your paper the following sentences, adding commas where necessary.

1. Every player likes George Egan the coach of our team.
2. "No I didn't invite them to join us" said Ms. Marvel.
3. We waited for a long time but the President never arrived.
4. Tim a tireless player would not rest until after the game.
5. The Declaration of Independence was adopted in Philadelphia Pennsylvania on July 4 1776.
6. The letter was addressed to Patrick Potter 3459 Potomac Place Lansing Michigan 80356.
7. Mom asked where we were what we had done and why we were out late.
8. We depend upon Duke our faithful dog to protect us.
9. Does the game begin at 7:30 or will we be late?
10. I am going to walk with Danielle in the parade and Fernando will walk with the governor.

B Using Punctuation Marks Write on your paper the following paragraphs, adding punctuation where necessary.

Ms Herbrook can you suggest any biographies of famous Americans asked Gary I have to read one

Why dont you read a book about Charles Lindbergh Gary I think youd find him interesting said Ms Herbrook

I cant remember who he was Can you Pete asked Gary.

Ms Herbrook asked Pete wasnt Lindbergh a famous flyer

He certainly was Pete He made the first solo flight across the Atlantic Ocean in a single engine plane continued Ms Herbrook Because of the fog sleet wind and total darkness he encountered he was forced to rely only on his instruments

Sounds exciting to me Gary said Ms Herbrook where can I find a biography of him

Look on the biography shelves Gary We have many books about him said Ms Herbrook

Cumulative Review

A Using Capitalization Find the words that contain capitalization errors in the sentences below. Write the words correctly.

1. my brother and i visit our aunt and uncle every saturday.
2. did you ask dr. shah for an appointment next week?
3. the first astronaut to become famous was john glenn.
4. the explorer john cabot sailed under the english flag.
5. has philip asked his mother and father to tell him the date of aunt helen's birthday?
6. the reverend hale told stories of jesus during church services.
7. Moslems always face east when they pray to allah.
8. the president of the united states awarded a medal to captain lindquist at a special ceremony.
9. the famous financier j. p. morgan made a fortune.
10. the statue of liberty is in new york city.
11. sue lives in the house at the south end of oakton avenue.
12. lee worked at grant hospital right after she graduated from high school.
13. next winter, will new year's day fall on a monday?
14. the brooks cabinet company sponsored a scholarship at cornell college.
15. on monday, we will study world war II.
16. was the constitution signed in philadelphia?
17. many oriental people practice buddhism.
18. many french people fly long distances on the concorde.
19. a packard was once a popular american car.
20. the huns invaded europe between a.d. 300 and a.d. 400.
21. the poem starts, "if you can keep your head when. . . ."
22. the leader said, "please stay in line."
23. "answer the phone," he said, "if it rings twice."
24. the letter began, "dear mrs. miller."
25. my favorite book is *the heart of darkness*.

B Using Punctuation Write the following sentences on your paper, adding correct punctuation where necessary.

1. Help Im stuck on the ledge
2. She earned her M A and Ph D degrees in six years
3. Dr R V Sontag arrived in Ft Lauderdale on Tues at 1030 A M to perform the rare operation
4. The appointment book entry read Gov Andrews Dec 1
5. Close the door said Mr Staley
6. He bought milk eggs and peanut butter at the corner store
7. Clouds will form the sky will darken and rain will come
8. Andy have you finished cleaning your room
9. Margaret Price a soprano sings opera all over the world
10. Eddie won the chess championship on August 12 1986 in Atlanta Georgia
11. Please bring these items scissors tape and cotton
12. The door opened Bill stalked in
13. The recipe says to use two thirds cups of sugar
14. Its too hot for the dog to wear its sweater
15. Jenny got eighty five percent of the test right
16. The concert starts at 830 PM come early for a good seat
17. Whos the student whose theme paper was lost
18. If the window opens said Jan well know theres a ghost
19. How many great uncles do you have asked Toni
20. Lynnes feet are cold but shes staying outside anyway

C Combined Review Write the following sentences on your paper, using correct capitalization and punctuation.

1. have you read *great expectations* by charles dickens?
2. oh no the *lusitania* has been sunk
3. marge gil and dan live at 12 e oak st in omaha nebraska.
4. the new show will start at 800 pm on the dot
5. well answered marsha i dont feel that well
6. bobs late again shouted his great grandfather
7. why asked captain wilson is that hatch open
8. my uncle gave dad and me a ride to chicago said anne
9. everyone saluted the prince of wales entered
10. is wall street the financial district of new york

Writer's Handbook

Ideas for Writing

Ideas for writing are everywhere, waiting to be discovered and explored. Read the following lists of ideas. For other writing ideas, see Starting Points, pages 43–55. Then use the thinking skills you learned in Chapter 2 to create interesting writing topics.

Ideas for Writing

Descriptive
a collection
an animal in flight
a snowstorm
a Halloween
  costume
a computer game
a moonlit night
a magician's trick
a park in autumn
the beach at noon
an interesting
  photograph
a father and son

Narrative
a competition
feeling left out
an unexpected
  visitor
unknown danger
performing on stage
a funny incident
in my own backyard
a spy among us
one dark, dreary
  night
the wrong number

Expository
(Process)
how an auto is built
how weather predic-
  tions are made
how doctors treat
  knee injuries
how radar detectors
  work
how sunken ships
  are raised
how to plant a
  garden

(Cause/Effect)
the causes of
  deafness
the effect of home-
  lessness on
  children
What causes paraly-
  sis?
What causes hunger
  pains?
the effects of
  fluorocarbons on
  the earth's
  atmosphere
the effects of
  malnutrition

(Compare/Contrast)
Compare/contrast . . .
travel by high-speed
  train/jet plane
designer clothes/
  regular clothes
two actors or
  actresses
photography/painting
record/music video
imported car/
  American car

Persuasive
Should animals be
  used in scientific
  research?
Are computer
  screens safe?
Should the min-
  imum wage be
  raised?
Should the U.S. and
  Russia explore
  space together?
Should young peo-
  ple be paid for
  household chores?
Should recycling be
  required by law?

Ideas for Writing in Subject Areas

Art
makeup artists
Russian ballet
how to draw and
   compose pictures
the treasures of
   Tutankhamen
special effects in
   motion pictures
how skyscrapers are
   built
glassblowing

Consumerism
Should you join a
   record or book
   club?
how to complain
   about a defective
   product
electronic shopping
saving your money

Health
What causes aging?
how plaque harms
   teeth
how doctors
   diagnose leukemia
how to improve
   your memory
starting an exercise
   program
the effects of
   pesticides on the
   environment
autism in children
What causes
   myopia?
treating insomnia
the causes/effects of
   an earache
Should smoking be
   banned in public
   places?

Math
how to use an
   abacus
mathematical instru-
   ments in
   navigation
the binary system of
   numbers
geometric patterns
   in art
real-life uses of
   math skills
how roller coasters
   are designed
how to measure the
   height of a house

Music
how an orchestra is
   conducted
Broadway musicals
computers in music
origins of rock and
   roll
tuning a guitar
careers in music
opera for children
blues festivals
Cajun music
how music videos
   are made
music in advertising
radio disc jockeys
New Orleans jazz
music for exercising
how to make your
   own musical
   instruments

Science
What is the green-
   house effect?
how dolphins help
   the U.S. Navy
how viruses attack
   the body
how a heart-lung
   machine works
lasers in surgery
What is a mutation?
how a submarine
   works
effects of steroids
   on the body
how astronauts
   exercise in space
new scientific
   discoveries

Social Studies
migrant farm
   workers
How should we
   dispose of nuclear
   waste?
How is the standard
   of living defined?
What is propaganda?
planned
   obsolescence
how fingerprints are
   used to solve
   crimes
how social security
   works
foster care for
   children
the American Dream
the current U.S.
   trade deficit
How does Great
   Britain choose its
   Prime Minister?

Outlines and Other Graphic Organizers

Graphic aids are excellent tools for organizing ideas and information. Outlines and other graphic organizers may be used to take notes or to plan a composition or speech.

Correct Outline Form

A **formal outline** presents the main points of a topic in a detailed way. These points are arranged to show the relationships between ideas.

Two types of formal outlines are sentence outlines and topic outlines. In a **sentence outline,** main points and subpoints are written in complete sentences. A **topic outline** uses words or phrases instead of complete sentences for each main point and subpoint. Here is a portion of a topic outline on volcanoes.

Volcanoes

I. Origin of volcanoes   (Main point)
   A. Magma formation   (First subpoint)
      1. Rock melted by earth's interior heat ⎫
      2. Magma pushed toward surface   ⎬ (Subdetails
      3. Reservoirs of magma formed   ⎭ for A.)

   B. Eruption   (Second subpoint)
      1. Caused by pressure of surrounding rock on reservoir
      2. Conduits where magma breaks through
         a. Central vent in crater ⎫ (Subdetails for 2.)
         b. Side vents   ⎭

II. Materials produced by volcanoes
   A. Fluid magma
      1. Lava when hot
      2. Rock when cooled
         a. Pahoehoe rock
         b. Aa rock
   B. Sticky magma
      1. Flows when hot
      2. Forms tephra when cool

Follow these steps when writing a sentence or topic outline.

1. Write the title at the top of the outline. The title, introduction, and conclusion are not considered parts of the outline.
2. Organize main points and subpoints as shown on the previous page.
3. Indent each division of the outline. Write the letter or the numeral directly below the first letter in the first word of the larger heading above.
4. Do not use a single subheading. A heading should not be broken down if it cannot be divided into at least two points. For example, if there is a *1* under *A,* there must be at least a *2*.
5. In a topic outline, keep items of the same rank in the same form. For example, if *A* is a noun, then *B* and *C* should also be nouns. Subtopics do not need to be in the same form as main topics.
6. Begin each item with a capital letter. Do not use end punctuation in a topic outline.

Writing an Information Outline

An **information outline** can be used to organize information quickly and in as few words as possible. Main ideas are listed as separate headings, with supporting details written below. Because informal outlines are generally for personal use, the format can vary widely. Any form is acceptable that helps you to clarify and organize information.

Use informal outlining when you want to take notes quickly during class discussions. An informal outline can also help you prepare a short speech, or study and review test material. Here is a portion of an information outline on submarines.

    I. Military use
       —carry torpedoes and guided missiles
       —sonar finds and tracks targets
       —attack enemy ships from below water's surface
   II. Scientific research
       —explore ocean depths
       —gather scientific information
       —conduct underwater experiments

Other Graphic Organizers

There are other types of graphic organizers that can help you explore topics and organize information.

Chronological Organization   Ideas that are related by time can be arranged in chronological, or time order. **Chronological order** is the order in which events happen. One way to arrange ideas chronologically is to place them on a **time line**.

To make a time line, write the event that happens first at the far left of the line. Then add details to fill in the order of events and identify when they occur. Here is a portion of a time line.

October 1957	May 1961	February 1962	July 1969
Soviets launch *Sputnik I,* the first satellite to circle Earth	U.S. astronaut Alan Shepard makes 15-minute space flight	John Glenn becomes first astronaut to orbit Earth	U.S. astronaut Neil Armstrong is first man to walk on moon

Charts   Another way to organize information is to make a chart. This allows you to show relationships and review information quickly and efficiently. The labels of a chart are similar to the headings of an outline. The following comparison/contrast chart explains some of the differences between white blood cells and red blood cells.

Red and White Blood Cells

	Main Job	Structure	Site of Production	Disorders
red blood cells	carry oxygen from lungs to body tissues and carry carbon dioxide from body tissues to lungs	mature cells have no nucleus	bone marrow	anemia— shortage of red blood cells
white blood cells	protect body from disease and infection by destroying bacteria and viruses	cells have nucleus	bone marrow	leucopenia— shortage of white blood cells

A **cause-and-effect chart** shows how one thing happens because of something else. The cause-and-effect chart below has been used to explain soil pollution.

Soil Pollution	
Cause	**Effects**
overuse of fertilizers	—prevents soil bacteria from destroying wastes
	—slows production of soil nutrients
pesticides	—destroy helpful bacteria
	—leave harmful chemicals
erosion	—wears away valuable soil

A **spider map** is similar to the cluster digram described on pages 25–26. The oval in the center of the spider map contains the topic. Various subtopics are written on the "legs" extending out from the main topic. Further divisions of the subtopics are placed on the lines branching out from each "leg" of the spider map. Here is a spider map used to illustrate the roles of various participants in a theatrical production.

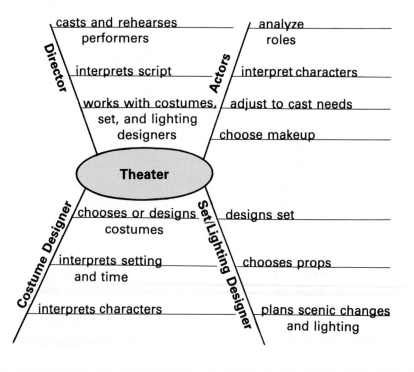

Common Usage Problems

This section identifies common writing problems. Use these pages as a means of review or as a proofreading guide.

Abbreviations

In most cases, abbreviations should be avoided in formal writing. The following are exceptions: titles (Mr., Mrs., Ms., Dr.), dates, and times (A.M., P.M., B.C., A.D.).

See also pages 603 and 617.

Clichés

A **cliché** is an expression that has been used too often. Avoid the clichés listed below and any others that come to mind. Instead, try expressing your thoughts in fresh new ways.

rub salt in the wound   down in the dumps
a sight for sore eyes   don't rock the boat

Double Negatives

Words that mean "no" are called **negatives**. A **double negative** occurs when two negatives are used where only one is needed. Always avoid using double negatives.

Incorrect   I do*n't* know *nothing* about photography.
Correct   I do*n't* know *anything* about photography.

See also page 535.

Jargon

People who share the same interests often use a special vocabulary called **jargon**. For example, auto mechanics use the words *butterfly valve, distributor,* and *vapor lock*. Although these words are easily understood by people within the same profession, jargon can be confusing to others. When you write, remember to use vocabulary that your readers will understand.

Modifiers

Adjective-Adverb Confusion If you do not know whether to use an adjective or an adverb, ask yourself which word is being modified. Adjectives describe nouns or pronouns by telling *which one, what kind, how many,* or *how much*. Adverbs modify verbs, adjectives, or other adverbs by telling *where, when, how,* or *to what extent*.

| Incorrect | Todd's painting looks *beautifully*. |
| Correct | Todd's painting looks *beautiful*. (*Beautiful* is a predicate adjective modifying the noun *painting*. |

| Incorrect | Those math problems were *real* hard. |
| Correct | Those math problems were *really* hard. (*Really* is an adverb modifying the adjective *hard*.) |

See also pages 532–533.

Good-Well Learn to use the words *good* and *well* correctly. *Good* is always an adjective. It modifies a noun or a pronoun.

> Matt felt good about his achievement. (predicate adjective—*felt good* refers to happiness or comfort)

Well is usually an adverb, modifying an action verb.

> Julio plays the drums *well*.

Well is an adjective when it means "in good health" and describes a noun or a pronoun.

> I haven't felt *well* all week. (predicate adjective—*felt well* refers to health)

Bad-Badly *Bad* is an adjective, modifying a noun or a pronoun. *Badly* is an adverb, modifying action verbs.

> Claire felt *bad* about your accident. (predicate adjective)
> The orchestra performed *badly*. (adverb)

Comparative and Superlative Forms Use the **comparative form** of an adjective to compare two things. Use the **superlative form** to compare three or more things.

> Brenda's cake is *moister* than mine.
> It is the *moistest* cake I have ever tasted.

> The museum is a *more impressive* building than the library.
> It is the *most impressive* building in town.

Do not use *-er* and *more* or *-est* and *most* together.

| Incorrect | Venus is the *most closest* planet to Earth. |
| Correct | Venus is the *closest* planet to Earth. |

See also pages 513–515, 530–531.

Pronouns

Agreement A pronoun must agree with its antecedent in number. Use a singular pronoun with a singular antecedent. Use a plural pronoun with a plural antecedent.

Incorrect	Any *traveler* must show *their* passport at the border.
Correct	*Travelers* must show *their* passports at the border.

Use a singular pronoun when two singular antecedents are joined by *or* and *nor*.

Neither *Jeff* nor *Joel* rode *his* skateboard in the contest.

Indefinite Pronouns An **indefinite pronoun** does not refer to a specific person or thing. The indefinite pronouns listed below are always singular and must be used with singular verbs.

Incorrect	*Everyone* in these rooms *were* waiting patiently.
Correct	Everyone in these rooms *was* waiting patiently.

another	each	everything	one
anybody	either	neither	somebody
anyone	everybody	nobody	someone
anything	everyone	no one	

Use singular indefinite pronouns with *his, her,* and *its*.

Did *anyone* in the dance groups lose *her* ballet slippers?
Nobody raised *his* or *her* hand to answer the questions.

The following indefinite pronouns are always plural: *both, few, many,* and *several*. Use them with the plural possessive pronouns *our* and *their* and with plural verbs.

Many in the crowd forgot *their* coats. (pronoun agreement)
Both of us carried *our* umbrellas. (subject-verb agreement)

The following indefinite pronouns may be either singular or plural depending on their meaning in a sentence: *all, any, most, none, some,* and *much*.

None of the silverware lost *its* shine. (singular)
None of the victims recovered *their* belongings. (plural)

Lack of Antecedents Do not use a pronoun without an antecedent. The meaning of the sentence will be unclear.

Unclear	When the movie ended, she turned it off. (turned what off?)
Clear	When the movie ended, she turned the television off.

Possessive Pronouns Do not confuse possessive pronouns with the contractions they resemble. A **contraction** contains an apostrophe and takes the place of two words. **Possessive pronouns** show ownership and are not formed with an apostrophe.

The leopard lazily opened its eyes. (possessive pronoun)
It's not my decision. (contraction meaning *it is*)

Subject and Object Pronouns The subject pronouns are *I, you, he, she, it, we,* and *they*. Use these pronouns as subjects of sentences and as predicate pronouns after linking verbs.

> *He* lost control of the car on the icy pavement. (subject)
> The most valuable player was *she*. (predicate pronoun)

Use the object pronouns *me, you, him, her, it, us,* and *them* as objects of verbs or prepositions.

> A swarm of bees surrounded *us*. (object of verb)
> Without *her*, our plan would fail. (object of preposition)

To use compound pronouns correctly, try each pronoun of the compound by itself.

Compound Subject	We and they went skin diving last summer. (*we* went, *they* went)
Compound Object	Give the recipe to *me* and *him*. (give to *me*, give to *him*)

Unclear Reference When a pronoun may refer to more than one word in a sentence, the reference is unclear.

Unclear	Scoop the salad out of the carton and throw *it* away. (throw the carton away or the salad?)
Clear	Scoop the salad out of the carton and throw the *carton* away.

Sentence Errors

Fragments A **sentence** is a group of words that expresses a complete thought. A **fragment** is a group of words that does not express a complete thought. A fragment may be missing a subject, a predicate, or both. To correct a fragment, add the missing part or parts. For more information, see pages 413–415.

Fragment	Sailed toward the Caribbean Sea. (missing subject)
Sentence	Three *ships* sailed toward the Caribbean Sea.

Run-on Sentences When two or more sentences are incorrectly written as one, the error is called a **run-on sentence**. To correct a run-on, place a period after the first sentence and begin the next sentence with a capital letter.

Run-on	The skaters completed their routine the audience applauded.
Correct	The skaters completed their routine. The audience applauded.
Run-on	The clown wore a curly yellow wig, he carried brightly colored balloons in each hand.
Correct	The clown wore a curly yellow wig. He carried brightly colored balloons in each hand.

Slang

Colorful words and expressions spoken during a particular time period or by a certain group of people are called **slang**. Slang is appropriate only in very informal situations. It should not be used in formal writing. Below are examples of slang.

> *cool* pleasing, excellent, admirable
> *wimp* weak or ineffective person

Verbs

Agreement with Subject in Number A verb must agree with its subject in number. In inverted sentences, the subject occurs after the verb, but the verb must still agree with the subject.

> In the arboretum *grow* many wild *flowers*.
> Here *are* the *tomatoes* from the garden.

When the parts of a compound subject are joined by *and,* use a plural verb. When the parts of a compound subject are joined by *or* or *nor,* the verb agrees with the subject closer to the verb.

> The *sailboat and lighthouse were* silhouetted by the sun.
> The dolphins or the *walrus is* performing next.
> Neither Lauren nor her *sisters have* pierced ears.

The verb must always agree with its subject even when a prepositional phrase separates the subject and verb.

Singular   One of Dad's blue socks *is* missing.
Plural   Both *flashlights* in the cabinet *are* broken.

Tense, Avoiding Unnecessary Changes *Tense* means "time." Most verbs change their forms to show present, past, and future time. Avoid changing tenses in the middle of a sentence.

Incorrect   We *sit* near the fire and *toasted* the marshmallows.
Correct   We *sat* near the fire and *toasted* the marshmallows.

Who and Whom

Who is the subject form of the pronoun: *whom* is the object form. For more information, see pages 454 and 549.

> *Who* drank the glass of milk? (subject of the verb *drank*)
> *Whom* did you invite? (direct object of the verb *did invite*)

You, Use Of

Avoid the pronoun *you* in writing unless you mean the reader.

Incorrect   *You* were unable to buy tickets at the door.
Correct   *Fans* were unable to buy tickets at the door.

Quick Guide to Capitalization

Proper Nouns and Proper Adjectives

1. Capitalize the names of persons and also the initials or abbreviations that stand for those names.
2. Capitalize titles used with names of persons and capitalize the initials and/or abbreviations standing for those titles. Capitalize the titles *Mr., Mrs., Ms.,* and *Miss.*
3. Capitalize titles of people in unique positions whose rank is very important, even when the titles are used without proper names: *The President will meet with his staff.* Do not capitalize titles that are used as common nouns.
4. Capitalize such words as *mother, father, aunt,* and *uncle* when these words are used as names.
5. Capitalize the pronoun *I.*
6. Capitalize all words referring to the Deity, to holy books, and to religious scriptures.
7. Capitalize personal pronouns referring to the Deity.

Geographical Names

1. Capitalize names of sections of the country but not directions of the compass.
2. Capitalize proper adjectives derived from names of sections of the country or the world. Do not capitalize adjectives derived from words indicating directions.

Organizations, History, and Time

1. Capitalize all the important words in the names of organizations and institutions, including their abbreviations.
2. Capitalize the names of historical events, documents, and periods of time.
3. Capitalize the names of months, days, and holidays, but not the names of seasons.

Languages, Peoples, Transportation, and Abbreviations

1. Capitalize the names of languages, races, nationalities, and religions, and also the adjectives derived from them.

2. Do not capitalize the names of school subjects unless they are languages or unless a course name has a number.
3. Capitalize the names of ships, trains, and aircraft. Capitalize brand names of automobiles.
4. Capitalize the abbreviations, *B.C., A.D., A.M.,* and *P.M.*

First Words

1. Capitalize the first word of every sentence.
2. Capitalize the first word in most lines of poetry.
3. Capitalize the first word of a direct quotation.
4. Capitalize all the important words in the greeting of a letter. In the closing, capitalize only the first word.
5. Capitalize the first word in each entry of an outline.
6. Capitalize the first word, the last word, and all important words in the titles of books, poems, short stories, articles, newspapers, magazines, plays, motion pictures, works of art, television programs, and musical compositions.

Quick Guide to Punctuation

The Period

1. Use a period at the end of a declarative sentence.
2. Use a period at the end of an imperative sentence.
3. Use a period at the end of an indirect question, that is, a question that reports what someone said without using the speaker's exact words.
4. Use a period after most abbreviations and after initials.
5. Use a period after the letters or numbers in an outline or list.
6. Use a period between numerals representing dollars and cents and before a decimal.

The Question Mark and the Exclamation Point

1. Use a question mark at the end of an interrogative sentence.
2. Use an exclamation point at the end of an exclamatory sentence and following an interjection.

The Comma

1. Use a comma before the conjunction that joins the two parts of a compound sentence. In a very short compound sentence, it is not necessary to put a comma before *and,* but one must be used before *but* or *or.*
2. Use a comma after each item in a series except the last.
3. When two or more adjectives precede a noun but do not express a closely related thought, use a comma after each adjective except the last one.
4. Use commas after the adverbs *first, second, third,* and so on, when these adverbs introduce items in a series.
5. Use a comma to separate an introductory word or phrase from the rest of the sentence.
6. Use commas before and after interrupters.
7. Ue commas to set off all nouns used in direct address.
8. Use commas to set off most appositives.
9. When writing dates, place a comma after the day of the month.
10. For geographical locations, place a comma between the name of the town or city and the names of the state, district, or country.
11. Use a comma after the greeting in a friendly letter and after the closing of a friendly or business letter.
12. Use a comma to set off the explanatory words of a direct quotation, such as *Ann asked, Larry said,* or *Jill replied.*
13. Use a comma to separate any sentence parts that might be improperly joined or misunderstood without the comma.

The Semicolon and the Colon

1. Use a semicolon to separate the parts of a compound sentence when you do not connect them with a coordinating conjunction.
2. Use a semicolon between the parts of a compound sentence when these clauses are long, complicated, or punctuated.
3. Use a colon to introduce a list of items.
4. Use a colon after the greeting of a business letter.
5. Use a colon between numbers that represent hours and minutes in expressions of time.

The Hyphen and the Apostrophe

1. Use a hyphen to separate the parts of a word at the end of a line.
2. Use a hyphen in compound adjectives when they precede the word they modify.

3. Add *'s* to form the possessive of singular nouns.
4. Add only an apostrophe to form the possessive of a plural noun that ends in *s*.
5. Add *'s* to form the possessive of a plural noun that does not end in *s*.

Quotation Marks

1. Use quotation marks to enclose direct quotations.
2. When a direct quotation is divided by explanatory words, begin the second part of the quotation with a lower-case letter, unless it is the beginning of a new sentence.
3. Place commas and periods inside quotation marks. Place semicolons and colons outside the quotation marks.
4. Place question marks and exclamation points inside quotation marks if they belong to the quotation. Place them outside if they do not belong to the quotation.
5. Use single quotation marks to enclose quotations within one another. If the quotation within the quotation ends the sentence, use both the single and double quotation marks after the last words of the quotations.
6. In a quotation of more than one paragraph, use quotation marks at the beginning of each paragraph and at the end of the final paragraph.
7. Use quotation marks to enclose the titles of poems, short stories, songs, reports, articles, and chapters of books.
8. Underline titles of books, plays, magazines, newspapers, television series, works of art, musical compositions, and motion pictures. Also underline the names of ships, airplanes (but not the type of plane), spacecraft, and trains.

Thesaurus

A thesaurus is a resource that writers use to make their choices of words more precise. In a thesaurus, synonyms—words with similar meanings—are listed in groups. These synonyms can help you find the best word to express an idea. They will also help you to develop your speaking and writing vocabulary.

Using This Thesaurus

To find synonyms for a word, first find the word in the index on pages 681–682, which lists, in alphabetical order, every synonym in the thesaurus. Notice the format of the following portion of the index.

> **elegant** *see* BEAUTIFUL
> **emigrate** *see* TRAVEL
> **enchanting** *see* BEAUTIFUL
> **END**
> **energetic** *see* ACTIVE
> **ENERGY**

Words printed in capital letters in the index are called **entry words.** *End* and *energy* are entry words. An entry word has a general meaning. It is the heading under which more specific synonyms are grouped.

Words printed in lower-case letters in the index are synonyms for entry words. Thus, *elegant* is a synonym for BEAUTIFUL.

If you wanted to find a synonym for the word *energetic,* you would find *energetic* in the index. The index would tell you to look at the entry for ACTIVE.

When you turn to the entry word, you will notice that it is defined and used in an example sentence. After each entry word, related synonyms are listed, with a definition and example sentence for each one. The entry word ACTIVE, for example, is followed by the synonyms *agile, energetic,* and *spirited.* Be sure to read through all the synonyms before you decide which word best expresses your idea.

At the end of most entries, there is a list of other synonyms that are not defined and not used in example sentences. Antonyms—words with opposite meanings—are also listed at the end of many entries. Be careful about using these words. Before you choose one, look it up in a dictionary and study its meaning.

ACTIVE The words in this group all mean "full of action" or "inclined to action." *Active*, the general word, includes both meanings. • She is an active person who enjoys soccer, swimming, and running.

agile Use *agile* to suggest quickness and a good ability at using one's arms and legs. • He made an agile leap to the top of the wall.

energetic Use *energetic* to show that a person has more energy than others who arc doing thc samc thing. • Chris is so energetic that I get tired just watching her.

spirited Use *spirited* to show that someone is especially lively. It also suggests independence and strong will. • The Cougar's spirited defense kept the defending champions from scoring.

Other Synonyms: acrobatic, athletic, busy, frisky, lively, nimble, spry, vigorous, vital, vivacious

Antonyms: inactive, lazy, sluggish

AFRAID *Afraid* and its synonyms mean "feeling fear." Use *afraid* to suggest a lasting fear that will probably continue. • Vera is afraid of heights.

aghast *Aghast* comes from an Old English word for "ghost"; it suggests the horror a person would feel upon seeing a ghost. • I was aghast when I saw the bear turn toward me.

fearful Use *fearful* to show fear of a potential danger. • We were fearful that Dan and Kate would be lost in the blizzard.

terrified *Terrified* suggests strong fear that overwhelms a person. • I was so terrified by the python that I couldn't move.

wary *Wary* suggests being cautious or concerned for a good reason. • Ever since the fire, I've been wary of turpentine and kerosene.

worried A worried person is mildly frightened by expecting something troubling to happen. • For a week, Dan worried about the exam.

Other Synonyms: alarmed, anxious, frightened, nervous, panicky, scared

Antonyms: calm, confident, relaxed, unafraid *see also* BRAVE

ALONE *Alone* and other words in this group mean "by oneself" or "by itself." • Mr. Jenkins lives alone.

lonely *Lonely* suggests unhappiness, even gloom. • A lonely cabin stood in the shadows of the huge pine forest.

lonesome *Lonesome* suggests a longing for companionship. • "I'll be lonesome without you," he said.

solitary *Solitary* emphasizes the idea of being the only one. • A solitary puppy remained in the pet shop cage.

Other Synonyms: isolated, single, solo, unique

ANGRY The words in this group mean "upset by something that hurts or opposes one." *Angry* is the general word for this feeling. • Dan's rudeness made me angry.

enraged To be enraged is to be extremely angry. An enraged person may shout or make wild gestures. • Enraged citizens gathered outside the dictator's headquarters.

furious *Furious* suggests a wild anger that may be out of control or even violent. • I'm too furious to speak to anyone now.

irritated To be irritated is to be mildly annoyed, usually by something that continues. • The constantly dripping water irritated me.

Other Synonyms: annoyed, cross, incensed, indignant, irate, mad, resentful, upset

Antonyms: glad, happy, pleased

ANSWER The words in this group mean "to react to a question or request." *Answer* means saying, writing, or doing something in the way required by a situation. • I'll answer Nettie's letter.

acknowledge To acknowledge is merely to show that a message has been received and understood. • Jack acknowledged my greeting with a nod.

reply *Reply* is more formal than *answer*. It also has a very specific meaning. It means "to answer completely, to satisfy the questioner." • Jenkins agreed to reply to all the charges.

respond *Respond* suggests cooperation or appropriate action. It is often used for "answering" something other than a question or request. • Thunder rumbled above us, and we responded by dashing inside.

retort *Retort* suggests answering in an angry or clever way. • "I'm taking a long time because I'm doing a good job," she retorted.

Other Synonyms: react, rebut, rejoin
Antonyms: see ASK

ASK

Ask and its synonyms mean "to request something that is wanted." A person may ask for the answer to a question, for information, or for help. • "When does the next bus arrive?" he asked.

beg To beg is to ask for something in an especially humble or earnest way. • "Won't you let me see him just once?" she begged the guards.

demand Use *demand* to show that a person believes that he or she has a right to what is requested. • "Tell me who is in charge here," she demanded.

inquire Use *inquire* to emphasize seeking information. It suggests a serious reason for asking and is more formal than *ask*. • "Has my membership application arrived?" he inquired.

request Use *request* to indicate asking in a polite and formal way. • "May I watch the recording session from the control room?" she requested.

Other Synonyms: beseech, entreat, implore, plead, question, quiz, seek
Antonyms: see ANSWER

BAD

There are two groups of synonyms for *bad*. One means "not satisfactory," and the other means "evil." • Melinda had a few bad grades, but she did well overall. Stealing and other bad behavior will not be tolerated. **Caution:** do not use *bad* carelessly. Describing what is wrong is usually better than using *bad* or a synonym. Think before you write.

careless Use *careless* to stress lack of attention or thought. • We didn't hire you to do careless work.

dreadful Something dreadful is so bad that it makes a person feel dread or terror. • The headlights revealed a dreadful shape.

evil Use *evil* to suggest deliberate wrongdoing. An evil person is one whose badness shows in nearly every act. • The knight was imprisoned by an evil king.

horrible *Horrible* describes something that makes a person feel horror or dread. • In the next scene, a horrible monster attacked the city.

incorrect When something is incorrect, it fails to meet certain requirements. • "I'm sorry," said the quiz show host, "but that answer is incorrect."

wrong *Wrong* has nearly the same meaning as *incorrect*, but is less formal. • "That's the wrong answer," he said.

Other Synonyms: detestable, malicious, poor, repulsive, revolting, vicious, vile, wicked, *see also* MEAN, WRONG
Antonyms: good, fine, right

BEAUTIFUL

The words in this group mean "pleasing the eye (or the ear, or another sense)." *Beautiful* suggests that a thing approaches the ideal for its type. • Ossie sent a dozen beautiful roses.

attractive *Attractive* suggests beauty that catches a person's eye or draws a person's attention. • She has a wonderfully attractive voice.

dazzling *Dazzling* suggests beauty that is brilliant and splendid. • The celebration ended with a dazzling fireworks display.

elegant *Elegant* describes refined beauty, good taste, grace, and excellence. • Patrice wrote an elegant description of a snowfall.

enchanting *Enchanting* is used to describe beauty that charms a person. Behind the porch is an enchanting flower garden.

gorgeous *Gorgeous* suggests bright, lively, almost gaudy beauty. • Peacocks have gorgeous plumage.

Other Synonyms: fair, handsome, lovely, pretty, stunning
Antonyms: hideous, homely, ugly

BEST The words in this group mean "as good as can be" or "better than any other of its type." *Best* emphasizes the idea that something is above all others of its type. • Grady Street is the best route to the stadium.

finest Use *finest* to emphasize the idea that something is best because its qualities are without flaw. • This is Mary Cassatt's finest painting.

foremost Use *foremost* to emphasize that something is first in a ranking of things. • Doug Benson is the foremost runner in the county.

incomparable Use *incomparable* to indicate that something is so much better than others of its type that there is almost no comparison. • We were awed by the incomparable power of the huge rocket.

superior Use *superior* to show that something is better than most, even if it is not the very best. • Lisa is a superior gymnast.

Other Synonyms: inimitable, supreme, unparalleled
Antonyms: inferior, least, worst

BRAVE *Brave* and its synonyms mean "fearless in meeting danger or difficulty." • Brave firefighters battled the huge blaze.

adventurous *Adventurous* suggests eagerness to get into dangerous or difficult situations. • She is an adventurous sailor who is planning a solo trip around the world.

bold A bold person is quick to meet a challenge or face trouble, perhaps too quick. • Wilson made a bold leap onto the ledge.

daring *Daring* suggests that a person likes to take risks and face danger. • The balloonists made a daring flight over the North Pole.

fearless Use *fearless* to show that a person acts without even thinking about personal safety. • The fearless tightrope walker performed without a net.

Other Synonyms: courageous, hardy, heroic, indomitable, plucky, resolute, valiant
Antonyms: see AFRAID

BREAK The words in this group mean "to cause to come apart." *Break* expresses the general idea of dividing something into pieces by force. • The pencil will break if you press too hard.

crack To crack is to split something without making the pieces come completely apart. • The window pane cracked in a long, thin line.

crumble To crumble is to break something into small bits. Often, a thing that crumbles is easy to break. • The old letter crumbled when I touched it.

crush To crush is to break something by squeezing it. Often, crushing does not separate pieces. • We crush the cans before recycling them.

demolish To demolish is to destroy something completely, often deliberately. • This building will be demolished to make way for a new one.

shatter Use *shatter* for a sharp blow that makes pieces scatter. • The windshield shattered in the accident.

wreck Originally, *wreck* referred to the remains of a shipwreck. Use *wreck* for the complete destruction of something large. • The earthquake wrecked six entire blocks.

Other Synonyms: dismantle, raze, smash, snap, split

BRIGHT *Bright* and its synonyms mean "reflecting light well" or "shining with its own light." • Bright lights lit the stage.

glistening Use *glistening* when something smooth reflects small gleams of light. • The morning sun shone on glistening drops of dew.

glowing Use *glowing* for warm, even light coming from the thing itself, especially something heated until it gives off light. Compare *radiant*. • The buildings were glowing in the rosy light of sunset.

radiant *Radiant* suggests a brighter light than *glowing* does, but the meanings are otherwise much the same. • We warmed ourselves in front of a radiant fire.

sparkling *Sparkling* suggests many tiny points of light that last a brief time, like sparks. • I couldn't take my eyes off the queen's sparkling jewels.

Other Synonyms: blazing, brilliant, gleaming, luminous, shiny
Antonyms: dark, dim

END *End* and its synonyms mean "come to a stop." • The program will end at nine o'clock.

conclude Use *conclude* to show that something came to an end as planned. • We concluded the meeting in full agreement.

finish Use *finish* to show that something is completed when it comes to an end. • We will begin on Tuesday, and should finish on Friday.

halt *Halt* suggests a sudden stop, a coming to an end that was not planned or expected. • A section of broken track brought the train to a halt.

Other Synonyms: bring to a close, cease, close, complete, stop
Antonyms: continue, keep up, persist

ENERGY The words in this group mean "the quality that is necessary to do work or be active." Use *energy* as the general term. • Ted just didn't have the energy to finish the job.

force Use *force* for energy that works against something. • The hurricane struck the Gulf coast with great force.

power Use *power* to indicate great energy, especially when it is put to use. • This engine has more power than last year's model.

strength Use *strength* for energy that is compared to a standard. • The instruments gauge an earthquake's strength.

Other Synonyms: might, stamina, verve, vigor, vim, vitality

ENTHUSIASTIC All the words in this group mean "having or showing interest." They vary in the degree and type of interest and the way it is shown. Use *enthusiastic* to show strong favorable feelings and intense interest. • Everyone I know is enthusiastic about the upcoming concert.

eager Use *eager* to emphasize the impatience a person feels when waiting for something desired. • Brownsville is eager for victory in Saturday's game.

fervent Use *fervent* to suggest burning enthusiasm; the word comes from a root meaning "burn." • Carl has a fervent interest in world peace.

Other Synonyms: avid, fanatical, passionate, sincere, zealous
Antonyms: bored, reluctant, unenthusiastic, uninterested

EXPLAIN

To *explain* is to make plain or understandable. • This book explains the causes of the Ice Age.

clarify Since *clarify* means "to make clear," it suggests that something was "murky" or confused before it was explained. • Senator Ross clarified her stand on new taxes.

criticize To criticize is to examine something carefully, explain it, and show where it is good and bad. • Mr. James Thompson criticizes books for the *New York Times.* Perhaps because many critics often find more to blame than to praise, *criticize* has the secondary meaning of "finding fault." • My friend Curtis criticizes everything I do.

critique *Critique* is a noun. A critique is what a critic produces when he or she criticizes something. • Did you read this critique of *The Old Man and the Sea?* Many people use *critique* as a verb in place of *criticize* because they want to avoid the suggestion of "finding fault." In formal writing, avoid using *critique* in this way. *Criticize* is the better choice.

demonstrate Use *demonstrate* when the explanation includes showing how something works or why something is so. • This model demonstrates the structure of DNA.

describe Use *describe* when the explanation paints a picture in words. • Her essay describes the river gorge in clear and precise language.

Other Synonyms: clear up, comment, define, detail, develop, interpret

FUNNY

The words in this group mean "inspiring smiles or laughter." *Funny* is the general word. • The play includes some funny scenes that relieve the seriousness.

hilarious *Hilarious* suggests liveliness and may suggest silliness or foolishness. • The movie ends with a hilarious chase that is full of slapstick.

humorous *Humorous* suggests gentle, friendly laughter. • The story is about a humorous episode in a "typical" school day.

laughable Something laughable is funny unintentionally. • After my laughable attempt to fix the sink, I called a plumber.

witty Something witty is funny because it is clever. Often, wit relies on the humorous use of words. • Mr. Kahn entertained us with witty stories about life as a television performer.

Other Synonyms: amusing, comical, droll, ludicrous, playful, silly, whimsical
Antonyms: grave, serious

GET

Get and its synonyms mean "to come to have." • You can get your supplies at Wilson's department store.

acquire *Acquire* is often used for collecting or accumulating things. It suggests that the act of getting took considerable time. • The museum has acquired a number of impressionist paintings.

gain Use *gain* for the getting of something valuable, especially when work is done. • Scientists gain important knowledge even from experiments that fail.

obtain *Obtain* means "to get possession of something." • After weeks of waiting, we obtained our passports.

procure *Procure* suggests that something was obtained only after considerable effort. • Finally, we managed to procure medical supplies.

Other Synonyms: amass, buy, collect, earn, purchase, realize, reap, receive, secure, take, win
Antonym: give

GROUP

Group and its synonyms mean "a number of people, animals, or things considered together." • A group of tourists waited in the lobby.

association An association is a formal group of people with similar interests. • Nan Hatch heads an association of physicists.

company *Company* originally meant "people sharing bread." That meaning survives in our use of *company* to mean "guests." • We'll be having company for dinner. *Company* also means a group organized for a purpose. • We formed a company of actors to perform new plays.

crowd *Crowd* suggests a large, disorderly group squeezed into a small space. • I will take a place in line, but I won't wait in a crowd.

gang Use *gang* for workers who do a job as a group, or for a group of lawbreakers. • Police broke up a gang of drug dealers.

mob A *mob* is a large, disorderly crowd, especially one that has gone beyond the limits of the law. • "If we tell them we're out of tickets, this crowd will turn into an angry mob," she said.

ANIMAL GROUPS Specific words are used for groups of animals; for example, army of frogs, bevy of swans, brood of chicks, cast of hawks, colony of ants, drove of cattle (or oxen), flight of birds, flock of sheep (or camels), gaggle of geese, herd of elephants, hoard of gnats, host of sparrows, pack of wolves or dogs, pod of seals (or whales, or walruses), pride of lions, school of fish, sleuth of bears, swarm of bees (or eels), troop of kangaroos (or monkeys, or lions).

HELP

Help and its synonyms mean "to make things easier or better." • A sudden downpour helped firefighters save hundreds of acres.

abet To abet is both to help and to encourage someone. It is often, but not always, used for wrongdoing. • You are accused of abetting the thieves.

aid Because *aid* is more formal than *help,* it is appropriate when the help is seriously needed. • Please give something to aid the homeless.

assist *Assist* suggests that the help given is less important than the rest of the work. • My job is to assist the director when we are on location.

bolster To bolster to provide support for someone's effort. *Bolster* suggests that the support is not absolutely necessary. • Your letter to the mayor bolstered our campaign for better street lighting.

support To *support* is to give approval or understanding or to meet a person's needs, either by giving money or what is needed. • Fifty-six percent of those surveyed supported Anderson.

Other Synonyms: foment, foster, rescue, serve, succor, sustain, tend
Antonyms: hinder, interfere

IMPORTANT

Important and its synonyms mean "having great meaning or great influence." • Dan's sister has an important job.

essential *Essential* indicates something so important that it is absolutely necessary. • Reading is an essential skill in our society.

serious *Serious* suggests a contrast between really important things and things that are not very important. • Now we must turn to serious matters.

urgent *Urgent* indicates something so important that it should get immediate attention. • An urgent message has just arrived.

vital Use *vital* for something absolutely necessary. Its original meaning is "necessary to life." • Light, air, and water are vital to a plant.

Other Synonyms: critical, grave, momentous, notable, prominent, remarkable, weighty

Antonyms: insignificant, trivial, unimportant

LIKE The words in this group share the general meanings of *like:* "to be pleased with, to enjoy." • I like long walks along city streets.

adore *Adore* is a strong word that suggests liking something to the point of honoring it. Don't waste *adore* by using it simply to mean "like very much." • Those who adore their freedom must honor the freedom of others.

cherish To cherish is to hold dear. It suggests tender affection for the thing liked. • I cherish the peace and quiet of summer afternoons.

enjoy To enjoy something is to get pleasure from it. • I enjoy talking with my friends about whatever topic comes up.

love *Love* indicates a strong, deep, and tender affection. • I love my brother, even though he sometimes annoys me. In speech, people may use *love* to exaggerate their feelings. • I love basketball! In formal writing, avoid using *love* that way.

prefer Use *prefer* to indicate a liking for one thing over another. • Esther prefers modern paintings.

Other Synonyms: admire, appreciate, fancy, favor, idolize, prize, relish, revere

Antonyms: despise, disdain, dislike

MAKE *Make* and its synonyms mean "bring into being." • All of these videocassette recorders were made in Japan.

assemble To assemble is to complete something by putting its parts together. • On this platform the space shuttle is assembled.

build To build is to make something large, especially a building, by putting materials or parts together. • Crews began building a bridge across the river.

construct To construct is to put parts together in an orderly way, according to a plan. • Using sheet metal, we constructed temporary shelters.

create To create is to bring into being something that did not exist before. • The author has created many amusing characters.

Other Synonyms: establish, fabricate, manufacture, produce

Antonyms: break, demolish, destroy, dismantle

MANY *Many* means "a great number of." **Caution:** whenever you can, tell how many, instead of using *many* or one of its synonyms, as in the second of the following sentences. • Many viewers watched the program. An estimated 40 percent of the viewers watched the program.

a lot Although the phrase *a lot* is used colloquially to mean "very many" or "very much," you should avoid it in most writing and speaking.

a number of This phrase is more formal than *a lot,* but it is just as vague. Avoid it. Instead, choose a more precise synonym or use a figure.

numerous *Numerous* suggests many more than expected. It is more formal than *many.* • Numerous candidates have announced their intention to run.

several *Several* means "more than two but not many." • I have several reasons for disagreeing with you.

various Use *various* to emphasize

the idea of many different things. • We saw an egret and various other birds.

Other Synonyms: countless, myriad, sundry
Antonym: few

MEAN *Mean* has two related meanings, "bad-tempered or unkind," and "stingy or miserly." • Juan complained that his brother had a mean temper. • Claudia is so mean that she won't lend me a nickel.

nasty Use *nasty* to indicate very unpleasant, harmful, or disgusting behavior. • Instead of answering the question, he made nasty remarks about the reporter who asked it.

selfish Use *selfish* for a person who cares too much for his or her own interests and not enough for others. • Donna chooses her friends for selfish reasons.

petty *Petty* indicates meanness about even the smallest things. • John still holds a petty grudge because I forgot his birthday last year.

unkind *Unkind* means, of course, "not kind." It indicates harsh or cruel treatment, often the result of thoughtlessness. • It was unkind of them to leave without you.

Other Synonyms: bad-tempered, contemptible, nasty, spiteful, vicious
Antonyms: considerate, generous, kind

OFFEND The words in this group share the general meaning of *offend:* "to hurt the feelings of, to make angry." • Lisa was offended when she wasn't invited.

annoy To annoy is to cause mild temporary pain or disturbance. • She annoys me when she talks about herself.

displease *Displease* is a mild word . It means "not to please," or to offend slightly. • Your lateness displeased me.

insult *Insult* suggests an offense so strong that it causes deep pain or an-

ger. • By calling me a liar, Terry insulted me more than I can bear.

Other Synonyms: affront, disgust, hurt, provoke, upset, vex
Antonym: please

QUIET The words in this group share the general meaning "without sound." *Quiet* also suggests freedom from excitement or confusion. • Life moves slowly in the quiet countryside of Vermont.

calm *Calm* suggests stillness, quiet, and serenity. • When the record ended, calm settled over the room.

noiseless *Noiseless* stresses the complete absence of noise and often suggests movement without sound. • A gentle, noiseless breeze drifted in across the bay.

silent Use *silent* to indicate that there is no sound of any kind or that a person makes no answer of any kind. • When we asked where he had gotten the money, he was silent.

still Use *still* to indicate that there is no sound or movement. • The storm passed, and the sea was still.

Other Synonyms: hushed, peaceful, restrained, serene, tranquil
Antonyms: loud, noisy

RIGHT The two general meanings of *right* are "correct" and "proper." • When you find the right answer, let me know. • You did the right thing.

accurate Use *accurate* to emphasize that something meets a standard very precisely. • Sylvia's estimate of the temperature was accurate.

correct Use *correct* to emphasize that something fits the facts, with no errors. • This is the correct time. Use it also to suggest that a thing is proper. • Did you follow the correct procedure?

fit Use *fit* to indicate that something is just what a situation or purpose requires. • This boat is fit for an Atlantic crossing.

proper Use *proper* for a thing that good judgment says is appropriate or suitable. • When you go hiking, wear proper shoes.

Other Synonyms: exact, fitting, just, precise, reasonable, suitable, true

Antonyms: see WRONG

RUN *Run* and its synonyms share the meaning "to go by moving the legs faster than in walking." • Bonnie ran to catch the last bus.

gallop Use *gallop* to suggest very fast running. This is the word for a horse's fastest gait, or way of running. • When the doors opened, we galloped to the nearest ticket booth.

race *Race* suggests moving too fast, too hastily, or too frantically. • Dick puts things off, and then races around at the last minute.

scamper Use *scamper* to suggest small, quick movements, like those of a small animal. • Terns scampered along the water's edge.

sprint Use *sprint* for very quick running over a short distance. • Dozens of commuters sprinted for the five o'clock train.

Other Synonyms: dash, jog, scurry, trot

SAY *Say* and its synonyms share the general meaning "to utter words; to speak." • "I'll be ready in a minute," she said.

assert To assert is to say something in a positive, forceful way. • "I'm going to win this award," he asserted.

comment To comment is to make a remark that explains, criticizes, or gives an opinion. • "Felicia has not played up to her ability," the coach commented.

declare To declare is say something emphatically. • "I intend to leave promptly at six," he declared.

state To state is to say in a definite, precise way, to specify. • She stated that the winner would be announced at noon.

Other Synonyms: announce, blurt, boast, cry, exclaim, growl, grumble, remark, roar, shout, whisper

SEE All the words in this group share the general meaning of *see:* "to get information through the eyes." • I saw Andy at the movies.

behold *Behold* means "to look at with awe or wonder." • In the evening, we beheld a magnificent sunset.

glimpse *Glimpse* means "to see briefly." • The clouds parted, and we glimpsed the sun.

inspect *Inspect* means "to look at closely, usually in an attempt to find something wrong or flawed." • A United Nations team inspected the refugee camp.

observe To observe is to look at with special attention or a special purpose • She observed the laboratory animals.

sight *Sight* means "to see something for which one has been looking." • High above us we sighted an eagle.

watch *Watch* means "to observe something closely for a purpose." • From towers, rangers watch for a sign of fire. However, *watch* also means "to look at something *without* paying close attention." • We passed the time by watching people pass by.

Other Synonyms: ascertain, discern, perceive, spot, view

SIGN A sign is something that stands for something else. • The first robin is a sure sign of spring.

mark Use *mark* for a sign that is an accepted indication of a certain quality. • Silky fur is the mark of a healthy puppy.

signal   Use *signal* for a sign made deliberately.   • Hold your arm high to signal a cab driver that you want a ride.

Other Synomyms: emblem, indication, omen, symbol, symptom, token, trace

SMART   The words in this group share the general meaning of *smart*: "intelligent, alert, clever." *Smart* is an informal word.   • You did the smart thing.

astute   Use *astute* to show cleverness combined with wisdom.   • She outlined an astute plan for getting a job.

clever   Use *clever* to suggest new or unusual ideas.   • Burt has some clever ideas for decorating the gym.

gifted   Use *gifted* to emphasize basic intelligence rather than learning or experience.   • Linda is a gifted actress.

intelligent   Use *intelligent* to emphasize the ability to learn or to adapt to new situations.   • He's inexperienced, but he's intelligent and eager to learn.

Other Synomyms: bright, perceptive, shrewd

STRANGE   The words in this group share the general meaning of *strange:* "out of the ordinary, peculiar, or odd."   • To the east, a strange green fire lit the sky.

bizarre   *Bizarre* suggests something extremely strange, startling, and unexpected.   • Her bizarre costume had the head of a rabbit and the body of a lizard.

fantastic   *Fantastic* suggests something so vastly different from experience that it seems to have come from a dream. • We wandered through a fantastic garden where flowers sang.

mysterious   *Mysterious* suggests the unknown, unexplained, or secret. • Ronnie stayed home yesterday for some mysterious reason.

peculiar   *Peculiar* suggests something puzzling or difficult to explain.   • A peculiar sound came from deep in the cave.

Other Synonyms: curious, eccentric, extraordinary, odd, quaint, unfamiliar, unusual, weird

Antonyms: familiar, ordinary, usual

TEACH   *Teach* and its synonyms share the general meaning "to show someone how to do something or help someone learn something."   • Dora taught me an interesting card trick.

educate   Use *educate* for teaching that covers various subjects over a long period.   • She was educated at UCLA.

instruct   Use *instruct* for teaching a particular subject or guiding a particular activity.   • Mr. Wells instructed us to set the chairs up in a semicircle.

train   Use *train* when the teaching develops a particular skill or prepares one for a particular job or career.   • Steve trains computer programmers.

Other Synonyms: coach, drill, enlighten, imbue, inform, school

TERRIFIC   Although *terrific* and the other words in this group are often used in casual speech to mean "unusually fine or enjoyable," this is not the best use for them. Each word has a specific meaning of its own. *Terrific,* for example, means "terrifying, horrifying."   • A terrific thunderclap shook the house.

amazing   Use *amazing* for something so surprising or astonishing that a person is momentarily confused.   • The news was so amazing that it left me speechless.

marvelous   Use *marvelous* for something that would make a person stop and marvel, or stare.   • In the shop was a marvelous gingerbread house, so large that customers could walk into it.

remarkable Use *remarkable* for something that is noticeably exceptional for its type. • This metal is remarkably light.

sensational Use *sensational* for something that causes strong feeling or great excitement. • Her sensational speech motivated everyone to pitch in and help.

wonderful Use *wonderful* for something that causes wonder or amazement. • The way bats dart around in the evening sky is wonderful.

Other Synonyms: astonishing, astounding, fabulous, miraculous

THINK The words in this group all mean "to use the mind" in one way or another. To think is to use the mind reasonably, to form ideas or reach conclusions. • I think Senator Carson's plan is a sound one.

believe To believe is to accept something as true, even when one cannot completely prove that it is. • I don't know all the facts, but I believe Al's story.

consider To consider is to think about something in order to reach a decision. • The jury retired to consider the evidence.

feel To feel is to believe something based on emotion, not on thinking. Avoid using *feel* when *think* is the appropriate word. • We feel certain that she will return.

speculate To speculate is to reason for incomplete information or guesswork, in order to decide what might be. • Scientists speculate about life on other planets.

Other Synonyms: contemplate, deliberate, meditate, ponder, reflect

TRAVEL *Travel* and its synonyms share the general meaning "to go from one place to another." • Mr. Connors has traveled throughout the Southwest.

emigrate To emigrate is to move from one country to stay permanently in another. • They emigrated from Korea to the United States.

immigrate To immigrate is to come into a country from another to stay permanently. • They immigrated to the United States from Korea.

journey Although *journey* once meant "a day's travel," to journey now is to make a long and difficult trip. • A team of explorers journeyed across the polar ice cap.

tour To tour is to travel for the purpose of sightseeing. • A group of students will tour Ireland by bicycle. It can also mean "to travel for the purpose of performing." • The group's summer tour will include twenty cities.

Other Synonyms: migrate; roam, traverse, wander

WALK *Walk* and its synonyms mean "to go on foot at a normal pace, not running." • I walk to school every morning.

amble To amble is to walk in a relaxed, easy-going manner. • We ambled along at the water's edge, talking and laughing.

saunter To saunter is to walk in a way similar to ambling. Use *saunter* to emphasize that the walk has no destination; it is aimless. • Beth sauntered through the mall, passing the time.

stride To stride is to walk with long steps, in a vigorous or bold way. • The astronauts strode confidently toward the space shuttle.

strut To strut is to walk in a proud or showy way. • The defending champions strutted onto the basketball court.

trudge To trudge is to walk as a tired or unhappy person would walk. • Mr. Richards trudged home after work.

Other Synonyms: hike, march, pace, parade, step, stroll, tramp, tread

WRONG The words in this group share the meaning "not what is true, correct, or wanted." *Wrong* is the general term. • The poster gave the wrong date for the performance.

erroneous Use *erroneous* for an idea that is based on an error. • Carl had the erroneous idea that I would help him.

false Use *false* when there is a suggestion that the lack of truth is deliberate. • What Denise said about me is false.

faulty Use *faulty* to indicate that there are errors which can be corrected. • Ed's ideas are clever, but his reasoning is faulty.

incorrect Use *incorrect* as a more formal and polite substitute for *wrong*. • A government source said that the figures were incorrect.

mistaken Use *mistaken* to suggest being wrong by accident. • I thought I knew you, but I was mistaken.

Other Synonyms: fallacious, groundless, illogical, inaccurate, untrue *see also* BAD
  Antonym: see RIGHT

Index

A

abet *see* HELP
accurate *see* RIGHT
acknowledge *see* ANSWER
acquire *see* GET
ACTIVE
adore *see* LIKE
adventurous *see* BRAVE
AFRAID
aghast *see* AFRAID
agile *see* ACTIVE
aid *see* HELP
ALONE
a lot *see* MANY
amazing *see* TERRIFIC
amble *see* WALK
ANGRY
ANIMAL GROUPS *see* GROUP
annoy *see* OFFEND
ANSWER
a number of *see* MANY
ASK
assemble *see* MAKE
assert *see* SAY
assist *see* HELP
association *see* GROUP
astute *see* SMART
attractive *see* BEAUTIFUL

B

BAD
BEAUTIFUL
beg *see* ASK
behold *see* SEE
believe *see* THINK
BEST
bizarre *see* STRANGE
bold *see* BRAVE
bolster *see* HELP
BRAVE
BREAK
BRIGHT
build *see* MAKE

C

calm *see* QUIET
careless *see* BAD

cherish *see* LIKE
clarify *see* EXPLAIN
clever *see* SMART
comment *see* SAY
company *see* GROUP
conclude *see* END
consider *see* THINK
construct *see* MAKE
correct *see* RIGHT
crack *see* BREAK
create *see* MAKE
criticize *see* EXPLAIN
critique *see* EXPLAIN
crowd *see* GROUP
crumble *see* BREAK
crush *see* BREAK

D

daring *see* BRAVE
dazzling *see* BEAUTIFUL
declare *see* SAY
demand *see* ASK
demolish *see* BREAK
demonstrate *see* EXPLAIN
describe *see* EXPLAIN
displease *see* OFFEND
dreadful *see* BAD

E

eager *see* ENTHUSIASTIC
earnest *see* ENTHUSIASTIC
educate *see* TEACH
elegant *see* BEAUTIFUL
emigrate *see* TRAVEL
enchanting *see* BEAUTIFUL
END
energetic *see* ACTIVE
ENERGY
enjoy *see* LIKE
enraged *see* ANGRY
ENTHUSIASTIC
ERRONEOUS *see* WRONG
essential *see* IMPORTANT
evil *see* BAD
EXPLAIN

F

false *see* WRONG
fantastic *see* STRANGE
faulty *see* WRONG
fearful *see* AFRAID
fearless *see* BRAVE
feel *see* THINK
fervent *see* ENTHUSIASTIC
finest *see* BEST
finish *see* END
fit *see* RIGHT
force *see* ENERGY
foremost *see* BEST
FUNNY
furious *see* ANGRY

G

gain *see* GET
gallop *see* RUN
gang *see* GROUP
GET
gifted *see* SMART
glimpse *see* SEE
glistening *see* BRIGHT
glowing *see* BRIGHT
gorgeous *see* BEAUTIFUL
GROUP

H

halt *see* END
HELP
hilarious *see* FUNNY
horrible *see* BAD
humorous *see* FUNNY

I

immigrate *see* TRAVEL
IMPORTANT
incomparable *see* BEST
incorrect *see* WRONG, BAD
inquire *see* ASK
inspect *see* SEE
instruct *see* TEACH
insult *see* OFFEND
intelligent *see* SMART
irritated *see* ANGRY

J

journey *see* TRAVEL

L

laughable *see* FUNNY
LIKE
lonely *see* ALONE
lonesome *see* ALONE
love *see* LIKE

M

MAKE
MANY
mark *see* SIGN
marvelous *see* TERRIFIC
MEAN
mistaken *see* WRONG
mob *see* GROUP
mysterious *see*
  STRANGE

N

nasty *see* MEAN
noiseless *see* QUIET
numerous *see* MANY

O

observe *see* SEE
obtain *see* GET
OFFEND

P

peculiar *see* STRANGE
petty *see* MEAN
power *see* ENERGY
prefer *see* LIKE
procure *see* GET
proper *see* RIGHT

Q

QUIET

R

race *see* RUN
radiant *see* BRIGHT
remarkable *see* TERRIFIC
reply *see* ANSWER
request *see* ASK
respond *see* ANSWER
retort *see* ANSWER
RIGHT
RUN

S

saunter *see* WALK
SAY
scamper *see* RUN
SEE
selfish *see* MEAN
sensational *see* TERRIFIC
serious *see* IMPORTANT
several *see* MANY
shatter *see* BREAK
sight *see* SEE
SIGN
signal *see* SIGN
silent *see* QUIET
SMART
solitary *see* ALONE
sparkling *see* BRIGHT
speculate *see* THINK
spirited *see* ACTIVE
sprint *see* RUN
state *see* SAY
still *see* QUIET
STRANGE
strength *see* ENERGY
stride *see* WALK
strut *see* WALK
superior *see* BEST
support *see* HELP

T

TEACH
TERRIFIC
terrified *see* AFRAID
THINK
tour *see* TRAVEL
train *see* TEACH
TRAVEL
TRUDGE *see* WALK

U

unkind *see* MEAN
urgent *see* IMPORTANT

V

various *see* MANY
vital *see* IMPORTANT

W

WALK
wary *see* AFRAID
watch *see* SEE
witty *see* FUNNY
wonderful *see* TERRIFIC
worried *see* AFRAID
wreck *see* BREAK
wrong *see* BAD
WRONG

Index

problems with, 454
subject, 446, 448, 662
substituted for nouns, 447
unclear reference of, 663
Pronunciation, 331–32
and spelling, 337
Pronunciation keys, in dictionaries, 331, 332
Proofreading, 87–88
descriptive writing, 173
narrative writing, 199–200
reports, 267
see also Revising/Editing
Proofreading symbols, 87–88
Proper adjectives, 508
capitalization of, 596–97, 599
Proper nouns, 425, 426, 508
capitalization of, 596–97, 599
Publishers, on library catalog cards, 316, 317, 318
Publishing. *See* Presenting
Punctuation, 405, 612–44, 666–68
apostrophes, 636
colons, 634
commas, 620–32
exclamation points, 615
hyphens, 635
periods, 614–15, 616–17
proofreading for, 87, 88
question marks, 615
quotation marks, 639–43
semicolons, 562, 565, 633
see also Commas
Purpose
and descriptive writing, 162
and prewriting, 61–62
and speaking, 296–97

Q

Question marks, 615
with quotation marks, 640
Questions
for creative thinking, 38–39
and determining purpose, 61
group, and revising, 84
for ideas for writing, 43
indirect, 614
for introductions, 121
for organizing persuasive writing, 239
for paragraph development, 104–105
for preparing to write, 74
and prewriting, 61

for topic sentences, 102
for using the senses in writing, 7, 8, 9, 10
see also Inquiring; Interrogative sentences; Test questions
Quick drafts, 78
quiet, quite, 343
Quotation marks, 639–43
in dialogue, 196, 641
with direct quotations, 639–40
with other punctuation marks, 639–40
with titles, 643
Quotations
capitalization in, 605
commas with, 629
direct, 629, 639–40
divided, 629
for ideas for writing, 43
indirect, 629
for introductions, 121

R

Readers' Guide to Periodical Literature, 322–23
Reading
aloud, 79
drafts, 79
scanning, 355
skimming, 355
see also SQ3R
Reasons, for paragraph development, 105
Reference books, writing and, 75
Reference section, 310, 320–23
almanacs, 321
atlases, 321
biographical reference books, 321–22
dictionaries, 320
encyclopedias, 321
Readers' Guide to Periodical Literature, 322–23
vertical files, 322
yearbooks, 321
Reflecting, 24, 65, 74, 79
Regular verbs, 483
Religious names/words, capitalization of, 597, 603
Repetition
in empty sentences, 144
for memorizing, 359
Reports, 248–69
drafting, 261–65
finding a subject, 250
gathering information, 253–57

Editorial Credits
Director of Program Planning and Development: Bonnie L. Dobkin
Senior Editor: Julie A. Schumacher
Associate Editor: Christine Iversen
Assistant Editor: Peter P. Kaye
Project Assistance: Ligature, Inc.

Acknowledgments

Sources of Quoted Materials

The authors and editors have made every effort to trace the ownership of all copyrighted selections found in this book and to make full acknowledgment for their use. Grateful acknowledgment is made to the following sources for permission to reprint copyrighted materials.
11–14: Random House, Inc. and Collins Publishers, London: For excerpts from "Elsa Meets Other Wild Animals," from *Born Free* by Joy Adamson; copyright © 1960 by Joy Adamson, reprinted by permission of Pantheon Books, a Division of Random House, Inc. **48:** Walker Gibson: For "Advice to Travelers" from *Come As You Are* by Walker Gibson first appeared in *Saturday Review,* May 5, 1956. **53:** COLGEMS-EMI Music, Inc.: For "You've Got a Friend" by Carole King; copyright © 1971 by COLGEMS-EMI INC, all rights reserved. **158:** Rand McNally & Company and George Allen & Unwin, Ltd.: For an excerpt from *Kon-Tiki: Across the Pacific by Raft* by Thor Heyerdahl; copyright © 1984, 1978, 1950, published in the United States by Rand McNally & Company. **181:** Jane and Paul Annixter: For an excerpt from "Last Cover," from *The Best Nature Stories of Paul Annixter;* **182–185:** Jan Andrews: For "The Vigil" by Jan Andrews, reprinted by permission of the author. **206:** Time, Inc.: For an excerpt from "Lights! Camera! Special Effects!" by Richard Zoglin, copyright © 1986 Time, Inc., all rights reserved; **207:** Kyle Counts: For an excerpt from "The Making of E.T." by Kyle Counts, which first appeared in *Cinefantastique,* Vol. 13 No. 2/ Vol. 13 No. 3, November–December 1982; **208–209:** Margaret Poynter: For excerpts from "Krakatoa," reprinted by permisson of the author; **210:** Random House, Inc.: For "Jar Terrarium," from *Mr. Wizard's Supermarket Science* by Don Herbert; copyright © 1980 by Don Herbert. **233:** Tribune Media Services: For Gene Siskel column, "The Fly;" **234–35:** The Lantz Office: For excerpts from *My Wilderness East to Katahdin* by William O. Douglas: copyright © 1961 by William O. Douglas. **257:** World Book, Inc.: For entry "Guide Dogs," from *The World Book Encyclopedia;* copyright © 1987 by World Book, Inc. **322:** The H. W. Wilson Company: For an entry from *Readers' Guide to Periodical Literature,* copyright © 1986 by H. W. Wilson Company. **328, 330, 332, 333, 334:** Simon & Schuster: For entries from *Webster's New World Dictionary,* Students Edition; copyright © 1976, 1981 by Simon & Schuster, Inc. **348:** Frank Music Company: for two lines from "Seventy-six Trombones," from *The Music Man* by Meredith Willson; copyright © 1957 by Frank Music Corp. and Meredith Willson Music, renewed 1985 Frank Music Corp. and Meredith Willson Music; international copyright secured, all rights reserved.

Unit Art

Unit 1: Christine Stanford, *Elmer's Farm.* New Jersey State Teen Arts Program (Nancy Roberts-Lawler) **Unit 2:** Courtesy of the International Collection of Children's Art, University Museums, Illinois State University **Unit 3:** Courtesy of the International Collection of Children's Art, University Museums, Illinois State University

Photographs

Assignment photography: Vito Palmisano: **4, 44–45,** *b* **49,** *b* **50,** *t* & *l* **52,** *cr* **53,** *r* **54, 97, 154, 291, 297, 327, 329, 349, 377, 577, 613,** Ralph Brunke, *l* **15, 18,** *t* & *c* **19, 27, 37,** *l* **39,** *c* **43,** *cl* **45,** *b* **46,** *t* **48,** *b* **48,** *tl* **53, 61,** *r* **85, 96, 104, 196, 211, 228, 231, 264, 304, 334,** *r* **345, 376, 427, 497,** *l* **500,** *r* **519,** *b* **536, 594, 608, 625,** *l* **632,** *l* **644 5:** © Fredrick D. Bodin/Stock, Boston **6:** © Charles Krebs, Aperture **8:** © Richard Steedman, The Stock Market **9:** © David Lissy, Click/Chicago **10:** © Sam Griffth, Click/Chicago **12:** © Bradley Smith, Gemini Smith, Inc. **14:** New Jersey State Teen Arts Program (Joseph Schembri) **15:** *c* © Stahman Studios, PhotoUnique **16:** *t* G & J Images, The Image Bank, *bl* T. Mayac. *Mallard Duck.* (Chris Arend, Alaska Photo) **17:** © Esto Photographics *t* Barry Herem. *Indian Mask.* (Aperture) **19:** *b* New Jersey State Teen Arts Program (Nancy Roberts-Lawler) **20:** *l* © Gerry Souter, Click/Chicago, *r* © Don Fleming, Click/Chicago **22:** © Michael Philip Manheim, Gartman Agency **23:** © Dale Jorgenson, Tom Stack & Assoc. **36:** T.D.F. Kendall* **39:** *r* © Gary Crallé, The Image Bank **40:** Three Lions **43:** *r* The Bettmann Archive, *l* © Schecter Lee, Esto Photographics **44:** *t* NASA, *c* The Bettmann Archive **45:** *t* Permission of King Features Syndicate, Inc., *cr* © Michael Beasley, Click/Chicago **46:** *t* © Ellis Herwig/Stock, Boston, *cl* © Tom Check/Stock, Boston **47:** *tl* © Roger Tully, After-Image, *tr* Ralph Brunke*, *c* © David Seman, Gartman Agency *b* © Lewis Portnoy, The Stock Market **48:** *c* © Springer/Bettman Film Archive, **49:** *t* The Bettmann Archive, *c* © Robert Frerck, Odessy Productions, **50:** *l*

© David Hiser, The Image Bank, *r* © Craig Aurness, Click/Chicago, **51:** *tl* Charlotte Warr-Anderson. Museum of American Folk Art, Scotchgard Collection of Contemporary Quilts *tr* © Chad Ehlers, After-Image, *c* © Janeart, The Image Bank, *b* © Jim Weiner **52:** *r* © Pat Curran-Miller, The Stock Shop **53:** *tr* Culver Pictures, *cl* © Jim Whitmer, *cm* © Jeffrey W. Myers, The Stock Market, **54:** *t* © R. Hamilton Smith, *l* © Schecter Lee, Esto Photographics **55:** *tl* © Leslie Wong, Archive Pictures, *tr* © James Kirby, Focus/Virginia, *c* Smithsonian Institution, *b* © Schecter Lee, Esto Photographics **56:** © Brian Payne, Stock Imagery **57:** © Richard Steedman, The Stock Market **66:** Historical Pictures Service, **67:** The Bettmann Archive, **69:** © Brent Petersen, The Stock Market **72:** © Robert Amft, Nawrocki Stock Photo **73:** © Nicholay Zurek, **80:** © Dan McCoy, Rainbow **82:** © Steve Lenord Click/Chicago, **83:** © Gary Benson, Aperture **85:** *l* Historical Pictures Service **93:** *l* © Bohdan Hrynewych, Southern Light *r* © Suzanne L. Murphy, *FPG* **100:** Artist Unknown. Abby Aldrich Rockefeller Folk Art Center, Williamsburg, VA. **103:** © Robert Rozinski, Stock Imagery **107:** SCALA/Art Resource **110:** *l* © Rui Coutinho, Nawrocki Stock Photo, *r* H. Armstrong Roberts **112:** Al Levine, Courtesy National Broadcasting Company **114:** © Ed Lee, Click/Chicago **115:** © Phil Degginer, Click/Chicago **118:** T.D.F. Kendall* **124:** © David Falconer, Stock West **130:** New Jersey Teen Arts Program (Joseph Schembri) **132:** © Globus Brothers, The Stock Market **133:** © Co Rentmeester, The Image Bank **145:** Art Resource **148:** © Jerry Berndt/Stock, Boston **151:** Photri/Gartman Agency **155:** Thomas Braise, The Stock Market **165:** © George Schneeger, Tom Stack Assoc. **170:** Paul R. Perry **175:** *l* SCALA/Art Resource, *c* Museo Stibbert, Florence (Amendola/Art Resource), *r* Historical Pictures Service **176:** Movie Still Archives **178:** © Bob Taylor, The Stock Shop **179:** © Michael Schoenfield, Royce Blair & Assoc. **190:** T.D.F. Kendall* **200:** © Brian Seed, Click/Chicago **201:** Vivianne Holbrooke, The Stock Market **202:** Nawrocki Stock Photo **204:** © John Lemker, Earth Scenes **205:** © Brent Cavedo, Focus/Virginia **209:** © Alastair Black, FPG **213:** J. Zehrt, FPG **219:** Chicago Historical Society **221:** Focus on Sports **223:** *t* © Brian Seed, Click/Chicago, *r* © George Von Kantor, PhotoUnique **227:** © Lee Waldman, Click/Chicago **230:** © George Mars Cassidy, Click/Chicago **233:** Shooting Star/20th Century Fox **235:** *l* FPG, *r* © E. R. Degginer, Earth Scenes **238:** T. D. F. Kendall* **248:** © Luis Villota, The Stock Market **249:** © Brian Seed, Click/Chicago **254:** © Paul Chesley, Photographers/Aspen **257:** © Peter Fronk, Click/Chicago **268:** *l* © J.G. Zimmerman, FPG, *c* © LPI, FPG, *r* © Mike Valeri, FPG **272:** © Wayne Eastep, PhotoUnique **273:** © Allan Seiden, The Image Bank **277:** SCALA/Art Resource **286:** © E.R. Degginer, Animals Animals **288:** © Scripps Clinic/Science Source, Photo Researchers **290:** © Lawrence Hughes, The Image Bank **303:** © J. Sloan, Gamma-Liaison **306:** © Wynn Miller, After-Image **307:** © Russ Kinne, Photo Researchers **309:** © Phil Cantor, PhotoUnique **326:** © Weinberg-Clark, The Image Bank **332:** © Donald Smetzer, Click/Chicago **341:** Three Lions **345:** *l* © Chris Jones, The Stock Market **346:** *l* © David Klutho, Focus West, *r* © John Terence Turner, FPG **348:** © R. Hamilton Smith **354:** © Grandma Moses Properties, New York **360:** © Bob Adelman, Magnum **362:** © Globus Brothers, The Stock Market **363:** © Neil Leifer, Sports Illustrated **365:** Photri/Gartman Agency **371:** Nawrocki Stock Photo. **385:** © Kathleen Taylor Campbell, PhotoUnique **386:** © Diana Rasche **390:** © George Von Kantor, PhotoUnique **391:** NASA **397:** © Robert Keeling **406:** © Vito Palmisano **408:** © Michael Philip Manheim, Gartman Agency **422:** © Tom David Zimberoff, PhotoUnique **423:** © Don Valentine, After-Image **431:** © Philip MacMillan James, Click/Chicago **433:** John Sinnok, *Hunter* (© Chris Arend, Alaska Photo) **434:** *l* © Arthur H. Bilsten, *r* © Abril Images, The Image Bank **444:** © Ray Morsch, The Stock Market **445:** © G&J Images, The Image Bank **447:** © Michael Philip Manheim, The Stock Market **457:** © Co Rentmeester, The Image Bank **468:** © Dick Luria, After Image **469:** © Jay Fries, The Image Bank **477:** SCALA/Art Resource **482:** *b* © Grafton Marshall Smith, The Image Bank, *r* © Andy Caufield, The Image Bank **500:** *bt* © Donald Smetzer, Click/Chicago **506:** © Henley & Savage, Click/Chicago **507:** © John Clayton **510:** © Kevin Schafer, Tom Stack & Assoc. **519:** *b* © Marie Ueda, Click/Chicago **520:** Movie Stills Archive **524–525:** © Michael Philip Manheim, Gartman Agency **527:** © Ellis Herwig, Gartman Agency **534:** Historical Pictures Service **536:** *l* © Ralph Oberlander/Stock, Boston **542:** © Kay Chernush, The Image Bank **543:** © Robert Frerck, Odessy Productions **546:** © Geoff Gove, The Image Bank **556:** Dave Shaefer, Jeroboam **560:** © Peter C. Poulides, PhotoUnique **561:** © Vito Palmisano **564:** © Francisco Hidalgo, The Image Bank **567:** © Steven Burr Williams, The Image Bank **568:** © Wayne Eastep, PhotoUnique **576:** © Roark Johnson, Click/Chicago **579:** © Michael O'Brien, Archive Pictures **587:** © Andy Caufield, The Image Bank **595:** FPG **601:** Photri/Gartman Agency **602:** © Cary Wolinski/Stock, Boston **605:** Three Lions **612:** © Vitro Palmisano **619:** © Michael Kevin Daly, The Stock Market **621:** The Bettmann Archive **628:** *l* Antonio Varese. Farnese Palace, Rome (SCALA/Art Resource), *b* Bettmann Archive **632:** *b* © IRA Gabriel **637:** © Robert Amft, Nawrocki Stock Photo **641:** © Vito Palmisano **642:** Culver Pictures **644:** *l* © Steve Prezant, Artista *r* © Alfred Gescheidt, The Image Bank

* Indicates exclusive property of McDougal, Littell & Company.

Illustrations

7, 70, 86, 137, 152, 310, 314, 315, 324, 374, 426: Jeff Mellander **32, 192, 252, 378, 393, 460, 485:** Avalyn Lundgren-Ellis **35, 168, 260, 278, 453, 598:** Debra Stine **78, 117, 412, 616:** Doug Schneider **94:** Dirk Hagner **129, 416, 529:** Pam Rossi **142, 143, 215, 356, 439, 515, 550, 572:** Judy Reed **160, 161:** Kenneth Crippen **183, 185:** Curt Hrabe **246, 259, 401:** Dianne Bennett **473, 588:** Ken Raney **475, 571:** Cathy Pavia **583:** Ross Adcock **Handwriting:** Michael Kecsez, Pen Graphics Studio, Inc.